# JUSTICE, LEGALITY, AND THE RULE OF LAW

# Justice, Legality, and the Rule of Law

*Lessons from the Pitcairn Prosecutions*

Edited by
DAWN OLIVER

OXFORD
UNIVERSITY PRESS

UNIVERSITY PRESS

Great Clarendon Street, Oxford OX2 6DP

Oxford University Press is a department of the University of Oxford.
It furthers the University's objective of excellence in research, scholarship,
and education by publishing worldwide in

Oxford  New York

Auckland  Cape Town  Dar es Salaam  Hong Kong  Karachi Kuala Lumpur  Madrid
Melbourne  Mexico City  Nairobi  New Delhi  Shanghai  Taipei  Toronto

With offices in

Argentina  Austria  Brazil  Chile  Czech Republic  France  Greece
Guatemala  Hungary  Italy  Japan  Poland  Portugal  Singapore
South Korea  Switzerland  Thailand  Turkey  Ukraine  Vietnam

Oxford is a registered trade mark of Oxford University Press
in the UK and in certain other countries

Published in the United States
by Oxford University Press Inc., New York

British Library Cataloguing in Publication Data

Data available

Library of Congress Cataloging in Publication Data

Justice, legality, and the rule of law : lessons from the Pitcairn prosecutions / edited by Dawn Oliver.

p. cm.

ISBN 978-0-19-956866-6
1. Law–Pitcairn Island. 2. Common law–Reception–Pitcairn Island. 3. Law–Great Britain–Colonies.
4. Trials (Rape)–Pitcairn Island. 5. Human rights–Pitcairn Island. 6. Criminal liability–Pitcairn Island.
I. Oliver, Dawn.

KWL46. 7. J87 2009
349.961'8–dc22

2009023761

Typeset by MacMillan Publishing Solutions
Printed in Great Britain on acid-free paper by
the MPG Books Group, Bodmin and King's Lynn

ISBN 978-0-19-956866-6

1   3   5   7   9   10   8   6   4   2

# Foreword

The final drama in the prosecutions with which this book is concerned took place many thousands of miles away from the tiny island community where the acts that gave rise to them were committed.

The conduct of the trials had been in the hands of the legal profession in New Zealand under an agreement between the governments of the United Kingdom and New Zealand. New Zealand judges were appointed to the Pitcairn Supreme Court and to a newly established Court of Appeal for Pitcairn, and it was in New Zealand that the trials were held. Preliminary objections had been taken to the Supreme Court's jurisdiction, to the procedures under which the defendants had been charged, and to the applicability of the English Sexual Offences Act 1956, under which the charges were brought, to Pitcairn. They were rejected by the Supreme Court for reasons that were set out in its written judgment in great detail. They were rejected, for no less detailed reasons, in its turn by the Court of Appeal.

The defendants sought and were granted special leave to appeal against the decision of the Court of Appeal to the Judicial Committee of the Privy Council. A request for the trials to be postponed until the appeals on the preliminary issues had been disposed of was refused on the ground that it was in the interests of justice, after the delay that had already occurred, that the trials should take place as soon as possible. So it was that by the time the preliminary objections came before the Judicial Committee in Downing Street, the defendants had already been tried, convicted, and sentenced. Undertakings were given that the sentences would not be enforced until the appeals had been disposed of. In the meantime, a further objection had been raised that the proceedings were an abuse of process.

The issues which the Judicial Committee had been asked to consider raised fundamental questions about the rule of law in remote communities and about the responsibilities of the colonial power which seeks to exercise its authority over them. One might have expected the Board to respond to the challenge that they presented, as the New Zealand judges had done, by engaging as closely as possible with the unique circumstances of the Pitcairn islanders. The United Kingdom, after all, is not without its own isolated communities and the Judicial Committee has a long tradition of acting as the final court of appeal for distant territories. That this did not happen, and the disappointment that this gives rise to, is a recurrent theme throughout this book. The following extract from my diary offers an explanation:

21 July 2006

These last two weeks should have been occupied by an eight day hearing of appeals from Pitcairn arising from prosecutions against several of the islanders in that remote and isolated community for what in our terms would be regarded as child sexual abuse but—as they go back over 40 years and were unchecked until police investigations by Kent Police in 1996—were, on the surface at least, apparently part of the lifestyle of the islanders' male population. Various points of interest were raised in the appeals, and a huge amount of effort had been put into the preparation of historical documents—over 4,000 pages of them—for us to look at, as we reviewed the decisions of the courts below as to the right of the UK to legislate for Pitcairn and whether the laws made for the island had been properly promulgated, as well as issues of abuse of process on a variety of grounds. Flat screens had been installed in the Committee Room for our benefit and memory sticks produced with the material stored on it, and a DVD was to be created as a record, both visually and in sound, of the entire proceedings to be shown on Pitcairn to the islanders and to interested parties in New Zealand.

To the great misfortune of counsel who had put such an effort into preparation, our Board in the Privy Council was presided over by Lord [Lennie] Hoffmann who had expressed to me a total disinterest in Pitcairn, its culture, and history, and was determined to cut to the bone the scope for any argument. The other members of the Board were Harry Woolf, Johan Steyn—both retired—and myself, and Bob Carswell on the wings. Lennie had reduced counsel, in a state of shock, to almost abject surrender and speechlessness within half an hour in a manner reminiscent of Lord Diplock. It did not help that—with the exception of David Perry, who had not yet got to his feet—they were all from New Zealand or New South Wales and unfamiliar with the ways of the Board. Nevertheless it was a devastating start to the proceedings, which resulted in the whole affair being over in under two days after the thinnest of arguments. I did my best to keep the thing alive, bearing in mind that our proceedings were to be on view by the islanders, and with some support from Harry Woolf. But the whole stuffing had gone out of the affair and Lennie had collapsed the whole event with his devastating ability to cut issues to the core and demonstrate that there was nothing of substance in any of them. He has just produced a draft judgment which is just as terse. The novelty and difficulty of the issues is not apparent from what he has written.

I am in a quandary. I felt that there was much more in the case than he had given credit for, and I am sure that if Tom Bingham or Donald Nicholls had been in the chair the issues would have been debated in much greater depth. I feel that I must write something, even—unusually—in a concurring opinion. But it is going to be difficult to do so without breaking all the conventions that dictate that the Privy Council does not go in for separate opinions. I am sad for the teams on both sides of the case who had put so much effort into it. They deserved more, and were understandably dismayed by the reception they received in the event after expecting to be heard in full for so much longer on issues which could have been regarded as some of the most interesting to reach the Privy Council in decades.

That Lord Hoffmann was so determined to find nothing of interest in the case was a complete surprise to me. One of the most intellectually gifted judges of his generation, he had so much to offer if I had been able to persuade him to take a different view. On this occasion, uncharacteristically, his was the flower that did not bloom. It is fair to say that none of us felt that there was any merit in the appeals, once the preliminary objections had been disposed of. The crucial decision was that which Baroness Scotland took, after considering the results of Woman Police Constable Gail Cox's investigations, that the men should be prosecuted. The objections had been considered with the greatest care and attention to detail by the judges in New Zealand and, as I said in the last paragraph of my opinion, the proceedings had been conducted throughout with conspicuous fairness and sensitivity by the public prosecutor. The evidence of guilt, assuming that the charges had been properly brought, was overwhelming. It was one of those cases that judges encounter from time to time when the problem was not so much what the result should be as how to get there. The clearer the view of the result, the greater is the urge to get there by the shortest route possible. I felt however that, if ever there was an occasion for making an exception to this approach, it was to be found in the Pitcairn case.

I am very pleased indeed therefore that the opportunity has now been taken to open up the issues with which we dealt so imperfectly in our judgment and to explore them in much greater depth than we could possibly have done, even if we had been minded to do so. It can no doubt be said that they are of academic interest only. No practical result can follow as far as the islanders are concerned, and the circumstances which gave rise to these prosecutions are unlikely to be repeated elsewhere. But these were real events and they gave rise to real problems which, had the events not actually happened, one would have been hard put to it to invent. This is the lifeblood of academic study. How is law made? Do laws that regulate the most basic things that people do to each other need to be promulgated? If so, how should this be done? Is it right that the behaviour of people who have been left to their own devices for centuries should be judged by the advanced standards of civilizations very different from their own? These are some of the questions that need to be answered. Those who are interested in the theory of the law will find much to interest them in the richness of this collection of essays.

David Hope
House of Lords

# *Preface*

In the case of *Steven Raymond Christian and Others v The Queen*,[1] six men from Pitcairn Island in the Pacific Ocean—a British colony with a population of only 48 souls—were convicted of a large number of sexual offences against *English* law that were committed against young girls and women on the island between 1964 and 1996. At the time the offences were committed there were no developed systems of government or of justice on the island.

When the Judicial Committee of the Privy Council in London delivered its judgments in this case in 2006, I and a number of colleagues in the Faculty of Laws at University College London were struck by the importance of the legal issues that the situation raised, but which received little attention in legal journals and columns at the time. Hence, we decided to put together a collection of essays on at least some of these questions.

The history of Pitcairn Island, since it was settled by *The Bounty* mutineers in 1790, and right up to the present day, has often been violent and lawless. The Pitcairn situation in effect provides an inter- and cross-disciplinary case study on the nature and sources of law which will be of interest to lawyers (including those interested in public and criminal law, and law and culture and feminism) and to philosophers, political scientists, anthropologists, and students of the history and sociology of the Pacific islands. The aims and rationale of this book are, then, to explore these often highly theoretical issues and to obtain insights into them from the fact that the courts and government have had to deal with them in the concrete, real-life situation of Pitcairn.

## Scope of the Book

The essays in this collection deal with the following questions raised by the Pitcairn situation.

---

[1] Privy Council Appeal No 109/2005 [2006] UKPC 47. (See Appendix I.)

## The nature of law

- First, and perhaps most fundamental, what, if any, law is there in a remote community such as that on Pitcairn in the period in question, which lacks any formal system of government or administration of justice? What, in other words, is 'law'? How does law develop in a lawless society? And what effect does the perspective of the person answering that question have on the answer?
- Related to that question, to what extent does law's existence depend on there being formal machinery for its enforcement at the time offences are committed?

## The development of law and a legal system

- How and why does law develop—if it develops at all—when settlers arrive on new territory, unaccompanied by any state officials or lawyers?
- Do those who settle uninhabited land bring the laws of the countries from which they come with them? What if those settlers are from more than one country (as in Pitcairn, where the original settlers were a combination of English subjects and Polynesians)? Whose law and what law applies then? And in what sense or senses are these 'laws'?
- What if there is no machinery of justice in this new settlement—no police, no judges, no law books, no lawyers? How does any 'law' that settlers bring with them develop after the settlement? What connection does it have with the law of the mother country? What if the settlers have rejected the authority of their state? Does customary or folk law have a place in such a situation? Indeed, to what extent is the common law (one of the foundations of the law in England and many Commonwealth countries which, it was claimed, the settlers took with them to Pitcairn) itself a form of customary law?

## Colonial power, authority, and responsibility

- How does a colonial power establish and maintain *authority* over a colony and how does it satisfy a court that it has authority? What continuing authority does a colonial power which neglects its colony have over that land? What authority did the British Crown have over Pitcairn?

- And, if a colonial power has authority over a territory, as the British government claimed to have in this case, what *responsibilities* does it have towards it? What were the responsibilities of the British Crown towards Pitcairn and its people? Did it include a responsibility to eliminate a culture of sexual abuse of women? Was prosecution of offenders an appropriate way of discharging such a responsibility?

## Public International Law

- How does a colonial power acquire sovereignty over a territory?

- What are the obligations in public international law of the colonial power in such a situation as that of Pitcairn, particularly in relation to the protection of the human rights of both the defendants and the complainants?

- What would be the implications for the protection of Pitcairn and its international status if the UK had accepted, or the court had found, that Pitcairn was not a colony?

## The rule of law, legality, criminal liability

- When, if ever, is it justifiable for a ruler to criminalize activity or to impose severe punishments for criminal activity which a local community does not consider to be criminal or seriously criminal (though it may be considered immoral)? When, if ever, do arguments about cultural relativism have any relevance here?

- What conditions must be met for a community or a ruler to use coercion against members, eg by prosecuting them? And what relevance, if any, do human rights have in such situations? Are certain forms of universal rights claims valid, even in circumstances of apparently strong cultural variation? Is it possible to determine what constitutes a violation of common and universal fundamental rights norms in particular cultural contexts?

- Is it an abuse of process and unfair to prosecute people for offences that have not been promulgated or published in the country in question, as was the case in relation to the Pitcairn prosecutions—especially if the population has no means of access to information about the content of the law? Does it make any difference if the law proscribes a *mala in se*—an intrinsically bad act? Is an unpromulgated law valid law? By what criteria is that question to be answered—by the laws of the legislator (in this case the UK Parliament and the British Crown), or according to principles of the common law? If those two are inconsistent, which is to prevail?

- Should judges trying such cases adopt a positivist approach and apply only 'the law on paper', or should they take into account broader matters such as justice and the principles of the rule of law? And what is positivism and what does it require?

Lord Hope of Craighead, who gave one of the judgments on the case in the Judicial Committee of the Privy Council, has kindly written a Foreword to the collection. Dame Marilyn Strathern, Emeritus Professor of Social Anthropology at the University of Cambridge, has provided an Afterword. We are grateful to both of them for putting the issues with which these chapters are concerned into, respectively, a judicial and an interdisciplinary context.

Finally, we are most grateful to Alex Flach and Chris Champion at Oxford University Press and two anonymous reviewers for their helpful suggestions and support.

Dawn Oliver
University College London
March 2009

# Summary Contents

| | |
|---|---|
| *Foreword* | v |
| *Preface* | ix |
| *Table of Cases* | xix |
| *Table of Legislation, Treaties, and Conventions* | xxi |
| *List of Contributors* | xxiii |

**1. Problems on Pitcairn**  1
*Dawn Oliver*

**2. The Pitcairn Prosecutions, Paper Legal Systems, and the Rule of Law**  23
*Dawn Oliver*

**3. Pitcairn's Tortured Past: A Legal History**  39
*Andrew Lewis*

**4. Pitcairn Island Law: A Peculiar Case of the Diffusion of the Common Law**  63
*Gordon Woodman*

**5. The Pitcairn Prosecutions: An Assessment of Their Historical Context by Reference to the Provisions of Public International Law**  93
*Dino Kritsiotis and A. W. B. Simpson*

**6. 'A Million Mutinies Now': Why Claims of Cultural Uniqueness Cannot be Used to Justify Violations of Basic Human Rights**  131
*Colm O'Cinneide*

**7. Rights and Duties on Pitcairn Island**  157
*George Letsas*

**8. Legality, Reciprocity, and the Criminal Law on Pitcairn**  183
*Stephen Guest*

*Afterword* 221
*Marilyn Strathern, DBE, FBA*

*Appendix I* 231
*Appendix II* 259
*Appendix III* 267
*References* 271
*Index* 285

# Contents

| | |
|---|---|
| *Foreword* | v |
| *Preface* | ix |
| *Table of Cases* | xix |
| *Table of Legislation, Treaties, and Conventions* | xxi |
| *List of Contributors* | xxiii |

**1. Problems on Pitcairn** — 1
*Dawn Oliver*

| | |
|---|---|
| A Thought Experiment | 5 |
| The Government and Governance of the Island | 10 |
| 'Operation Unique': Investigation of Alleged Offences | 13 |
| Trials and Convictions | 15 |
| The Next Chapters | 16 |

**2. The Pitcairn Prosecutions, Paper Legal Systems, and the Rule of Law** — 23
*Dawn Oliver*

| | |
|---|---|
| *Steven Raymond Christian and Others v The Queen* in the Judicial Committee of the Privy Council | 23 |
| The Colonial Status of Pitcairn | 24 |
| The Machinery of Justice Points | 27 |
| Legality and the Rule of Law | 28 |
| Reflections | 35 |
| And Afterwards ... | 36 |

**3. Pitcairn's Tortured Past: A Legal History** — 39
*Andrew Lewis*

| | |
|---|---|
| The Settlement: 1790–1814 | 41 |
| A savage society | 41 |
| A biblical monarchy | 48 |
| Recognition: 1814–56 | 51 |
| Intervention: 1856–98 | 54 |

Settled Government: 1898–Present     56
Conclusion     61

4. **Pitcairn Island Law: A Peculiar Case of the Diffusion of the Common Law**     63
   *Gordon Woodman*

   The History of the Sources of Law in Pitcairn     66
       The law originally in force in Pitcairn     67
       Legal development after the original settlement     72
   The Abuse of Process Issue     82
   A Concluding Comment     89

5. **The Pitcairn Prosecutions: An Assessment of Their Historical Context by Reference to the Provisions of Public International Law**     93
   *Dino Kritsiotis and A. W. B. Simpson*

   Jurisdiction: A Brief Conceptual Analysis     96
   On Territorial Acquisition     106
   Sovereign Title and Sovereign Obligations     119
   Concluding Reflections     127

6. **'A Million Mutinies Now': Why Claims of Cultural Uniqueness Cannot be Used to Justify Violations of Basic Human Rights**     131
   *Colm O'Cinneide*

   Narrating Pitcairn     134
       The alleged failure to respect the uniqueness of Pitcairn     136
       The incoherence of the cultural narrative and the reality of the sexual abuse that occurred on Pitcairn     138
       The distorting influence of the emphasis on Pitcairn's isolation     141
   'Cultural' Arguments in Relation to Pitcairn     143
       Minority group rights claims     146
       'Cultural defence' claims     150
       'Cultural relativism' claims     151
   The Dangers of Exaggerated Respect for 'Culture'     154
   Conclusion     155

7.  **Rights and Duties on Pitcairn Island** 157
    *George Letsas*

    Cultural Relativism, Universality, and Blameworthiness 159
    Legal Positivism and Natural Law 169
    Legality and Community 176
    Conclusion 182

8.  **Legality, Reciprocity, and the Criminal Law on Pitcairn** 183
    *Stephen Guest*

    Crown Jurisdiction in Pitcairn: Community and
    Legal Theory 186
    *Mala in se* 197
       The importance of promulgation 199
       Promulgation and *ignorantia* 201
       Two values of promulgation and legal positivism 204
    Return to Pitcairn 207
       Fairness 210
    The Limits of Criminal Law 214
       Rights of victims 216
       The value of certainty in the criminal law 218
    Summary and Conclusion 219

*Afterword* 221
*Marilyn Strathern, DBE, FBA*
    How are Islands Made? 221
    Speculations 222
    Comparisons 226
    End 228

*Appendix I*
*Steven Raymond Christian and Others v*
*The Queen* [2006] UKPC 47 231

*Appendix II*
Official Correspondence
(a)  Paul Treadwell, Honorary Legal Adviser to the
     Governor of Pitcairn Island, Kerikeri, New Zealand,
     to CD Shute, First Secretary, British High Commission,
     Wellington, New Zealand, 5 January 1997 260

(b) Paul Treadwell, Honorary Legal Adviser to the Acting
Governor of New Zealand, to Mrs K Wolstenholme,
Acting Governor of Pitcairn, Wellington, New Zealand,
29 April 2000                                                                                    262
(c) Martin Williams, Governor of Pitcairn, London,
to Mrs K Wolstenholme, Deputy Governor,
British High Commission, Wellington, New Zealand,
2 May 2000                                                                                      264
(d) Clare Short, Secretary of State for International
Development, London, to The Rt Hon Robin Cook,
Secretary of State for Foreign and Commonwealth
Affairs, London                                                                               265

*Appendix III*
   Outline: Pitcairn Island Chronology                                       267

*References*                                                                                    271
*Index*                                                                                            285

# Table of Cases

Advocate-General of Bengal v Ranee Surnomoye Dossee (1863) 15 ER 811 . . . . . . 68
Al-Kateb v Godwin 208 (2004) ALR 124 . . . . . . . . . . . . . . . . . . . . . . . . . . . . . 193
Angu v Attah, 1916 Gold Coast Privy Council Judgments (1874–1928). . . . . . . . . 80
Attorney-General of British Honduras v Bristowe (1880) 6 App Cas 143 . . . . 73, 106
Campbell v Hall (1774) 98 ER 1045, 20 State Tr. 239 . . . . . . . . . . . . . . . . . 67, 77
Carl Zeiss Stiftung v Rayner and Keeler Ltd. (No. 2) [1967] 1 AC 853 . . . . . . . . 108
Christian v R (No.2) [2005] PNSC 1 . . . . . . . . . . . . . . . . . . . . . . 139, 140, 142, 153
Fagernes, The [1927] P 311 . . . . . . . . . . . . . . . . . . . . . . . . . . . . .25, 58, 79, 107, 233
Fothergill v Monarch Airlines Ltd [1981] AC 251 . . . . . . . . . . . . . . . . . . . . . . . 256
Grant v Borg [1982] 1 WLR 638 . . . . . . . . . . . . . . . . . . . . . . . . . . . . . . . . . . . 241
Hesperides Hotels v Aegean Holidays Ltd. [1978] QB 205, CA . . . . . . . . . . . . . 108
Island of Palmas Arbitration: Netherlands v United States,
    2 RIAA 831 . . . . . . . . . . . . . . . . . . . . . . . . . . . . . . . . . . . . . . . 110, 115, 119
Joyce v Director of Public Prosecutions [1946] AC 347 . . . . . . . . . . . . . . . . 50, 101
Nyali Ltd v Attorney-General [1956] 1 QB 1 . . . . . . . . . . . . . . . . . . . . . . . 234, 254
Queen, The v 7 Named Accused [2004] PNSC 1 . . . . . . . . . . . . . . . . . . . . 99, 106
R v Bailey [1964] Crim LR 671 . . . . . . . . . . . . . . . . . . . . . . . . . . . . . . . . . . . . 89
R v Byfield [1967] Crim LR 378 . . . . . . . . . . . . . . . . . . . . . . . . . . . . . . . . . . . . 89
R v Court [1989] AC 28 . . . . . . . . . . . . . . . . . . . . . . . . . . . . . . . . . . . . . . . . . 211
R v Finlay [1963] Crim LR 299 . . . . . . . . . . . . . . . . . . . . . . . . . . . . . . . . . . . . 89
R v Latif [1966] 1 WLR 104 . . . . . . . . . . . . . . . . . . . . . . . . . . . . 124, 236, 237
R v Rimmington [2005] UKHL 63; [2006] 1 AC 459 . . . . . . . . . . . . . . . 125, 256
R v Seven Named Accused, Pitcairn Court of Appeal, CA 1-7/2004,
    5 August 2004 . . . . . . . . . . . . . . . . . . . . . . . . . . . . . . . . . . . . . . . . . . . . 16
Republic of Somalia v Woodhouse Drake Carey Suisse S.A. [1993] QB 54 . . . . . . 108
Sammut v Strickland [1938] AC 678 . . . . . . . . . . . . . . . . . . . . . . . . . . . . . 80, 114
Steven Raymond Christian and Others v The Queen
    (Appeal No 109/2005) [2006] UKPC 47; [2007]
    2 AC 400, [2007] 2 WLR 120 . . . . . . . . . . . . . . . 1, 4, 11, 23–37, 39, 59, 63,
                                                                65,71, 75, 81, 83, 85, 90, 93,
                                                                96, 112, 136, 175, 183, App 1
Steven Raymond Christian and Others v The Queen, Pitcairn Court of Appeal,
    CA 1-7/2004, 5 August 2004 and CA 1-6/2005, 2 March 2006 . . . . . . . . 63, 65
Western Sahara (1975) ICJ Rep. 12 . . . . . . . . . . . . . . . . . . . . . . . . . . . . . . . . . 98

# Table of Legislation, Treaties, and Conventions

Australian Courts Act 1828 . . . . 88, 102
Colonial Laws Validity Act 1865 . . . . 77
British Nationality Act 1730 . . . . . . . 51
   s 2 . . . . . . . . . . . . . . . . . . . . . . 56
British Nationality Act 1736 . . . . . . . 99
British Settlements Act 1843 . . . . . . 104
British Settlements Act 1860 . . . . . . 104
British Settlements Act 1887 . . . . . . 24,
         25, 58, 76, 77, 78, 81,
     104, 108, 109, 111, 174, 179,
     193, 231, 239, 243, 250
   s 2 . . . . . . . . . . . . . . . . . 248, 267
   s 4 . . . . . . . . . . . . . . . . . . . . . 105
British Settlements Act 1945 . . . . . . . 76
British Settlements Act 1952 . . . . . 104,
          239, 250
Foreign Enlistment Act 1870
   s 12 . . . . . . . . . . . . . . . . . . . . . 99
Foreign Jurisdiction Act 1890 . . . . . 104
   s 2 . . . . . . . . . . . . . . . . . . . . . 103
Human Rights Act 1998 . . . . . 127, 145
Incitement to Mutiny Act 1797 . . . . 102
Judicature (Courts) Ordinance 1999
   s 16 . . . . . . . . . . . . . . . . . . . . 127
Judicature Ordinance 1961 . . 104, 232,
          250, 268
   s 7 . . . . . . . . . . . . . . . . . 234, 249
   s 8 . . . . . . . . . . . . . . . . . . . . . 249
Judicature Ordinance 1970 . . . . . . 104,
         117, 243, 250, 253
   s 14 . . . . . . . . . . . . . . . . 233, 240
   s 14(1) . . . . . . . . . . . . . . 127, 234
Merchant Shipping Act 1894 . . . . . . 102
Mutiny Act 1689 . . . . . . . . . . . . . . 100
Mutiny Act 1797 . . . . . . . . . . 101, 102
Mutiny Act 1872 . . . . . . . . . . . . . . 101

Offences against the Person Act 1861
   . . . . . . . . . . . . . . . . . . . . . . 87
   s 9 . . . . . . . . . . . . . . . . . . . . . . 57
   s 48 . . . . . . . . . . . . . . . . 252, 257
   s 52 . . . . . . . . . . . . . . . . 252, 257
Pacific Islanders Protection Act 1873
   . . . . . . . . . . . . . . . . . . . . . 102
Pacific Order in Council 1893 . . . . 104,
         111, 231, 248
   Art 6(1) . . . . . . . . . . . . . . . . . 232
   Art 20 . . . . . . . . . . . . . . . 232, 234
Pacific Order in Council 1970
   . . . . . . . . . . . . . . . . . 104, 232
Pitcairn Island Government Regulations
   1940 . . . . . . . . . . . . . . . . . . . 104
Pitcairn Court of Appeal Order 2000
   (SI 2000/1341) . . . . . . . . . . . . 117
Pitcairn Criminal Justice Ordinance 1966
   s 82 . . . . . . . . . . . . . . . . . 93, 256
   s 88 . . . . . . . . . . . . . 93, 240, 256
Pitcairn Order in Council 1952
   . . . . . . . . . . . . . . 232, 239, 268
Pitcairn Order in Council 1970
   . . . . . . . . . . . . . . . . . . 239, 268
   Art 5(3) . . . . . . . . . . . . . . . . . 255
Sexual Offences Act 1956 . . . . . . 17, 21,
   24, 25, 28-30, 33, 37, 65, 77, 78,
   86, 95, 117, 127, 128, 169, 173,
   197, 212, 233, 242, 252, 255-258
   s 1 . . . . . . 15, 31, 34, 82, 167, 211,
         238, 239, 245
   s 5 . . . . . . . . . . . . . . . . . . . . . 244
   s 10 . . . . . . . . . . . . . . . . . . . . . 82
   s 14 . . . . . 15, 31, 34, 82, 211, 238,
       239, 242, 245, 246, 252,
       255-258

s 50 . . . . . . . . . . . . . . . . . . . . 118
s 54 . . . . . . . . . . . . . . . . . 93, 118
Sexual Offences Act 2003
s 137. . . . . . . . . . . . . . . . . . . 118
s 142. . . . . . . . . . . . . . . . . . . 118

European Convention on Human
  Rights 1950 . . . . . . . . . . . . . 18, 145
  Art 7(1) . . . . . . . . . . . . . . . . . 125
  Art 7(2) . . . . . . . . . . . . . . . . . 125
  Art 56(1). . . . . . . . . . . . . . . . . 126
Geneva Convention on the High
  Seas . . . . . . . . . . . . . . . . . . . . . 100
Montevideo Convention on the Rights
  and Duties of States
  Art 5. . . . . . . . . . . . . . . . . . . . 103
  Art 9. . . . . . . . . . . . . . . . . . . . 103
Treaty of Utrecht 1713 . . . . . . . . . . 114

United Nations Convention on the
  Rights of the Child 1989 . . . . . . 122
  Art 19(1). . . . . . . . . . . . . . . . . 121
United Nations Covenant on Civil and
  Political Rights 1966 . . . . . 18, 120,
                                  121, 144
  Art 15(1). . . . . . . . . . . . . . . . . 125
  Art 15(2). . . . . . . . . . . . . . . . . 125
  Art 27. . . . . . . . . . . . . . . . . . . 146
United Nations Covenant on Economic,
  Cultural and Social Rights . . . . . 120
United Nations Convention on the
  Elimination of All Forms of
  Discrimination Against
  Women . . . . . . . . . . . . . . . . 18, 120
Universal Declaration of Human Rights
  1948 . . . . . . . . . . . . . . . . . 123, 125
  Art 15. . . . . . . . . . . . . . . . . . . 122

# List of Contributors

**Stephen Guest** is Professor of Legal Philosophy at University College London (UCL) and a member of the English and New Zealand bars. His books include *Positivism Today* (editor, 1996) and *Ronald Dworkin* (2nd edition, 1997). In 2006–2007 he held a British Academy/Leverhulme Trust Senior Fellowship. He has been co-chair of the Dworkin Colloquium for Legal and Social Philosophy at UCL for many years. He was academic advisor to the Public Defender in the Pitcairn case.

**Dino Kritsiotis** is Reader in Public International Law at the University of Nottingham, and he has been the L. Bates Lea Visting Professor of Law at the University of Michigan (2003, 2005–2008). His main research commitments lie in the fields of the international legal regulation of force, international humanitarian law, and the history and theory of public international law. He sits on the editorial boards for the *Journal of Conflict and Security Law* (Oxford University Press), the *Human Rights Law Review* (Oxford University Press), *Human Rights and Human Welfare* (www.hrhw.org) and the *African Yearbook of International Humanitarian Law* (Juta Publishing). Kritsiotis served as the founding rapporteur of the Theory of Committee of the International Law Association (British Branch), from 1998 to 2001.

**George Letsas** is Lecturer in Laws at University College London. He researches in the fields of jurisprudence and human rights and his work has been published in the *Oxford Journal of Legal Studies*, the *European Journal of International Law*, and the *European Human Rights Law Review*. He is the author of *A Theory of Interpretation of the European Convention of Human Rights* (OUP, 2007).

**Andrew Lewis** is Professor of Comparative Legal History at University College London. He has recently edited (with Dr Iris Cox) Montesquieu's early and unpublished text *Collectio Juris* (2 volumes, Voltaire Edition, Oxford, 2006) as part of the Société Montesquieu's ongoing edition of the *Complete Works*. In 2007 he contributed to a special number of the *Journal of Legal History* devoted to the case of *The Zong*.

**Colm O'Cinneide** is a Senior Lecturer in Laws at University College London. His work has been published in *Industrial Law Journal*, *Irish Human Rights Law Journal*, *Northern Ireland Legal Quarterly*, and

*Current Legal Problems* and *Public Law*, in the fields of human rights and anti-discrimination law. Other publications for public bodies include: *Equivalence of Rights and the Belfast Agreement* (2005); *Age Discrimination and European Law* (2005); and *Taking Equal Opportunities Seriously* (2003). He was a member of the UK Task Force on the establishment of the new Commission for Equality and Human Rights. He is currently a member of the Committee of Independent Experts that supervises state compliance with the European Social Charter.

**Dawn Oliver**, FBA, is Professor Emeritus of Constitutional Law at University College London. Her research interests include UK constitutional reform, judicial review, the public private divide, and human rights. Publications include: *Common Values and the Public-Private Divide* (Butterworths, 1999); *Constitutional Reform in the UK* (Oxford University Press, 2003); *The Changing Constitution* (edited with Jeffrey Jowell, 6th edn, Oxford University Press, 2007); *Human Rights and the Private Sphere* (edited with Joerg Fedtke, Routledge-Cavendish, 2007).

**A. W. B. (Brian) Simpson** is Charles F. and Edith J. Clyne Professor of Law at the University of Michigan Law school, where he has taught since 1987. He has held chairs at Cambridge and in other institutions. He was made an honorary QC in 2001. His main publications and research have been in the fields of legal history and theory, the British Empire, human rights, and international law. Publications include: *A History of the Common Law of Contract* (1975); *Cannibalism and the Common Law* (1984); *Legal Theory and Legal History* (1987); and *Human Rights and the End of Empire: Britain and the Genesis of the European Convention* (2001).

**Dame Marilyn Strathern**, FBA, is Emeritus Professor of Social Anthropology at the University of Cambridge, and Mistress of Girton College. Her publications include: *The Gender of the Gift* (1988); *After Nature* (1992); and *Kinship, Law and the Unexpected* (2005).

**Gordon R. Woodman** is Emeritus Professor of Comparative Law at the University of Birmingham. He is the author of *Customary Land Law in the Ghanaian Courts* (Ghana Universities Press, 1996), co-editor with A O Obilade of *African Law and Legal Theory* (Dartmouth, 1995), and co-editor with U Wanitzek and H Sippel of *Local Land Law and Globalization* (LIT, 2004). He has published a number of articles on the reception, application and adaptation of the common law in Commonwealth countries, and has taught courses on this subject in Ghana, Nigeria, Papua New Guinea, Mauritius, and Birmingham.

# 1

# Problems on Pitcairn

## *Dawn Oliver*

The discussions in this book centre around the prosecution of a number of men on Pitcairn Island in the Pacific Ocean for offences committed between 1964 and 1999 against women and young girls there.

Few people have heard of Pitcairn Island. Stamp collectors may know of it, since stamps are one of its few exports.[1] And some may connect it with the Mutiny on HMAV *The Bounty* in 1790. Wikipedia tells us that there is speculation that Coleridge's *Ancient Mariner* may have been modelled on the leader of the mutiny, Fletcher Christian. Those who do know about the mutiny and that some of the mutineers settled on Pitcairn may have a romantic picture—derived perhaps from having seen the 1935 Clark Gable and Charles Laughton film *Mutiny on 'The Bounty'*—of a rebellion by Fletcher Christian against the Crown and the brutal Captain Bligh of *The Bounty*, and of a rather idyllic tropical island on which the mutineers settled and on which to this day hardworking people live in harmony without a government.[2] But that is the extent of most people's knowledge of the island. So where is it? And what is special about it? Why bother to write a collection of essays about it? And is the idyllic picture true?[3]

---

[1] For information see <http://www.stamps.gov.pn>.

[2] See for instance W.Y. Fullerton, *The Romance of Pitcairn Island*, London: Carey Press, 1921; Dea Birkett, *Serpent in Paradise*, New Zealand: Anchor Books, 1997; Trevor Lummis, *Life and Death in Eden: Pitcairn Island and the Bounty Mutineers*, Aldershot: Ashgate, 1997.

[3] There are a range of sources for the information in this and subsequent chapters about life on Pitcairn. This account draws partly on the judgments in the Privy Council case of *Christian v The Queen*, below, and on Kathy Marks, *Trouble in Paradise: Uncovering Decades of Sexual Abuse on Britain's Most Remote Island*, London: Harper Perennial, 2008.

Where is it? Pitcairn is one of a collection of four islands in the South Pacific. It is some 3,000 miles from, respectively, New Zealand and South America. It is two square miles in area. The other islands are uninhabited. There is no harbour there and visiting ships—of which there are few—have to anchor offshore. Visitors are then ferried ashore by the islanders in longboats. Nor is there an airstrip.

What is special about Pitcairn? The island was settled in 1790 by nine of the English mutineers who had been responsible for the mutiny on HMAV *Bounty*, and 19 Polynesians—six men, 12 women, and a child—they brought with them, mostly against their will. At the time of settlement the island was uninhabited. Its current population is about 50.

Why should lawyers bother to write a collection of essays about all this? Because the situation on the island raises so many fascinating and fundamental questions about the existence and nature of legal systems, justice, and the law. The English law doctrine is that English subjects 'take the common law with them' when they settle in new territories.[4] Many of the settlers on Pitcairn were not English: if the Polynesians took any law with them it was not English law. So what law did the settlers take with them—if any? Of course the Pitcairn settlers did not take any machinery of justice with them—no lawyers, judges, or police. Can there be law without any formal machinery for enforcing it?

In the early years of the settlement the community was in many respects lawless: within 10 years most of the original English and Polynesian male settlers had been murdered. Thus the history of Pitcairn[5] provides an illustration of how law and a system for its administration of the kinds we are accustomed to in a Western democracy may wither away or not develop in a small, remote, acephalous island society lacking contact with the outside world.

The original settlers and their descendants have been joined from time to time by further British subjects—and by others. Over the years some members of the community—including many women now aged between 30 and 50—have left Pitcairn for Australia, New Zealand, Canada, and other countries. The maximum size of the population since the settlement has been about 200. In the relevant period, between the 1960s and today, the population has been around 50. It consists of

---

[4] See discussion in Woodman, chapter 4 below.     [5] See Lewis, chapter 3 below.

seven intermarried families and a few resident visitors such as the Seventh Day Adventist pastor and his wife, and the schoolteacher.

The British government has claimed since the mid-nineteenth century at least that Pitcairn is a British colony—a British Overseas Territory. The UK has kept its colonial legal paperwork in order (Acts of Parliament, Orders in Council and Ordinances, and appointment of a Governor). It has paid, out of a Pitcairn fund[6] fed largely by the sale of stamps, coins etc, for the running costs of the island—travel of Pitcairners to New Zealand (on British Dependent Territories passports issued by the UK) for education and health care, capital items such as longboats, tractors, and generators, and the salaries of those holding 'government jobs'—the island police officer (who was appointed by the Crown), the postmaster, the teacher, the tractor driver, and various other office-holders on the island.

But there has—until recently—been no permanent or resident independent Crown presence on the island. The islanders have been left to govern themselves—until the last decade or so. The Governor of Pitcairn is resident in New Zealand. Most importantly for our purposes, the system of justice has been neglected. At the time of the convictions there were still no lawyers or judges resident on the island. There was until recently only one law book—containing local laws—there. There is a local Magistrate, whose jurisdiction is limited to minor offences, which did not include the serious offences with which the defendants in the case were charged. And there is a local police officer, appointed by the Crown. Neither had received any training at the time the alleged offences were committed. And both the Magistrate and the police officer were related to almost all the other members of the community, including many of those charged with offences.

And yet the Pitcairners, Marks noted during her visit to the island at the time of the trials, are rather patriotic:[7] portraits of the Queen and the Duke of Edinburgh were displayed in the court house; the Union Jack forms part of the Picairn flag, and both the Pitcairn flag and the Union Jack are often hoisted; the national anthem is sung at public meetings, school concerts, and film shows; some islanders are MBEs. These facts appear to contradict assumptions which were implicit in the

---

[6] Marks, *Trouble in Paradise*, chapter 5.
[7] Ibid, chapter 3.

defendants' denial at the trials of the colonial status of the island that the islanders were hostile to the Crown—that it was not a colony at all.

Since the 1960s a legal drama has been played out in Pitcairn, New Zealand, and London. In a process starting in 1999 and culminating in an appeal to the Judicial Committee of the Privy Council in London in 2006, *Steven Raymond Christian and Others v The Queen*,[8] a number of male Pitcairn Island residents have been investigated, prosecuted, and convicted of sexual offences against young girls. Many of these attacks have been violent, including repeated rapes and gang rapes. In many instances the perpetrators were considerably older than their victims. The cases were not about adolescent experimentation.

Girls on the island were liable to be abused—including being indecently assaulted and subjected to oral sex—from the age of about five, some even from the age of three. Virtually all the young girls on the island were sexually abused. Some were left barren as a result of the injuries they suffered in these assaults. Many of the victims left the island.[9] Thus the popular idyll of life on Pitcairn has been grossly misleading, for women and girls on the island at least.

The interesting issues for the lawyers in the case—judges, barristers, solicitors—were not to do with whether the men charged had committed the acts they were accused of. (Only one of the defendants gave evidence.) The men's cases were either that the assaults they were accused of had not occurred at all, or that their victims had consented to them. None of the accused actually suggested that sexual abuse of young girls and women was not wrong, or that it was part of their culture and that for that reason it should not be regarded as criminal. The situation of Pitcairn does, however, raise issues to do with that very point—cultural relativism. Some of these are considered in chapters 6, 7, and 8 below.

The most interesting points for the lawyers in the case were rather to do with whether the UK had authority over the island as a colony; with what—if any—law relating to sexual offences there was on Pitcairn at the time the acts took place; and with whether it was in any way inconsistent with the principles of justice and the rule of law for the defendants to be prosecuted in the rather exceptional circumstances of the cases. In this collection of essays, we explore some of these issues and

---

[8] Privy Council Appeal No 109/2005 [2006] UKPC 47.
[9] Marks, *Trouble in Paradise*, chapters 3–6.

the questions—some of them highly theoretical but nonetheless of central importance for lawyers, as well as anthropologists, philosophers, and others—generated by the situation of an isolated island community such as Pitcairn. The Pitcairn case and the situation of the community provide concrete sounding-boards against which to test the various possible answers to these questions—and indeed to many other questions that would be of interest to those working in disciplines other than law.

## A Thought Experiment

Let us put ourselves in the position of the government of any Western democratic colonial power that receives information about the kind of abuse that had taken place on Pitcairn having occurred on one of its remote colonies. Having taken legal advice the government will realize that, if prosecutions are brought against those suspected of acts of rape, incest, and indecent assault, it will be met by quite substantial objections: (i) the defendants may argue that the territory is not to be treated as a colony because the original settlers explicitly rejected the authority of the colonial power; (ii) even if it is a colony, the mother country has effectively lost its authority over the territory by neglect; (iii) the defendants may challenge the validity of the laws under which they will be prosecuted; and (iv) they may argue that, even if the laws are valid, it is unfair to prosecute them for offences under legislation of which they could not be aware.

What is the colonial power to do?

Option 1: Should it accept that because of its neglect and the fact that the original settlers were rejecting its authority it has no claim to authority over the territory? That would meet the demands of the defendants. But what about the other members of the community? It would mean that there would be no legal provision for the prosecution of people who had committed, by the legal standards of every civilized country, serious offences against their fellows; there would be no deterrence against continuation of the culture of abuse and no retribution or amends for the victims of these acts; and the reasons for the colonial power to provide financial support to the community would disappear.

Alternatively, option 2: the colonial power could maintain its authority over the island, but decide not to prosecute the alleged offenders; instead it could decide to pay compensation to the victims of sexual abuse and to put in place arrangements for the future protection of children and young women on the island:[10] for instance, a Family and Community Advisor, child protection training for the island teacher and doctor, education programmes for the Family and Community Advisor and teacher, and appointment of a full-time Community Police Officer from outside the island.

Lastly, option 3: our colonial power could maintain its position that the island is a colony, and put in place the machinery for the prosecution of defendants for sexual offences, despite the facts that laws were not published on the island and that the system of justice has been neglected. It could do so on the basis:

1) that the acts the defendants are accused of are in any event *mala in se* and contrary to the law of any civilized country;

2) that—given that its own legal paperwork is in order—it has the legal authority to make and enforce laws for the peace, order, and good government of the territory in question; that right and the validity of such laws are not dependent upon the people of the territory being part of the community of the mother country, or having been parties to the law-making process, nor upon the people having been informed of the existence and terms of the laws to be applied to them, nor upon those subject to the law accepting that what they were doing was immoral, or sufficiently immoral to attract criminal sanctions.

Of course there may be political pressures on the government to decide one way or the other: women in the government may feel strongly that only prosecution, conviction, and punishment can provide satisfaction to the victims of the abuse and alter the unacceptable culture of the community.[11]

None of those courses—abandoning claim to authority over the colony in these matters, taking steps to compensate victims and ensure that such offences are not committed in future, or asserting law-making and law-enforcing authority over it—is self-evidently—from a moral point of view—the only right or wrong one. And the strict or technical legal position may be debatable. Indeed as we shall see, it is not easy to

---

[10] See discussion by Kritsiotis and Simpson in chapter 5 of the obligations in international law of colonial powers towards women and children.

[11] See chapter 8 and Appendix II, document (c).

separate moral and legal arguments in a situation of legal uncertainty. There are moral and legal objections to each of these three options taken in isolation, and some things to be said in favour of each. So the issue, ultimately, is what is or are the least wrong or most right courses of action for the government of this colonial power to take?

I guess that, given that we know that the thought experiment is taking place in the context of the Pitcairn prosecutions, many of us are quite sympathetic to the decision of the colonial power to put in place the machinery for the prosecution of the accused. Surely, we might think, the men on the island cannot get away with what by any decent standards are revolting acts against the womenfolk in their community? Where's the problem about prosecuting them?

But let us move the pieces on the chess-board and then ask ourselves again what our responses are. Imagine that some fugitives from an oppressive regime—Iraq in 2000, Afghanistan under the Taliban, the USSR during the Stalinist period—escaped and settled on an uninhabited island in, say, the Indian Ocean. Some years later the regime in their 'mother country'—not a Western democracy—claims sovereignty over that island and creates legal paperwork giving effect to that claim. Perhaps it sends a priest or preacher to the community or provides electricity-generating equipment to the island. But it does not provide or maintain a system of justice. Some years later, the mother country asserts the right to prosecute residents on the island for criminal offences against the law of the mother country or laws made by the mother country for the colony. Where would our sympathies lie today?

The argument might well be put that the government of the mother country is a mere busybody if it intervenes in the affairs of a community it has had nothing much to do with for many years. And it may be argued that the law of the mother country should not apply in the new settlement: the population was not involved in the law-making process, and at any rate, the culture of the population has now evolved from what it was at the time of the settlement. It is no longer regarded (as it was at the time the islanders' forbears settled there) as an offence on this island to criticize the government of the colonial power, or to have sex outside marriage, or for women to leave their homes unveiled. Many of us would instinctively sympathize with that argument. But this takes us into debate about what the law in that island is—if indeed there is any law on such matters there—or what we think the law ought to be. It is not easy to separate the two issues in this kind of situation where the actual legal position is itself very debatable.

The women were, at various times, in open rebellion against the men and, generally, a source of conflict between the men. Both these factors were related to the circumstances which brought them to Pitcairn seemingly against their will. Soon after their arrival, the Tahitian companion of John 'Jack' Williams died and he demanded that he be given one of the three women allotted to the 'blacks' as a replacement. After some discussion, this was agreed and lots were cast to determine which woman Williams should have: the lot fell upon Toofaitii or Nancy. The Polynesian to whom she was attached immediately left the settlement. He later returned and carried Nancy off, determined to have revenge. This fact was communicated by the rest of the women to the mutineers. Christian tried to take action but succeeded only in alienating another of the Polynesian men. A temporary solution was arrived at when a third Polynesian was persuaded to confront and shoot dead the two renegades. Williams got Nancy back and this initial crisis terminated.

The final crisis did not occur until September 1793 when Isabella Christian was expecting her third child. The Polynesians, who worked as servants for Quintal and McKoy determined upon their deaths and recruited the other two to assist. They borrowed a gun to hunt for wild pigs. Whilst the women, all but Isabella Christian, were away from the village looking for eggs, and the mutineers were at work in their gardens, the four Polynesian men set out to kill them all. First to die was Williams, followed by Christian who was shot from behind as he dug out a root in his garden. McKoy and Quintal, alerted, fled the settlement. Mills was then killed when he sought to approach the Polynesians (according to Teehuteatuaonoa, McKoy was with Mills when he was killed but escaped). Martin was shot and then beaten to death when he took refuge with Brown, who was next to die.

There were now eight men left on the island, the four Polynesians and four of the mutineers. Adams had been warned by one of the women and hid himself, but was wounded when he showed himself. He fled but was eventually persuaded to return to Christian's hut where the women were now assembled. Also there under their protection was Young.

With Quintal and McKoy still in hiding, a truce was established. There were now, at least, more than enough women to go round. But there was rivalry between the Polynesians which eventually led one of them, Manarii (or Menalee), to kill one of his fellows and then flee to join McKoy and Quintal. A message was got to these that they would be welcomed back if they disposed of Manarii: this they did but remained in

If, furthermore, the evidence was that the law which the mother country now seeks to apply on the island had not been published or promulgated on this remote island, we may be even more opposed to the prosecution of the accused. Alternatively we may take the view that as long as these laws were roughly consistent with the law at the time the settlers arrived on the island, there is no need for their publication: it is sufficient that the settlers and their offspring to whom they are taken to have passed on this information know that what they have done is criminally punishable; cultural transmission of the values underlying the laws of the mother country substitutes for actual publication of those laws on the island.

But what if the mother country's laws now require, for instance, the stoning to death of women found to have committed adultery, or the prosecution and incarceration of those who criticize the ideology—Marxist-Leninism, or Taliban teaching, for instance—of the mother country? I suggest that we would not be comfortable with the enforcement of those laws on the later generations of people on this island in any event, and particularly if they had come to reject such laws and developed a different (perhaps more liberal—but is that relevant?) culture. Our concerns would not only have to do with the fact that the population had not participated in the making of these draconian laws, but with the fact that they seem to deny the interests of individuals in their autonomy and dignity.

Alternatively, what if the law or the culture at the time that the fugitives settled on the island permitted the sexual abuse—indecent assault, incest, and rape—of young girls and women, and such behaviour remains part of the tradition and culture of the population? Perhaps there was a presumption that young girls enjoy and consent to such acts. But the law of the mother country now criminalizes such abuse. Where do our sympathies lie now? Can we avoid confronting the fact that the substance of the law dictates our response to it? Which of the three options set out above should the mother country follow?

When dealing, at least in the abstract, with the question of the authority of a colonial power, we might assert that there are universal principles, among which the protection of children and women[12] or freethinkers with a new perspective against violent actions by the state or other individuals is one, which a body in legal or de facto authority

---

[12] See discussion of international law by Kritsiotis and Simpson in chapter 5.

over a territory ought to apply, even if democratic or participatory processes have not been followed in making the laws which lay down the consequences of these 'offences' and even if many of the inhabitants would object. We would likely take the view that laws of the mother country that are inconsistent with these universal principles should not apply to the colony; *first*, because to do so would be *antidemocratic*, the laws not having been made by the people on the island; and *secondly*, because in any event, 'democratic' or not, it would be 'unlawful' to apply such rules, the substance of such rules being contrary to universal principles of equality, respect for individual autonomy and non-discrimination, of proportionality of punishment, and legal certainty. And conversely we might argue that the laws of the mother country that are consistent with these universal principles ought to apply, again regardless of whether they have been democratically made or endorsed by those to be subjected to them.

If we adopted that position we might find ourselves accused of cultural arrogance, the colonial power maintaining that it was no business of any other body to intervene in the affairs of this remote territory and its people: we would, I anticipate, reject such claims, feeling that universal principles are indeed our business.

The point of all this is that our responses to such situations are likely to be coloured by our own culture and traditions. And if we are also trying to decide what the law *is* in such a situation, our moral and legal responses may conflict with one another. It is not easy, even—or perhaps especially—for lawyers, to separate out moral from legal responses to such situations. Indeed in a small, remote community lacking any real machinery of justice it may be very difficult to decide if there is any law at all save that 'might is right'—the might in this case being that exercised by the men in the community against the girls. The dry legal answer for a court based in the mother country might be to give effect to the legal paperwork that has been produced by its own government and legislature regardless of issues of principle and morality, such as whether the substance of the law was known to the defendants. To a court or lawyers practising in another jurisdiction, however, the issues might be seen differently, and questions of the substantive justice of the law would be relevant. To a court, lawyers, and defendants in the actual community, such issues would naturally be of central importance.

Bringing all these points home, how would we want or expect the British government to respond in such a situation—the Pitcairn situation in the late 1990s? If it accepts the argument that the settlement is not a colony (option 1) it will be accused of washing its hands of its responsibilities to all those on the island, in particular the women, and later generations. Not only that, but it will be forbearing, when it has a colourable excuse for doing so, from intervening in the affairs of a territory where life is, at least for the girls and young women on the island, Hobbesian—nasty and brutish. And, furthermore, if it abandons all claims to authority over the island, and given that no other state has a claim to such authority, it will expose the island and its inhabitants to the risk of plunder by the modern equivalent of the marauding whalers who plagued Pitcairn Island in the nineteenth century.[13]

The colonial power could decide against prosecution and instead put in place the arrangements set out in option 2 above. (As we shall see in chapter 8, the British government did indeed consider various alternatives to prosecution for Pitcairn—and ultimately it put them in place: it went for options 2 *and* 3.[14])

If, after appropriate argy-bargy about these issues, the colonial power asserts its authority and arranges for prosecutions to be launched (option 3) how would we expect a court hearing them to respond? Having satisfied itself that the offences charged are in any event contrary to the standards of any civilized community, should a court adopt a formalistic, legalistic approach, focusing on whether the colonial paperwork complied with the mother country's formal legal requirements; or should it confront and deal with the deep issues of democracy and constitutional and moral theory that underlie the case? Where that consideration would lead them is not certain, as is demonstrated by the differences of view put forward by O'Cinneide, Letsas, and Guest in this collection.[15] But that unpredictability is not itself an argument against taking this principled approach.

These were the dilemmas facing the Crown and the courts in the Pitcairn case.

## The Government and Governance of the Island

Let us turn now from the thought experiment to some of the realities on Pitcairn. Reference was made earlier to a 'legal drama' being played out in Pitcairn, or in associated locations, in recent years. So who are the

---

[13] See Lewis, chapter 3, and Kritsiotis and Simpson, chapter 5, below.
[14] See chapter 2 below.     [15] Chapters 6, 7, and 8 below.

characters in this drama? A number of bodies have been involved in Pitcairn over the years. But by no means all of them have been actors in any real sense in the legal events from the 1960s to the present with which we are concerned. Many have, in effect, been paper characters in a paperwork legal system.[16]

Although technically Pitcairn has been governed by the British Crown since its annexation in 1838 or, on some accounts, 1887,[17] there was no effective civil authority presence on the island[18] from the date of settlement until the prosecutions in question were launched. (The island's teacher was paid by the Crown, but he had no legal authority on the island. The population itself elected its Mayor, but he did not exercise authority on behalf of the Crown.) Over the years there were very occasional, irregular, and short-term visits from officials representing the Crown. For the most part, these officers were resident in New Zealand. A Governor was appointed—in practice in recent years, this has been the UK High Commissioner to New Zealand. (For some years before 1970, the Governor had also been the Governor of Fiji.)

On the matter of governance on the island, provision was made in 1940 by Island Government Regulations for a Council of the Island and a Mayor. That Council met in 1965 to consider a draft of what became the Justice Ordinance 1966, made on behalf of the Crown. The meeting discussed, among other things: the law relating to sexual offences; the fact that English law applied; and that carnal knowledge of a female under 12 would be an offence of rape. A motion to approve the draft Ordinance was accepted and the Magistrate informed the Commissioner who represented the Crown that it had been approved by the Council. Thus the community was involved in the making of this law. But no such procedure was followed when, in 1970, an Ordinance was made by the Governor subjecting Pitcairn to English law, including the laws under which the defendants were to be prosecuted in *Christian*.

---

[16] The Pitcairn Supreme Court however stated that: 'We find that English administration of justice over Pitcairn Island was not a paper administration operating on an occasional and ad hoc way, but a reality when considering how civil and criminal disputes were dealt with through the 20th century.' (para. 110).

[17] See discussion by Woodman, chapter 4 below.

[18] This was the view taken in a letter from the Legal Adviser to the Acting Governor, dated 29 April 2000: see Appendix II, document (b); and see letter from the Acting Governor to the Foreign and Commonwealth Office, dated 1 May 2000, referred to in para. 74 of the Privy Council report in Appendix I, below.

Before the arrival of two Kent police officers on Pitcairn in 1996 (on which see below) there was no British police presence on the island. There was in practice no operative internal legal system in Pitcairn. The local police officer must have known about the ways in which the men on Pitcairn treated girls there. He may have been imbued with a local culture or attitude according to which the sexual offences with which these prosecutions were concerned were not particularly serious. (On the other hand, the evidence was that the girl victims of the abuse were told by the perpetrators not to tell anyone, indicating that this behaviour was known to be wrong.) The local island Magistrate and two assessors had no legal training. They constituted the Island Court that was established by the Crown under the Justice Ordinance 1966, with jurisdiction over certain minor criminal and civil matters. Its sentencing powers were limited to fines of £25 or 100 days' imprisonment. The limitation period for prosecuting offences was six months from when the matter of the complaint arose. The offences over which it had jurisdiction included assaults and underage sex. In fact, however, there were almost no prosecutions on the island during the period we are concerned with (from the 1960s onwards) and no one had been arrested since the 1950s. For more serious offences there was, in theory, recourse to the Pitcairn Supreme Court. But it was a paperwork court; no judge had ever been appointed to it before these trials. (A judge had been appointed to the Fiji-based High Commissioner's Court to hear a trial of one of the islanders for murder in 1898.[19])

So there were a number of important-sounding characters in the legal drama: the Crown; the Governor; the Council of the Island; a local Pitcairn police officer; an island Magistrate, elected by the community; and his Court. None of these important-sounding characters was involved in the prosecutions with which essays in this collection are concerned, save that the Crown secured that the legal paperwork was in order, and save for the Magistrate and the Mayor—who were defendants. (The Magistrate was acquitted; the Mayor was convicted on many counts of rape and indecent assault on two victims.) The actual characters in the drama, apart from the accused, were officers of Kent Police acting as Pitcairn police officers; the Woman Police Constable (WPC) Gail Cox who visited the island in 1997 and again in 1999–2000; the witnesses (including victims of the offences) who gave

[19] See Lewis, chapter 3 below.

evidence in the prosecutions, some of them by satellite link from New Zealand; the specially appointed judges of the Pitcairn Supreme Court and the specially created Pitcairn Court of Appeal; the specially created Pitcairn Bar and those who were called to it; and judges of the Judicial Committee of the Privy Council in London.

## 'Operation Unique': Investigation of Alleged Offences[20]

Two officers of Kent police visited the island as Pitcairn police officers (again the paperwork was in order) in 1996 to investigate a complaint that had reached the Foreign Office that a young woman had been raped on the island. The person suspected of offences at that time admitted having consensual intercourse with a girl before and after her twelfth birthday on six occasions. (Intercourse after the twelfth birthday was an offence under the Justice Ordinance 1966, and, if it applied (on which see later), under the English Sexual Offences Act 1956, which made it an offence to have sexual intercourse with a girl under the age of 13.) The complainant, an Australian girl who had lived with her family on the island for a time, had by now left the island. It was decided not to prosecute but to caution the suspect for underage sex[21] because of concern about the weak state of the criminal law on Pitcairn and the implications for the liberty of the inhabitants if prosecutions were brought.

The two Kent Police officers reported to the Foreign Office that the island needed to be properly policed. Thereafter the Foreign and Commonwealth Office (FCO) decided that a police officer should be sent to Pitcairn for three months to train and support the island police officer. WPC Gail Cox arrived in 1997. She stayed for over 12 weeks, and visited again for further training in 1999–2000. On that second visit she discovered extensive sexual abuse of girls and young women over some 30 years. Offences (or what would be offences if English law applied) included rape, indecent assault, and incest. Most were assaults by older men of girls from the age of five, and even three years old. Many offences involved violence. These included a gang rape of a 12-year-old girl by

---

[20] The following account is taken from a range of sources, including the judgment of Lord Hope in the Privy Council (Appendix I below), the only member of the committee to go into the facts, and from Marks, *Trouble in Paradise*, especially chapter 3.
[21] See Marks, *Trouble in Paradise*, at pp. 37–38.

boys of 14 to 16, and many rapes of girls between 10 and 18 by teenaged boys and older men.

On receipt of WPC Gail Cox's report, the Foreign Office in April 2000 sent two Kent police officers to investigate further. This was the start of 'Operation Unique'. They interviewed complainants and men against whom complaints were made in Australia and in Norfolk Island. They interviewed all 20 women who had grown up on Pitcairn since 1980. By then, most of them were in their late teens or were aged up to 40 years old. Most of them were living in Australia or New Zealand, and a few were living in the United Kingdom or the USA. All stated that they had been victims of sexual abuse to varying degrees. In some cases, the abuse started when they were between three and five years old.

Considering how widely the abuse had been spread, the police officers decided to draw a line at 1960: they identified 31 victims, including two men, and some 30 named offenders, of whom 27 were native Pitcairners—nearly every Pitcairn male. Some 12 women accused their brothers, uncles, or first cousins. However, with such a small population, most women were related to most of the men on the island.

Kent police reported on their findings to the FCO. Consideration was given to various options, including a general amnesty, and a South African style Truth and Reconciliation Commission, but these were rejected.[22] Baroness Scotland, the minister in the British Cabinet with responsibility for overseas territories, demanded prosecution.[23] The British Cabinet decided that the legal machinery should be put in place to facilitate a prosecution. An agreement was reached with New Zealand that their judges would sit as the Pitcairn Supreme Court for the trials, and as the Pitcairn Court of Appeal to hear the expected appeals. A Pitcairn Public Prosecutor and Public Defender were appointed. A Pitcairn Bar was established and New Zealand lawyers were called to it. And in due course, the trials took place.

The Pitcairn community mobilized public opinion on the island, among the Friends of Pitcairn Association and among the large numbers of people around the world who were committed to the Pitcairn idyll, to campaign against the prosecutions.[24] The concerns of the islanders—including many women who had been victims of abuse as had their mothers—were for the survival of the community itself. This

---

[22] See Marks, *Trouble in Paradise,* chapter 6.

[23] See Guest, chapter 8 and Appendix II, document (c) below.

[24] See Marks, *Trouble in Paradise*, chapter 6.

appeared to outweigh any concerns for the victims of the abuse. As Kathy Marks put it: 'The unforgivable crime, in the Pitcairners' eyes, was not sexually assaulting children, but betraying the island'.[25] And 'the necessity to cooperate, whatever the circumstances, is the most fundamental reality of Pitcairn life ... the pressure to conform to communal norms is intense'.[26] These comments provide fascinating insights into the psychology of small, isolated communities. A number of women who had previously complained to the police and given statements refused to testify, presumably for that very reason. Some of the female victims no longer lived on the island and gave evidence by video link from New Zealand. Thus, not all of the men about whom complaints were made to the investigators were prosecuted.

### Trials and Convictions

The trials were heard on Pitcairn by the Pitcairn Supreme Court. Points of law were argued separately some time later in Auckland, New Zealand.

Of the seven men prosecuted at this time, one was cleared of all charges and six were convicted of some 35 offences. The six included the Mayor. The charges were in practice, specimen charges, representing in many instances, courses of conduct repeated many times over against the same complainant. The charges were only the tip of the iceberg.

Four defendants were convicted of offences of rape under section 1 of the Sexual Offences Act 1956. The offences had been committed from 1964 to the present, mostly in the 1960s and 1970s. These defendants had been boys or young men at the time of the offences except for one male who was in his forties. Their victims had been between 10 and 19 years old.

Four of the six defendants were convicted of indecent assault and/or incest under section 14 of the 1956 Act. Their ages had ranged from 15 to 37 at the times of the offences. Their victims ranged in age from five to 15 years. The offences had been committed at various times between 1972 and 1999. Two of those offenders were also convicted of rape.

Four of the offenders were sentenced to terms of imprisonment ranging from two to six years, to be served on the island in the six-cell

---

[25] Ibid, at p. 99.          [26] Ibid, at pp. 259–260.

jail which had been constructed during the period of investigation, preparation for the trial, and prosecution. These prison sentences were far more lenient that they would have been for such offences if committed in England or New Zealand. (In fact, the men, who have by now completed their sentences, were released from the jail on the island when needed, for instance to bring visitors ashore.) Two who had expressed remorse were sentenced to community work.

The defendants appealed to the Pitcairn Court of Appeal.[27] This court was established in 2000 in preparation for these anticipated appeals. The convictions were upheld, the Court of Appeal broadly agreeing with the Supreme Court. From there the defendants appealed to the Judicial Committee of the Privy Council in London.

## The Next Chapters

The next chapter summarizes the Privy Council decision.[28] The judgments do not convey much about the realities of life on Pitcairn and of the relationship between the island and the British government. The focus is on the colonial paperwork. What is interesting, however, is that the judges adopted quite different ways of reasoning. The opinion of the majority, delivered by Lord Hoffmann, was based on a formalistic, positivist, peremptory approach which did not engage with some of the troubling issues to do with the rule of law and justice which the case raised. Two of the judges however, Lord Woolf and Lord Hope, did enter the arena and engage with those issues, though they agreed with the opinion of the others in the result, namely that the convictions should be upheld.

In chapter 3 on 'Pitcairn's Tortured Past: A Legal History', Andrew Lewis gives us an account in some detail of the colourful early history of Pitcairn and its people. Many of the original settlers were murdered, and their Tahitian womenfolk were ill-treated—and there was no machinery of justice, at least of the kind that modern lawyers would recognize as such—to deal with these activities. There was much coming and going of residents, the addition of new blood from time to time, a brief forced deportation to Tahiti in 1831, and a transportation to

---

[27] *R v Seven Named Accused*, Pitcairn Court of Appeal, CA 1-7/2004, 5 August 2004.
[28] See Appendix I.

Norfolk Island (a penal colony until 1855) in 1856. There were various assertions of authority over Pitcairn by the British Crown from 1813, and particularly from 1856. And, from about 1886, Seventh Day Adventist practices were adopted on Pitcairn. In 1898, the Crown brought Pitcairn within the operation of the British Settlements Act, and within its definition of a colony, in response to the need to try Harry Christian for the murder of two people on the island. Thereafter some measures were taken by the British to put in place a criminal justice system, at least on paper. But there was still no British presence on the island until the criminal proceedings in *Christian* were under-way, and there were only a couple of brief visits—one by a legal adviser in 1958 and one by the Governor in 1973. This, suggests Lewis, looks like laxity on the part of the British to the point of turpitude.

In chapter 4 on 'Pitcairn Island Law: A Peculiar Case of the Diffusion of the Common Law', Gordon Woodman considers some of the diffi-culties in determining what was the law of Pitcairn at the time the offences were committed and tried. The issues here are rather more technical than those considered in this chapter and chapter 2, but their importance will be obvious. Much depended on colonial law, and the discussion gives us insights into some of the knotty problems raised by the UK's colonizing past.

The law of Pitcairn is not necessarily the same as the law of England. So it needed to be determined on what basis, if any, the English Sexual Offences Act 1956, under which the defendants were prosecuted, applied to Pitcairn. The criteria for this decision are provided by the common law—the interaction of the common law and Acts of the UK Parliament is thus crucial to the question. And this in turn raises the questions whether the common law is the same in whatever jurisdiction it operates, and to what extent the common law itself is 'customary law', and whether, alongside the common law, a system of customary law can operate.

Woodman expands on the point that the Judicial Committee of the Privy Council was prepared to accept the statement by the Crown as to the status of Pitcairn as a settled colony, exploring the implications if the judges had taken a less deferential line on this. He then goes on to discuss the abuse of process point, taking on the 'ignorance of the law is no excuse' doctrine. Lord Hope's approach in the Privy Council, that rape and indecent assault were offences at common law at the date of settlement and that the defendants must be taken to have known that they were crimes, is, Woodman suggests, more attractive than the blunt approach of the other judges. It is nevertheless formalistic. No evidence was presented to any of the courts dealing with the case that the inhabitants of the island realized that these were offences. Indeed the failure to link the many assumptions in the case to actual evidence—particularly as to the possible development of a local customary law—is a weakness, perhaps typical of lawyers, in the reasoning of the judges in this case. It may be, for instance, that even if the inhabitants considered rape or indecent assault or both to be criminal, their view as to the ages below which the victims were especially vulnerable, so that strong criminal penalties for the perpetrators were justified, might—as a matter of supervening customary law—be lower in Pitcairn than in England. These are matters on which legal anthropologists might contribute to the discussion. Finally, and in concluding comments, Woodman raises questions of relevance to the United Kingdom itself and most developed multicultural democracies as to how state law should deal with or accommodate cultural diversity and legal pluralism.

In chapter 5, 'The Pitcairn Prosecutions: An Assessment of Their Historical Context by Reference to the Provisions of Public International Law', Dino Kritsiotis and Brian Simpson consider the Pitcairn prosecutions in the light of public international law. In particular, the chapter explores the jurisdictional relationship that the United Kingdom developed with Pitcairn Island and its people, taking on the history from the time of the settlement of the *Bounty* mutineers in January 1790 to the more recent charges arising under the Sexual Offences Act 1956. They examine how jurisdiction came to be asserted in changing but more obvious ways, before considering whether sovereign title existed over the territory, and how this might have come to pass given the various modes of territorial acquisition acknowledged in public international law. The authors regard these assertions of jurisdiction as somehow demonstrative of sovereignty in the long term, before considering what obligations might exist as between the sovereign and its territory (or territories). They then turn, in the penultimate section of the chapter, to the human rights obligations of the United Kingdom, stemming as they do from a range of different sources (such as the 1950 European Convention on Human Rights, the 1966 United Nations Covenant on Civil and Political Rights, and the 1979 United Nations Convention on the Elimination of All Forms of Discrimination Against Women). In the final section they offer some concluding thoughts and reflections.

The last three chapters move into more theoretical territory.

In chapter 6, ' "A Million Mutinies Now": Why Claims of Cultural Uniqueness Cannot be Used to Justify Violations of Basic Human Rights' Colm O'Cinneide discusses issues of cultural relativism and vulnerability raised by the Pitcairn situation. It was argued by some commentators that the Pitcairn prosecutions unjustifiably imposed a set of cultural and legal norms upon individuals who did not accept those norms, and put at risk the continuation of the community and its culture on the island. O'Cinneide rejects this approach. First, it was not the case that the community as a whole rejected the norms implicit in the criminalization of rape and the other offences with which the prosecutions were concerned: the women victims did not reject them. The offenders knew that these assaults were 'wrong'. The trial court found that they were aware that English law applied. The prosecutions were brought to vindicate the basic human rights of vulnerable members of the community.

Even if abuse had been part of the accepted culture of the island, and that culture was 'vulnerable', that consideration would not, O'Cinneide suggests, justify failure to protect the basic human rights to autonomy of the women on the island. Nor could the fact, if it had been the case, that the very survival of the community was threatened by the possible imprisonment of offenders, justify non-prosecution of these offences. (These issues were taken into account in the sentencing of the offenders.) The case should rather be seen as illustrating the validity of certain forms of universal rights claims, even in circumstances of apparently strong cultural variation. In particular, it is an example of how the application of human rights norms can serve to expose oppressive and abusive power relationships sheltering under the cloak of cultural difference. There is no doubt that the language of human rights can be abused to justify illegitimate Western intervention. There is also no doubt that there are certain applications of human rights standards that only have validity in certain cultural contexts. However, neither of these two arguments should be used to justify the suspension of the human rights project in general when it runs up against particular cultural differences. In the Pitcairn situation, O'Cinneide concludes, the prosecutions were properly brought and did not constitute violations of such norms.

In chapter 7, 'Rights and Duties on Pitcairn Island', George Letsas discusses two major philosophical debates that have a bearing on the legitimacy of the Pitcairn prosecutions. The first is the debate between cultural relativism and moral universalism, and the second is the debate between positivist and non-positivist theories of law. In relation to the first, Letsas argues that the acts for which the defendants were prosecuted are universal moral wrongs that cannot be justified on the grounds of cultural relativism. He distinguishes, however, moral wrongfulness from moral blameworthiness and argues that judgements of moral blameworthiness are culture-specific, requiring a detailed and careful examination of local circumstances. In Letsas' view, the British government's decision to prosecute the Pitcairn offenders for the moral wrongs they had committed and to impose legal punishment involved a distinctive element of moral disapprobation that was disproportionate to their degree of blameworthiness, taking into account the island's unique circumstances.

Letsas next examines whether the Crown had jurisdiction to prosecute the islanders under English law. He argues that the question of whether the Crown had jurisdiction over Pitcairn was not, as legal positivists would assume, an *empirical* question, to do with whether the British government enjoyed de facto legal authority. Following a nonpositivist approach, Letsas argues that there is a *moral* test governing whether individuals are under the legal authority of a government and whether coercive enforcement of a norm is justified, *qua* an exercise of legal authority. The test turns on, among other things, whether coercers and coercees belong to the same political community which has displayed an attitude of equal respect and concern towards the coercees. Letsas claims that no such relationship of an egalitarian and reciprocal community existed between the islanders and the United Kingdom, and that, as a result, it was illegitimate for the government to assert criminal jurisdiction over the islanders.

In chapter 8, 'Legality, Reciprocity, and the Criminal Law on Pitcairn', Stephen Guest considers a range of possible meanings of legality. Moral wrongness in itself is insufficient to ground a legal claim, he argues. Rather, legality introduces the additional requirement of a morally legitimate right on the part of a community to impose collective coercive force on individuals. One conception of legality lies in an English doctrine of legal positivism which sharply distinguishes nonfactual moral claims from factual legal ones. While that doctrine seems compatible with basing legality on an historical account of the constitutional connection between the UK and the remote island of Pitcairn, Guest argues that it is not. It is more than a question of mere history whether the UK Crown had sufficient authority in the sense of 'speaking for' the Pitcairn islanders. More sophisticated versions of positivism characterize law by reference to its practical point, but these also fail. If the purpose of law is efficiency in achieving desirable social goals, then positivism must centrally endorse, as Jeremy Bentham thought, the efficient communication of the law's requirements to the defendants. That would mean, given the isolation of Pitcairn, and the different culture of acceptability of child abuse, a particularized and special promulgation. An additional purpose is discernible in the work of H. L. A. Hart, who made legal certainty crucial to respecting the moral independence of citizens. He argued that it would only be in conditions of clear and certain promulgation that citizens would have the capacity to confront abuse of authority. Given the lack of presence of the British Crown on Pitcairn, recognition of the moral independence of individuals would likewise require particularized promulgation for the English Sexual Offences Act 1956 to apply. Guest concludes that even according to the theory that appears to be most congenial to the prosecution's position, the convictions were unjustified.

Arguing that legality is more richly defined through supposing it to have moral value, Guest favours an approach closer to that of Fuller, who saw legality as a morally legitimate claim arising where reciprocal fair dealings existed between law-makers and addressees of the law. The history of the British Crown's activity in Pitcairn, particularly in relation to the suppression of sexual abuse, demonstrates unfairness through failure to make clear any intention to prosecute, to hold trials, and in other ways to treat the Pitcairn islanders as equal to its citizens in the United Kingdom. Guest concludes that under this conception of legality, too, the convictions were wrong. He adds that there were other means of securing a better sexual culture on the island, means that were in fact considered by officials in both the UK and New Zealand. These were along the lines of 'truth and reconciliation' type hearings, or by a concentrated social care programme coupled with a compensation package, or some mixture of the two approaches. Such measures, he argues, combined with a genuine demonstration that sexual abuse would not in future be tolerated, would have solved matters, and showed sufficient respect for the rights of the victims and with the appropriate degree of sympathy and sensitivity to all concerned.

Together the chapters provide a sociological and legal history of the island and an analysis of some of the fundamental legal and philosophical issues which the situations of Pitcairn and other remote, acephalous communities raise.

# 2

# The Pitcairn Prosecutions, Paper Legal Systems, and the Rule of Law

*Dawn Oliver*

In this chapter we home in on the decision of the Judicial Committee of the Privy Council on the appeals of the six Pitcairn men who were convicted of sexual offences against women on the island. (The decision is in Appendix I.) While some of this account contains material of a rather technical legal kind, much of it raises in concrete form important issues to do with justice, legality, and the rule of law—the themes of this collection.

## *Steven Raymond Christian and Others v The Queen* in the Judicial Committee of the Privy Council

The Judicial Committee of the Privy Council sitting in London is a peculiar court. It hears appeals from the remaining British colonies and from some Commonwealth countries. At the time of the appeals, the judges were current and retired Lords of Appeal in Ordinary (Law Lords), who also sat on the Appellate Committee of the House of Lords, the top UK court. Other senior judges from the Commonwealth are also qualified to sit on the Judicial Committee. The Appellate Committee of the House of Lords was replaced by the UK Supreme Court with effect from 1 October 2009.

It is the custom for the Privy Council to deliver one 'advice'—and to decide unanimously. In the *Christian*[1] case, the five judges—Lords

---

[1] Privy Council Appeal No 109/2005 [2006] UKPC 47.

Hoffmann (who delivered the main advice), Carswell, Hope, Steyn, and Woolf—were unanimous as to the result: the convictions should be upheld. But two of the five, Lord Hope and Lord Woolf, departed from custom and gave separate opinions setting out their different reasons for upholding the convictions. The advice of the other three judges was given by Lord Hoffmann. As we shall see, Lord Hoffmann, for the majority, took a formalistic approach, relying on the colonial paperwork produced by the government. Lord Hope and Lord Woolf were more concerned about the rule of law issues in the case than the others: the implications of the fact that the defendants in these prosecutions could not know what law, precisely, applied to their conduct at the time of the alleged offences.

The defendants raised four important points. First, that Pitcairn was not a UK colony, with the result that the UK had no authority over the community. Secondly, even if Pitcairn was a colony, English criminal law could not apply there in the absence of a functioning system of justice. Thirdly, the criminal 'law' on which the prosecution relied was not valid law in Pitcairn because the colonial legislation did not provide for its application to a 'ceded' rather than a 'settled' colony (a technical point which is discussed in chapters 4 and 5, below) and because the 'law' in question had not been published there. And fourthly, even if that law was in principle valid law on Pitcairn, it was an abuse of process to prosecute the defendants under it: the Pitcairn Supreme Court, the Court of Appeal, and the Pitcairn Bar, had all been specially brought into being for the purposes of prosecuting the defendants. And in any event, the defendants did not know that their assaults on their victims were contrary to this particular law, and they should not therefore have been prosecuted.

## The Colonial Status of Pitcairn

The starting point in the defendants' case was that Pitcairn was not a colony and thus the UK had no jurisdiction over it. The point was put as follows: since the original settlers were mutineers who had rejected the authority of the Crown it would not be right to treat the previously uninhabited, unclaimed land as a British colony once they settled there. Thus, they argued, the UK legislation, the British Settlements Act 1887, and the Sexual Offences Act 1956, on which the prosecutions were based, did not apply on Pitcairn. In the alternative, the defendants argued that if Pitcairn was a colony, it was a ceded rather than a settled one, their point being that the British Settlements Act 1887 and Sexual Offences Act 1956 only applied in terms to settled colonies.[2]

These issues were resolved by the Privy Council—and indeed by the Pitcairn Supreme Court and the Court of Appeal—in favour of the Crown. It was held that Pitcairn was a colony, and a colony by settlement—a colony as from the date the mutineers and their companions arrived—and not by cession, when the islanders called upon passing Royal Navy ships to provide them with the protection of the UK.[3] In his judgment Lord Hoffmann relied upon statements of the executive—the UK government—including a 'direction' or statement of 1898 made under the Pacific Order in Council 1893,[4] and the making of the 1970 Order in Council—as determinative of the status of Pitcairn. He referred to and applied the judgment of Atkin LJ in *The Fagernes*[5] to the effect that: 'What is a territory of the Crown is a matter of which the Court takes judicial notice ... Any definite statement from the proper representative of the Crown as to the territory of the Crown must be treated as conclusive.'[6] This is an extremely formalistic approach. Lord Hoffmann did not deal with any of the evidence of the history of the island and of the actual relationship between the UK and Pitcairn in support of his finding that Pitcairn was a colony by settlement rather than a ceded colony.[7]

The actual evidence on that issue points in both directions: in brief, the history of the settlement indicates that the original English settlers in 1790 were rejecting the authority of the Crown—they were fugitives from English justice—and that their Polynesian companions owed no loyalty to the Crown in any event. That evidence would suggest that it was incompatible with the intentions of the settlers that they were settling on Pitcairn with a view to it being a British colony. If this were true it would seem to follow that they believed they were establishing a new independent state. It may nevertheless have been the case under English

---

[2] See discussion by Woodman in chapter 4 and Kritsiotis and Simpson in chapter 5 below.
[3] Privy Council decision paras 9–10. This point is discussed by Woodman in chapter 4 and Kritsiotis and Simpson in chapter 5 below.
[4] This Order in Council is discussed by Lewis in chapter 3 and Woodman in chapter 4 below.     [5] [1927] P 311, at 324.     [6] Lord Hoffmann, at para. 9.
[7] For discussion of this point see Woodman in chapter 4 and Kritsiotis and Simpson in chapter 5 below.

law that they were to be treated as colonial settlers. That point was not made or even explored in any of the Privy Council judgments.[8]

The Pitcairn islanders sought the protection of the Royal Navy to defend themselves against marauding whalers during the early nineteenth century: Captain Eliott of *The Fly* provided them with a Union Jack flag which might deter the whalers, and with a constitution and some written laws when he visited the island in 1838 (this is discussed in chapters 3, 4, and 5). That visit is probably the incident which supported the defendant's fall-back argument that the island became a colony, if at all, by cession in that year, or on a later occasion of a Royal Navy visit. But Lord Hoffmann did not go into these issues and relied instead upon executive statements—statements in effect from the Foreign and Commonwealth Office (FCO) in London—as to the colonial status of Pitcairn.

However, Lord Hoffmann did observe that: 'for over a hundred years Pitcairn has been administered by the Crown as a British possession' and added that factor to his conclusion that it was 'unthinkable that the Judicial Committee … would not accept an executive statement affirming it to be part of the territory of the Crown'.[9] That statement does not of course deal with the crucial question whether it was a settled or ceded—or annexed—colony. The fact of the matter was that Pitcairn had not been actually 'administered by the Crown' save very sporadically before the prosecutions were launched. Although a system of colonial government existed on paper, it was inactive and remote from the island. There was no Crown presence on the island, no provision at all for the promulgation of laws other than the Ordinances, no independent system of justice, and no law library or any other access to information as to the law.

To the extent that judgments are supposed to communicate the justifications for a decision to the parties and to the public, the formalistic approach falls short and leaves the court vulnerable to criticisms of, in this case, undue deference to the executive. Concern about this may account for the different approaches of Lord Woolf and Lord Hope in the case, both of whom made reference to the evidence.

Lord Woolf in his judgment on the colonial status issue gave consideration to the implications of the acceptance of statements by the British government as conclusive on the question of the status of

---

Pitcairn as part of the 'act of state' doctrine, according to which, on the orthodox view, the courts should not go behind executive statements on such issues. Lord Woolf considered that the 'evidence' that Pitcairn was a British possession was overwhelming. (Perhaps he was referring to factual information which had been before the lower courts and on the record before the Privy Council but which is not referred to expressly in the judgments. If so, it is a pity that the evidence was not summarized in the judgment and that the CD containing 4,000 pages of documents which had been prepared for the trial is not publicly available.) It was not necessary, therefore, Lord Woolf decided, to explore further the limits of the act of state doctrine. But, Lord Woolf indicated, it would be necessary to do so in a less obvious case: 'it can no longer be taken for granted that the courts will accept that there is any action on the part of the Crown that is not open to any form of review by the courts if a proper foundation for the review is established'.[10] This proposition is, of itself, an important pointer to possible future judicial activism in relation to such issues.[11]

## The Machinery of Justice Points

The defendants argued that, given that there was no English police presence on the island at the time of the offences, jurisdiction could not be asserted on the basis of English criminal law.[12] In other words, law in the sense in which the courts understand it does not exist in the absence of machinery of justice to enforce it. This challenge was also rejected— the statutory provisions and Ordinances were accepted to be sufficient authority for the prosecutions. While in most jurisdictions the common law is underpinned by formal legal enforcement provisions and machinery, according to Lord Hope, even in the absence of such machinery it remains law.[13] This represents a conventional legal view. But it raises significant questions for philosophers and anthropologists as to the actual nature and meaning of 'law' if it is not accompanied by any enforcement provisions, whether formal or social.

The defendants further claimed that the importation by the Crown of the New Zealand machinery of justice[14] for the purposes of the trials

---

[10] At para. 33.
[11] See further discussion of this by Kritsiotis and Simpson in chapter 5.
[12] At paras 18, 23–24.     [13] At para. 85.
[14] See the account of this in chapter 5.

was legally invalid, so that the Pitcairn Supreme Court was not properly constituted. This challenge too was rejected, again on the positivist basis that the legislation authorizing the New Zealand involvement was valid and the paperwork was in order. On both these points about the machinery of justice then the courts followed a formalistic approach—one that is not unusual where points are taken about the machinery rather than the substance of the legal system, but nevertheless one which might generate debate, especially among legal sociologists and anthropologists.

## Legality and the Rule of Law

The main issues of general principle in the case were to do with legality and the rule of law. The defendants pointed to the fact that the UK Ordinances purporting to apply the English Sexual Offences Act 1956 to Pitcairn had not been published or adequately communicated in Pitcairn—and nor had the 1956 Act itself. They argued first, that it was a precondition of the application of Acts of the UK Parliament on Pitcairn that they had been published there, and since the Sexual Offences Act 1956 had not been published on Pitcairn it was *not valid legislation* for Pitcairn;[15] and secondly, in the absence of publication on the island, even if the legislation itself was valid law on Pitcairn, it was an *abuse of process* to prosecute.[16] Their case was that the policing of the inhabitants was rudimentary; the impression was conveyed to the inhabitants that English law would not be enforced; it would thus be an abuse of process to enforce it, especially retrospectively; the prosecutors had been specially put in place to pursue the cases, the judges of the Supreme Court had been appointed specifically for the trials, the Court of Appeal had been specifically created for the expected appeals, a prison had been built on the island in anticipation of convictions and prison sentences, and all this many years after most of the offences had been committed. This, they argued, amounted to targeted justice and an abuse of process.[17]

The *legal invalidity* argument was rejected at every level as the case passed through the court hierarchy, though for varying reasons. Lord

---

[15] At paras 16–17.       [16] At paras 18–24.
[17] Other grounds were delay and inequality of arms, but we shall not consider them here.

Hoffmann, giving the opinion of the majority in the Privy Council, held that the subjection of Pitcairn to the Sexual Offences Act was properly authorized by statute and Ordinances, and that these did not require publication for their validity.[18] It followed that the UK Sexual Offences Act 1956 applied on Pitcairn under the 1970 Ordinance, there being no local circumstances which made it inappropriate to apply the provisions about rape, indecent assault, and incest there.[19] Further, the fact that the Act had not been published in the island did not prevent it from applying, since the publication requirement in the Order in Council applied only to laws made by the Governor, and the Sexual Offences Act 1956 was not made by him. This, again, is a formalistic, positivist approach to the questions.

On the *abuse of process* point Lord Hoffmann, for the majority, relied in part on findings of fact by the Pitcairn Supreme Court to the effect that at all relevant times Pitcairn was a developed society in which rape and various sexual offending were known to be criminal, and that there was no reason to doubt that this knowledge extended to sexual offending generally, including indecent assault and incest. English administration of justice, he found, was not a paper administration but a reality. Lord Hoffmann thus purported to deal with this point in the light of his understanding of the evidence that had been before the trial court—a different approach from the one he adopted in relation to the colonial status of Pitcairn, where he relied on the formal paperwork rather than the factual evidence of realities on Pitcairn. The Judicial Committee did not accept that Pitcairn was an anarchic or lawless society. The roles of Island Police Officer and Island Magistrate had frequently been high profile and the law and its enforcement had 'loomed large'.[20] This is a remarkably laid-back approach, given that the many offences with which the defendants had been charged had been committed over a period dating from the mid-1960s, and self-evidently they had not attracted any penalties at all until these proceedings were instituted some 30 years later. The reliance on 'evidence' in this part of the judgment was thus rather uncritical.

Dealing with the lack of publication of the 1956 Act on Pitcairn, the Pitcairn Court of Appeal had held that this did not matter as there was

---

[18] Lord Hoffmann also maintained (this time on the abuse of process point) that in any event, the defendants knew that their activities were contrary to the criminal law so that it was not an abuse of process to prosecute them—see below.
[19] At para. 13.     [20] At para. 21.

never any contention that the defendants did not know that the allegations constituted serious criminal offences and it was self-evident that they would attract substantial terms of imprisonment. Again, this is difficult to accept given that the offences went back to 1964 and no steps were taken to prosecute the defendants before the investigations leading to these trials.

Lord Hoffmann accepted that the fact that a law had not been published and could not have been known to exist may, in certain circumstances, be a ground for staying a prosecution as an abuse of process; but he held that in this case 'it is ... unnecessary to discuss the philosophical basis or legal limits of such a principle' because of the findings of the lower courts with which it would be impossible to persuade the Privy Council to interfere.[21] Here the findings of fact by the trial court are regarded as relevant, indeed highly persuasive, but it is hard to see how factual evidence necessarily makes the philosophical bases of principles irrelevant, or less relevant than they would be without the factual evidence.

In his separate advice, Lord Woolf too considered whether it was an abuse of process to prosecute when the 1956 Act had not been published in Pitcairn. Having been indicted under the Sexual Offences Act the defendants could not, he recognized, be convicted of common law or other offences of a similar nature; thus it was important to determine whether the 1956 Act was part of the law of Pitcairn at the time of the offences, and whether the defendants were sufficiently aware of the nature of the offences of rape and indecent assault charged under the Act to justify prosecuting them.[22] Lord Woolf agreed with Lord Hoffmann that the publication requirement under the 1970 Ordinance did not apply; but he went on to consider whether the failure to publish the 1956 Act in Pitcairn was a breach of the rule of law so as to make the prosecutions unjustifiable—an abuse of process. His conclusion was that it was not. The question was whether the defendants were aware that their conduct was contrary to the criminal law.[23] He found—as did the trial court— that they were. The test, he held, should be whether it was an affront to justice to proceed. Lord Woolf was satisfied that it was generally known that rape and possibly indecent assault were offences and that these would be prosecuted before the Pitcairn Supreme Court because they required greater punishment than would be possible in a trial before the Island

---

[21] At para. 24.     [22] See Lord Woolf's judgment from paras 30–45.
[23] At paras 41–42.

Magistrate's Court. (Let us remind ourselves that no judge had ever been appointed to the Pitcairn Supreme Court, so no one had ever been prosecuted before it. It was, until this case, a paper court.) Lord Woolf was satisfied that information as to the actual law was available to Pitcairn islanders if they sought it. Evidence about these matters had been before the Pitcairn Supreme Court, the Pitcairn Court of Appeal had considered the matter, and Lord Woolf felt bound by the findings of those courts. Thus, he held, actual promulgation was not necessary for the validity of a law or to avoid the defect of abuse of process.

We need to remind ourselves, however, that these facts had been hotly disputed by the defendants and that, from at least a sociological or anthropological point of view, the actual availability of accurate and precise information about the law must remain important issues when dealing with the existence or validity of a 'law'. This issue of validity is not the same as the 'ignorance of the law is no excuse' argument—discussed in chapter 8—which arises only in relation to valid laws.

Lord Hope was particularly concerned about some of the 'fundamental issues about the rule of law in remote communities and about the responsibilities of the colonial power which seeks to exert its authority over them'[24] that were raised by the case.

He agreed with Lord Hoffmann that Pitcairn was established as a colony by settlement, but he was concerned about technical issues such as the legislative powers of the Governor under the 1970 Ordinance, and whether sections 1 and 14 of the 1956 Sexual Offences Act were in force on Pitcairn at the times that the offences were committed. But his concern was not by any means solely about technical legal issues. He emphasized that 'abhorrence at the nature of these crimes must not blind us to the rule of law'.[25]

The expression 'the rule of law' is here used by Lord Hope in relation to the burden that lies on the Crown to establish that the law under which a person is prosecuted is a valid law, validly made. But the expression also carries another meaning, 'law and order', and in that sense, the rule of law had not existed on Pitcairn—at least in relation to sexual abuse of girls and young women—for many years. Lord Hope was, as we shall see, concerned about both aspects of the legal system. (The 'law and order' aspect must have been most influential in the mind of the Crown when it decided to prosecute.)

---

[24] At para. 47.    [25] At para. 48.

It is clear from Lord Hope's judgment that evidence about the shocking realities of life for girls and women on Pitcairn, outlined in chapter 1 above, weighed heavily with him. He noted that the case was about child sexual abuse on a grand scale, which was deeply disturbing. 'Conduct of that kind cannot be regarded as other than criminal and deserving of punishment.'[26] He observed that the offenders must have known that they were doing wrong (the evidence that the men told their victims not to tell anyone about the assaults bears this out), and—significantly—that it was scarcely credible that the population of the island as a whole was unaware of what was going on. The inference we can draw is that this kind of abuse of young girls and women was part of the culture of the islanders. However, as we noted in chapter 1, it was no part of the defendants' case that such abuse was cultural and should not therefore have been prosecuted, or that there was nothing wrong with it. Those facts do not of course mean that the abuse was not cultural, only that if it was, the defendants were unwilling to admit it, or were in denial about it. There may have been—we do not know—tactical reasons for the defendants not relying on the cultural defence, if for instance it was expected that the New Zealand judges hearing the case would not be sympathetic to such arguments in relation to such serious offences. The fact that the abuse had been tolerated for so long was, Lord Hope said, 'an indication of the poor state of supervision exercised over its affairs by the colonial authorities'.[27]

That did not, however, lead Lord Hope to the conclusion that the prosecutions were unjustified. He grounded his decision on the reasons why the decision had been taken to prosecute under the 1956 Act, and in the common law. He noted that, as a matter of English law, the settlers took the common law with them when they decided to settle.[28] (The fact that Polynesians were among the settlers and that they were not English subjects was not apparently considered at this stage of the case.) Rape and indecent assault were, Lord Hope noted, offences at common law at the time of the settlement, and indeed they still are in England; the defendants could have been charged under the common law, but were not; they could also have been charged, for instance, with rape where there had been carnal knowledge of complainants over 12 years old, under the Justice Ordinance 1966, though the available

---

[26] Ibid.
[27] At para. 56. Issues as to culture are explored by O'Cinneide in chapter 6 below.
[28] This principle is discussed by Woodman in chapter 4 below.

penalties were lenient and there were problems over the timing of such prosecutions.[29]

So why, Lord Hope asked, were the prosecutions brought under the 1956 UK Act instead of at common law, and did these reasons reveal an abuse of process? The reasons for the decision to prosecute under the 1956 Act were set out in correspondence over the matter between the FCO and the Governor, and between the Deputy Governor and the legal adviser which had been referred to by the Supreme Court. They are very illuminating. The concerns were, on the one hand:

1) the need for severe penalties for such offences;[30]

2) given the time that had elapsed since many of the offences were committed and the short limitation period for trials before the Magistrate, the need to treat the defendants even-handedly; and

3) if the line of offending were a cultural trait, the need to put an end to it once and for all—a 'law and order' argument.

These considerations, Lord Hope found, pointed in favour of prosecution under the 1956 Act. There is also the point that a number of the victims of offences had shown considerable courage in coming forward to the police with their complaints and it would be unfair to them to drop the cases.

On the other hand there was:

1) the possibility of the collapse of the community if many of its menfolk were imprisoned;

2) awareness that the neglect of the colonial power to exercise any meaningful civil authority and thus control the 'unbridled sexual licence'[31] of the men on the island may have been partly responsible for the abuse.

These considerations pointed against prosecution on abuse of justice grounds. Ultimately, the decision to prosecute under the 1956 Act,

---

[29] At para. 72.

[30] Note that sentences of only six months imprisonment were imposed on four of the convicted defendants, and of community service on the other two.

[31] This phrase was taken from the letter of 29 April 2000 from Paul Treadwell, the legal adviser to the Acting Governor appointed for the trial, to Karen Wolstenholme, Acting Governor of Pitcairn at that time. The legal adviser's role included advising the Crown in much the way as the Attorney-General in England would do: see Appendix II, Document (b) below.

Lord Hope found, had been taken with a view to treating all accused even-handedly. Alternatives to prosecution such as an amnesty had been considered and rejected.[32] In conclusion, Lord Hope did not find the arguments in favour of prosecution to have been abusive.[33]

Lord Hope accepted that the 1956 Act applied in principle in Pitcairn under the provisions of the Judicature Ordinance 1970. On the question whether the Act had been sufficiently promulgated in Pitcairn for it to be permissible to deal with the offences in this way, he emphasized that it was a matter of the rule of law[34] and whether this technique of incorporation by reference satisfied the principles on which the rule of law was founded. It seemed that the Governor when making that Ordinance had never applied his mind to whether it was appropriate to apply the 1956 Act or any parts of it to Pitcairn, given that, unlike other territories, which had ample resources for people to find out what the law was and obtain advice about it, Pitcairn was tiny, remote, and isolated, lacking any such resources. 'The requirement of ascertainability is an essential element of the rule of law,'[35] he held. There was a strong negative comparison to be made between the procedure adopted for the 1966 Ordinance (which, as was noted earlier, had been put out to consultation and discussion by the Island Council) and the 1970 one, the latter having involved no consultation at all.

However, despite his misgivings about the rule of law and the principle of legality in this case, Lord Hope concluded that reliance on the 1956 Act in the prosecutions could be justified, but on a basis quite different from that adopted by the other judges. The offences were in reality, he held, common law offences; the settlers had taken the common law with them, the common law did not need to be promulgated, and the defendants must have known that these offences were criminal. All that the Sexual Offences Act did was deal with the procedures for prosecution and sentencing, not with the substance of the common law offences. 'Here we are dealing with conduct which the common law has regarded as criminal for centuries, and the appellants cannot have been in any doubt that what they were doing amounted to criminal conduct.'[36] The 1956 Act was not creating new offences but was providing for the fact that the common law offences were no longer felonies, that category having been abolished. '[A]s sections 1 and 14 of the 1956 Act were not creating new crimes it was open to the prosecutor to bring the prosecutions under the statute

---

[32] See Appendix II, Document (c) below.     [33] At para. 75.
[34] At para. 81.        [35] At para. 81.        [36] At para. 83.

notwithstanding its lack of promulgation.'[37] The 1970 Ordinance was thus only making provision for punishments for existing common law crimes rather than changing the substance of common law offences. This is an ingenious argument.

The implications that only statutory and other formal written provisions that change the law by creating new crimes need to be promulgated, and that it is not necessary for there to be ready access to written accounts of the common law, appear to attribute to the common law a cultural as well as a legal character, as something that is handed down from generation to generation in a community as part of the socializing process. This is an interesting insight into the nature of common law as, in effect, customary law, possibly to some extent cultural in nature.[38] It highlights the fact that 'law' has many meanings and degrees and methods of enforceability.

Yet more tantalizing is Lord Hope's comment that: 'We are dealing here with acts which were wrong in themselves.'[39] Another term would be *mala in se*, which means, broadly, something sufficiently bad to override any consideration of the community's culture.

Thus all judges in the Judicial Committee of the Privy Council found the convictions of the defendants to be lawful. The defendants have by now served out their sentences and are at liberty once more in the community.

## Reflections

The ways in which the members of the Privy Council dealt with the case reveal two very different approaches to the questions and indeed to the judicial function. Lord Hoffmann adopted an approach that is rather peremptory, unengaged—positivist—and deferential to the executive. We have already noted his comment that it was unnecessary to consider the philosophical basis and legal limits of the abuse of process doctrine. But the main thing that is missing from his judgment is a picture of the Hobbesian realities of life on Pitcairn when the offences were committed.

Lord Woolf and Lord Hope, though reaching the same conclusions as Lord Hoffmann, articulated and dealt with their concerns about the unjusticiability of acts of state and the rule of law more fully. In the end

---

[37] At para. 86.    [38] This point is noted by Woodman in chapter 4 below.
[39] At para. 85.

they too adopted a formalistic approach, accepting the paperwork as authorizing the prosecutions. They were, however, explicit about the reasons of legal principle against upholding the convictions. Lord Hope was most open about the fact that, ultimately, a balance had to be reached between conflicting principles and considerations of public policy. The practical implications of not dealing with the sexual abuses that had taken place would have been horrendous for the female half of the population for generations to come. But that powerful consideration does not point unambiguously towards prosecution as opposed to other ways of dealing with the problems.

The choices that judges have to make in such a situation are sensitive and difficult. They need to balance (i) justice to the accused with (ii) justice to the victims of, in this case, extremely serious and violent offences, (iii) the principle of the rule of law—itself a matter of public policy and public interest—with (iv) public policy and interest in changing a culture of violence and sexual exploitation. And all this against a background—not of the judges' making—of colonial, non-democratic government. It is not open to courts to require, instead, the adoption of measures such as compensation to victims and provision of community support. That would be a matter for the executive.

In chapter 1 we considered the dilemma in which the British government found itself once these offences came to its notice. Many of the issues that must have concerned them also concerned the courts. In effect, the government passed the ultimate decision to the courts. Thus, the government avoided direct political criticism for its decisions—to arrange for prosecution. It did its best to ensure, however, that the issues were at least dealt with openly, after argument, and in accordance with the law as found by independent judges at each stage of the case. In a dilemma this may be the best way for a responsible government to have such issues resolved. But it is regrettable that Lord Hoffmann did not in fact deal with all the issues in the case.

## And Afterwards . . .

Since the convictions of the defendants, the British government has put a number of measures in place to provide protection for the young people on the island. It has appointed a full-time Family and Community Adviser and a full-time Community Police Officer on secondment from New Zealand Police; and it has arranged child protection training for the island teacher and doctor, and education programmes led by the Family and Community Adviser and teacher.[40] There is now a Pitcairn Island government website, which includes information about the laws of Pitcairn: but there is no general heading 'criminal law' and no criminal law ordinance or reference to the Sexual Offences Act 1956 on that website.[41] A new school has been built, a wind turbine has been installed, and a breakwater is being built to improve access to the island. The British government is encouraging outsiders to settle on the island. The British government has spent some two million pounds a year on a population that stands at some 54 people—and that does not include expenditure on the infrastructure.[42]

In October 2008, the British government announced that it had established 'a mechanism to compensate the victims of past child sex abuse on Pitcairn' who had been identified during the investigation of the offences—Operation Unique.[43] The UK Criminal Injuries Compensation Authority will advise on the levels of compensation to award, linked to the amounts awarded in the UK. The payments of compensation to victims of offences, whether the perpetrators were convicted or not, will not be available to victims who failed to cooperate with the authorities in attempting to bring assailants to justice, or if the applicant fails to give all reasonable assistance to the authorities in connection with applications for compensation.[44]

So what has been achieved by the prosecution of the defendants? The community has been confronted with the evidence of serious abuse; some of the offenders have been publicly shamed; they have been punished, albeit lightly; the community has survived; the British government has been shamed for its neglect of the community and has taken steps to prevent recurrences of the abuse.

Returning to the thought experiment with which we opened the first chapter in this collection, in the end the British government adopted options 2 and 3 sequentially—prosecution and compensation and future protection. But it has been bit by bit and reluctantly, in a typically British, ad hoc, incremental way.

---

[40] See <http://ukun.fco.gov.uk/en/newsroom/?view=PressR&id=7221944>.
[41] See <http://www.government.pn/Laws/index.html>.
[42] K Marks, *Trouble in Paradise: Uncovering Decades of Sexual Abuse on Britain's Most Remote Island*, London: Harper Perennial, 2008, chapter 21.
[43] <http://www.fco.gov.uk/en/newsroom/latest-news/?view=PressS&id=7221966>.
[44] Note: *Framework for Compensation*, 9 October 2008 at <http://www.pitcairn.pn>.

# 3

# Pitcairn's Tortured Past:
# A Legal History

*Andrew Lewis*

Pitcairn's meagre legal history can scarcely be separated from its general history over the past two hundred years. Nearly all the significant events in its history have actual or potential legal significance. The acts for which the six islanders were prosecuted in *Christian* must, on any honest judgement, have seemed more or less vile. To understand why, nevertheless, the prosecution should have been regarded as unjustifiable and, in the words of Lord Hope, the most empathetic judge to hear the case, 'whether the law under which the offenders were to be prosecuted had been sufficiently promulgated in Pitcairn for it to be permissible for them to be dealt with in this way',[1] one needs to understand a little of the turbulent and disturbed history of the place.

The story of Pitcairn begins in Africa. In 1789 the *Bounty,* under the command of Captain Bligh, was dispatched to Tahiti to collect breadfruit plants and to carry them to the West Indies where it was hoped they would provide a cheap staple there to feed slaves brought from Africa by the slave trade. An enforced stay at Tahiti, occasioned by the growing cycle of the plant and the lengthy outward voyage, familiarized the crew of the *Bounty* with a style of life different from that they experienced either on board ship or at home. They were by no means the last Europeans to be seduced by the exotic. On the return journey, some of the men mutinied, led by the senior master's mate, Fletcher Christian. Bligh, together with 21 of the senior members of the crew,

---

[1] *Christian v The Queen* [2006] UKPC 47, Lord Hope at para. 75.

were turned away in a small launch.[2] The 25 left on board the *Bounty* returned to Tahiti whence Christian and eight men then set sail for a remoter refuge.[3] Even among the vast spaces of the Pacific, Pitcairn (formerly Pitcairn's) Island is remote. It is over 3,000 miles from the coast of South America and another 3,000 miles from New Zealand. The eponymous Pitcairn was a midshipman aboard the *Swallow*, commanded by Captain Carteret, who in 1767 first sighted the island in latitude 25° south. The sighting was reported in John Hawkesworth's 1773 *Account of the Voyages in the Southern Hemisphere*, a copy of which was carried by Bligh aboard the *Bounty*.[4] Carteret gave the longitude as 133°W24 which was repeated in Hawkesworth. In fact, Pitcairn lies in 25°S 130°W25, some 180 nautical miles further to the east. Fletcher Christian almost certainly learned of the island's existence from reading Bligh's copy of Hawkesworth and probably found it by running eastward along the 25° line of latitude until he came to it.[5]

The pattern of legal history of Pitcairn is dictated largely by constitutional questions and, for this purpose, I propose the following chronological divisions:

• The settlement: 1790–1814
• Recognition: 1814–56

---

[2] Not the least remarkable feature of the *Bounty* story is the fact that Bligh then sailed the grossly overcrowded and underprovisioned launch some 3,600 miles to Kupang in Timor. See W. Bligh, *A Voyage to the South Sea* (London: George Nicol, 1792). The *Bounty*'s log, which includes this open boat journey, is in the National Archives: NA/PRO Adm 55/151.

[3] Fourteen of those who remained on Tahiti were captured by HMS *Pandora*, Captain Edwards, which had been dispatched by the Admiralty for the purpose of pursuing the mutineers. Of these, four died when *Pandora* herself sank on the Great Barrier Reef, and 10 were brought back to England and court-martialled. Six were condemned for mutiny though only three were hanged. Two were freely pardoned on the recommendation of the Court-martial; a third, William Muspratt, a mere able seaman and the cook's assistant aboard the *Bounty* won a pardon on a technical issue of evidence. One of those freely pardoned, Peter Heywood, rose to become a Captain RN.

[4] J. Hawkesworth, *An Account of the Voyages Undertaken by the Order of His Present Majesty for Making Discoveries in the Southern Hemisphere etc.*, 3 vols (London: Strahan and Cadell, 1773) vol 1, 561.

[5] Before modern times the finding of longitude, degrees east or west, was problematic: latitude, position south or north, by contrast could be relatively easily found by celestial observation. A popular account of the problem of longitude and attempts at a solution is D. Sobel, *Longitude* (London: Fourth Estate, 1996). Nevertheless Captain Pipon in 1814 reported his surprise that so great an error had been made in the longitude of Pitcairn: Banks Archive ser. 71, State Library of New South Wales, see below note 14.

- Intervention: 1856–98
- Settled government: 1898–present

## The Settlement: 1790–1814

Within this period it is necessary to distinguish the first years of uneasy and eventually brutal relationships between the original settlers from the transition to a period of seemingly benign paternal governance of the emerging second generation of islanders by John Adams. The term 'settlement' here is deliberately ambiguous: the initial settling of the mutineers was anything but settled and much of the subsequent difficulties in assessing the nature and legal structure of Pitcairn society stems from the characterization of the events of these years.

### A savage society

The first 10 years of the settlement on Pitcairn was a troubled time. The mutineers were a heterogeneous lot brought together only by their marine occupation. Christian, who remained the recognized leader, had pretensions to gentility. His barrister brother Edward became Downing Professor of the Laws of England at Cambridge, the editor of Blackstone's *Commentaries*, and Chief Justice of the Isle of Ely.[6] Young, who had shipped in the *Bounty* as a supernumerary midshipman, was the nephew, probably illegitimate, of Admiral Sir George Young. He was born in the West Indies and contemporary descriptions suggest that his mother was of African descent. All the other mutineers on Pitcairn were seamen. The circumstances of the *Bounty*'s commissioning in peacetime ensured that all (with the exception of the gunner's mate, John Mills) were rated able but they were ill-educated in non-maritime matters. In a ship which by the standards of the time was relatively free of

---

[6] See *Minutes of the Proceedings of the Court-Martial held at Portsmouth, August 12, 1792. On ten persons charged with mutiny on board His Majesty's Ship the Bounty. With an appendix [by Edward Christian], containing a full account of the real causes and circumstances of that unhappy transaction, etc. [Compiled by Stephen Barney]* (London, 1794) (Stephen Barney was Muspratt's counsel); W. Blackstone, *Commentaries on the laws of England . . . with notes and additions by Edward Christian*, twelfth edn (London: Cadell, 1793–5); E. Christian, *The Charge of the Chief Justice Edward Christian, Esq. to the Grand Jury at the Assizes held at Ely . . . on 9th of March 1804* (Cambridge: Hodson, 1804). Fletcher Christian's other brother Charles was a naval surgeon.

punishments (Hollywood and popular imagination notwithstanding) four of the nine men Bligh had ordered to be flogged were amongst the mutineers on Pitcairn.[7]

There are a number of sources for life on Pitcairn in the early years. Edward Young appears to have kept a journal which came into the hands of Captain Beechey of HMS *Blossom*, who visited Pitcairn in 1825. Although the journal has since disappeared, Beechey incorporated elements into his account of his voyage.[8] Beechey also interviewed the sole surviving member of the crew, John Adams (otherwise known as Alexander Smith). But Adams told his story on numerous occasions, including to another member of the *Blossom*'s crew, Lt Edward Belcher, and was not always consistent in his tale.[9] A third eyewitness was Teehuteatuaonoa or Jenny who had been Adams' companion during the *Bounty*'s time at Tahiti and accompanied the mutineers to Pitcairn only to be passed over to Isaac Martin. She left Pitcairn in 1817 aboard the *Sultan*, under Captain Reynolds, and her oral history was reported in *The Sydney Gazette* on 17 July 1819.[10]

Of these accounts, the least reliable but most dominant are Adams'. It must be supposed that Young did not take the trouble to commit an inaccurate account to paper and Jenny had no particular reason to embellish what was in any case a remarkable tale. But Adams' accounts were all given orally to visitors, including some of the Royal Navy. Whatever assurances they may have provided, he must have realized that he was in some small danger of being called to account for his part in the mutiny and, quite possibly, for the bloody deeds committed on Pitcairn. The most recent historian of the *Bounty* considers it likely that Adams was responsible for Fletcher Christian's death.[11] Even if this

---

[7] Another four were amongst the rest of the mutineers: Churchill and Thompson who had been killed on Tahiti, and two who remained on Tahiti only to be captured by the Navy—Millward was executed by verdict of court martial whilst Muspratt was convicted of mutiny but pardoned on an evidential technicality (his counsel successfully argued that he had been deprived of the evidence of his fellow accused). Robert Lamb, butcher, who had also been flogged at Bligh's order, accompanied him in the launch only to die on Timor. [8] See below note 17.

[9] Earlier accounts of Adams were reported by Mayhew Folger of the American whaler *Topaz*. See note 13.

[10] A fuller account is to be found in *United Services Journal* (1829), part 1, 589–593 copied from a Bengali journal, *Bengal Hurkaru* for 2 October 1826. It is reproduced at <http://library.puc.edu/Pitcairn/pitcairn/jenny.shtml>.

[11] C. Alexander, *The Bounty* (New York: Viking Books, 2003), 372, 441. The case was fully argued by Fletcher's descendant Glynn Christian in the revised edition of his *Fragile Paradise* (Sydney & London: Doubleday, 1999), 340 ff.

conclusion is regarded as unsupported speculation, such considerations may well underpin the very diverse accounts Adams gave over the years of the fate of his companions.

An account of the events in the years immediately following the settlement has largely to be drawn from the impressions gained by subsequent visitors. It appears that in the ten years after the mutineers' landing, a sequence of vessels was seen off Pitcairn and that one at least landed some men briefly. According to Teehuteatuaonoa an attempt was made, without success, to contact this ship after its boats had returned on board.[12]

In February 1808, the American *Topaz*, under Captain Folger, hunting for seal in the Pacific, came upon land unexpectedly. Guessing that it might be Pitcairn's Island from Carteret's description, despite the wrong location, he was surprised to find it inhabited, and even more surprised that the inhabitants spoke English. Folger landed and spent some five hours on the island talking to the sole surviving mutineer, John Adams, whom he knew under the alias of Alexander Smith which Adams had adopted on the *Bounty*.[13]

In 1814 HMS *Briton*, under Captain Sir Thomas Staines, and HMS *Tagus*, under Captain Pipon, chanced upon Pitcairn where no island was 'laid down in the Admiralty, or other charts'. They were greeted from a boat by Thursday October Christian and George Young, the

---

[12] Those who, since 1796, have been led to believe that Fletcher Christian left Pitcairn to return eventually to England are sometimes minded to assume that his departure on one of these vessels was deliberately suppressed: *Letters from Mr. Fletcher Christian, etc.* (London 1796) (a spurious account); K. Curry, ed., *New Letters of Robert Southey*, vol 1, 1792–1810 (New York: Columbia University Press, 1965), 519 ff (genuine letters from the poet Robert Southey alluding to a sighting of Christian in Cumbria around 1804).

[13] Folger and others of his crew reported his visit on arrival at Valparaiso and this eventually reached the ears of the senior British naval officer on the South American station, Admiral Sir Sydney Smith who in turn reported the news to the Admiralty: T. Pocock, *A Thirst for Glory: The Life of Sir Sydney Smith* (London: Aurum Press, 1996), 210. Although the news became public in England in the pages of the *Naval Chronicle* 21 (1809) 454–455, no official action was taken. The *Topaz's* log is now in Nantucket Hist. Assn. Research library MS 220: ships logs, no 105. A copy of a copy of the relevant section of the *Topaz's* log made by Lt. Fitzmaurice in Valparaiso in 1808 is preserved among the papers of Sir Joseph Banks and available online on the State Library of New South Wales website at <http://www.sl.nsw.gov.au/banks/series_71/71_01.cfm/>. A further account is given in a private letter from his wife: Folger Family Papers in the Nantucket library MS 118 folder 32: see W. Hayes, *The Captain from Nantucket and the Mutiny on the Bounty* (Ann Arbor, Mich.: The William Clements Library, 1996). For this and other references I am indebted to the very full description of sources in C. Alexander, *The Bounty* (New York: Viking Books, 2003), 411 ff.

sons respectively of Christian and Young, and both captains landed on the island and spent time talking to John Adams, who now revealed his true name, and the younger members of the community.[14] A third visitor was the captain of the American whaler, the *Sultan*, Captain Reynolds, who visited the island in 1817. He induced Adams to visit him on board his ship and took away a number of artefacts belonging to the *Bounty*, including a notebook in which Adams had begun a personal memoir.[15] He also, as we have seen, gave passage to Jenny, one of the original women settlers.

Thereafter there were a number of visiting ships, to most of which Adams offered a differing account. So frequent indeed were visitors that John Adams was able to conduct a correspondence with his brother Jonathan in England.[16] In 1825, HMS *Blossom*, under Captain Beechey, on a survey expedition, spent some 16 days anchored off the island. A number of officers from the ship went on shore, including Lieutenant Edward Belcher, and left various accounts, whilst Beechey himself interviewed Adams in his cabin aboard the *Blossom*, with a clerk to take notes.[17]

Piecing together these fragmentary and differing accounts the following picture emerges.[18]

Pitcairn was uninhabited in January 1790.[19] It was settled by nine men of the *Bounty* crew, six Polynesian men who had joined the mutineers

[14] This time their reports were given more general publicity. Pipon's was published in the *Quarterly Review* 13 no 26 (1815) 352–383 and an account of this and Staines' appears in *Naval Chronicle* 35 (1816) 17–25. Mss reports of Pipon's account are preserved in the Banks Archive online at <http://www.sl.nsw.gov.au/banks/series_71/71_05.cfm> [hereafter Pipon with references to the online frames]. Based on these accounts a review called *Pitcairn's Island, A new Melo-dramatic Ballet of Action*, appeared on stage in London in April 1816.

[15] An account was published in a letter to *The New England Galaxy* for 12 January 1821.

[16] Printed in the *European Magazine*, September 1819, 210–211 and reproduced in part in Alexander, *The Bounty*, 359.

[17] Beechey published his account in his *Narrative of a Voyage to the Pacific . . . to co-operate with the Polar Expeditions* (London: Colburn and Bentley, 1831). The manuscript draft is preserved in the Mitchell Library, Sydney, NSW, Australia, ML.A1804. Belcher's account, first utilized by Alexander, *The Bounty*, is in the Alexander Turnbull Library, Wellington NZ, MS 0158.

[18] It is worth noting that the variety of testimony about the early years on Pitcairn results in a number of various reconstructions of events. For a recent attempt which differs in part from what follows see T. Lummis, *Pitcairn Island: Life and Death in Eden* (Aldershot: Ashgate, 1997).

[19] It had not always been so: there are remains of settlers who had left or died out around 1350.

during the *Bounty*'s wandering in search of a refuge, together with 12 Tahitian women (and one child). The habitable and cultivable extent of Pitcairn was small, some 90 acres in all in an island that was scarcely one mile by two in extent. This was divided into nine shares. The 'blacks', as the mutineers instinctively called the male Polynesians, were reduced to the position of servants. Each mutineer took a woman to wife, and not necessarily those to whom they had been formerly attached on Tahiti.[20] Although subordinated to their male companions by the contemporary mores of both English and Tahitian society, the women were never referred to as 'blacks'.[21] Nor had all the women come voluntarily. Apart from Jenny Teehuteatuaonoa, Isabella Mauatua, Christian's 'wife', and Quintal's companion, Tevarua/Sarah, the others had been members of a group visiting the *Bounty* off Tahiti when Christian made his decision to leave by cutting the anchor cable. One of these women had jumped into the sea and six others, the more elderly of the group, were eventually landed on an island close to Tahiti. The others remained on board, quite probably against their will.

The mutineers signalled their intention to remain on Pitcairn by burning the *Bounty*: apart from other considerations, it was essential not to leave it as an indication to any visitors of their origin.

Fletcher Christian was, according to Adams' account to Folger, the first mutineer to die on Pitcairn, killed by one of the Polynesians in 1793. According to the version he told to Folger's mate, Christian had committed suicide, an inconsistency which has fuelled speculation that, in fact, Christian had found some way to leave the island. There was a tale later current on Pitcairn itself that Christian had been accidentally killed by Adams whilst he tried to prevent Christian putting to sea in *Bounty*'s remaining boat.[22]

---

[20] Alexander Smith (born John Adams to which name he reverted on Pitcairn) had tattooed his initials on Teehuteatuaonoa, nicknamed Jenny, when he lived with her during the *Bounty*'s initial stay at Tahiti. On Pitcairn, she at first associated with Isaac Martin.

[21] Later visitors to Pitcairn commented on the fact that whilst the male descendants of these liaisons appeared to them European in appearance, their female siblings were perceived as Tahitian.

[22] G. L. Becke and W. Jeffery, *The Mutineer: a Romance of Pitcairn Island* (London: Fisher Unwin, 1898). Although a novel, by Jeffery, it claims authentic information derived from Becke, who defended the details in a exchange of correspondence with reviewers. According to Glynn Christian, the topographical detail fits ill with the reality on Pitcairn, *Fragile Paradise* (1st edn, London: Hamish Hamilton, 1982; 2nd edn, Sydney & London: Doubleday 1999; 3rd edn, The Long Riders Guild, 2005), 239. In any case, there are numerous other, equally improbable, tales of Christian's end.

hiding. Next, one of the two remaining Polynesians was murdered by one of the women as he slept. Shortly after, the other was shot by Young. Quintal and McKoy now returned and a new arrangement was agreed upon. The women were allowed to choose with whom they would live: Young and Adams were each joined by three of them, Quintal and McKoy by two each but a pattern of promiscuity was established as the women occasionally left those who dissatisfied or maltreated them. It was now October 1793 and, with seven children all aged under three, it may be said that the first community on Pitcairn began to be established. It was a racially and culturally mixed community in which all four adult males were European, all the adult women Polynesian, and all the children of mixed race.

During the next year there were two significant developments, both of which were emblematic of the shifting influences in the community. In March, the women were discovered to have kept and tendered the skulls of a number of those killed: the men were scandalized and insisted on their being buried. The women responded by insisting on leaving the island and to this end, led by Jenny who dismantled her house to the purpose, started to build a boat. Perhaps mindful of the impracticality of the idea, the men assisted them only to see the boat overturned when it was launched. Given the extent to which their quarrels seem to have been generated by sexual jealousy, it is difficult to believe that the men were serious in their endeavours to help the women leave. The failure was the occasion for an assertion of male dominance. The day after the unsuccessful launch, the skulls were buried. In November, the women planned an attack on the men but in the end determined on an act of secession, gathering up their children and leaving the men to look after themselves. This tactic seems to have been temporarily effective in restoring some measure of stability in relations. The community continued to grow throughout and despite these developments.

By the late 1790s, both McKoy and Quintal took to distilling alcohol.[23] McKoy threw himself off a cliff in a drunken fit whilst Quintal was shot dead by Young when he threatened to kill all

---

[23] Adams told Pipon in 1814 that 'from a Root in this Island he could extract a Spirit equal if not superior to our Jamaica rum [but] he has very prudently abstained from making any lately': Pipon CY 3011/333.

Christian's children if he could not have Isabella, who had subsequently had three children by Young, for himself. These were the last violent deaths on Pitcairn for a century.[24] Young survived until 1800, dying peaceably enough of asthma. He had taught Adams to read and, following Young's death, Adams underwent a religious conversion. Basing himself upon the Anglican *Book of Common Prayer* and the Bible, both among the books rescued from the *Bounty*, supplemented it would seem by memories of earlier practice—he taught the community to pray before and after meals—he instructed the young in a form of Christianity sufficient to impress subsequent visitors. By the time of the *Topaz*'s visit in 1808, he was capable of being perceived as the patriarch of the community, a role he cultivated until his death in 1829.

## A biblical monarchy

When Captains Staines and Pipon came to Pitcairn in 1814 they found what seemed to them a paradisiacal society. It should be borne in mind that they were only on the island for some few hours and had to spend some time in satisfying Adams' concern that they had come to take him back to England. Despite his evident anxiety that Folger's story would have reached the Admiralty, as indeed it had, no specific information was made available to naval vessels proceeding into the Pacific and Pipon and Staines were quite ignorant of Folger's discovery.

Between Young's death and their rediscovery by the rest of the world, Adams seems to have exploited his superiority of generation and education to dominate the community. Throughout the early visits, the rest of the islanders seem to have been conscious of a need to protect him. Down until his conversation with Beechey of the *Blossom*, Adams seems to have harboured fears that he might yet be seized and returned to England to stand trial. Before Bligh's death in 1817 this indeed seems to have been a reasonable assumption. When Pipon and Staines landed they were first greeted by one of his daughters who only led them to Adams on being reassured that they had not come to take him away. Precisely how Adams managed to convey his vulnerability to capture whilst maintaining his authority is uncertain. What seems likely is that,

---

[24] In 1898 Harry Christian killed Clara Warren and her baby daughter, for which he was tried and hanged. This was the first occasion, and the last before *Christian*, in which English criminal law was applied on Pitcairn. See below, at note 42.

despite his daughter's claim that he mistreated her mother, he was in general supported by the womenfolk of the original settlers. He may have been, or may have grown into, a less rebarbative companion than some of his shipmates had proved.

Although Young's journal (which only survives in the extracts made by Beechey) and Jenny Teehuteatuaonoa's oral accounts offer some control on our information, the general impression we have of the early years is almost entirely coloured by Adams' various statements. There can be little doubt that at first for reasons of self-preservation and latterly for self-aggrandizement, Adams suppressed and elaborated his tales. Nevertheless, some facts speak for themselves. Adams was the sole survivor of the mutiny and he did thereafter lead a seemingly virtuous life by Pitcairn standards. That the community on Pitcairn survived at all in its early years was due in some measure and for whatever reasons to his care.

In 1814 there were some 40 persons living on Pitcairn. All the original settlers were dead save Adams and six or seven of the original women.[25] Of these latter some, including Adams' wife Mary, seemed quite old: 'blind with age' was Pipon's description of her. Others, including Jenny Teehuteatuaonoa, whom Pipon does not mention, must have been a good deal younger as she survived to return to Tahiti in 1821. Adams himself had four children under 18, one of whom was married, and a step-daughter whose husband, presumably another first generation descendant, was dead. Fletcher Christian's two sons were still living: his first child was born on a Thursday in October 1790 and named Thursday October Christian.[26] The choice of name is perhaps emblematic of a willingness to forgo the past by not using a name common in the Christian family whilst not choosing to adopt a name more redolent of a Polynesian present and future. Subsequent children, both in the Christian and other mutineers' families, bore common Christian names. Fletcher's second son, born in 1792, was named Charles after his uncle. There were to be 24 children of these liaisons. No children were seemingly born of liaisons between the male Polynesians and the three women they shared. Perhaps none were permitted

---

[25] The uncertainty arises from Pipon's statement that there were originally 11 women of whom five had died and alternative claims that there were 12 Tahitian women (and a child, Teatuahitea or Sarah called Sully) which are now generally accepted.

[26] When he subsequently learned from visitors that his father Fletcher had been out in his reckoning he changed his name to Friday October.

to survive. These factors suggest the framing of a society after a European or at least English model.

Two features stand out in all the accounts of the settlement period. Most of the male members of the original Pitcairn community met violent deaths at their own or others' hands. The women on the whole survived but they suffered persistent violence at the hands of their male companions.

What can be said of the constitutional status of Pitcairn during these years? It is a necessary paradox that the dominant influence on the early community on Pitcairn was that of the mutineers, though outnumbered in point of personnel by the Polynesians both men and women. The language of the developing community was English, though it is unlikely that the original women ever spoke much of that language—Jenny Teehuteatuaonoa's accounts were translated for publication. The first generation of islanders would of necessity be bilingual but thereafter the language of Tahiti gave way to English, an English moreover which to this day preserves some distinct eighteenth century features of both language and pronunciation. The use of English Christian names for the descendants born after Thursday October Christian betrays a commitment to English tradition. The paradox lay in the fact that the mutineers were of necessity escaping from the English cultural and legal context: their lives were else forfeit as the fate of those captured on Tahiti demonstrates.[27]

There is authority for the proposition that British-born subjects cannot divest themselves of this status.[28] Blackstone cited a decision in Salkeld's reports for the statement that: 'In case of an uninhabited country newly found out by English subjects, all laws in force in England are in force there.'[29] It was ingeniously argued by the defence for Stevens Christian that in any event, such considerations did not apply either to the Tahitian women nor to their offspring, who were

---

[27] Of those who were tried for mutiny the four who were acquitted, Norman, McIntosh, Coleman, and Byrn, were all able to demonstrate that they had been detained on the *Bounty* against their will. Heywood and Morrison, who claimed to have done nothing to assist the mutineers were condemned to death (though later pardoned) for simply not doing their best to resist. Adams later admitted that he had been among those armed by Christian and as much if not more was true of the other Pitcairn settlers.

[28] *Joyce v Director of Public Prosecutions* [1946] AC 347.

[29] W. Blackstone, *Commentaries on the Laws of England*, vol I (Oxford: Clarendon Press, 1765), 104 citing Salk 411, 666 2 Salk 356 at 357: 'In case of an uninhabited country newly found out by English subjects, all laws in force in England are in force there, so it seemed to be agreed.'

illegitimate by English law and thus unable to take the nationality of their fathers from which they were, in any event, statutorily barred by the provisions of the British Nationality Act 1730.[30] It would be odd if the dominant factor in determining the constitutional position of such a community were to be the régime of a minority of its members who were actively seeking to escape its working and who, before any settled community had been established, were reduced to a group of four men who remained, from the example of Adams, in fear of capture if discovered.[31]

## Recognition: 1814–56

In his report of the discovery of Pitcairn, Captain Pipon recommended that the settlement should be permitted to continue: 'It remains to be determined whether it would be politic to withdraw them from the settlement altogether and destroy it. In my opinion such an act would be very unwise.'[32]

There succeeded a number of curious settlers on Pitcairn, the remoteness of which does not seem to have preserved it from the attentions of the most eccentric. It must be remembered that this was the peak period of whaling in the Pacific which brought both whaling vessels and those determined to police or harry them. The first new settler to arrive was John Buffett who was a seaman aboard the whaler *Cyrus*, under Captain Hall, which called at Pitcairn in 1823. Buffett and his friend John Evans asked to be left behind when the ship sailed. Apparently, Buffett was given permission but Evans was not. However, Evans managed to conceal himself on the island and remain. Buffett immediately took a prominent role as teacher and undertook church services. Both he and Evans married into the community.

In 1828, a quite different character, George Hunn Nobbs, arrived on the island having sailed himself from the coast of South America. Following the death of John Adams in March 1829, Nobbs obtained some ascendancy over the community, ousting Buffett as leader.

---

[30] 4 Geo 2 c 21, s. 2 of which provided that natural children whose fathers 'were or shall be liable to the penalties of high treason or felony' should be ineligible for British subject status.
[31] The Privy Council declined in *Christian* to permit argument on the issue of whether Pitcairn had ever been a British possession but simply assumed the force of Blackstone's remark: Lord Hoffmann at paras 9 and 16. [32] Pipon CY 3011/333.

At this juncture, the authorities in England determined to react to Adams' earlier request to Captain Beechey for relief to the islanders, with the result that an expedition was mounted from Sydney, consisting of HMS *Comet*, with Captain Sandilands, and a barque, the *Lucy Anne*, with instructions to remove the islanders to Tahiti. The last visitor before the arrival of the *Lucy Anne* was Captain Waldegrave in HMS *Seringaptam*. He was to report that the community were happy in their situation and no longer desired to leave: a change which may be attributed in part to the death of Adams and the coming of Nobbs.[33] But it was too late to countermand the *Lucy Anne* and so on 6 March 1831, amid protests, the whole population of the island was embarked and carried to Tahiti. Though they were made welcome there they did not settle. Exposed to disease to which they had no natural protection a number, including Thursday (Friday) October Christian, died. Almost immediately a small group made their way back to Pitcairn, arriving on 27 June. Later in the year, the remaining 65 members of the community persuaded an American whaler, the *Charles Doggett*, to carry them back to Pitcairn, where they arrived on 3 September 1831.[34]

Following the return to Pitcairn, Nobbs seems to have lost some of his former authority: perhaps he was too closely associated with the decision to emigrate to Tahiti. Moreover it appears from reports from ships visiting that the community had developed a taste for alcohol during their stay on Tahiti. The vacuum in the leadership of the community was filled by the arrival of Joshua Hill, who was initially welcomed by the islanders. Saying he was sent by the government in London, a wholly fictitious claim, Hill proclaimed himself President and proceeded to marginalize and impose restrictions upon Buffett, Evans, and Nobbs, whom he identified as potential sources of opposition to his rule. Matters came to a head when he sentenced both Evans and Buffett to a flogging which he proceeded to administer himself. It seems all too probable that Hill was mentally unstable.[35] In the end Nobbs, Buffett, and Evans left Pitcairn aboard the *Tuscan*, under

---

[33] Waldegrave made a record of local written laws which went back to those introduced by Adams. See D. McLoughlin, 'The Development of the System of Government and Laws of Pitcairn Island From 1791 to 1971' in *Laws of Pitcairn, Henderson, Ducie and Oeno Islands*, Rev. Ed., 1971, online at <http://library.puc.edu/Pitcairn/pitcairn/govt-history01.shtml> and see also Waldegrave, 'The Pitcairn Islanders' (1833) 3 *Journal of the Royal Geographical Society*.

[34] McLoughlin, 'Development' gives the date as 2 September.

[35] McLoughlin, 'Development'.

Captain Stavers, in March 1834. Hill then proceeded to behave so badly that by the end of the year, he had been forcibly deposed by the islanders who then summoned Nobbs, Buffett, and Evans to return, which they did by October 1834. Hill was neutralized though his conduct was not investigated until HMS *Actaeon* arrived in 1837 when arrangements were made to remove him to South America aboard HMS *Imogene*, under Captain Bruce, in early 1838.

HMS *Fly*, under Captain Eliott, was then dispatched (from the British Naval Station at Valparaiso) to assist the islanders. Among their concerns was the fact that visiting American whalers were in the habit of imposing upon them, owing to their supposed lack of status as a British colony. To strengthen their position, the leading islanders sought from Captain Eliott the protection of the British Crown. Eliott seems to have considered the community independent at the time of his visit and one version of the *Pitcairn Island Register* records that: 'The island was taken possession of by Capt Eliott on behalf of the Crown of Great Britain on the 29th of November.'[36] A different version in island folklore has Pitcairn adopted into the British Empire (an anachronistic term) on November 30th, when a constitution settled with the assistance of Captain Eliott was signed on board the *Fly*. This document, which incorporates a number of existing local laws recorded earlier by Captain Waldegrave, is notable for granting universal suffrage to both men and women for the election of an annual Magistrate and for imposing compulsory schooling on children.[37]

Although Captain Elliot was commended by his immediate superior on the Pacific Station, Rear-Admiral Ross and by the Admiralty Board, the Colonial Office, when apprised of Elliot's report, were less enthusiastic. The Permanent Under-Secretary minuted:

I confess I know not how anything can be done for the inhabitants of Pitcairn's Island. It is impossible to establish an independent Govt or Colony there, nor do I know how the Island could with any propriety be annexed to the Govt. of New South Wales, which has no sort of connection with it. Yet if neither of these measures be practicable we are I believe at the end of our resources.

---

[36] See W. Brodie, *Pitcairn's Island and the Islanders* (London: Whittaker, 1851). Brodie visited Pitcairn in 1850 and published his version of the *Register* on his return. The *Register* is an informal record maintained by the islanders.

[37] In the judgement of McLoughlin, 'Development': 'the people of Pitcairn Island, with the ready assistance of Captain Elliott, formally acknowledged their status as a British possession and, as a natural consequence, placed themselves under the protection of the British Crown'.

George Nobbs remained the leader of the community, though the terms of the 1838 Constitution precluded his becoming Chief Magistrate as he was not native-born. Since the disastrous interlude of Hill, his talents as teacher and religious leader were once more appreciated and he became headmaster of the school. He left the island briefly in the early 1850s to return in 1852 as an ordained priest of the Church of England, and was appointed Chaplain to Pitcairn.

## Intervention: 1856–98

Interventions came from a number of quarters. The most significant was the decision of the British government in 1856 to deport the entire population of 194 persons on Pitcairn to Norfolk Island.[38] These plans may well have been drawn up under the influence of George Nobbs who, in 1847, had written to General Williams, British Consul-General for the Pacific Islands in Hawaii, to ask for assistance in relocating the population.[39] The concern was that the size of the community was again outpacing the resources on the island. Arrangements were negotiated during a visit to Pitcairn in May 1853 by Admiral Moresby, the Commander-in-Chief of the Pacific Station. Norfolk had some attractions despite its grim reputation.[40] Initially settled in 1788 as part of the New South Wales colony, from 1825 to 1855, Norfolk Island was exclusively a penal colony for those transported to Australia from Britain who persisted in crime. The prisoners had cultivated the island but the abandonment of the penal colony made it available for civilian settlement. After their experience on Tahiti, it was an attraction to the Pitcairners that it was currently uninhabited. The whole community was transported to Norfolk Island in May 1856.

---

[38] The whole community of 193 were transported to Norfolk Island but numbered 194 on arrival owing to the birth of Reuben Christian on board the *Morayshire*.

[39] McLoughlin, 'Development' citing H. E. Maude, 'History of Pitcairn Island', in A. S. C. Ross and A. W. Moverley, *Introduction to the Pitcairnese Language* (London: Andre Deutsch, 1964), 77–78.

[40] See, for example, the popular account in R. Hughes, *The Fatal Shore* (London: Collins Harvill, 1986). Only during the period 1840–44 when the governor of Norfolk Island was Alexander Maconochie, formerly professor of geography at University College London, was a more enlightened penal regime attempted: J. Clay, *Maconochie's Experiment* (London: John Murray, 2001).

Some Pitcairners immediately set about trying to return. A small party of 16, members of the Young and McCoy families, of whom 12 were children, returned aboard the *Mary Ann* in early 1859. In 1864, a larger party sailed back aboard the *St Kilda*. Nobbs remained on Norfolk Island together with John Buffett and the greater part of the community who seem to have welcomed the greater security and material well-being offered. Thereafter there were two Pitcairn populations, those, the majority, who remained on Norfolk Island, unquestionably under British rule, and those who returned to their homeland. The resettlers included members of the Christian, Young, and McCoy families together with some Buffetts (but not John) and some new blood in the person of Samuel Warren, an American from Rhode Island who had married Agnes Christian on Norfolk Island.[41]

This third settlement, it may be argued, was as spontaneous and unofficial as the first and raises similar questions about the status and role of the British government. There is this difference. In 1790, Pitcairn's Island was in traditional international law terms *terra nullius* and open to the first taker, and an important issue arises as to whether the mutineers' settlement constituted a British seizure. This we have considered above. By 1856 it may be assumed that this question had been settled in the British Crown's favour, at least from the perspective of English law. Once a British possession, it would require a deliberate act of abandonment or cession to another to change its status. Did the resettlement of the population amount to an abandonment of the island? The issue never seems to have been argued, though the returnees of 1858 claimed that they had arrived just in time to prevent a French vessel taking the seemingly abandoned island. It seems reasonable to suppose that in this they saw themselves protecting British rather than their own mere personal interests. In practice, the British government continued to claim sovereignty over Pitcairn whilst largely ignoring its immediate needs.

Some 10 years after the resettlement, a party from Norfolk Island, including the elderly John Buffett, paid a visit and encouraged the Pitcairners once more to emigrate but to no avail. This was despite the fact that island life was harder than it had been previously. The substantial falling off of the whaling allied to the interruption in trade caused by the abandonment of the island for three years during the

---

[41] Of these resettler families, the names of Buffett and McCoy were to die out.

Norfolk Island period left the islanders in a more subsistence economy than had prevailed earlier in the century. Matters improved after a visit in 1878 from Rear-Admiral de Horsey in HMS *Shah* in 1878: thereafter regular visits by Royal Navy vessels resumed and continued until the First World War. The islanders acquired fresh blood in the persons of sailors wrecked in the vicinity throughout the 1880s. Unfortunately one of these incomers managed to offend local sentiment by making love to an already affianced girl: he was ordered to leave the island aboard HMS *Sappho*, under Captain Clark. At the same time a new law was passed, again with Royal Naval blessing, forbidding any new settlers to the island. In October 1886, a Mr John Tay, a Seventh Day Adventist missionary, landed on Pitcairn. Earlier some Adventist missionary material had been sent to the island which paved the way for his acceptance. The community adopted the Adventist practice of Sabbath (ie Saturday worship). Tay was not authorized to baptize and after a stay of some weeks he left, promising to return. This he did in 1890 in an Adventist mission ship called *Pitcairn* and all the islanders were (re) baptized. All pigs on the island were slaughtered, for Adventists do not eat pork, and alcohol and smoking were abandoned.

Two years later, Pitcairn introduced, for a brief spell, a parliamentary form of government in which judicial and executive functions, formerly combined in the chief Magistrate, were separated. In time-honoured fashion this change was made with the cooperation of a visiting naval captain, Captain Rooke, of HMS *Champion*. Since at least the time of the visit of HMS *Fly* in 1838, Pitcairn had considered that changes of a fundamental nature could only be introduced with the assistance of outside authority, however irrelevant.

## Settled Government: 1898–Present

In 1887, the British Settlements Act gave power by section 2 to Her Majesty in Council to establish all such laws and institutions necessary for the peace, order, and good government of Her Majesty's subjects and others within British settlements. The Act defined as a British Settlement any British possession not 'acquired by cession or conquest' which lacked its own legislature. In 1893, the Pacific Order in Council was made in accordance with this Act but it only applied to islands specified in Article 6(1) of the Order—which did not include Pitcairn. However Article 6(2) gave the Secretary of State power to add islands and in 1898, Pitcairn was added in accordance with this provision. Whether this was done in ignorance of the revision of the island constitution in 1892 to include a 'parliament' is unclear, but in any case, this body lacked full legislative capacity. The 1893 Order had established a High Commissioner's Court for the Western Pacific with both civil and criminal jurisdiction which was empowered to apply the law 'for the time being in force in and for England' so far as circumstances permitted. It was under these provisions that the only prosecution for a breach of the English criminal law prior to *Christian* took place: the trial for murder of Harry Christian in 1898. Harry Christian was convicted by the High Commissioner's Court sitting on Pitcairn and taken to Suva to be executed. It should be noted that, as in 1996, the regularization of Pitcairn's position was achieved under the prompting of events. The killing of Clara Warren and her child Eleanor by Harry Christian in June 1897 required some action and, failing any existing machinery, Pitcairn was brought within the operation of British Settlements Act.[42] The sense of expediency and retroactivity created by the events of 1898 were to be repeated on a larger scale in the period 1996–2006.[43]

From 1898, therefore, there could be little doubt but that Pitcairn was a British settlement in the eyes, at least, of the British government. Subsequent alterations in the detailed administration of Pitcairn did not alter the position. During the early part of the twentieth century, attempts were made to provide a degree of local criminal apparatus for Pitcairn. In 1904, a revised set of laws for Pitcairn were promulgated by the Deputy Commissioner for the Western Pacific, R. T. Simons, in the course of a visit to the island. Amongst other things, this restored the function of Chief Magistrate in place of the seven-member parliament. In 1940, the Pitcairn Island Government Regulations were established by the then-Deputy Commissioner, H. F. Maude, which, inter alia, created an Island Court. These regulations were found in 1951 to be ultra vires the Deputy Commissioner. In 1952, the Pitcairn Order

---

[42] It was recognized that, on the assumption that Harry Christian was a British subject, he could have been tried in England by virtue of s 9 of the Offences against the Person Act, 1861, 24 & 25 Vict. c.100.

[43] On the question of the delay in bringing proceedings in *Christian* the Privy Council casually observe: 'The main period of delay (between a year and two years) was caused by the need to determine a venue for the trials and appoint Supreme Court judges to conduct them. This required a diplomatic agreement between the United Kingdom and New Zealand, followed by primary legislation ... ' (Lord Hoffmann at para. 25).

revoked the application of the Pacific Order to Pitcairn and substituted as the governing authority the Governor of Fiji who was also to be Governor of Pitcairn, granting a power to make provision for 'peace, order and good government'. Following the Pitcairn Order, the 1940 Regulations were re-established by Ordinance.

In 1961, by the Judicature Ordinance, the jurisdiction of the High Commissioner's Court for the Western Pacific was replaced by that of the Supreme Court of Fiji. A subordinate or Magistrate's Court (replacing the earlier Island Court) was created by the Justice Ordinance 1966 which replaced the 1940 Regulations. This was enacted by the Governor of Fiji as Governor of Pitcairn. When Fiji became independent, the Pitcairn Order 1970 reverted to the pattern of giving the Governor of Pitcairn power to make laws for 'peace, order and good government'. At the same time the Pitcairn Royal Instructions were issued by Her Majesty the Queen which contain rules and guidance to be followed by the Governor in legislating.[44] By Instruction 5, the Governor was forbidden to introduce divorce. The particular nature of Pitcairn society was reflected in other of its local laws, which did not conform to British norms. As recently as 1966, the Justice Ordinance included criminal penalties for adultery and cohabitation.[45]

From 1970, effective administration was handled from New Zealand, the Governorship of Pitcairn being conferred upon the UK High Commissioner based in Wellington. The Governor established a Supreme Court of Pitcairn by the Judicature Ordinance 1970 with the jurisdiction of the High Court in England.[46] No judge was immediately appointed to the court.

---

[44] For example, Instruction 4 (2) provided inter alia that: 'Matters having no proper relation to each other shall not be provided for by the same law'—a principle which can be traced back to the Roman *lex Caecilia Didia* of 98 BC.

[45] Justice Ordinance 1966 ss 89 and 90. The Ordinance is now replaced by the 1999 Ordinance which lacks such provision. This may be taken to reflect the changes worked upon Pitcairn by the massive intervention in the wake of the *Christian* prosecutions.

[46] Although it was argued in *Christian* that the Ordinance was ultra vires the 1887 Act because Pitcairn was either not a British possession at all, or, if it were, it was so by cession and so outwith the provisions of the Act, the Privy Council, following *The Fagernes* [1927] P 311, declined to allow the first proposition to be argued on the grounds that, as far as the courts were concerned, the status of Pitcairn was conclusively determined by the British government's statement: Lord Hoffmann delivering the judgment of the Council at para. 9. At para. 10 the Privy Council concluded that the powers of the Crown with regard to a ceded territory, even supposing Pitcairn to have fallen into this category, were even more extensive than those granted by the 1887 Act.

In the period up to 1996 there were various prosecutions under local criminal law, though seemingly no civil proceedings of any kind. There were no professional judges or magistrates or trained police on the island and no lawyers. Nor were there any copies of books on or of English law.[47] Until the proceedings in *Christian* there was no right of appeal from the Supreme Court: a Pitcairn Court of Appeal (with membership drawn from the Court of Appeal of New Zealand) was created for the purpose by the Pitcairn Court of Appeal Order 2000. The air of unreality which surrounds the whole proceeding in *Christian* is enhanced on realizing that there is now a Pitcairn bar, with rights of audience before these Pitcairn courts, whose members are wholly drawn from New Zealand some 3,000 miles distant and whose convenience was undoubtedly considered in the arrangements made to permit the Supreme Court to sit in New Zealand after the initial hearings on the island. One cannot help feeling that one-tenth of the cost of the legal proceedings could have been more usefully employed in direct educational and other provision on Pitcairn—a consideration which seems to have weighed with Paul Treadwell, the lawyer with most acquaintance with the island before *Christian*.[48]

It is striking that throughout this period there were only rare official visits to the Island. Only one Governor of Pitcairn has ever visited the territory for which he was responsible.[49] Even the sympathetic Mr Treadwell, legal adviser to the Governor since 1979, had not done so.

---

[47] There is now apparently a copy of Halsbury's *Laws* (4th edn) on Pitcairn but it may be wondered whether this is not, in Lord Woolf's words in *Christian*, 'a meaningless gesture': Lord Woolf at para. 39. And see the Pitcairn Court of Appeal's seemingly realistic assessment of the previous situation (Lord Woolf in the Privy Council at 41 *dubitante*) at para. 108: 'It seems to us that accessibility [of legal advice] through a government agency may not always be sufficient . . .'. With the greatest of respect to his lordship, Lord Woolf's statement (at 41) that 'the criminal law can only operate . . . if the onus is firmly placed on a person, who is or *ought to be* on notice that conduct he is intending to embark on may contravene the criminal law, to take the action that is open to him to find out what are the provisions of the law' (emphasis added) amounts only to the old maxim that *ignorantia haud excusat*. It is scarcely an observation of sociological probability or even possibility.

[48] Treadwell also foresaw that the proceedings might result in the destruction of the tiny island community: see Appendix II, document (b).

[49] In his privately printed personal memoir Sir David Scott, British High Commissioner in New Zealand, records a visit which he made as Governor in 1973 at the time of French nuclear tests in the Pacific: *A Window into Downing Street* (London: The Memoir Club, 2003), 169–178.

The last visit by a legal adviser was by Mr McLoughlin in 1958.[50] There is now a permanent Governor's representative on Pitcairn.

There was no medical doctor on Pitcairn until 2000: previously it had been the practice for the wife of the pastor appointed by the Seventh Day Adventist Church to provide nursing services. Before 1997, the local police officers were untrained (and their number included two of the defendants in *Christian*).

The British position on Pitcairn is not universally accepted. The website of the Pacific Union College, a Seventh Day Adventist institution in the Napa Valley, California, which maintains strong links with the island, contains the following entry:

Pitcairn Island, claimed by the United Kingdom as one of its 'Overseas Territories', was previous to 2002 claimed as a 'Dependant Territory' of the United Kingdom. It is governed from the United Kingdom by an appointed Governor whose offices are in Wellington, New Zealand. A Commissioner for the island who handles most on-going, practical matters for Pitcairn is located in Auckland, New Zealand.

On Pitcairn Island there is the Island Council which meets with the island's Mayor in charge. Under ideal circumstances the Council is in complete charge of governing the island locally. In the last two years, though, there has arisen some tension between the Island Council, representing the Pitcairn people, and the Governor, as failures have occurred in seeking the Council's views on matters that importantly affect Pitcairn's present and future.

...

In point of fact, Pitcairn's Governor has in 2003 issued a flurry of ordinances, regulations, orders, and rules, some of which have been put into effect without counsel with the Pitcairn Island Council. This governance without full consultation has resulted in an exacerbation of tension, the Pitcairn people feeling that their culture and remote island conditions need to be carefully factored into any law or regulation that affects them.

---

[50] McLoughlin produced a report which contains some account of the history of Pitcairn: D. McLoughlin, *Report on Judicial and Administrative Visit to Pitcairn Island, 1958*. MS.103 Western Pacific Archives, Suva. H. E. Maude similarly wrote up a history in the light of his 1940 visit: H. E. Maude, *History of Pitcairn Island* in A. S. C. Ross and A. W. Moverley, *Introduction to the Pitcairnese Language* (London: Andre Deutsch, 1964), 45–101.

## Conclusion

The legal history of Pitcairn is inseparable from its social history. The original settlement was not a promising one: the men were either mutineers from the *Bounty* or their Polynesian followers, who were reduced to the status of servants; the women were their largely reluctant mates. The early history was violent, and most of the mutineers and Polynesian men were murdered or committed suicide. Some 20 years after the original landing, however, a small civic society had developed under the leadership of the surviving mutineer, John Adams. Fearful of recapture, Adams did not encourage visitors but increasingly during the early nineteenth century the Royal Navy provided a channel of communication with the outside world and a measure of administrative oversight. The island was troubled by the arrival of adventurers and missionaries and on two occasions the whole population was evacuated, first to Tahiti in 1831 and then to Norfolk Island in 1856. On both occasions, a section of the population returned to begin life on the island again. The British Crown exercised a tenuous authority over Pitcairn, initially through the interventions by the Royal Navy, and has always been reactive in its attitude to Pitcairn's problems, a pattern which has continued into the present. In 1898, in order to provide a mechanism for trying one of the islanders for murder, Pitcairn was brought within the operation of the British Settlements Act as a colony. Thereafter there have been various modifications to the formal constitutional position of Pitcairn but until recently these had little direct effect upon life on the island. The very real concerns felt by some commentators, and most ably reflected in Lord Hope's opinion in *Christian*, arise from the fact that the government of Pitcairn has been lax to the point of turpitude. It is these failings which should form the basis of our collective human responsibility to the female population of Pitcairn.

# 4

# Pitcairn Island Law: A Peculiar Case of the Diffusion of the Common Law

*Gordon Woodman*

*Steven Raymond Christian and Others v The Queen*[1] raises issues both in general legal theory and in respect of the fundamental principles of legal practice. This chapter considers its relevance to the principles of legal practice on choice of law. Judges are expected and generally endeavour to make decisions according to law. This requires them to decide according to an existing normative order. There are often problems, such as those considered in some other chapters in this collection, as to how a chosen normative order is to be interpreted and applied to a particular case. But a prior question in every case is which normative order is to be chosen out of those currently in existence? In most cases the answer seems obvious, but the question needs consideration in a significant minority of cases.

An existing normative order is an integral part of the culture of the population which observes it. Normative orders are characterized by, inter alia, their places on a continuum of formality. At one extreme are the formal, technically elaborated orders observed in the professional culture of the officials of the modern state, which may also be embedded in a wider culture of the state's population ('state law', or 'positive law' in a narrow sense). At the other extreme are the unofficial orders formed

---

[1] *R v Steven Raymond Christian and Others*, Pitcairn Supreme Court, various proceedings and judgments of 2004 and 2005; *Steven Raymond Christian and Others v The Queen*, Pitcairn Court of Appeal, CA 1-7/2004, 5 August 2004 and CA 1-6/2005, 2 March 2006; *Steven Raymond Christian and Others v The Queen*, Privy Council Appeal No 109/2005 [2006] JCPC 47, [2007] 2 AC 400, [2007] 2 WLR 120.

by social practice in the cultures of acephalous communities, called here 'customary law' (being forms of 'folk law' or 'living law').[2] It is unnecessary to debate here the appropriateness of the label 'law'. It may seem obvious that the law courts of a state will choose one of the former for application to any case before them. Even then there may still be problems of choice of law. The population of this professional culture may appreciate that the officials of other states observe different normative orders, and may decide that in some cases their own courts should either decline jurisdiction or recognize and apply other states' laws. Such choices between different systems of state law comprise the area of private international law.

But private international law includes only one part of the field of choice of law. Judges and lawmakers often feel a need to relate 'their' normative orders to the less 'official' orders observed by populations outside the limits of professional official cultures. Thus English common law has traditionally been ready to recognize and enforce customary laws arising from social practice, such as local customs and the customs of trades, professions, and international commerce, presumably in part because the common law itself consists in large measure of a form of customary law.[3] At a relatively early date, the English courts had already formulated rules to the effect that customary laws were to be recognized if they met the qualifications that they were of ancient origin, not contrary to reason, and sufficiently certain.[4] Thus there are choice of law issues even when a case is within the confines of the common law.

These 'internal' choice of law issues are especially numerous and acute in jurisdictions which are or have been British colonies. The inception of colonial rule in almost all territories was accompanied by

---

[2] The various terms which have been used are noted in G. R. Woodman, 'Folk Law' in *Dictionnaire encyclopédique de théorie et de sociologie du droit*, 2nd edn, dir. A.-J. Arnaud (Paris: Librairie Générale de Droit et de Jurisprudence, 1993), 262–265.

[3] A. W. B. Simpson, 'The Common Law and Legal Theory' in *Oxford Essays in Jurisprudence*, ed. A. W. B. Simpson (Oxford: Clarendon Press, 1970), 77–99; G. R. Woodman, 'The Involvement of English Common Law with Other Laws' in *La quête anthropologique du droit: Autour de la démarche d'Étienne Le Roy*, eds C. Eberhard and G. Vernicos (Paris: Éditions Karthala, 2006), 477–500.

[4] J. H. Baker, 'Custom and Usage' in *Halsbury's Laws of England*, 4th edn, 1998 re-issue, 12(1), 153–259; Woodman, 'Involvement'.

a diffusion (or reception, transfer, or transplantation) of English state law.[5] But where there were already indigenous populations, the common law readiness to recognize other bodies of customary law usually operated. It was generally provided that each state legal system, formed in the British, common law mould, was to observe and enforce indigenous customary and religious laws, except where they infringed the British notion of minimum moral standards. Hence there was created in these territories a ruling colonial, official culture which was often vastly different from those of the societies the officials attempted to control, but which they were also supposed to recognize and apply. The officials of the now independent states in Africa and Asia which participated in the diffusion of the common law, themselves frequently living in both the state culture and a popular culture, continue to wrestle with these issues.

Questions of choice of law arising from the difference between the official and popular cultures are well illustrated by the case of Pitcairn. Here the social gap has been exacerbated by a large spatial separation and lack of communication between governing officialdom and the island descendants of the settlers of 1790. Consequently *Christian v The Queen* has lessons for other colonial and former colonial territories. It is also relevant to modern, technologically advanced societies in which there is a gap between the educational, social, and economic environment of the governing officials and that of other parts of the population who follow 'street' and other unofficial cultures.

The case illustrates two broad questions about choice of law. The first arose from the issue whether the defendants could be validly convicted under the Sexual Offences Act 1956 of the UK for acts done in Pitcairn. It concerns the principles according to which a state court chooses the law for application in a case, and follows from the history of the sources of law in Pitcairn. The second arose from the argument that the

---

[5] The term 'diffusion' has been proposed by William Twining, 'Diffusion of Law: A Global Perspective', *Journal of Legal Pluralism* 49 (2004), 1–45, especially at 5, and 'Social Science and Diffusion of Law', *Journal of Law & Society* 32 (2005), 203. The term 'reception' was widely used in the past, eg A. N. Allott, *Essays in African Law* (London: Butterworths, 1960), chapter 1; M. Doucet and J. Vanderlinden, eds, *La réception des systèmes juridiques: implantation et destin,* (Brussels: Bruylant, 1994). The terms 'transplant' and 'transplantation' have also been much used, eg A. Watson, *Legal Transplants: An Approach to Comparative Law*, rev. edn (Edinburgh: Scottish Academic Press, 1993). In German the term *Übertragung* (carrying over) is used in H. Janssen, *Die Übertragung von Rechtsvorstellungen auf fremde Kulturen am Beispiel des englischen Kolonialrechts: ein Beitrag zur Rechtsvergleichung* (Tübingen: Mohr Siebeck for Max-Planck-Institut für ausländisches und internationalisches Privatrecht, 2000).

prosecutions were an abuse of the process of the court. It concerns the possible need for the general principles of choice of law to be modified to secure justice in particular circumstances. The principal aspects of these issues are examined in this chapter.

The courts involved were constituted under the authority of the legislature of the UK, on the basis that Pitcairn was a territory of the British Crown. Consequently they were required to apply English law to the initial questions of whether they had jurisdiction and the choice of the law which they should apply.

## The History of the Sources of Law in Pitcairn

The doctrines designating the laws to be applied in colonial territories were developed in relation to the diffusion of English law in many parts of the world over several centuries. After the initial diffusion to a territory at the inception of colonial rule, there has usually been a continuing communication and exchange of ideas, concepts, practices, judicial decisions, and statutory texts, such that it is realistic to continue to refer to these territories as belonging to 'the common law world'. On the other hand, there has always been some adjustment of the English law to local circumstances, both at the moment of reception and subsequently. There is here a continuing globalization of localisms, continuing the earlier globalization of English legal localisms. And with each instance of diffusion there has been a localization of the globalism, or glocalization.[6]

In the case of Pitcairn the starting-point for argument was the proposition that the territory was a British possession. This status was said to result from the facts that the *Bounty* mutineers were the first settlers, and that the island was annexed by the Crown in consequence of that settlement. The reasoning of the courts on this point is considered below, but it would seem clear that as a matter of historical fact Pitcairn had indeed become subject to the British Crown, even though it had not been actively administered by Britain, well before the events which gave rise to the case. Consequently British colonial law was applicable.

---

[6] B. de Sousa Santos, *Toward a New Legal Common Sense: Law, Globalization and Emancipation*, 2nd edn (London: Butterworths, 2002), 177–179; U. Wanitzek and G. R. Woodman, 'Relating Local Legal Activity to Global Influences: A Theoretical Survey' in *Local Land Law and Globalization: A Comparative Study of Peri-urban Areas in Benin, Ghana and Tanzania*, eds G. R. Woodman, U. Wanitzek, and H. Sippel (Münster: LIT Verlag, 2009), 1–79.

## The law originally in force in Pitcairn

The principles for the determination of the law in a newly acquired colony were stated thus by Blackstone around the time of the Pitcairn settlement:

Plantations, or colonies in distant countries, are either such where the lands are claimed by right of occupancy only, by finding them desert and uncultivated, and peopling them from the mother country; or where, when already cultivated, they have been either gained by conquest, or ceded to us by treaties. And both these rights are founded upon the law of nature, or at least upon that of nations. But there is a difference between these two species of colonies, with respect to the laws by which they are bound. For it is held, that if an uninhabited country be discovered and planted by English subjects, all the English laws are immediately there in force. For as the law is the birthright of every subject, so wherever they go they carry their laws with them. But in conquered or ceded countries, that have already laws of their own, the king may indeed alter and change those laws; but, till he does actually change them, the ancient laws of the country remain, unless such as are against the law of God, as in the case of an infidel country.[7]

Thus the English state law doctrines governing the courts' choice of law contain an initial presumption in favour of the law which already governs a community. It thus adopts the relatively conservative stance to legal change which the rule of law also requires.[8] But to identify the existing laws of populations, the doctrine uses primarily not a territorial criterion but the concept of personal law. This underlies especially the rule for colonies acquired through the migration of settlers, expressed in Blackstone's statement that English settlers 'carry their laws with them'.

---

[7] W. Blackstone, *Commentaries Upon the Laws of England*, Vol. 1, 1st edn (Oxford: Clarendon Press, 1765), 104. The corresponding text in the 12th edn, edited by Christian (1793) differs in the following respects: the words 'wherever they go they carry their laws with them' are omitted, although the reference to 'birthright' is retained; the English laws which are in force in settled colonies are qualified as those 'then in being'; and, also with reference to settled colonies, a passage (quoted below) qualifies the rules of English law which are transferred. Blackstone amplified and qualified his statement of 1765 following the decision in *Campbell v Hall* (1774, 98 ER 1045, 20 State Tr. 239; the most relevant part of those reports is the judgment of Lord Mansfield; there are valuable passages in the arguments of counsel in the latter report at cols. 264–266, 287, 288–290). On the basic rules on the diffusion of English law to colonies, see: K. Roberts-Wray, *Commonwealth and Colonial Law* (London: Steven & Sons, 1966), 539–544; K. Patchett, 'Reception of Law in the West Indies', *Jamaican Law Journal* (1973), 17–35, 55–67; K. McNeil, *Common Law Aboriginal Title* (Oxford: Clarendon Press, 1989), especially chapter 4; G. R. Woodman, 'The Peculiar Policy of Recognition of Indigenous Laws in British Colonial Africa. A Preliminary Discussion', *Verfassung und Recht in Übersee* (1989) 22, 273–284, 276–279; J. M. Finnis, 'Commonwealth and Dependencies' in *Halsbury's Laws of England,* 4th edn, Vol. 6, 2003 Reissue, Part 5, 'The Extension of English Law', 515. [8] Guest, chapter 8 below.

The concept of personal law, existing long before the rise of the modern state and its laws, entailed the notion that every person had a law, usually developed by custom and rarely containing significant legislation, which applied to that individual wherever they went. As state laws developed, the concept came to be expressed in terms of the state law with which a person was primarily associated, and it was in this sense that it came to be employed in private international law. However, the importance of observing the personal, non-state laws of indigenous peoples even when the English law of settlers was imported was robustly stated a century after Blackstone in a judgment of Lord Kingsdown. Considering the Indian subcontinent, he said that there had been there:

a settlement made by a few foreigners for the purposes of trade in a very populous and highly civilized country . . .

If the settlement had been made in a Christian country of Europe, the settlers would have become subject to the laws of the country in which they were settled. It is true that in India they retained their own laws for their own government within the Factories, which they were permitted by the ruling powers of India to establish; but this was [because they did not intermingle with the indigenous population . . . ].

But the permission to use their own laws by European settlers does not extend those laws to Natives within the same limits, who remain to all intents and purposes subjects of their own Sovereign, and to whom European laws and usages are as little suited as the laws of the Mahometans and Hindoos are suited to Europeans.[9]

Although there are references there to the laws of the local 'sovereign', it was well established that it might be also appropriate for local indigenous laws which were not state laws to be recognized, just as in England. The principle was given extensive effect in the legislation establishing colonial courts, in the Pacific as elsewhere, which required them to apply English law, but also to observe and enforce the observance of 'native laws and customs', especially in cases between 'natives'.[10] Moreover, in these cases,

[9] *Advocate-General of Bengal v Ranee Surnomoye Dossee* (1863) 15 ER 811.

[10] On Africa see generally Allott, *Essays*, chapter 7. On the recognition of customary law in common law legal systems of the Pacific, the main literature is directed to the current law but in most cases refers to the development from the colonial periods. See especially: J. Corrin-Care and J. G. Zorn, 'Legislating Pluralism: Statutory "Developments" in Melanesian Customary Law', *Journal of Legal Pluralism* 46 (2001), 49–101, 49; J. G. Zorn and J. Corrin-Care, *Proving Customary Law in the Common Law Courts of the South Pacific* (London: British Institute of International and Comparative Law, 2002); K. Brown, *Reconciling Customary Law and Received Law in Melanesia: the Post-Independence Experience in Solomon Islands and Vanuatu* (Darwin: Charles Darwin University Press, 2005); Law Commission, New Zealand, *Converging Currents: Custom and Human Rights in the Pacific*, Study Paper 17 (Wellington, New Zealand: Law Commission, 2006).

unlike those arising in England, there was no condition imposed that the customary laws in question should be ancient, although it was required that they should not be contrary to reason, or not 'repugnant to natural justice, equity and good conscience', or some such phrase.[11]

The one field in which this deference to other laws was excluded was in the structures and processes of colonial state government. The machinery of government was established through the overriding legislative power taken by the colonizing state. English law shaped and regulated the apparatus of this state and the actions of officials administering it, who were British personnel for most of the colonial period.

Colonial legal policy was thus in broad outline to impose English law as the only appropriate law for government but to recognize personal laws, whether state, customary, or religious, as appropriate for other fields of social ordering. This policy was confirmed in legislation enacted for many British Pacific territories in the nineteenth and twentieth centuries, where separate regimes were provided for 'natives' and others, the distinction being largely racial.[12]

The application of the principle of personal law to Pitcairn encounters difficulties. It was not entirely obvious that English law and English law alone should have applied on this basis in the first years of settlement. Of the 28 settlers, 19 were Tahitians.[13] Perhaps the Tahitians

---

[11] See also Law Commission, *Converging Currents*, para. 4.24.

[12] The initial definition provision in the Pacific legislation on choice of law stated: ' "native" means every person in the West Pacific not of European descent' (*Western Pacific Queen's and King's Regulations 1879–1912*, Regulation 4 of 1888). The definition later settled upon was contained in the Definition (Native) Regulation 1907 (Regulation 3 of 1907), which provided in s. 2 that 'native' meant:

'(1) Any aboriginal native of any island in the Pacific Ocean.
(2) Any person of mixed European and aboriginal native descent who shall not have been registered by a Deputy Commissioner or whose registration shall have been cancelled in the manner provided [in s. 3]'

S. 3 required the Commissioner to register a person 'as being of status equivalent to Europeans' if they or their 'European parent or guardian' applied, unless the Commissioner was satisfied that he had 'contracted or not abandoned native habits of life and provided always that such applicant speaks one European language'. But the registration was to be cancelled if a Deputy Commissioner represented to the High Commissioner that a person 'has abandoned European for native habits of life'.

The literature cited in the previous note generally does not give specific attention to Pitcairn (see eg Law Commission, *Converging Currents*, 248, note 1). There is possibly a comparable case in the body of 'Indo-Fijians' who settled in Fiji in the late nineteenth and early twentieth centuries. A distinctive culture arose within that community, and some consideration has been given to the recognition of that customary law: Law Commission, *Converging Currents*, paras 10.36–37).   [13] Lewis, chapter 3 above.

were in the process of being absorbed into a British cultural group, but there is no strong evidence that this was happening in the early decades. Indeed, it appears that both the English and Tahitian languages were still in daily use in 1830,[14] a fact which suggests that there was a mixing of cultures. It is not unusual for people of different personal laws to live intermingled, as for example, in many African countries today. On the other hand, it could have been difficult to argue that two different bodies of personal law continued to coexist for such a minute community as that on Pitcairn.[15] It is impossible for the researcher today to be certain what practices prevailed within the community. As we shall see later, the courts and officials showed little interest in investigating the question.

Another difficulty in applying the principle of personal law to the nine Britons is the fact that they were mutineers, so cannot have seen themselves as unconditionally committed to the observance of English law as their personal law. The answer to this may be that according to English law a person cannot divest themselves at will of their personal law, at least unless they unequivocally adopt another. Here the notion that personal law is a state law seems particularly strong. A person who has a personal law may succeed in changing it for another, typically by permanent settlement in another community, defined in private international law as a change of domicile. But there are no instances of a person quitting their personal law without simultaneously acquiring another. Changing roles is permitted, but dropping out is not an option. Furthermore, there is a particular difficulty, according to English law, in changing one's personal law of birth if it is English law. Its observance is not only a 'birthright' but a part of one's identity, and a duty. This view had been vigorously contested shortly before the Pitcairn settlement by the American colonists in the period leading up to the War of Independence,[16] but it was hardly to be expected that the British legal authorities would accede to their arguments, and it is clear that they did not.[17]

---

[14] J. Barrow, 'Recent Accounts of the Pitcairn Islanders', *Journal of the Royal Geographical Society of London* 3 (1833), 156–168, 160.

[15] Nevertheless we may recall Llewellyn's reflection that the 'law jobs' needed to be done even for two-person groups: K. Llewellyn, 'The Normative, the Legal, and the Law-Jobs: The Problem of Juristic Method', *Yale Law Journal* 49 (1940), 1355–1400, 1374.

[16] J. Adams, 'Novanglus' in *The Works of John Adams*, ed. Charles Francis Adams (Boston: Little, Brown & Co., 1851), Vol IV, 3–177, 102–105, 122, 148–149 (first published 1775).          [17] Lewis, chapter 3. Cf Patchett, 'Reception', 17.

The courts in *Christian v The Queen* did not explicitly consider these difficulties. In so far as they considered the question they concluded that the first settlers on Pitcairn must be deemed to have brought English law with them. From this a further question followed: which version of English law was imported in 1790? Blackstone, in a later edition which expanded the passage quoted above, asserts that the transfer of English law:

must be understood with very many and very great restrictions. Such colonists carry with them only so much of the English law, as is applicable to their own situation and the condition of an infant colony; such, for instance, as the general rules of inheritance, and of protection from personal injuries. The artificial refinements and distinctions incident to the property of a great and commercial people ... are neither necessary nor convenient for them, and therefore are not in force.[18]

This is the basis of the rule on the importation of English legislation, stated repeatedly in reception statutes including those considered in *Christian v The Queen*, that only English statutes which are 'of general application' are received.

It seems likely that the courts would hold that English law as it stood at settlement in 1790, shorn of elaboration unsuitable for local circumstances, was introduced into Pitcairn at that date as the law exclusively applicable. It may be questioned whether the principle relating to settlement by British subjects as used by English courts is suitable for the Pitcairn case. A principle devised for migration on a much larger scale, in cases where the British government expected to concern itself from an early date with the legal control and development of the territory, was applied here to quite different conditions. A realistic view of the events of 1790 might have recognized that the settlers arrived with only fragments of different laws between them, the British having effectively discarded some of their English personal law. That would have required a departure from the preference for state laws as personal laws—although not a departure from the ancient English legal culture of recognition of other laws. It would also have complicated the necessary process of reaching a justifiable conclusion on the system of law which was in force in Pitcairn at later dates.

---

[18] Blackstone, *Commentaries*, 12th edn (London: Cadell, 1793), 107.

## Legal development after the original settlement

According to the doctrines set out by Blackstone, the English law brought to Pitcairn in 1790 did not carry with it any provision whatever for its subsequent development. Blackstone states that law which is imported by English settlers consists of 'English laws then in being', that is, at the date of settlement.[19] Statutes enacted in England after 1790 did not take automatic effect in the colony.[20] Presumably this rule was formulated to enable territories to make their own subsequent developments, according to their particular needs. However, in Pitcairn no formal legislative institutions were established to enable changes to be made, just as there were no formal judicial institutions to determine which parts of English law were to be excluded as unfitted to local conditions.

It is relevant to consider what may have been the internal legal circumstances of Pitcairn in the years immediately following 1790, taking the period which Lewis names 'The Settlement' (1790–1814).[21] It was, not surprisingly, a disorderly society. As Lewis notes, of the nine mutineers who settled, only two died natural deaths.[22] Nevertheless it would seem likely that some social development must have occurred. It was reported by the occasional visiting ship's captain that John Adams, the final survivor of the mutineers, from 1800 until his death eventually in 1829 'exercised patriarchal rule; no system of government seems to have been required, and no law but his word'.[23] This suggests that after 1800 life was relatively ordered and peaceful. If in the first decade it was almost a Hobbesian state of nature, thereafter the analogy may have

---

[19] Blackstone, *Commentaries*, 12th edn, 107; not in 1st edn.

[20] It is not necessary for the present purpose to consider whether the rule excludes developments in case law brought about by judicial decision in England after the reception. This question is discussed in eg: Allott, *Essays*, 30–31; F. A. R. Bennion, *The Constitutional Law of Ghana* (London: Butterworths, 1962), 393–394; A. E. W. Park, *The Sources of Nigerian Law* (London: Sweet & Maxwell and African Universities Press, 1963), 20–24; Roberts-Wray, *Commonwealth and Colonial Law*, 545–546; A. N. Allott, *New Essays in African Law* (London: Butterworths, 1970), 63–69; A. Castles, *An Introduction to Australian Legal History* (Australia: Law Book Co., 1971); J. E. Coté, 'The Reception of English Law', *Alberta Law Review* 15 (1977), 29–92, 55–57; G. W. Bartholomew, 'English Law in *Partibus Orientalium*' in *The Common Law in Singapore and Malaysia*, ed. A. J. Harding (Singapore: Butterworths, 1985), 1–30, 19–27; P. Wesley-Smith, 'The Reception of English Law in Hong Kong', *Hong Kong Law Journal* 18 (1988), 183–217, 207–210.           [21] Lewis, chapter 3 above.

[22] Lewis, chapter 3 above; see also Roberts-Wray, *Commonwealth and Colonial Law*, 907.           [23] Roberts-Wray, *Commonwealth and Colonial Law*, 907.

been rather with Locke's concept. Although Adams may have needed to intervene in such conflicts as arose, all the inhabitants must have followed a body of norms of behaviour to enable them to live together and survive. There are only scanty records of developments during this period, but it seems that some rules were drawn up by the inhabitants with the assistance of those captains of passing ships,[24] giving rise to informal legislation which was customarily accepted. It has been further suggested: 'In general it seems that the cultural pattern of Pitcairn society evolved from Polynesian or European practise according to the traditional role of male and female', that is, that norms governing male activities tended to be European, and those governing female activities, Polynesian.[25] It is likely that the developments would have seemed relatively familiar not only to social psychologists but also—and crucially for the present purpose—to legal anthropologists. This was the making of a body of folk law, or customary law.

The English common lawyer also should find the process recognizable, given the requirement on courts from the earliest times to recognize and give effect to customary laws. There is a case for concluding that English law would have characterized the law of Pitcairn in this period as consisting of two laws: the English law of 1790; and a body of customary law which itself recognized English law in most respects and for most purposes, but as developed and modified by the customary practices of the inhabitants. This may have been the condition to which the inhabitants aspired, according to the evidence of the flag which they had designed for themselves, containing both the British Union flag and the symbol of their mutiny against British rule on the *Bounty*.[26]

An alternative view, which reaches a similar practical conclusion, is that there continued to be only one body of law in Pitcairn, but that it was the English law of 1790 as developed and amended by local custom. The argument for this may be strengthened by analogy with the case of Belize (then British Honduras). That territory was settled by British subjects in 1638, and not formally established as a colony until 1862, although there is some authority that it was Crown territory by 1817.[27]

---

[24] Lewis, chapter 3 above.

[25] T. Lummis, *Pitcairn Island: Life and Death in Eden* (Aldershot: Ashgate, 1997), 119. However, the various texts which speculate about life on Pitcairn in the early years differ both in the factual detail and the broad outlines of the accounts which they propose. Cf. the discussion based on a study of archival materials by Lewis, chapter 3 above.

[26] Lewis, chapter 3 above; see also Guest, chapter 8 below.

[27] *Attorney-General of British Honduras v Bristowe* (1880) 6 App Cas 143.

It was not until the 1860s that the imperial power provided a relatively adequate range of governmental institutions.[28] It appears that long before then the settlers had set up institutions of government, including some with legislative powers, which continued to function until replaced. It has been argued that these settlers' institutions would have been recognized by English law:

> The settlers must carry with them English law as in force at the time of settlement, otherwise they have no law at all. If the home government is indifferent or inactive and takes no steps to provide them with organs of government, has the common law nothing to say? Are the settlers unable to change or amplify the law they take with them to meet their own needs? It can be asserted, not without a fair degree of confidence, that the answers to these questions are in the negative and that in such circumstances settlers have a common law right to set up a body to make such laws as they require and Courts to enforce them.[29]

The argument regarding Pitcairn need not go so far. It suggests not that the common law would have recognized the acts of courts and a legislature set up by the settlers, but merely that it would have recognized their developments of the received law through customary norms, including minor legislative acts validated by customary norms.

However, on the balance of probability this latter characterization of early Pitcairn law may accord less with social reality than that which sees the unchanged English law of 1790 coexisting with a customary law which bore it some resemblance but diverged in various respects. If the probable development of customary norms in Pitcairn is to be taken into account, it may be more satisfactory to depict Pitcairn law as a legally plural arena than to try to force the two bodies of competing norms into a unitary frame.

To uncover the development (if any) of the law of Pitcairn in the later periods of 'Recognition' (1814–56), 'Intervention' (1856–98) and 'Settled government' (1898–present),[30] it is necessary to examine the process whereby the British Crown acquired legislative authority over Pitcairn, and then exercised, or purported to exercise, that authority.

---

[28] Roberts-Wray, *Commonwealth and Colonial Law*, 818–826.
[29] Ibid, 153–154. Another account, comparable in some respects to the pre-annexation period of Pitcairn, is given in respect of Tristan da Cunha by Roberts-Wray, *Commonwealth and Colonial Law*, at 806 so also on land law on Pitcairn, McNeil, *Common Law*, 147–157.       [30] Lewis, chapter 3 above.

Settlement of and the diffusion of English law to Pitcairn may have occurred in 1790, but it did not follow that the island became a territory of the Crown at that date. Settlers do not by the fact of settlement secure the annexation of the territory. It is apparent from instances where the British government did not wish a territory to be annexed that annexation requires an acceptance by the British Crown of sovereignty.[31] In the case of Pitcairn, the British government was not opposed to annexation, but rather was uninterested in the territory. It appears that annexation was not approved until 1838, or, according to some reports, 1887.[32] So according to English doctrine there was a period of at least 48 years during which the law of England of 1790 applied in Pitcairn, simplified to render it suitable to the conditions of life on the island, but during which Britain had not assumed sovereignty.

The question of the date of annexation has a bearing on the question of the mode of acquisition. Blackstone, in the passage quoted above, distinguished between territories acquired by settlement and those acquired by cession or conquest. If the island had been annexed immediately after the settlement in 1790, there would have been no doubt that it was acquired by settlement. But it was not annexed until at least 48 years later, by which time the inhabitants had fashioned a law and rudimentary form of administration for themselves. This renders it arguable that it could have been acquired by cession.

This aspect of the history of Pitcairn law was crucial to arguments in *Christian v The Queen*. The charges were brought under the UK Act of 1956, not under any other English law. So it needed to be shown that under English law the rules of choice of law required the courts to apply a body of English law which included that Act. It needed to be shown

---

[31] The case of Belize has just been mentioned. Similarly, Tristan da Cunha was settled in 1817 but not formally recognized as a colony for many years: Roberts-Wray, *Commonwealth and Colonial Law*, 805–807. Again, when in 1883 the Premier of the colony of Queensland sent an official to Papua (then New Guinea) to annex the territory, the British government refused to ratify the act. The next year the Government authorized the establishment of a protectorate there, but only in 1888 was the territory effectively proclaimed a colony: R. B. Joyce, 'British New Guinea: Government' in *Encyclopaedia of Papua and New Guinea*, general ed. P. Ryan, Vol. 1 (Clayton Victoria: Melbourne University Press in Association with the University of Papua and New Guinea, 1972), 115. See also generally on this issue, Roberts-Wray, *Commonwealth and Colonial Law*, 100–101.

[32] Lewis, chapter 3 above; Roberts-Wray, *Commonwealth and Colonial Law*, 906; McNeil, *Common Law*, 116; Lummis, *Pitcairn Island*, 153.

that the Act was part of the law of Pitcairn for the times when the alleged offences occurred, that is, for the period 1964 to 1999. The Act, as enacted in the UK, applied in England throughout the period, but did not in its own words apply in Pitcairn. To establish that Pitcairn had been annexed did not lead inevitably to the conclusion that the UK Act of 1956, or any other particular portion of English law, applied in Pitcairn. Annexation meant only that British legislative authority could determine what law applied.

The essence of the prosecution argument for claiming that the UK Act of 1956 applied was the following. For the period 1961 to 1970, the Judicature Ordinance 1961 for Pitcairn provided that 'the substance of the law for the time being in force in and for England shall be in force in [Pitcairn].'[33] That Ordinance was made by the Governor of Fiji under the authority of the Pitcairn Order in Council, 1952 (SI 459). That Order in Article 4(1) declared the Governor of Fiji to be the Governor of Pitcairn, and provided in Article 5(1): 'It shall be lawful for the Governor to make laws for the peace, order and good government of [Pitcairn].' The Order itself was stated to be made 'under the powers vested in Her Majesty by the British Settlements Act 1887 and 1945, or otherwise'. The Act of 1887 authorized the establishment of 'all such laws and institutions . . . as may appear to Her Majesty in Council to be necessary for the peace, order and good government of Her Majesty's subjects and others within any British settlement'. It defined 'British settlement' as 'any British possession which has not been acquired by cession or conquest', and which did not already possess its own legislature.

For the period from 1970 the Judicature Ordinance 1970 took effect, repealing the Judicature Ordinance 1961. The 1970 Ordinance, which was still in force at the time of the trials, provided in section 14(1): ' . . . the common law, the rules of equity and the statutes of general application as in force in and for England at the commencement of this Ordinance shall be in force in [Pitcairn]'. The 1970 Ordinance was enacted by the Governor of Pitcairn under the authority of the Pitcairn Order in Council 1970 (SI 1434). That Order, replacing the Order of 1952, provided in Article 4(1) for the appointment of a Governor of Pitcairn, and in Article 5(1) that the Governor 'may make laws for the

---

[33] The original texts referred to 'the Islands'. That term was defined to mean the Pitcairn Islands of Pitcairn, Henderson, Ducie, and Oeno, of which Pitcairn alone is continuously inhabited.

peace, order and good government of [Pitcairn]'. The 1970 Order stated its source of authority in the same words as the 1952 Order.[34]

Because of the importance of the distinction between colonies acquired by settlement and those acquired by cession or conquest, their government is regulated by different Acts. The Act of 1887 provided means of legislation for the government of settled colonies only. Regulation of the government of a conquered or ceded colony was, according to a common law rule confirmed by the Colonial Laws Validity Act 1865, within the authority of the royal prerogative until the Crown exercised its power to establish a local representative legislative body, at which point the prerogative ceased to be exercisable unless it had been expressly reserved.[35] The Act of 1887 was intended to define, regulate, and partially replace the royal prerogative powers over settled colonies. In both types of colonies, legislation was usually enacted to define the law to be applied in the courts, but this normally restated, with minor changes, the common law rules for settled colonies.

A series of arguments was advanced for the defendants attacking the links in the prosecution argument for applying the Sexual Offences Act 1956. For the present purpose, the most important issues are those which questioned whether the Orders of 1952 and 1970 were within the powers conferred by the Act of 1887, as they claimed to be. The most crucial question in this respect was whether Pitcairn was a 'British settlement' within the terms of the Act of 1887, or had been acquired by cession.

If the defendants had succeeded on this point, then, Pitcairn not being a settled colony, the Act of 1887 would not have applied, and hence the Orders of 1952 and 1970, and the Ordinances of 1960 and 1970, which arguably depended on that Act for their validity, could have been invalid.[36] It would then have been arguable that on

---

[34] There were some subsequent changes of no relevance to these cases. An Ordinance of 1983 amended s. 14(1) of the 1970 Ordinance by changing the date of the received English law from the date of commencement of the 1970 Ordinance to 1 January 1983. The Judicature (Courts) Ordinance 1999 replaced the 1970 Ordinance, and provided that the English law to be applied was once more to be the law 'for the time being in force' in England.

[35] *Campbell v Hall* (1774) 98 ER 1045, 20 State Tr. 239; Roberts-Wray, *Commonwealth and Colonial Law*, 157–163.

[36] There was a further possibility of holding that, even if Pitcairn were not a settled colony, the Orders of 1952 and 1970 were valid. The Orders cited their enabling authority as the British Settlements Acts 'or otherwise'. In the view of the Privy Council ([2006] JCPC 47, para. 11, Lord Hoffmann), if Pitcairn had been a ceded colony, the Crown would still have had powers to legislate for it under the Prerogative, and these words would have been sufficient to import that Prerogative power as validating authority for the Orders.

annexation the pre-existing law as developed by the settlers had continued in force. Pitcairn might still today have a fairly rudimentary law, and the UK Act of 1956 would not be part of it. The Privy Council rejected the contention that Pitcairn was a colony by cession. The consideration of this question was combined with the court's consideration of the question whether Pitcairn was within the Crown's territories, a question which, it is suggested above, had to be answered in the affirmative. The court decided both questions in the affirmative on two grounds. First, it held that courts were bound by statements by the Crown to the effect that Pitcairn was a settled colony. Secondly, it held that the historical evidence showed that the territory had in fact been acquired by settlement, not cession.

The conclusive nature of statements by the Crown was the primary ground. The first such statement relied upon dated back to the nineteenth century. The Pacific Order in Council 1893, providing for the government of certain British settlements in the Pacific, had been made under the Act of 1887. The Order had not initially referred to Pitcairn, but it had conferred on the Secretary of State power to direct that it should apply to other British settlements in the region. A direction to this effect had been made in 1898. (The Order was eventually repealed and replaced for Pitcairn by the Pitcairn Order in Council, 1952.) The Privy Council held that the direction of 1898 'was therefore a statement by the Crown that Pitcairn was a British settlement'.[37] Lord Hoffmann said that the court declined to investigate the question whether as a matter of historical fact the islanders had ever acknowledged allegiance to the Crown, because it considered that successive statements by the executive concluded the matter.[38] He concluded:

[W]hatever its history or the inclinations of its people may have been, it is unthinkable that the Judicial Committee of Her Majesty's Privy Council would not accept an executive statement affirming it to be part of the territory of the Crown. The directions of 1898 and the Orders in Council of 1952 and 1970 are statements of this kind.[39]

However, Lord Woolf added that today it could not be taken for granted that there was any action on the part of the Crown that was not open to review by the courts, and preferred to base his conclusion on the 'overwhelming' evidence.[40] Lord Hope of Craighead stated that he

---

[37] [2006] JCPC 47, para. 4, Lord Hoffmann.     [38] [2006] JCPC 47, para. 9.
[39] [2006] JCPC 47, para. 10.     [40] [2006] JCPC 47, para. 33.

agreed with all that had been said by Lord Hoffmann on this issue. He commented on the necessity of consistency on the issue of the classification of colonies into settled, conquered, and ceded, saying that 'once made by practice or judicial decision it will not be disturbed'. He concluded that 'as long standing practice has established Pitcairn's status as a settled colony, [historical research] must be held irrelevant to the issue of classification raised in these appeals'.[41]

There are grounds for doubting this view. While statements of the executive have been taken as conclusive of the question whether a territory was within the Crown's dominions, this has not been done regarding the further question whether a territory within those dominions was acquired by settlement or by cession or conquest. Moreover, when a statement from the Crown on the status of a territory has been followed, this has normally been an express statement, often made in reply to an inquiry for the purpose of that litigation. Thus the judgment quoted by Lord Hoffmann as showing the rule referred to a 'definite statement' by the executive.[42] The statements relied upon in the present cases were not 'definite'. They were merely instances of the executive exercising over Pitcairn a power which had been granted it in respect of settled colonies. One may wonder whether the purported exercise of a power is enough to confirm that the power exists. As Guest argues, in this context 'saying so does not make it so'.[43] Lord Woolf's observation suggests a less than enthusiastic support for this view and casts doubt on the extent to which the courts will accept a statement without question if they have reason to consider that it could be incorrect. The implications of the classification of a territory as settled, ceded, or conquered for its legal system are such that it may well be desirable to establish this definitively, as Lord Hope indicated, when the question first arises. But this does not show that the view of the executive must be followed. It is possible for the courts to determine the issue through evidence on the first occasion when it arises, after which they can take judicial notice of that initial decision. This has long been the practice when proof of the content of a rule of a customary law is required, as established by the Privy Council for

---

[41] [2006] JCPC 47, para. 47.

[42] 'Any definite statement from the proper representative of the Crown as to the territory of the Crown must be treated as conclusive' (*The Fagernes* [1927] P 311 at 324, quoted [2006] JCPC 47, para. 9, Lord Hoffmann). [43] Guest, chapter 8 below.

colonial territories in which the legal systems recognized existing customary laws.[44]

What might have been the outcome if the court had looked to the evidence of historical fact? The objection to holding on this basis that the territory had been ceded was expressed thus by Lord Hoffmann:

> Cession by whom? The notion of cession contemplates a transfer of sovereignty by one sovereign power to another. So, for example, by the Treaty of Utrecht in 1713, Gibraltar was ceded to Great Britain by the Kingdom of Spain. In *Sammut v Strickland*[45] the Privy Council recognised the possibility of a cession by the people of a territory (in that case Malta, during the Napoleonic wars) who had assumed sovereign authority over themselves. But the analogy with the people of Pitcairn seeking the protection of the Crown seems to their Lordships somewhat far fetched.[46]

The case of Malta is indeed different from that of Pitcairn, as Malta had had a history of many centuries as a distinct polity, for some periods subordinate to another power, for some an independent state, before its Congress ceded sovereignty to the UK in order to obtain the protection of the Crown.[47] Possibly closer cases are those African territories which are regarded as having been acquired by the British by cession, especially Basuto (now Lesotho),[48] and Lagos (later merged into Nigeria),[49] both of which were regarded as having been ceded by treaties with their traditional rulers. For the purpose of cession, '[n]o formal document is necessary, the manifestation of the wish of the people or their Ruler being sufficient'.[50] It would appear, then, that a community which has developed its own law, which may be customary law, may cede sovereignty through the agreement of its representatives holding the appropriate authority under that law. It has been said the events of 1838 in Pitcairn were 'at the urgent request of the inhabitants for steps to be taken to regularise their status and their government' and that Captain Eliott of *The Fly* in response to these requests devised a constitution and written laws for them and presented them with a Union Flag to signify their status within the

---

[44] *Angu v Attah, 1916 Gold Coast Privy Council Judgments (1874–1928)*, 43. The rule originally required a series of cases proving a rule before judicial notice could be taken, but the practice became to require little more than one previous case: G. R. Woodman, 'Some Realism about Customary Law—The West African Experience', *Wisconsin Law Review* (1969),128–152.                   [45] [1938] AC 678.

[46] [2006] JCPC 47, para. 11.

[47] Roberts-Wray, *Commonwealth and Colonial Law*, 683–688.

[48] Ibid, 777–779.          [49] Ibid, 793, 795.          [50] Ibid, 101.

British Empire.[51] This, or indeed a later recognition of sovereignty, could be seen as the acceptance of a proposal of cession. Since in all cases of cession the law previously in force in the territory continues to apply until amended or repealed by legislation, these are cases where the prior existence of a system of law is especially significant.

The principal problem in applying this analysis to Pitcairn would appear to be the fact that the islanders were regarded as being already subjects of the Crown at the time of settlement. If English law recognized a cession in these cases, it would concede that those who had been subjects had somehow succeeded in becoming an independent community by virtue of the fact that they had settled and remained in territory outside the dominions of the Crown. The general opinion of commentators is that settlers 'have no constitutional right to establish a separate independent state'.[52] This view follows from the same ground as the rule, noted above, which prevents British emigrants from discarding their personal English law. The effect is to draw a distinction between British subjects and others, or perhaps between the subjects of European states and others. This distinction is indeed common in colonial law. It has already been noted that the recognition of personal laws had the effect of distinguishing, especially in the Pacific and Africa, between 'natives' and 'non-natives'. The effect was, rules of private international law apart, to make English law, of the prescribed type in force in a colony, the personal law of all persons of non-native descent, generally whether they wished it or not. This was the effective rule of English law as it governed colonial territories. According to this the islanders of Pitcairn could not have ceded their territory to the Crown, and it must have been acquired by settlement.

The arguments thus far considered as to the choice of law in *Christian v The Queen* may be summarized thus. The court concluded that the Sexual Offences Act 1956 had been law in Pitcairn throughout the relevant period because this had been validly provided for under the authority of the British Settlements Act 1887. This depended on the proposition that Pitcairn had become a British territory by settlement. The founding of that proposition on the opinion of the executive was open to question, and if a serious investigation had been made of the early history of Pitcairn there would have been grounds for holding that

---

[51] Roberts-Wray, *Commonwealth and Colonial Law*, 907–908. And see Lewis, chapter 3 above. [52] Roberts-Wray, *Commonwealth and Colonial Law*, 100.

it had been acquired by cession by the community of the inhabitants. But the legal professionals involved in the case seem not to have wished to explore this history, preferring to adhere to formal legal doctrine. The decision on this issue meant that, again according to legal doctrine, legislation had replaced whatever law previously existed. This rendered irrelevant questions as to the law (if any) introduced in 1790, as to changes subsequently made in Pitcairn law during the following century, and as to whether any aspects of that observed law should have been refused recognition as unreasonable or 'against the law of God', as Blackstone put it. It was, however, still possible that these questions might be relevant to the second main issue in the case, to which we now turn.

### The Abuse of Process Issue

The second main issue in *Christian v The Queen* was whether the prosecutions were an abuse of the process of the criminal law. The wider issues of policy involved in the preliminary debate over whether to prosecute are considered elsewhere in this volume.[53] Here discussion is limited to the arguments on this issue which led or could have led to questions about the diffusion of common law to Pitcairn and the existence of a different, customary law there.

A principal basis for the abuse of process claim was the contention that the defendants had not had means of access to the text of the provisions defining the crimes with which they were charged, and thus the principle of the rule of law was infringed.[54] The defendants had been convicted on counts of rape and indecent assault brought under sections 1 and 14 respectively of the UK Act of 1956. (Two counts of incest under section 10 of the Act brought against one defendant do not seem to have introduced additional features into the reasoning.) The Act was not known to the defendants at the times of the offences. It was arguable that the provisions of the Judicature Ordinances 1961 and 1970, by virtue of which the Act was claimed to be in force in Pitcairn, were also not known to them, and that even if they had known the texts of the Ordinances they would not have understood the implications.

---

[53] See Guest, chapter 8 below.     [54] As considered by Guest, chapter 8 below.

This argument points to a widespread problem inherent in the diffusion of the common law through the process of colonization. Populations in colonized territories have been subjected to and punished for infringements of a law which, at least in the early years, was unknown to them. It was the policy of the colonizing mission that colonized peoples should be instructed in the laws and other aspects of the culture of the colonizing power, but the resources devoted to this were often inadequate. The problem was palliated by the practice of giving recognition to the personal laws of colonized peoples. However, it was not thought compatible with colonial control to give recognition to all branches of personal laws, and it was not given extensively to criminal laws. The policy regarding criminal law was implemented for the majority of colonies, although not for Pitcairn, by the enactment of comprehensive codes of criminal law modelled on English criminal law, which explicitly superseded all other criminal law.[55] This problem of the alien nature of the diffused law was apparently absent in one large category of cases: those where the colonial population was formed by settlers from England. It is, as we have seen, debatable whether the Pitcairn settlers of 1790 fell into this category.

This issue in many colonial laws may also be seen as a strong instance of a universal problem in state laws. A law developed, interpreted, and administered by a body of officials with a developed professional culture distinct from the culture or cultures generally observed within the subject population, is not likely to be well known or understood by its subjects. But the maintenance of state rule depends to some extent on a partial disregard of the resultant injustice. The response of state law to the knowledge gap is, on the one hand, sometimes to make efforts to teach 'the public' about the provisions of state law, especially those parts supported by criminal sanctions. On the other hand, state law also adheres to the rule that ignorance of the law is no excuse, taking the view that justice must cede to the practical necessity of maintaining state government. The issue is revealed in an especially acute form in *Christian v The Queen* when the abuse of process argument is examined. All

---

[55] The development is noted in T. Angelo and F. Wright, 'Pitcairn: Sunset on Empire?', *New Zealand Law Journal* (2004), 431, cited in *Christian v The Queen* [2006] JCPC 47, para. 70, by Lord Hope. The two models of criminal codes, one of which was adopted for nearly every territory, were the Indian Penal Code, 1860 and the Queensland Criminal Code, 1899 (the 'Griffith Code').

the courts rejected the claim of abuse of process. Their reasons fall into three categories.

First, Lord Woolf in a part of his judgment took a position on the policy issue of justice against practical necessity just mentioned:

> The criminal law can only operate on Pitcairn, as elsewhere, if the onus is firmly placed on a person, who is or ought to be on notice that conduct he is intending to embark on may contravene the criminal law, to take the action that is open to him to find out what are the provisions of that law.[56]

Secondly, the Court of Appeal reached a conclusion, accepted by a majority of the Privy Council, on the basis of evidence given at the trials that the defendants had had sufficient knowledge of the applicable law. The Supreme Court had found that the inhabitants of Pitcairn had been aware that for serious criminal offences English law applied. Thus they knew that in 1898, a Pitcairn man had been tried by the British authorities for the murder of a woman and her child, convicted, and executed.[57] British government officers had made clear to island representatives that the Island Court consisting of local inhabitants, which occasionally functioned in the mid-twentieth century, did not have jurisdiction in serious matters such as cases of rape, which would therefore need to be sent to the Supreme Court.[58] Further, the Supreme Court had concluded from evidence from members of the community that 'at all relevant times Pitcairn was a developed society in which rape and various sexual offending [sic] were known to be criminal'.[59] The court also quoted Lon Fuller's summary of a related argument:

> [T]o the extent that the law merely brings to explicit expression conceptions of right and wrong widely shared within the community, the need that enacted law be publicized and clearly stated diminishes in importance.[60]

There appear to be two different arguments here. One was that the accused must have known that their actions were criminal offences under the applicable English law. The other was that their actions were widely thought in the community to be wrong. The two were apparently taken together by the Privy Council, and were not pursued in detail. That court held that it was 'unnecessary to discuss the philosophical basis

---

[56] [2006] JCPC 47, para. 41.   [57] Lewis, chapter 3 above.
[58] Pitcairn Court of Appeal, CA 1-6/2005, 2 March 2006, paras 114–116.
[59] Pitcairn Court of Appeal, paras 114–115
[60] L. L. Fuller, *The Morality of Law*, Rev. edn (New Haven and London: Yale University Press, 1969), 92, quoted by the Pitcairn Court of Appeal, para. 109.

or legal limits of [the principle of abuse of process]'. Since there were concurrent findings of fact by the courts below, and both had agreed on the manner of exercise of discretion on this issue, the Privy Council could not be persuaded to interfere.[61]

Questions of fact about knowledge or opinion within the community again raise the question of the existence of a Pitcairn customary law or observed normative order. If it had been shown that the acts of the defendants were regarded as acceptable within the local normative order, several further questions would have needed consideration. It would have been arguable that the defendants were unlikely to have realized that they were committing crimes under the applicable English law. It would have been arguable that they were unlikely to have seen their actions as 'wrong'. But it would also have been necessary to consider whether the acts, or some of them, were so morally obnoxious that a local normative order which did not disapprove them must be disregarded.

A few witnesses were found willing to state that the acts of the accused were regarded as wrong, criminal, or both in Pitcairn. There is evidence to the contrary. A major factor in the prosecution case, especially regarding indecent assault, was the age of the victims. But evidence from Pitcairn and other Pacific societies shows that there the boundary between various stages of childhood and between childhood and adulthood may be drawn at different ages from those that are determinative in modern English law.[62] More generally there is evidence that a different view was widespread as to what constituted indecent assault, and that rape was viewed less seriously than at common law.[63] Reports from Tahiti and neighbouring islands in the nineteenth century suggested that

---

[61] [2006] JCPC 47, para. 24, Lord Hoffmann. Lord Woolf added that the evidence showed that the defendants 'were aware ... that their conduct was contrary to the criminal law': [2006] JCPC 47, para. 41.

[62] W. Prochnau and L. Parker, 'Trouble in Paradise', *Vanity Fair* (January 2008), 95–103, 136–139. I am grateful to William Twining for finding this report and making it available to me. It is a useful survey of the case by journalists who interviewed many of the persons involved. They were unable themselves to visit Pitcairn, but they rely partly on reports by journalists who were there during the trial, and which may be found in *The International Herald Tribune* (*IHT*) in the period 20 October 2004 to 26 October 2004, and *The Independent* in the period 27 July 2004 to 31 October 2004. (However, Prochnau and Parker are in error when they state at 137 that according to *The International Herald Tribune* Charlene Griffiths lost her virginity at 10: the report in the *IHT*, 20 October 2004, states that she was 13.) See further Law Commission, *Converging Currents*, paras 8.9–10, noting also that non-European customs in the Pacific differ in their definition of a child from international human rights law; see also Guest, chapter 8 below. [63] Law Commission, *Converging Currents*, paras 7.40–43.

very different sexual mores existed there from those of contemporary England.[64] The comments by Lord Hope, that the offences which had been proved were 'almost certainly the tip of the iceberg', and had been tolerated for long, and that it was 'scarcely credible that the population of the island as a whole was unaware of what was going on'[65] tend to suggest that the acts were not seen as criminal or wrong, or not so seriously criminal or wrong in Pitcairn as in England. However, since there was no scientific investigation of the question we do not know the true situation.

The suggestion that the acts of the accused, which had caused great suffering to the victims, might not have been seen as criminal or greatly wrong in the community, might seem perverse. But in investigating a customary law it is necessary to avoid assumptions that it is morally pure or egalitarian, or willingly accepted by all members of the community in which it is observed. Some customary laws may be admirable, but some endorse practices such as slavery, patriarchy, and exploitative or cruel treatment of the vulnerable. It is unfortunately possible that the acts of the accused were not contrary to the prevalent customary law. Moral criticism may need to be directed also towards the British government for its prolonged refusal to take seriously its responsibility towards Pitcairn. In the result, while it was clearly incumbent on government to aid the recovery of the victims as far as possible, it was also necessary to decide whether in the circumstances the prosecutions were an abuse of process against the perpetrators. This depended to some extent on whether they could fairly be considered to have known that they were committing crimes.

A third line of reasoning in response to the defence claim of abuse of process was advanced by Lord Hope. He observed that the conduct in question had been widespread and generally known in Pitcairn. That it had continued for so long was 'an indication of the poor state of supervision over its affairs exercised by the colonial authorities'.[66] The contents of the 1956 Act were not ascertainable by the islanders, and there had been no serious attempt to explain its provisions to them. He continued:

[64] W. Waldegrave, 'Extracts from a Private Journal Kept on Board HMS *Seringapatam*, in the Pacific, 1830', *Journal of the Royal Geographical Society of London* (1833) 3, 168–196, 170–171, 173, 179–180, 183.   [65] [2006] JCPC 47, para. 56.
[66] [2006] JCPC 47, para. 56.

These considerations would have led me to conclude that it was an abuse of process for these prosecutions to be brought under sections 1 and 14 of the 1956 Act, but for one fact which in the end has persuaded me that the use of these provisions can be reconciled with the principles of legality.[67]

This was the fact that these sections of the Act of 1956 did not create these crimes. They were derived from sections of the UK Offences Against the Person Act 1861. This Act also did not create new crimes, since rape and indecent assault were crimes at common law. The Acts of 1861 and 1956 had only prescribed penalties, identified which of the offences were felonies, and provided for their prosecution and punishment. Lord Hope then took the argument back to the principle considered earlier, saying: 'the islanders brought the common law of England with them when they settled there'. Thus rape and indecent assault had been crimes in Pitcairn since 1790, and 'no objections could have been taken on the ground of lack of promulgation if the prosecution of the defendants had been brought under the common law'. It was therefore not an affront to justice to prosecute the defendants under this Act.[68]

Lord Hope in this passage first vanquishes the formalistic argument which said that the prosecutions under the Act of 1956 were justified by the fact that the islanders could have discovered its provisions if they had inquired. But his judgment then succumbs to the formalistic argument contained in the rule on the applicability of English law in settled colonies. It would have been possible for a prosecutor to inquire whether the inhabitants of Pitcairn were aware of that rule, and knew that it applied to Pitcairn; and, indeed, whether they had the means of ascertaining the substance of English criminal law of 1790. It is possible that the answers, as to the crimes charged in these cases, might have been affirmative, but the matter had not been investigated. It seems to have been assumed that in any common law country everyone must know or have access to knowledge of the common law of crimes in the particular version which applied in that country. Alternatively there was at this point in the argument a reversion to the policy exemplified in Lord Woolf's judgment, according to which lack of knowledge of the criminal law cannot be accepted as a defence.

The argument, that the law of 1790 was in force prior to the Ordinance of 1961, also assumed that there could be no change in the law

---

[67] [2006] JCPC 47, para. 83.    [68] [2006] JCPC 47, paras 83–86.

after the initial date of settlement, except by formal legislation, or, possibly, case law of formally established courts. It was suggested in the previous section that changes in a received common law may be brought about by the development of customary law between the date of settlement and the date of annexation. There could be a further possibility of changes brought about by the same mode within the community after annexation. Changes in the received English law of 1790 through local customary law were rendered more likely by the governmental neglect of Pitcairn which Lord Hope had emphasized. It is also likely that any customary law formed in the earliest years was subsequently developed and changed by the population in response to external stimuli, either through the adoption of new practices or through the acceptance of legislative interventions such as visiting captains' rules. Customary laws in general are not static, whatever external representations of them may suggest.[69] The possibility would have raised again the question whether English law would have recognized these developments through customary law, either by accepting that they had modified the applicable English law, or by recognizing that they had given rise to another law coexisting with the English law of 1790.[70]

This is not to deny that, if such development had been revealed, affecting the criminal nature of the acts charged, the customary law might have been rejected as contrary to reason, or might have been held to be so morally obnoxious that it could not support the conclusion that the prosecutions had been an abuse of process. There would have been strong grounds for taking such a step. The question remains whether it was justified to assume that in 1790 the English law of that date had come into force in Pitcairn and had remained unchanged for more than a century until British legislation had intervened.

Another factor which could have been considered was the practice in common law jurisdictions of reducing the punishment for crimes committed under the influence of the cultures, or the customary laws,

---

[69] O'Cinneide, chapter 6 below. Lummis, considering the period to 1856, argues that development of what he has called 'the local cultural pattern of Pitcairn society' (Lummis, *Pitcairn Island*, 119) continued during this time, although he considers it to have been mainly through external European influences: 'The Tahitian element of the culture was, however, to be eroded by contact with the outside world' (Lummis, 130).

[70] On the considerable difficulty experienced in Australia in determining whether and how the received English law had been modified (although by legislative enactments issued by the Governor, not by customary law) after settlement in 1788 and prior to the enactment of clarifying legislation by the UK Australian Courts Act 1828, see Castles, *Introduction*, 114–130.

of the offenders. For example, in English cases, young men found guilty of sexual relations with girls aged as young as 12 have been given relatively light sentences on the ground that they were recent immigrants coming from societies in which social customs did not regard such conduct as criminal.[71] This practice could have been cited to support the argument that prosecution in some such cases was an abuse of process.

In sum, the defence claim that the prosecutions were an abuse of process demonstrated the conflict between justice for the accused and the necessity of maintaining state authority. Initially this raised questions as to whether the state, having failed to intervene at an earlier date to prevent the harm which had been done, should then have dealt with the problem in some way other than by prosecution.[72] The prosecutions having been brought, the courts needed to consider whether established legal doctrines of abuse of process should be employed. The maintenance of state authority, and a preference for English state law seem to have prevailed to the extent of obviating any serious investigation of social reality, including the customary law prevailing in the jurisdiction.

## A Concluding Comment

It is likely that there existed in Pitcairn a customary law, and that, like all customary law, it changed over time. Legal doctrine may perhaps compel us to say that in 1790 the settlers imported the law of England as it then stood, although it has been argued that this is an unsatisfactory legal interpretation of events. But legal doctrine need not compel us to deny that that law was subject to the qualification that the subsequently

---

[71] *R v Bailey* [1964] Crim LR 671; *R v Byfield* [196/] Crim LR 378. Cf *R v Finlay* [1963] Crim LR 299. Numerous cases of this type from a large number of jurisdictions are examined in detail in A. Dundes Renteln, *The Cultural Defense* (New York: Oxford University Press, 2004). The issue is examined further with respect to English law in G. R. Woodman, 'The Culture Defence in English Common Law: The Potential for Development' in *Multicultural Jurisprudence: Comparative Perspectives on the Cultural Defense*, eds A. Renteln and M.-C. Foblets (Oxford: Hart Publications, 2009), 7–34. K. Amirthalingam, 'Culture, Crime, and Culpability: Perspectives on the Defence of Provocation' in *Multicultural Jurisprudence*, 35, also contains a useful discussion of the Pitcairn cases. For a valuable study of one system of criminal law in a Pacific territory, see S. Dinnen, 'Sentencing, Custom and the Rule of Law in Papua New Guinea', *Journal of Legal Pluralism* 27 (1988), 19–54.

[72] See Chapters 2, 3, and 8 for discussion of compensation of victims and other possible responses open to the Crown.

developed customary law of the inhabitants was to be recognized and would not necessarily be overridden by received law whenever the two diverged. In the courts in common law jurisdictions it is not unusual for indigenous customary laws to be applied. The proof and application of customary law gives rise to various problems,[73] but there is a store of understanding of these, in the Pacific as elsewhere.[74]

Lord Hope remarked that the Pitcairn cases 'raise some fundamental issues about the rule of law in remote communities ... '.[75] In some respects they raise a question relevant to every society which is to any extent multicultural: how far should the law of the state be applied without qualification to members of cultural groups with customary laws, or normative orders, which differ from that of the group for whom state law has been designed? Beyond even this, it has been suggested that the case is also relevant to modern societies in which there is a gap between the legal culture of the governing officials and that of all other parts of the population. Acceptance of cultural diversity in a state entails acceptance of a degree of legal pluralism. For this the legislators and judiciary need to be well informed about the customary laws of minority communities, and to be aware of the dangers of ethnocentrism.

Finally it must be acknowledged that cases like the present, concerning the relationship between different laws in situations of legal pluralism, give rise to worries as to the maintenance of universal standards of justice. The modern multicultural state may accept diversity, but cannot afford to accept an extreme moral and cultural relativism. Some principles must be regarded as universally valid.[76] What then is it best to do with regard to particular cases in which customary practices challenge universal principles? To ignore the entire community, and to allow the victims to continue to suffer, as in this case, is not justifiable.

---

[73] These are examined with particular reference to certain African jurisdictions in Woodman: 'Some Realism'; 'Judicial Development of Customary Law: The Case of Marriage Law in Ghana and Nigeria', *University of Ghana Law Journal* 14 (1977), 115–136; 'Customary Law, State Courts, and the Notion of Institutionalization of Norms in Ghana and Nigeria' in *People's Law and State Law: the Bellagio Papers*, eds A. Allott and G. R. Woodman (Dordrecht: Foris, 1985), 143–163; 'How State Courts Create Customary Law in Ghana and Nigeria' in *Indigenous Law and the State*, eds B. W. Morse and G. R. Woodman (Dordrecht: Foris, 1988), 181–220.

[74] Allott, *Essays*; Corrin-Care, Cain, and Paterson, *Introduction*; Corrin-Care and Zorn, 'Legislating Pluralism'; Zorn and Corrin-Care, *Proving Customary Law*; Brown, *Reconciling Customary Law*; Law Commission, *Converging Currents*.

[75] [2006] JCPC 47, para. 47.

[76] See further O'Cinneide, Letsas, and Guest, at chapters 6, 7, and 8 below.

The objective of state law must sometimes be to effect changes in the observed normative order of a social group, minority or majority. What is the best way to achieve this? A direct onslaught, by prosecuting and punishing severely all conduct contrary to state law which is permitted by the objectionable norms may be ineffective, may damage the entire society of the state, and may destroy much else in the culture of the group which is good. On the other hand, a gradual approach involving acceptance and efforts at persuasion may allow social evils to continue indefinitely. The appropriate answer will no doubt vary according to the circumstances of each case. But it may be suggested that a strict adherence to legal doctrines formulated without consideration of this problem, and without a careful investigation of the non-state normative orders, is not the best procedure.

# 5

# The Pitcairn Prosecutions: An Assessment of Their Historical Context by Reference to the Provisions of Public International Law

*Dino Kritsiotis and A. W. B. Simpson*

Cast in the most uncontroversial light, the Pitcairn prosecutions that brought us the appeal of *Stevens Raymond Christian & Others v R* (2006) are no more and no less than a simple assertion of jurisdiction by the government of the United Kingdom.[1] The appeal marked the culmination of charges of rape, indecent assault, and incest brought under the Sexual Offences Act 1956,[2] legislation that had sought to consolidate 'the statute law of England and Wales relating to sexual crimes' according to its preamble—but also 'to make such adaptations of statutes extending beyond England and Wales as are needed in consequence of that consolidation'.[3] And yet in quite another sense, this was no ordinary set of prosecutions and no ordinary set of convictions. Quite the contrary, for the trials, producing jurisprudence from Pitcairn's Supreme Court and Court of Appeal as well as the Privy

---

[1] See Power, H., 'Pitcairn Island: Sexual Offending, Cultural Difference and Ignorance of the Law', *Criminal Law Review* (2007), 609–629 (noting, at 611, that 'the apparent scale and seriousness of the problem ultimately led to the decision to prosecute under England and Wales' [Sexual Offences Act], rather than under Pitcairn's local laws'). We would argue that the exercise of this jurisdiction is akin to the prosecutions anticipated following the raid on the Yearning for Zion Ranch in Eldorado, Texas, in April 2008: Johnson, K., and Dougherty, J., 'Sect's Children to Stay in State Custody for Now', *New York Times*, 19 April 2008, A11.

[2] See, also, ss. 82 and 88 of Pitcairn Criminal Justice Ordinance 1966.

[3] Concerning Scotland (s. 54 (1)) and Northern Ireland (s. 54 (2)).

Council, came to pass following the conclusion of an international agreement in October 2002 between the United Kingdom and New Zealand. This provided for 'the sitting and proper functioning' of the Pitcairn Court in New Zealand and for 'the serving or enforcement in New Zealand of sentences imposed by the Pitcairn Court in any such trial'.[4] Furthermore, the trials would occur under 'Pitcairn law',[5] a phrase that appears throughout the text of the agreement and which is also evident from its title.

It is the recurrence and meaning of this phrase that must give us good pause to wonder whether Pitcairn Island is able to claim, on account of its power to promulgate these laws but also on account of the loose structure of the organization of its own affairs,[6] some separate juridical status under public international law—for it has been said that '[t]he logic of government *is* the logic of jurisdiction',[7] where jurisdiction marks out the broad parameters of sovereign *competence* to both enact and to execute such laws.[8] Such a conclusion would in turn demarcate the outer edges of the competence of the United Kingdom to legislate *for* Pitcairn Island because, in truth, it is a defining element of the sovereign that it exercises prescriptive and prerogative powers *within* its territories; these powers are and

---

[4] Agreement between the Government of the United Kingdom of Great Britain and Northern Ireland and the Government of New Zealand Concerning Trials under Pitcairn Law in New Zealand and Related Matters, Cm. 5944; done at Wellington, New Zealand, 11 October 2002, Art. 2 (1) (a) and (b) respectively; Art. 2 (2) (a) made provision for 'any trial arising from investigations into allegations of sexual offending on the Islands, conducted by the Kent Police from 1999 to 2001', although the door was left open in Art. 2 (2) (b) for 'any other trial' that the Government of New Zealand agreed to host 'after being requested to do so by the Governor [of the Pitcairn Islands]'.

[5] Ibid, Art. 1 (v). See, also, Art. 15 (1); Art. 16 (6) (a); Art. 17 (3); Art. 18 (11). Consider, further, the Revised Edition of the Laws of Pitcairn, Henderson, Ducie, and Oeno Islands (2001) at <http://www.government.pn/Laws/index.html>.

[6] Identified as an Island Council, comprising a Magistrate, the Island Secretary, the Government Adviser and, in an advisory capacity, the Pastor of the island: Birkett, D., *Serpent in Paradise* (London: Picador, 1997), 80–81.

[7] Ford, R. T., 'Law's Territory (A History of Jurisdiction)', *Michigan Law Review* 97 (1999), 843–930, 851 (emphasis in original).

[8] The emphasis on the 'allocation of competence' in respect of jurisdiction is drawn from Higgins, R., *Problems and Process: International Law and How We Use It* (Oxford: Clarendon Press, 1994), 56. Although, as has been observed by Vaughan Lowe, 'if the Pitcairn Islands (population, 45) were to become independent and seek admission to the United Nations, States might re-examine the relationship between the principle of sovereign equality and common sense'. See Lowe, V., *International Law* (Oxford: Oxford University Press, 2007), 154.

remain exclusive to the sovereign in question.[9] After all, 'the first and foremost restriction imposed by international law is that—failing the existence of a permissive rule to the contrary—it may not exercise its power in any form in the territory of another State'.[10] That, in part, is what we have understood that *sovereign* has come to mean; that, in part, is what we have come to *expect* from a sovereign.[11] At one and the same time, however, and notwithstanding the demographic oddities and geographical remoteness for which Pitcairn Island is so well known,[12] its beguiling and multifaceted background calls out for an alternative appreciation of events, one in which the United Kingdom has come to assert jurisdiction in a more obvious and more regular manner over time—one in which the invocation of the Sexual Offences Act 1956 seems more inevitable than it does accidental or out of place. Or are these prosecutions by the United Kingdom better understood as the last throes of an imperial reflex

---

[9] We use the term Pitcairn Island here to designate the actual territory to which the charges under the Sexual Offences Act 1956 related; note, however, that, in the 2002 Agreement between New Zealand and the United Kingdom, reference is made to 'any trial arising from investigations into allegations of sexual offending *on the Islands*, conducted by the Kent Police from 1999 to 2001' (above note 4, Art. 2 (a) (emphasis added)) where 'Islands' are defined as 'the Islands of Pitcairn, Henderson, Ducie, and Oeno' (ibid, Art. 1 (h)). Henderson, Ducie, and Oeno comprise an island and two atolls which have never been continuously inhabited, but have, from time to time, been visited by Pitcairners—over which the United Kingdom first formally asserted sovereignty in 1902: see Roberts-Wray, K., *Commonwealth and Colonial Law* (London: Stevens & Sons, 1966), 906 (fn. 59). In 1988, Henderson was designated a World Heritage Site under the UNESCO World Heritage Convention: <http://whc.unesco.org/en/list/487>. See, also, Birkett, above note 6, at 82. Old Polynesians referred to Pitcairn Island as *Hiti-au-revareva* ('border of passing clouds'); Oeno lies 76 miles to the northwest of Pitcairn Island; Henderson 107 miles to the east-north-east and Ducie is 290 miles due east. Taken together, these have been collectively referred to as the Pitcairn Islands or the Pitcairn Island group: see Wahlroos, S., *Mutiny and the Romance in the South Seas: A Companion to the Bounty Adventure* (Topsfield, MA: Salem House Publishers, 1989), 347.

[10] *The Case of the S.S. "Lotus"* (1927) PCIJ Ser. A, No. 10, p. 18.

[11] Beckett, W. E., 'The Exercise of Criminal Jurisdiction over Foreigners', *British Yearbook of International Law* 6 (1925), 44–60. See, also, Cassese, A., *International Law* (Oxford: Oxford University Press, 2nd edn, 2005), 98.

[12] With a population of 48 in an area of 6.6 sq km. See Crawford, J., *The Creation of States in International Law* (Oxford: Clarendon Press, 2nd edn, 2006), 634. The total land mass of the Pitcairn Island group (above note 9) is 45.16 sq km (according to the Joint Nature Conservation Committee which advises the Government of the United Kingdom). See <www.jncc.gov.uk/page-4405>. Pitcairn Island lies some 17,000 miles from the United Kingdom. See Birkett, above note 6, at 59. See, also, Bockarth, J., 'Law on Remote Islands: The Convergence of Fact and Fiction', *Legal Studies Forum* 27 (2003), 21–81.

action, an attempt to secure once and for all a territorial claim that has proved so intractable and so elusive?[13]

It is around these (and related) questions that this chapter will take shape. It commences with an assessment of the *basis* or *bases* for the assertion of jurisdiction by the United Kingdom over Pitcairn Island as understood in public international law. The chapter does so by a brief analysis of the concept of jurisdiction and how public international law constructs the *idea* of the assertion of jurisdiction by States. As it does so, we shall reflect on the jurisdictional position of the United Kingdom in respect of Pitcairn Island from a historical as well as modern perspective, though this discussion all the while assumes that the United Kingdom does indeed have sovereign title over the territory (or territories) at issue. We shall need to engage this assumption further, so the next section of our contribution proceeds to tackle the question of territorial acquisition—of how public international law has provided over time for modes of acquisition of sovereign title, and through what process or processes title in respect of Pitcairn Island might have come to reside *in ultimo* in the United Kingdom. It will be apparent, however, that sovereign title itself opens up the vexed matter of the legal obligations of States in respect of their territories and, here, we consider the nature and extent of human rights obligations of States under public international law. We develop these themes in the penultimate section of the chapter to contemplate how this experience might inform or shape notions of the concept of law itself,[14] and what it tells us in general terms about the application of the law in anomalous or unusual spaces.[15] The final section of the chapter offers an opportunity for our concluding thoughts and reflections.

## Jurisdiction: A Brief Conceptual Analysis

There is a strange ironic twist to our consideration of the Pitcairn prosecutions from a jurisdictional perspective; the original task of

---

[13] See, further, Farran, S., 'The "Re-Colonising" of Pitcairn', *Victoria University of Wellington Law Review* 38 (2007), 435–464.

[14] Very much the concern of the Privy Council in October 2006, when it delivered its judgment in *Steven Raymond Christian & Others v R* [2006] UKPC 47 (ie, that the central issue before it 'relate[d] to the validity of the laws creating the offences and the question of whether the bringing of the prosecutions was an abuse of process') (per Lord Hoffmann (para. 1)).

[15] See Boyle, A., and Chinkin, C., *The Making of International Law* (Oxford: Oxford University Press) (2007), 39.

HMAV *Bounty*[16] as it set sail for the South Pacific in October 1787 was one of 'imperial proportions',[17] in the sense that its mission was to acquire a natural resource—breadfruit—as an alternative source of food for English slaves on sugar plantations in Jamaica and the Lesser Antilles,[18] and yet, following an act of mutiny and the subsequent landing of the *Bounty* on Pitcairn Island in January 1790,[19] we find ourselves over two centuries later attempting to configure the relationship between a former colonial power and, perhaps, one of the most unusual let alone remote outposts of its empire.[20]

With its renowned isolation, Pitcairn Island therefore stands as a fitting metaphor for the flight and final destination of the mutineers for, at the time of their settlement there in January 1790, it represented a place *beyond* the territory and, thus, we can assume, the jurisdiction of the United Kingdom—a space, that is, free of the laws of the United Kingdom. In addition, and as far as we can now tell, the territory was not in the control of any other State during that period,[21] which would have meant

---

[16] The *Bounty*, formerly *Bethia*, was HM's Armed Vessel, being a former merchantman and not a man-of-war.                [17] See Birkett, above note 6, at 8.

[18] In consequence of the loss of supplies of dried fish from the newly independent colonies in North America—again, a further testament of the shifting tides, demands, and fortunes of empire: see Madison, R. D., 'Introduction' in Bligh, W., and Christian, E., *The Bounty Mutiny* (New York: Penguin, 2001), ix at xi. See, also, Schine, C., 'Adventures in the Opium Trade', *New York Review of Books*, Vol. LVI, No. 1, 15 January–11 February 2009, 39–41 at 40. In their instructions to Lieutenant Bligh in November 1787, the Commissioners for executing the office of Lord High Admiral of Great Britain and Ireland wrote that the vessel in Bligh's command had 'been stored and victualled for that service, and fitted with proper conveniences and necessaries for the preservation of as many of the said trees as, from her size, can be taken on board her'. See Appendix A: Bligh's Orders and A Description of the Breadfruit, ibid., at 197. Knowledge of the breadfruit had been transmitted from Captain James Cook's voyage to Tahiti (where he arrived in April 1769): ibid., at 198 (that 'the bread-fruit tree is to be found in the most luxuriant state'.)

[19] Not the first landing on Pitcairn Island, for Captain Philip Carteret has written an account of his 1767 visit there in *An Account of the Voyages Undertaken by the Order of His Present Majesty for Making Discoveries in the Southern Hemisphere, and Successively Performed by Commodore Byron, Captain Carteret, and Captain Cook, in the Dolphin, the Swallow and the Endeavour* (London: W. Strahan & T. Cadell, 1773)—in which he described the island as 'scarce better than a large rock in the ocean'. See Birkett, above note 6, at 13. See, also, below note 21.

[20] Pitcairn Island has been said to compete with Easter Island for the title of 'the most remote inhabited island' in the world; it has no airport, no hotel, and no anchorage. See Wahlroos, above note 9, at 348.

[21] This is not to suggest that it had had no contact with humans: Polynesians had made use of (the) Pitcairn Island(s) centuries before the arrival of the *Bounty*. See Birkett, above note 6, at 99.

that there were no possibilities or infrastructures for an act of extradition of the mutineers.[22] For even at that point in time, public international law had constructed the jurisdictional powers of States around the nucleus of their territories and territorial possessions: '[t]he territorial sovereign has the strongest interest, the greatest facilities, and the most powerful instruments for repressing crimes, whether committed by native-born subjects, or by domiciled aliens, in his territory.'[23] This set of practices came to be reflected in what is called the territorial principle of jurisdiction (or 'territoriality') in public international law,[24] which had constitutional importance for the relationships that States would then develop with each other. The position was however different in respect of *terra nullius*, or those territories not in the claim or within the sovereignty of any State.[25]

---

[22] According to Boatswain's Mate James Morrison, Fletcher Christian chose to: 'Cruise for some Uninhabited Island where he would land his Stock . . . and set fire to the Ship, and where he hoped to live the remainder of His days without seeing the face of a European but those who were already with him.' See Birkett, above note 4, at 13. Though the mutineers did live 'in perpetual fear of discovery and capture': see Bockarth, above note 12, at 40. On the developing theoretical basis of extradition, see Koskenniemi, M., *The Gentle Civilizer of Nations: The Rise and Fall of International Law 1870–1960* (Cambridge: Cambridge University Press, 2002), 50.

[23] Lewis, G. C., *On Foreign Jurisdiction and the Extradition of Criminals* (London: J. W. Parker & Son, 1859), 30. See, also, and in general terms, Cormack, B., *A Power to Do Justice: Jurisdiction, English Literature, and the Rise of the Common Law, 1509–1625* (Chicago: University of Chicago Press, 2007).

[24] Whereby '[a] State has jurisdiction with respect to any crime committed in whole or in part within its territory.' As stated in Art. 3 of the Draft Convention on Jurisdiction with Respect to Crime, contained in the Harvard Project on Jurisdiction with Respect to Crime, *American Journal of International Law* (Supplement) 29 (1935), 435–651, at 480.

[25] And used as a classic trope for furthering the endeavours of the colonial enterprise: see the discussion in Knop, K., *Diversity and Self-Determination in International Law* (Cambridge: Cambridge University Press, 2002), 120–129. See, also, Boyle & Chinkin, above note 15, at 14 and 28–29. Koskenniemi, above note 22, at 129, observes that both of the major French studies on this topic as the nineteenth century drew to its close, Charles Salomon's *L'occupation des territoires sans maître. Etude de droit international* (Paris: Giard, 1889), and Gaston Jèze's *Etude théoretique et pratique sur l'occupation comme mode d'acquérir les territoires en droit international* (Paris: Giard & Brière, 1896), 'concluded that if only savages lived in a more or less organized community, their land would escape being labeled as *terra nullius* and colonial title could be created only by cession'. As a matter of historical interest, so thought the International Court of Justice in its advisory opinion in *Western Sahara* (1975) ICJ Rep. 12, when it concluded that 'the state practice of the relevant period indicates that territories inhabited by tribes or peoples having a social and political organization were not regarded as *terra nullius*' and that, in light of this fact and information furnished to the Court, 'at the time of colonization Western Sahara was inhabited by peoples which, if nomadic, were socially and politically organized in tribes and under chiefs competent to represent them'. Finally, consider Mason, A., 'The Rights of Indigenous People in Lands Once Part of the Old Dominions of the Crown', *International & Comparative Law Quarterly* 46 (1997), 812–830.

To be sure, some accommodation was made for extraterritorial assertions of jurisdiction in the form of the principle of nationality which provided for prosecutorial competence of States over their own nationals notwithstanding the fact that the offence had been committed outwith their territories: section 4 of the Offences Against the Person Act 1861 provided, for instance, that: 'whosoever shall solicit, encourage, persuade, or endeavour to persuade, or shall propose to any Person, to murder any other Person, whether he be a Subject of Her Majesty or not, *and whether he be within the Queen's dominions or not*, shall be guilty of a Misdemeanor'.[26] Nationality, then, would have had considerable import in this context,[27] although its relevance would have diminished over time with the gradual demise of the mutineers since their descendents were considered illegitimate and would not have been entitled to British nationality under the laws of that time.[28] Additional to the nationality principle is the so-called protective or security principle, concerning a State's competence to prosecute crimes committed against itself,[29] as well as the principle of universality (which justifies 'the repression of some types of crime as a matter of international public policy').[30] The classic example of this latter principle in

---

[26] Emphasis added. See, also, s. 12 of Foreign Enlistment Act 1870 and Lauterpacht, H., 'Revolutionary Activities by Private Persons Against Foreign States', *American Journal of International Law* 22 (1928), 105–130, 113–114. Consider, also, Art. 11 of the 1958 Geneva Convention on the High Seas, where 'no penal or disciplinary proceedings may be instituted against ... persons [in the service of a ship involved in a collision or any other incident of navigation on the high seas] except before the judicial or administrative authorities *either of the flag State or of the State of which such person is a national*' (emphasis added): 450 UNTS 82. See, also, Art. 97 of the 1982 United Nations Law of the Sea Convention: UN Doc. A/CONF.62/122 (1982).

[27] See Jennings, R., and Watts, A. (eds)., *Oppenheim's International Law* (Vol. I: Peace) (London & New York: Longman, 9th edn, 1992), 480.

[28] See British Nationality Act, 4 Geo. II, c. 21 (1736); 13 Geo. III, c. 21 (1772). See, further, Farran, above note 13, at 437. The Pitcairn Supreme Court stated in its judgment of April 2004 that '[a]t law, illegitimate children took the nationality of their mothers at birth, which in this case would have been Tahitian. The mutineers and their descendants did not undergo naturalization procedures, nor did they become subjects by conquest.' *The Queen v 7 Named Accused* [2004] PNSC 1, para. 35.

[29] Ie, its security, credit, political independence, or territorial integrity—which, though capable of abuse, holds 'a firm place in the practice of a number of States'. See Jennings, R. Y., 'Extraterritorial Jurisdiction and the United States Anti-Trust Laws', *British Yearbook of International Law* 33 (1957), 146–175, 155.

[30] Brownlie, I., *Principles of Public International Law* (Oxford: Oxford University Press, 7th edn, 2008), 305 (noting, at 306, somewhat cryptically, that hijacking and offences related to traffic in narcotics 'are probably subject to universal jurisdiction').

action was piracy.[31] A final principle, the subject of considerable debate in the *Cutting Case*, is that of passive personality—where jurisdiction is asserted on the basis that the victims of an offence are nationals of the State that is seeking to exercise jurisdiction.[32]

All of this is by way of background to the recent assertion of jurisdiction by the United Kingdom in respect of the Pitcairn prosecutions. The position on jurisdiction that exists under this set of circumstances must be contrasted with that which would have prevailed at the time of the mutiny on HMAV *Bounty* on 29 April 1789, and the arrival of the mutineers on Pitcairn Island in January 1790. At that moment, the United Kingdom would have had sufficient jurisdictional claim over the mutineers either on the basis of the territorial attributes of the HMAV *Bounty*,[33] and an expansive reading of the territorial principle of jurisdiction,[34] or on account of the nationality of the mutineers: by virtue of the Mutiny Act 1689, it was 'enacted' that:

---

[31] See Jennings, above note 29, at 156. Consider, however, Kontorovich, E., 'The Piracy Analogy: Modern Universal Jurisdiction's Hollow Foundation', *Harvard International Law Journal* 45 (2004), 183–237.

[32] (1887) US For. Rel. 751; see, also, Moore, J. B., *Report on Extraterritorial Crime and the Cutting Case* (Washington, DC: US Dept. of State, 1887).

[33] Smith, II, G. P., 'From Cutlass to Cat-O'-Nine Tails: The Case for International Jurisdiction of Mutiny on the High Seas', *Michigan Journal of International Law* 10 (1989), 277–303. See, also, Clark, R. S., 'Steven Spielberg's *Amistad* and Other Things I Have Thought About in the Past Forty Years: International (Criminal) Law, Conflict of Laws, Insurance and Slavery', *Rutgers Law Journal* 30 (1999), 371–440, 388. Note that, in the *Lotus Case*, the *locus classicus* on jurisdiction, the Permanent Court of International Justice stated that: '[a] corollary of the principle of the freedom of the seas is that a ship on the high seas is assimilated to the territory of the State the flag of which it flies, for, just as its own territory, that State exercises its authority upon it, and no other State may do so.' Above note 10. Art. 6 (1) of the 1958 Geneva Convention on the High Seas went on to provide that: '[s]hips shall sail under the flag of one State only and, save in exceptional cases expressly provided for in international treaties or in these articles, shall be subject to its exclusive jurisdiction on the high seas. A ship may not change its flag during a voyage or while in a port of call, save in the case of a real transfer of ownership or change of registry.' See above note 26. See, also, Art. 92 of the 1982 Law of the Sea Convention: above note 26. See, further, Harris, D. J., *Cases and Materials on International Law* (London: Sweet & Maxwell, 6th edn, 2004), 280.

[34] For later ratifications of this practice, see Harris, above note 33. See, however, Curtis, G. T., *The Case of the Virginius, Considered with Reference to the Law of Self-Defence* (New York: Baker, Voorhis & Co., 1874), 21. ('The regular ships of a nation at sea are within its personal jurisdiction, and they are without its territorial jurisdiction. The flag that is over them is the emblem of the personal jurisdiction; but it is no emblem or sign of the territorial jurisdiction.')

From and after the Twelfth day of April in the Year of our lord One thousand six hundred eighty nine, every Person being in Their Majesties Service in the Army, and being Mustered and in Pay as an Officer or Soldier, who shall at any time before the Tenth day of November in the Year of our Lord One thousand six hundred eighty nine, Excite, cause or joyn in any Mutiny or Sedition in the Army, or shall Desert Their Majesties Service in the Army, shall suffer Death, or such other Punishment as by a Court-Martial shall be Inflicted.

It is this basic formula that provided the foundation for subsequent statutory stipulations on mutiny—Mutiny Acts were adopted in 1797 and then again in 1872—and their focus was the official status of the vessel concerned: their application was not relevant to merchant vessels.[35] Coupled with this factor was, of course, the fact that the mutineers were nationals of the United Kingdom,[36] and we can appreciate how the nature of certain crimes by a State's nationals might dictate their commission *outside* the territorial confines of a State—to mutiny, we could add the crime of treason.[37] It should therefore come as no surprise that mutiny became ripe for criminalization, especially in those States with distinguished or evolving records of naval power.[38]

We therefore see the crime of mutiny coming into its own as a matter of the jurisdiction of sovereigns: in this sense, it offers an important contrast to piracy which was regarded as an offence against *both* national *and* public international law. As such—as a crime *hosti humani generis*—it was prosecutable in all jurisdictions, that is, as a crime *jure gentium* with the pirate as an enemy of mankind subject to the regime of universal jurisdiction.[39] (Note, though, that in Lassa Oppenheim's treatise on public international law, Hersch Lauterpacht maintained a definition of piracy as 'every unauthorized act of violence against persons or goods committed on the open sea either by a private vessel against another vessel or by a mutinous crew or passengers

---

[35] See Mutiny Act 1797 and Mutiny Act 1872. See, further, Smith, above note 33, at 287. [36] Above note 28.

[37] 35 Hen. VIII, c. 2—and as reflected in the facts in *Joyce v Director of Public Prosecutions* [1946] AC 347. See, further, Shaw, M., *International Law* (Cambridge: Cambridge University Press, 6th edn, 2008), 667.

[38] Very much the theme of Smith, above note 33.

[39] See above note 31 and Smith, above note 33, at 294. See, also, Shaw, above note 37, at 668.

against their own vessel'.)[40] Nevertheless, it is clear that, through creative design and deployment of their national laws, States with overseas commitments and ambitions were able to sustain and protect their respective (and changing) interests: the United Kingdom, for instance, made considerable use of the principle of nationality at that time when compared with other countries (who sought to place certain limitations on the *sort* of nationals to whom jurisdiction was extended (ie, public functionaries)).[41] However, we can also observe that, in terms of the sheer scope and range of legislative coverage, the United Kingdom also made abundant use of the nationality principle of jurisdiction: it was pressed into service for offences by nationals on British ships or on foreign ships to which they did not belong (the Merchant Shipping Act 1894) as well as for the Incitement to Mutiny Act 1797.[42] Furthermore, provision was made for the criminalization of the kidnapping of Pacific Islanders,[43] and, more pertinent to present purposes, the Australia Courts Act 1828 gave special jurisdiction to Australian courts over British subjects on Pacific Islands that did not form part of any State.[44]

This latter legislation hints at the limitations of the nationality principle and, indeed, of other extraterritorial forms of jurisdiction, since the *enforcement* of national laws has always been exclusively territorial as a matter of public international law.[45] These other

---

[40] Lauterpacht, H., *Oppenheim's International Law: A Treatise* (Vol. I: Peace) (London: Longmans Green & Co., 7th edn, 1948), 608–609 (§272). Cf. Jennings and Watts, in their edition of *Oppenheim*, above note 27, at 746 (§299) (noting that '[p]iracy, in its original and very strict meaning, is every unauthorised act of violence committed by a private vessel on the high seas against another vessel with intent to plunder (*animo furendi*).')

[41] As was the case with Argentina and Cuba: see Harvard Project on Jurisdiction, above note 24, at 530.

[42] 37 Geo. III, c. 70—both of the examples listed here are drawn from the Harvard Project on Jurisdiction: above note 24, at 530.

[43] Pacific Islanders Protection Act 1873: 35 & 36 Vict., c. 19.

[44] 9 Geo. IV, c. 83, s. 4.

[45] Consider how Art. 16 of the Harvard Draft Convention on Jurisdiction with Respect to Crime framed its notion of 'apprehension': 'In exercising its jurisdiction under this Convention, no State shall prosecute or punish any person who has been brought within its territory or a place subject to its authority by recourse to measures in violation of international law or international convention without first obtaining the consent of the State or States whose rights have been violated by such measures.' See Harvard Project on Jurisdiction, above note 24, 442. Consider, also, the implications for this understanding of the concept of *terra nullius*: above note 25.

principles therefore identified the *prescriptive* competences of States, that is their competence to legislate with a view to the enforcement of these laws as and when nationals once again found themselves within the prerogative purview of the State: the relationship between the State and its nationals had been described as one of 'compelling observance by punishment if a person who has broken [its laws] *returns within its jurisdiction*'.[46] And so it was that the Harvard codification project on jurisdiction concluded, in 1935, that it was 'universally conceded' in respect of the principle of nationality that:

> By virtue of such jurisdiction the State is enabled to prosecute its nationals while they are abroad and to execute judgments against them upon property within the State or upon them personally when they return, or the State may prosecute its nationals after they return for acts done abroad. Under existing international practice, a State is assumed to have practically unlimited legal control over its nationals. This competence is justified on the ground that a State's treatment of its nationals is not ordinarily a matter of concern to other States or to international law.[47]

This line of analysis emphasizes the jurisdiction of States *in relation to one another*,[48] but we should perhaps make some allowance for the fact that the concept and consequences of Statehood were only given a conventional standing in December 1933 with the adoption of the Montevideo Convention on the Rights and Duties of States.[49] What we observe in respect of the mutineers is a singular effort by the British Government to bring them to book for their actions of April 1789: in August 1790, Captain Edward Edwards, RN, was given command of

---

[46] Hall, W. E., *A Treatise on International Law* (Oxford: Clarendon Press, 8th edn, 1924) (Higgins, A. P., ed.), 56 (emphasis added). See, also, Higgins, above note 8.

[47] See Harvard Project on Jurisdiction, above note 24, at 519.

[48] S. 2 of the Foreign Jurisdiction Act 1890 provided that: '[w]here a foreign country is not subject *to any government from whom Her Majesty the Queen might obtain jurisdiction* in the manner recited by this Act, *Her Majesty shall by virtue of this Act have jurisdiction over Her Majesty's subjects for the time being resident in or resorting to that country*, and that jurisdiction shall be jurisdiction of Her Majesty in a foreign country within the meaning of the other provisions of this Act' (emphases added).

[49] 49 Stat. 3097 (which stated, amongst other things, that '[t]he jurisdiction of States within the limits of national territory applies to all the inhabitants' (Art. 9), and that '[t]he fundamental rights of states are not susceptible of being affected in any manner whatsoever' (Art. 5)).

the HMS *Pandora* and entrusted with the task of apprehending those responsible for the mutiny. A vivid account of its travails appeared in Lady Diana Belcher's *Mutineers of the Bounty and their Descendants in Pitcairn and Norfolk Islands* (1870).[50] This was no ordinary mission if one bears in mind the phenomenal distances and the sort of commitment involved—HMS *Pandora* set off for the Pacific from Portsmouth Harbour on 7 November 1790 with Captain Edwards in charge of a crew of some 134 men. It was as if all of the available machineries of State were being brought to bear on violators of the laws of the land—albeit at a distance of some several thousand miles from the mainland of the United Kingdom.[51]

The episode stands as a choice example of an attempt to *enforce* the law of the United Kingdom of that time, but it is only subsequent to these developments that we can begin to appreciate the *change* that occurred in the British relationship with the *territory* of Pitcairn Island—rather than just its relationship with those who had taken up habitation there.[52] It is a narrative as unique in fact as it is intriguing in its breadth and scope, told through the span of legislative actions taken which included the British Settlements Acts 1843, 1860, and 1887; the Foreign Jurisdiction Act 1890; the Pacific Order in Council 1893; an executive direction of 1898; the Pitcairn Island Government Regulations 1940; the British Settlements Act 1945 and 1952; the Pitcairn Order in Council 1952; the Judicature Ordinance 1961; the Justice Ordinance 1966; the Pitcairn Order in Council 1970; and the Judicature Ordinance 1970.

---

[50] At 77–87; and *reproduced as* Appendix B of Bligh & Christian, above note 18, at 205–212. See, also, Birkett, above note 6, at 14.

[51] After reaching Tahiti on 23 March 1791, five of the mutineers left on Tahiti surrendered to Captain Edwards; nine others were apprehended by armed shore parties. Two were murdered, though it is obscure in one instance whether one of the mutineers surrendered or was captured: see Alexander, C., *The Bounty: The True Story of the Mutiny on the Bounty* (New York: Viking, 2003) (an excellent and respectable modern account, equipped with a good select bibliography). The HMS *Pandora* was to meet its final fate by running aground on the Great Barrier Reef in August 1791. Four of the prisoners perished in the wreck; the 10 remaining prisoners were subsequently tried for the mutiny. Six were found guilty and, of these, three were executed.

[52] Cf. Farran, above note 13, at 437 (that '[i]n order to bring the accused within British jurisdiction[,] it was necessary to establish that Pitcairn Islanders were British subjects who remained subject to imperial law').

Prime among these was the British Settlements Act 1887,[53] but these formal manoeuvres on behalf of the United Kingdom must be read in the fuller context of which they were forming so integral a part: they accompanied the 'forms of government' that came to exist on Pitcairn Island in the nineteenth century, which the Privy Council deemed 'rudimentary, consisting of rules drawn up locally or with the assistance of the commanding officers or ships of the Royal Navy which made infrequent visits'.[54] So, in effect, we are presented with a series of intricate and expanding entanglements between the United Kingdom and Pitcairn Island that occurred over a significant interval of time, where initial assertions of jurisdiction led to further and more aggressive jurisdictional actions and claims as time went on—and it is these actions and claims which moved

[53] Which proved to be the enabling legislation around which all later legislative action concerning Pitcairn Island took shape: the Act, after noting in its preamble that 'divers of Her Majesty's subjects have resorted to and settled in, and may hereafter resort to and settle in, divers places where there is no civilized government, and such settlements have become or may hereafter become possessions of Her Majesty, and it is expedient to repeal and re-enact with amendments the existing Acts enabling Her Majesty to provide for such government,' provided in s. 4 that:

> It shall be lawful for Her Majesty the Queen in Council to confer on any court in any British Possession any such jurisdiction, civil or criminal, original or appellate, in respect of matters occurring or arising in any British settlement as might be conferred by virtue of this Act upon a court in the settlement, and to make such provisions and regulations as Her Majesty in Council may think fit respecting the exercise of the jurisdiction conferred under this section on any court, and respecting the enforcement and execution of the judgments, decrees, orders, and sentences of such court, and respecting appeals therefrom; and every Order of Her Majesty in Council under this section shall be effectual to vest in the court the jurisdiction expressed to be thereby conferred, and the court shall exercise the same in accordance with and subject to the said provisions and regulations: Provided always, that every Order in Council made in pursuance of this Act shall be laid before both Houses of Parliament as soon as conveniently may be after the making thereof.

For the importance awarded to the British Settlements Act 1887 in the thinking and reasoning of the Privy Council, see above note 14, at para. 3 (per Lord Hoffmann).

[54] Above note 14, at para. 2 (per Lord Hoffmann). Though, on this point, it is worth citing Roberts-Wray's observation that '[i]t is permissible to wonder how far English law has in fact been effective ... [I]t seems likely that the Island's magistrates have never known much about it and have formed their own written laws sufficient for most purposes.' See Roberts-Wray, above note 9, at 909. According to Farran, by the time of the British Settlements Act 1887, Pitcairn Island had two—if not three—written constitutions, known by the names of their respective authors: Elliott (1838) and Moresby (1852). Above note 13, at 443. The third constitution that is mentioned is that of Rookes (1892), on which see below note 92.

the matter from consideration as one of the mere exercise of jurisdiction to one of territorial acquisition and control.

## On Territorial Acquisition

The assertion of jurisdiction does, of course, presuppose that sovereign title exists over a specified territory, for jurisdiction is a manifestation or a *consequence* of that sovereignty.[55] In other words, what should occur *before* any appreciation of the scope of a State's jurisdictional powers is the demonstration of 'State sovereignty in respect of territory'.[56] Though this fact was recognized in the jurisprudence resulting from the Pitcairn prosecutions, the finer legal points as to the actual timing or moment of territorial acquisition were not regarded as essential to, or determinative of, the prosecution's case and, for all intents and purposes, British possession of Pitcairn Island was treated as an existing or going concern:

It is not necessary to define with accuracy the time at which Pitcairn Island did become a British possession. Sometimes there may be a gradual extension of jurisdiction over a territory, as was recognized in *Attorney General for British Honduras v Bristowe* (1880) 6 App Cas 143. British Honduras was formally annexed in 1862, but there were grants of land by the Crown made as early as 1817. The Privy Council held that sovereignty was acquired on or before that earlier year. Similarly, a formal act of acquisition is not required. It is the intention of the Crown, gathered from its own acts and surrounding circumstances, that determines whether a territory has been acquired for English law purposes. The same principle applies in the resolution of international disputes as to sovereignty.[57]

As for the Privy Council in *Christian*, it satisfied itself with the *fact* of possession on the say-so of the British government; it relied on the

---

[55] Bowett, D. W., 'Jurisdiction: Changing Patterns of Authority over Activities and Resources', *British Yearbook of International Law* 53 (1982), 1–26. '[T]he holding of a criminal trial is a sovereign act': see Aust, A., 'Lockerbie: The Other Case', *International & Comparative Law Quarterly* 49 (2000), 278–296, 283.

[56] Jennings, R. Y., *The Acquisition of Territory in International Law* (Manchester: Manchester University Press, 1963), 2 (as distinct from, at 8, 'the beneficial enjoyment of territory in the physical sense')—or what Malcolm Shaw has called 'the question of sovereignty over land in international law'. See Shaw, M., 'Speaking Volumes: The Acquisition of Territory in International Law', *Times Higher Education Supplement*, 17 November 1995.

[57] Or so held the Pitcairn Island Court of Appeal in August 2004: *Queen v 7 Named Accused* [2004] PNCA 1, para. 46.

*dictum* of Atkin LJ from *The Fagernes* (1927) that '[a]ny definitive statement from the proper representative of the Crown as to the territory of the Crown must be treated as conclusive'.[58] In fact, the Privy Council addressed itself in so robust a manner on this question that it left no doubt as to where it stood on *its* interpretation of the facts: '[f]or over a hundred years,' Lord Hoffmann said for the majority, 'Pitcairn has been administered by the Crown as a British possession and whatever its history or the inclinations of its people may have been, it is unthinkable that the Judicial Committee of Her Majesty's Privy Council would not accept an executive statement affirming it to be part of the territory of the Crown.'[59] In this form, the act of state doctrine is presented not as a doctrine expressing the domestic constitutional power of the Crown to decide at its discretion whether or not to acquire territory, but as a doctrine according to which the question whether territory has or has not been acquired is non-justiciable. Yet, though Lord Hoffmann's opinion does hint that there might be circumstances in which a court might go behind such a statement,[60] neither he nor any of the judges in the Privy Council gave any clear indication as to when this might (or might not) be appropriate. His own statement is rather puzzling, since it appears to suggest that since, in the view of the Privy Council, Pitcairn Island has been administered as a British possession for 'over a hundred years'— which seems like an adjudicative opinion as to the facts of the matter— the executive statement that it was a British possession has as a consequence to be accepted. Which all sounds as if the executive statement is non-justiciable because, in the adjudicative opinion of the court, it is plainly correct. Whatever may be said about the case, it has certainly not shed any light on either the theory or the rationale of the act of state doctrine.[61]

---

[58] [1927] P 311, at 324.  [59] Above note 14, at para. 10 (per Lord Hoffmann).

[60] Ibid ('[t]his is not the occasion on which to explore the limits of this doctrine, but their Lordships consider that the present case falls squarely within it') (per Lord Hoffmann). See, also, below note 64.

[61] For a recent and illuminating discussion as to the deep mysteries surrounding the doctrine of act of state, see Perreau-Saussine, A., 'British Acts of State in English Courts', *British Yearbook of International Law* 78 (2007), 176–254, in which the author presents three rationales for the English act of state doctrine. The decision of the Privy Council, unfortunately not informed by her analysis, does not appear to conform to any of them. The first rationale she mentions is that acts of state are non-justiciable because they are not regulated by law, but the Privy Council opinion, which assumes that in some circumstances they are justiciable, entails the view that they *are* regulated by law—presumably public international law or some combination of public international law, domestic, commonwealth, and colonial law.

The approach taken might appear unduly deferential from the bench given the matters at stake and the interests involved, but it does sit at one with other judicial practices—one thinks immediately of the recognition of governments—where the courts have adopted an identical attitude in taking their cue from the executive.[62] That said, it might be useful to consider the actual circumstances in which the courts have been prepared to tap open the door to more of a pragmatic outlook;[63] Lord Woolf did make the observation that where 'overwhelming' evidence did not underpin or support official pronouncements, there would be good cause for the courts to question an act of state:

> Recent developments, mainly in relation to judicial review have demonstrated a greater willingness on the part of the courts to scrutinize the use by the Crown of prerogative powers and so far the limits, if any, of the courts' power of review has not been clearly determined. So today it can no longer be taken for granted that the courts will accept that there is any action on the part of the Crown that is not open to any form of review by the courts if a proper foundation for the review is established.[64]

What issues were ripe for deliberation here? Given the particulars of the British Settlements Act 1887, which related to any British possession 'which has not been acquired by cession or conquest',[65] and which, as we have noted,[66] set the official foundations for the eventual governance of Pitcairn Island, it seems appropriate that a basic tracing of the lineage of title to the island would not have gone amiss—not least of all to confirm that subsequent developments had indeed fallen within

---

[62] See Harris, above note 33, at 167–168, and at 95–97. See, also, Grey, F. T. and Bellot, H. H. L., 'The Relations of the Executive and the Judiciary', *Transactions of the Grotius Society* 15 (1929), 139–161.

[63] See, for instance, Lord Wilberforce's remark in *Carl Zeiss Stiftung v Rayner and Keeler Ltd. (No. 2)* [1967] 1 AC 853, that 'the courts may, in the interests of justice and common sense, where no consideration of public policy to the contrary has to prevail, give recognition to the actual facts or realities found to exist in the territory in question'. See, also, the position of Lord Denning in the Court of Appeal in *Hesperides Hotels v Aegean Holidays Ltd.* [1978] QB 205, 218 and the more recent case of *Republic of Somalia v Woodhouse Drake Carey Suisse S.A.* [1993] QB 54, where the formal pronouncements of the executive (in the form of a Foreign Office certificate, for example) were found to be 'not conclusive', but, rather, 'just one consideration for the court to take into account' in deciding whether a government exists as the government of a State: see Harris, above note 33, at 167.

[64] Above note 14, at para. 33 (per Lord Woolf). See, also, above note 60.

[65] Above note 53.     [66] Ibid.

the *vires* of the British Settlements Act 1887.[67] That line of thinking would allow us to determine whether territorial acquisition had occurred for the United Kingdom as a matter of fact as well as of law—and, if so, *when* and *how* this had occurred. In his seminal treatment of this topic in *The Acquisition of Territory in International Law*, which appeared in 1963, R. Y. Jennings identified three other modes of acquisition additional to those of *cession* and *conquest*. These were: the *occupation* of territory not under the sovereignty of any State (or *terra nullius*); *prescription*, where title emanates from effective possession over a period of time; and, finally, *accession* or *accretion* which resulted from geographical modifications to the territory of a State.[68]

To undertake such an exercise would involve us coming to terms with the rules and associated proofs required for the acquisition of territory (and, therefore, of sovereign title) under public international law of that time—what is known as the doctrine of intertemporal law.[69] According

---

[67] Since the Act makes explicit reference to the *forms* of British possession to which it applies in respect of how it *defines* a 'British settlement': see above note 14, at para. 3 (per Lord Hoffmann). The Privy Council was fully aware of the importance of the Act, but thought the matter 'quite academic' since 'there is no doubt that the power of the Crown to legislate for a conquered or ceded possession is more extensive than its power to legislate for a settled colony: see Blackstone's *Commentaries* (4th edn, 1770) at p. 107': ibid, at para. 11 (per Lord Hoffmann). In truth, therefore, the *mode* of acquisition defined the scope of the Crown's 'power to legislate' as much as it did the *vires* of the British Settlements Act 1887.

[68] Jennings, above note 56, at 6 (where, at 19, accession or accretion relates to the 'augmentation or loss of territory by the processes of nature'). Cession was here described, at 6, as the 'transfer of territory by a treaty provision' whereas conquest—or subjugation—entailed 'the successful deployment of armed force [which] might serve not only to wrest the territory from the rightful sovereign but also to invest the conqueror with a superior title' (at 3–4). A sixth mode of acquisition—that of adjudication—is briefly mentioned by Jennings, at 7, but this identifies the *process* during which these modes of acquisition are invoked, or used as the basis of decision. These modes of acquisition were outlined with some scepticism it must be said, for, at 7, 'the facts of contemporary history' made one realize how 'incomplete' this scheme actually was: 'it has little or no place for some of the most important territorial changes of the last few years. The reason is not far to seek. The scheme is based upon the civil law modes for the transfer of property *inter vivos*; it does not provide, therefore, for the situation where a new State comes into existence.' See, further, Lee, S., 'Continuing Relevance of Traditional Modes of Territorial Acquisition in International Law and A Modest Proposal', *Connecticut Journal of International Law* 16 (2000), 1–22.

[69] See Elias, T. O., 'The Doctrine of Intertemporal Law', *American Journal of International Law* 74 (1980), 285–307 ('it seems true to say that the doctrine of intertemporal law may be regarded as a substantive rule of law in one sense and as a rule of interpretation in another sense'). For critical engagement with this position, see Lim, C. L., 'Neither Sheep Nor Peacocks: T. O. Elias and Post-colonial International Law', *Leiden Journal of International Law* 21 (2008), 295–315.

to the most famous exposition of this doctrine, in the *Island of Palmas* arbitration in 1928, 'a juridical fact must be appreciated in the light of the law contemporary with it, and not of the law in force at the time when a dispute in regard to it arises or falls to be settled'.[70] That said, these rules were framed in terms of the specific relations *between* States if one recalls the actual constructs of *occupation* or of *cession* or of *conquest*,[71] with competition for title occurring between 'the original state' and 'the subsequent claimant state'.[72] Title thus stood to be *acquired* by States and by States alone with no accommodation made for personal or private acquisitions. The matter is quite apart from how raw or how advanced localized arrangements for governance came to be in these territories.[73] This point is driven home in persuasive fashion if one reflects upon the broader historical sweep of territories in the Pacific Ocean,[74] so that the initial settlement on Pitcairn Island is best viewed as an act of 'private venture',[75] similar, we would maintain, to what happened with British Honduras[76]—as well as the attempt by the first settler on Ilha de Tristáo da Cunha, Jonathan Lambert, to declare the islands as his personal property.[77]

---

[70] Island of Palmas Arbitration: *Netherlands v United States*, 2 RIAA 831, 845.

[71] Above note 68.

[72] See Elias, above note 69, at 292. Note that in his oral argumentation before the International Court of Justice in November 2007 regarding sovereign title over Pedra Banca, Professor Ian Brownlie claimed that '[p]rior to 1847 Pedra Branca was *terra nullius*, and had never been the subject of a prior claim, or any manifestation of sovereignty by other means, *by any sovereign entity*.' See CR 2007/21, at 24 (§4): <http://www.icj-cij. org/docket/files/130/14179.pdf?PHPSESSID=00045397fef82cfdf25e400bce1272c0> (emphasis added).

[73] See above note 54. See, further, Wilford, J. N., 'Twilight of the Forest People', *New York Times* (Wk. Rev.), 8 June 2008, 5.

[74] And captured in Orent, B., and Reinsch, P., 'Sovereignty over Islands in the Pacific', *American Journal of International Law* 35 (1941), 443–461. See, also, Banner, S., *Possessing the Pacific: Land, Settlers, and Indigenous People from Australia to Alaska* (Cambridge, MA: Harvard University Press, 2007).

[75] The opinion of the Supreme Court of the Pitcairn Islands, above note 28, at para. 68.          [76] Above note 57 and below note 77.

[77] Lambert, from Salem, Massachusetts, had arrived on the islands in December 1810. For the discussion of unauthorized settlements, see Roberts-Wray, above note 9, at 100–101, who suggests that the list of those colonies in relation to which the original settlement was unauthorized comprises British Honduras, Pitcairn Island (which he thought was acquired in 1790 by settlement), and Tristan de Cunha. Another possible example is the Cocos Keeling Islands, where settlements by British subjects date back to 1823 and 1827, whilst the first formal authorization by the Crown dates back from 1857. See Roberts-Wray, above note 9, at 882. Roberts-Wray had worked as a lawyer for the Colonial Office and Dominions Office from 1931, and became Legal Adviser to the Colonial Office from 1945 until 1966, when it ceased to exist as a separate department of government.

This is not to negate the possibilities of formal consequences emanating from such private actions at some future point in time—that is, of the state taking over the running in respect of given territories in increasing measure through official and deliberate actions, representations, or ratifications. The United Kingdom had some record on this it must be said,[78] but, as the curious arrangements of Pitcairn Island began to emerge, it is apparent that the moment of acquisition is difficult to pin down; it is rather difficult to place. For this reason—and perhaps for this reason alone—the Privy Council ought to have given more concerted reflection to the matter,[79] and it was in fact invited to do so when counsel for three of the appellants presented the radical argument that the earliest the British Government could lay claim to Pitcairn Island was 1898. This was the year that the then-Secretary of State for the Colonies, Joseph Chamberlain, directed that the Order in Council of 1893, adopted for instituting governmental structures in possessions in the Pacific,[80] be applied to Pitcairn.[81] The occasion for this direction had been the occurrence of a murder on Pitcairn Island; one Harry Christian was accused of murdering his wife Clara Warren and infant daughter.[82] It represented a most public actualization of the inchoate or assumed power found in the Pacific Order in Council 1893, which had itself been promulgated under the British Settlements Act 1887.[83]

---

[78] Orent and Reinsch reporting that '[i]n cases where discoveries were made by her own subjects, Great Britain took formal possession only of those islands over which she desired to assume sovereignty.' One such example was that of Christmas Island, 'discovered' by Captain Cook in December 1877; another is that of Ducie Island, following its sighting by Captain Edwards of HMS *Pandora* in 1791: above note 74, at 443–444.

[79] Especially in a case so overwhelmed by the dictates of legal certainty!

[80] The Order in Council did not originally apply to Pitcairn Island. See s. 6 (1) of the Order. See, also, above note 14, at para. 4 (per Lord Hoffmann).

[81] For which allowance was made in s. 6 (2) of the Order. See, also, above note 14, at para. 4 (per Lord Hoffmann).

[82] Harry Christian was tried and convicted by a Judicial Commissioner from the Western Pacific High Commission, Hamilton Hunter. He was then taken off the island and executed in Suva. See Case for the Respondent, para. 2.23 (d) and see, also, McLoughlin, D., 'The Development of the System of Government and Laws of Pitcairn Island from 1791 to 1971,' in McLoughlin, D., *Laws of Pitcairn, Henderson, Ducie and Oeno Islands* (Govt. of the Islands of Pitcairn, Henderson, Duecie & Oeno: rev. edn, 1971), 34.

[83] See above note 14, at para. 3 (per Lord Hoffmann). See, also, above note 53. As was the Pitcairn Order 1970. Indeed, it is on the basis of these two actions—the 1898 direction and the Order of 1970—that the Privy Council moved to decide that 'the legal status of the island as a British possession is concluded by successive statements of the executive, starting with the direction of the Secretary of State in 1898 and ending with the making of the 1970 Order in Council.' Above note 14, at para. 9 (per Lord Hoffmann). See, also, the Order in Council 1952: above note 14, at para. 10 (per Lord Hoffmann).

So the position of counsel for the appellants in *Christian* in 2000 was that from 1790 onwards the Pitcairn community had managed its own affairs and had thereby constituted an independent sovereign state within the regime of public international law. The general appeal of this line of argument remains that British governmental power in Pitcairn Island, if that is what it was, had been intermittent and practically insignificant: to a considerable extent, the community resident there had been left alone to manage its own affairs. There had, for example, never been a British official of any sort resident on the island and by 1808—the year of the landing of *Topaz*—only one of the original mutineers, John Adams, survived.[84] He had become a benevolent and devout autocrat who ruled by a system of individual decisions, like the Homeric *themistes*, informed either by the Bible or the *Anglican Book of Common Prayer*. Government, in so far as it existed, was therefore theocratic and patriarchal. Adams died in 1829 and was succeeded as leader of the community by George Hunn Nobbs. By about 1829 or 1830, the islanders had promulgated some general written laws, and established a Court of Elders. Thereafter, the most basic of democratic infrastructures came to exist on Pitcairn Island, and local law-making, sometimes under the supervision of visiting naval officers and sometimes not, is a continuous and unmistakable theme.[85]

One problem with this interpretation of events is that it takes no account of the fact the majority of the 1790 settlers, 19 of them, were Tahitian—though whether they came of their own volition or not is not of course known.[86] In consequence, there was no exploration of the status of Pitcairn Island as a possible Tahitian settlement.[87] Another

---

[84] See Wahlroos, above note 9, at 208.

[85] See, generally, McLoughlin, above note 82, at 14–15, 17–24, 29–30, and 31–33.

[86] The *Bounty* had in fact dropped anchor in Matavi Bay, Tahiti, in October 1788, in accordance with its original mission for collecting breadfruit (above note 18); it then, in April 1789, set sail for the West Indies: see Birkett, above note 6, at 11. Following the mutiny on 28 April 1789, the *Bounty* headed for Tubai, an island 350 miles south of Tahiti's Elysian fields, but the attempt to found a settlement there was foiled because of living conditions and occasioned the return of the *Bounty* to Tahiti. After a recouping of supplies, the *Bounty* returned to Tubai but, within three months, it had returned to Tahiti where 16 of the mutineers decided to remain. Eight men, together with 12 Tahitian women and six Polynesian men and one child, joined the *Bounty* as it left Tahiti—arriving on Pitcairn Island on 21 January 1790. See Birkett, above note 6, at 12.

[87] Back in 1790, Tahiti (*O'tahiti*) was an independent kingdom; the French protectorate dates only to 1842 when Queen Pomare IV reached an agreement with Admiral Dupetit Thouars, but this arrangement had not been authorized by the metropolitan French Government. Tahiti was annexed by or ceded to France in June 1880 by King Pomare V (1842–1891). See Wahlroos, above note 9, at 394–403.

problem was that no evidence was produced to the effect that the Islanders had ever conceived of themselves as anything other than British subjects; nor had any other State claimed sovereign title, or the exercise of sovereign rights etc. over Pitcairn Island—or extended protection to its inhabitants. This includes Tahiti. It is of no surprise, then, that the case for the respondents quotes an affidavit by the Island Secretary, Betty Christian, that: '[t]here has never been an "independence movement" on Pitcairn, and Pitcairn has never been considered an independent State in its own right. The first I ever heard of Pitcairn not being British was when [counsel for the appellants] raised the idea in 2004.'[88]

For six of the appellants, the public defender made the more modest claim that Pitcairn Island was a territory acquired by cession in 1838. According to this appreciation of events, it was during this year that Pitcairn Island was visited by HMS *Fly*, under the command of Captain Elliott—whose assistance the islanders solicited in respect of the regulation of their affairs. The request was issued in the wake of the attempt by a newcomer, Joshua Hill, to establish and exercise 'self-proclaimed authority' over the islanders prior to his removal by Captain Bruce of HMS *Imogene*, also in 1838.[89] Apparently, '[t]his request stemmed not only from a desire to prevent the possibility of another self-appointed dictator usurping control of their community but also from a desire by the Islanders for protection from the depredations of American whaling crews who were visiting the Island in rapidly increasing numbers.'[90] Captain Elliott's response was to draft a constitution and code of laws for the islanders and, in what came to be the first formalization of a political arrangement for Pitcairn Island, an elected magistrate was established together with an elected council, with the latter equipped with powers to overrule the former: '[b]y that brief document the people of Pitcairn Island, with the ready assistance of Captain Elliott, formally acknowledged their status as a British possession and, as a natural consequence, placed themselves under the protection of the British Crown.'[91] The most significant postscript to this

---

[88] Case for the Respondent, para. 2.25 (a).
[89] The description of the Supreme Court of Pitcairn Island: above note 28, at para. 37.                    [90] See McLoughlin, above note 82, at 20.
[91] McLoughlin, above note 82, at 21. Cf., however, Farran—that 'it is not at all clear that Captain Elliott was acting within a particular mandate from the Crown to make rules for Pitcairn or simply responding to an immediate demand by the islanders': above note 13, at 440–441.

arrangement occurred in 1892 when Captain Rookes, of HMS *Champion*, revised the constitution with the creation of a parliament of seven individuals with the power to legislate.[92]

In the Privy Council, Lord Hoffmann questioned the potential worth of an argument of cession in this context: 'Cession by whom?' he asked probingly,[93] recalling the public international law particulars for this mode of territorial acquisition:[94]

The notion of cession contemplates a transfer of sovereignty by one sovereign power to another. So, for example, by the Treaty of Utrecht in 1713, Gibraltar was ceded to Great Britain by the Kingdom of Spain. In *Sammut v Strickland* [1938] AC 678 the Privy Council recognized the possibility of a cession by the people of a territory (in that case, Malta during the Napoleonic Wars) who had assumed sovereign authority over themselves. But the analogy with the people of Pitcairn seeking the protection of the Crown seems to their Lordships somewhat far-fetched. In any case, the question appears to their Lordships to be quite academic, since there is no doubt that the power of the Crown to legislate for a conquered or ceded possession is more extensive than its power to legislate for a settled colony.[95]

The invocation of Malta is a useful comparator for our purposes,[96] but it is clear that the Privy Council was not prepared to accept this version of events on account of the fact that cession 'contemplates a transfer of sovereignty *by one sovereign power to another*'.[97] In law, this would thus render a very different designation to the letter Arthur Quintal, Chief Magistrate of the Islands, wrote to Queen Victoria in a later development, in July 1853, 'humbly trust[ing] that we may be allowed to consider ourselves your Majesty's subjects, and Pitcairn's Island a British colony, as long as it is inhabited by us, in the fullest

---

[92] For earlier developments on this score, see above note 54.

[93] Above note 14, at para. 11.

[94] Above note 68. '[A] bilateral mode of acquisition,' writes Jennings, 'in that it requires the co-operation of the two States concerned, whereas all other modes are unilateral.' See Jennings, above note 56, at 16.     [95] Above note 14, at para. 11.

[96] See Crawford, above note 12, at 231 (on the double cession of the Sovereign Order of St. John of Malta—first to Napoleon in June 1798 over Russian protest; then, in the 1814 Treaty of Paris, from France to the United Kingdom (Art. 7)). As for Gibraltar, Art. X of the 1713 Treaty of Utrecht provided that '[t]he Catholic King does hereby, for himself, his heirs and successors, yield to the Crown of Great Britain the full and entire propriety of the town and castle of Gibraltar, together with the port, fortifications, and forts thereunto belonging; and he gives up the said propriety to be held and enjoyed absolutely with all manner of right for ever, without any exception or impediment whatsoever.'     [97] Above note 95 (emphasis added).

sense of the word.'[98] This letter did not yield an official or direct response from the Queen it is true, though a response was forthcoming from the office of the Secretary of State of the United Kingdom in October 1854 which stated that '[t]he manner in which England has always responded to the Pitcairn Islanders as claimed by them as their Fatherland is the best proof no doubt has ever existed as to the sovereignty of your Island and will I trust be accepted by you as a sufficient answer.'[99] Nevertheless, for the islanders, it was proclaimed at one point that they had 'never effectively claimed a relationship with the British Government or its Monarchs which would support jurisdiction being exercised over them'.[100]

As we turn to the more detailed provisions of public international law on territorial acquisition, it becomes clear how tenuous and how negotiable the requirements for acquisition actually were (and were meant to be) in practice. The 'international substantive law of real property',[101] as announced in the *Island of Palmas* arbitration,[102] did not require (as might be thought or imagined) a 'precise epoch' for proof of sovereignty but a 'critical period' that preceded 1898—or the year of the supposed territorial transfer from Spain to the United States by the Treaty of Paris.[103] This was the 'critical date' as it has been called,[104] and what developed was a need for sovereign acts that corresponded to the nature of the territory itself, enough to 'constitute a beginning of establishment of sovereignty by continuous and peaceful display of state authority or a commencement of occupation of an island

---

[98] See Murray, T. B., *Pitcairn: The Island, the People, and the Pastor: To Which Is Added A Short Notice of the Original Settlement and Present Condition of Norfolk Island* (New York: E. S. Gorham, 1909), 209—a letter in which Captain Fly was said to have taken 'formal possession of our little island'. The letter is reproduced in full in the judgment of the Supreme Court of Pitcairn Island: above note 28, at para. 51. Nor would it appear to be the case that the islanders could demonstrate that they had formed 'a more or less organised community' that would disrupt impressions that the territory was *terra nullius* (above note 25). Perhaps the history of the mutiny lingered long and hard to preclude any such claim being (successfully) made.

[99] From the hand of Toup Nicholas, on behalf of the Secretary of State—also reproduced in full in the judgment of the Supreme Court of Pitcairn Island: above note 28, at para. 52.

[100] See Supreme Court of Pitcairn Island: above note 28, at para. 53.

[101] The phrase coined by Jessup, P. C., 'The Palmas Island Arbitration', *American Journal of International Law* 22 (1928), 735–752.    [102] Above note 70.

[103] Done on 10 December 1898. See Award of Tribunal in *Island of Palmas*, above note 70, at 867.

[104] See Goldie, L. F. E., 'The Critical Date', *International & Comparative Law Quarterly* 12 (1963), 1251–1284.

not yet forming a part of the territory of a state'.[105] This was separate to an *act* of discovery.[106] Arbitrator Huber maintained that these facts would then lead to an evaluation of the 'relative strength of the titles invoked by each party',[107] a point very much emphasized in the judgment of the Permanent Court of International Justice in the *Legal Status of Eastern Greenland* between Denmark and Norway:

> Another circumstance which must be taken into account by any tribunal which has to adjudicate upon a claim over a particular territory is the extent to which sovereignty is also claimed by some other Power. In most of the cases involving claims to territorial sovereignty which have come before an international tribunal, there have been two competing claims to sovereignty, and the tribunal has had to decide which of the two is stronger . . . . It is impossible to read the records of the decisions in cases as to territorial sovereignty without observing that in many cases the tribunal has been satisfied with very little in the way of the actual exercise of sovereign rights, provided that the other State could not make out a superior claim.[108]

This *dictum* reinforces the context in which the United Kingdom has come to make its claim over Pitcairn Island—that it has done so in the relative absence of 'some other Power',[109] as Arbitrator Huber put it, and this has perhaps eased the evidential burden that it has had (or felt obliged) to make over time. We might wish to term this as *relative* possession, in the sense that Arbitrator Huber suggested that the question of territorial acquisition involves an essential weighing-up or contrasting of competing claims. The test is relative in an additional sense, however, for Arbitrator Huber also stated that '[m]anifestations of territorial sovereignty assume, it is true, different forms, according to conditions of time and place.'[110] This would

---

[105] See Award of Tribunal in *Island of Palmas*, above note 70, at 870.

[106] 'Not since the 16th century,' maintains Jennings, 'has it been possible to argue that a mere discovery, coupled with the intention eventually to occupy, is sufficient to create a title.' See Jennings, above note 56, at 4. Discovery therefore held its own in accounts of the acquisition of title in classical international law—and came with very clear legal consequences: Anghie, A., *Imperialism, Sovereignty and the Making of International Law* (Cambridge: Cambridge University Press, 2005), 82.

[107] See Award of Tribunal in *Island of Palmas*, above note 70, at 869.

[108] PCIJ Rep. Ser. A/B, No. 53, at 46.

[109] See the Pacific Order in Council 1893, which applied in part to '[i]slands and places which are for the time being *under no civilised government*' (s. 4 (c)) (emphasis added) and that, amongst those groups of islands singled out for particular mention, were the Solomon Islands—but '*so far as they are not within the jurisdiction of the German Empire*' (s. 6 (1) (emphasis added)). See, further, Farran, above note 13, at 442.

[110] See Award of Tribunal in *Island of Palmas*, above note 70, at 840.

imply that acts of sovereignty are to be constructed, understood, and calculated in accordance with the overall conditions in which they take place and that what might not meet the standard in one set of circumstances might well do so in another: 'Although continuous in principle,' Arbitrator Huber reasoned, 'sovereignty cannot be exercised in fact at every moment on every point of a territory. The intermittence and discontinuity compatible with the maintenance of the right necessarily differ according as inhabited or uninhabited regions are involved, or regions enclosed within territories in which sovereignty is incontestably displayed or again regions accessible from, for instance, the high seas.'[111]

That sovereignty would have been exhibited or demonstrated— or, again, to refer to Arbitrator Huber, 'exercised'—over Pitcairn Island in a manner not identical to how it is used within the base territory of the United Kingdom is not sufficient to disrupt or derail any claim to sovereignty; if anything, it would be a living testament to what Arbitrator Huber envisaged with his formulation in 1928. So, in our view, the development of separate and distinct infrastructures of governance within a single polity stand to be regarded as instances of what has been called *intraterritoriality*: '[j]ust as extraterritoriality has long been a way to conceptually draw maps, to redefine what is inside and outside the scope of a sovereign's law, intraterritoriality has served to delineate differences within national borders.'[112] That very much appears to be what was envisaged by the Judicature Ordinance 1970, made by the Governor of Pitcairn Island,[113] which provided that 'the common law, the rules of equity and the statutes of general application as in force in and for England at the commencement of this Ordinance shall be in force in

---

[111] Ibid.

[112] Raustiala, K., *Does the Constitution Follow the Flag? Territoriality and Extraterritoriality in American Law* (2009), 3 (draft copy on file with authors).

[113] Pursuant to the Pitcairn Order 1970 which had been occasioned by the independence of Fiji in 1970; the Pitcairn Order 1970 replaced the Pitcairn Order in Council 1952. Through to that point, the Pitcairn Order in Council 1952 provided that the Governor of Fiji should also serve as Governor of Pitcairn as well as some neighbouring though uninhabited islands. The Judicature Ordinance 1970 is also responsible for creating a Supreme Court for Pitcairn Island—with the same jurisdiction there as the High Court of Justice has in England; the Pitcairn Court of Appeal was created by virtue of the Pitcairn Court of Appeal Order 2000, SI 2000/1341. See, further, the territorial terms of the Sexual Offences Act 1956: above note 3.

the Islands'.[114] We see here scope for a varied—or variable—application of the law of the United Kingdom,[115] a feature not altogether absent from the Sexual Offences Act 1956 itself.[116] We might draw a certain equivalence with Norfolk Island, where the entire Pitcairn population moved in June 1856; a community has nevertheless continued to exist on Norfolk Island and the territory today is under legislation of 1979 as an external territory of Australia with extensive autonomy in domestic affairs.[117] What is important for this assessment is that it bears witness to the chequered and incremental assertions of jurisdiction of the United Kingdom over Pitcairn Island, tied in as these were with the arrangements—political, economic, cultural, and otherwise—the islanders had made and were making for themselves. There was, to be sure, an ineluctable admixture of these two processes, as if they were running parallel to one another. Yet what is striking from this

---

[114] S. 14 (1). Further, in s. 14 (2) of the Ordinance, it was provided:

All the laws of England extended to the Islands by the last preceding subsection shall be in force therein so far only as the local circumstances and the limits of local jurisdiction permit and subject to any existing or future Ordinance and for the purpose of facilitating the application of the said laws it shall be lawful to construe the same with such formal alterations not affecting the substance as to names, localities, courts, offices, persons, moneys, penalties and otherwise as may be necessary to render the same applicable to the circumstances.

Note, further, the Judicature (Courts) Ordinance 1999, adopted by the Governor of Pitcairn, which stipulates that 'the common law, the rules of equity and the statutes of general application as in force and for England for the time being shall be in force in the Islands . . . so far only as the local circumstances and the limits of local jurisdiction permit and subject to any existing or future ordinance' (s. 16 (1)).

[115] A practice—and formulation—not, it would seem, unusual for the United Kingdom: 'this language has been used in legislation for British overseas possessions for many years without causing difficulties'. See above note 14, para. 11 (per Lord Hoffmann). See, also, Roberts-Wray, above note 9, at 545. For Lord Denning, in *Nyali Ltd v Attorney General* [1956] 1 QB 1, such a stipulation was a 'wise provision' for the management of overseas territories: ibid, at 17. See, however, Angelo, A. H. and Townend, A., 'Pitcairn: A Contemporary Comment', *New Zealand Journal of Public International Law* 1 (2003), 229–243, 234–235.

[116] With its provision that the Act shall not extend to Scotland (s. 54 (1)) and only exceptional application (ie, s. 50) to Northern Ireland (s. 54 (2)). See above note 3. More recently, the Sexual Offences Act 2003 extends to England and Wales only, subject to s. 137 and subsections (2) to (4) of that Act (s. 142 (1)); there is qualified application to Northern Ireland (s. 142 (2)) and to Scotland (s. 142 (3)).

[117] The Supreme Court of Pitcairn noted that the Governor of New South Wales was appointed with delegated powers to legislate for Norfolk Island, 'but also with the added instruction to refrain from making any laws other than those desired by the Pitcairners'. See above note 28, at para. 64. See, also, Wahlroos, above note 9, at 335.

relation of events is that the United Kingdom's various assertions of jurisdiction occurred neither prior to nor were they consequent upon some magical moment of the acquisition of territory; at each point along the way, they came to resemble an 'exercise of sovereign rights'[118]—on the terms of the *Island of Palmas* arbitration[119]—that somehow came to be constitutive of the territorial sovereignty that we now so take for granted.

## Sovereign Title and Sovereign Obligations

Once we have dealt with the basics of territorial acquisition, our attentions should focus on the *consequences* of sovereign title—for while certain rights and entitlements might emerge or be created in respect of territorial acquisitions,[120] it is an inescapable fact that public international law also stipulates certain obligations in respect of those States with (or proclaiming) sovereign title. These obligations can arise from international custom, or from the conventional commitments of States—such as the 1945 Charter of the United Nations which contains, in Chapter XI of its text, the 'Declaration Regarding Non-Self-Governing Territories'.[121] According to the Charter, such territories are those 'whose peoples have not yet attained a full measure of self-government',[122] and there can be no doubt that Pitcairn Island is such a territory for the purposes of the Declaration; not even the United Kingdom has questioned this and the territory is indeed listed in General Assembly Resolution 66(I).[123]

---

[118] Above note 108.         [119] Above note 70.

[120] Where cession involved a transfer of title between states, or an 'effective conveyance of . . . rights', the creation of 'original title' would occur by virtue of the other modes of territorial acquisition: Jennings, above note 56, at 16–17.

[121] 892 UNTS 119. Chapter XI comprises two articles—and two articles alone: Art. 73 and Art. 74. See, further, de Deckker, P., 'Decolonisation Processes in the South Pacific Islands: A Comparative Analysis Between Metropolitan Powers', *Victoria University of Wellington Law Review* 26 (1996), 355–371.

[122] On what follows, see Chapter 14 of Crawford, above note 12 ('Non-Self-Governing Territories: the Law and Practice of Self-Determination'); Crawford provides references to all of the important literature on this topic, though he singles out for special mention Sureda, A. R., *The Evolution of the Right of Self-Determination. A Study of United Nations Practice* (Leiden: Sijthoff, 1973). See, further, Franck, T. M. and Hoffman, P., 'The Right of Self-Determination in Very Small Places', *New York University Journal of International Law & Politics* 8 (1976), 331–386.

[123] See Crawford, above note 12, at 752.

The United Nations Charter also mentions the *concept* of human rights,[124] but the full scope of this canon awaited more detailed specification in the 1966 United Nations Covenants on Civil and Political Rights,[125] and, then, on Economic, Cultural and Social Rights.[126] At the same time, the concept of human rights was fleshed out in a series of regional treaties, among which we would include the 1950 European Convention on Human Rights,[127] and an important bulwark of thematic instruments—such as the 1979 United Nations Convention on the Elimination of All Forms of Discrimination Against Women.[128] This latter instrument, which entered into force in September 1981, does not directly address the challenges arising out of the Pitcairn prosecutions, but the General Assembly Declaration on the Elimination of Violence Against Women, adopted without a vote in December 1993, does.[129] The Declaration is of immediate relevance to the protection of women against sexual offences involving rape, or the abuse of children, though it is not clear that it engages the question of incest. Under Article 4 of the Declaration, State Parties have a number of broad obligations; for example, it is provided that 'States should pursue by all appropriate means and without delay a policy of eliminating violence against women.' This provision catalogues the numerous avenues for

---

[124] As one of its purposes in Art. 1 (3). See, also, Art. 13 (1) (b), Art. 55 (c), Art. 62, Art. 68 and Art. 76. See Farer, T. J. and Gaer, F., 'The UN and Human Rights: At the End of the Beginning' in Roberts, A. and Kingsbury, B. (eds), *United Nations, Divided World: The UN's Roles in International Relations* (Oxford: Clarendon Press, 2nd edn, 1993), 240. For a detailed concentration on this matter in respect of the Pitcairn prosecutions, see Trenwith, A., 'The Empire Strikes Back: Human Rights and the Pitcairn Proceedings', *Journal of South Pacific Law* 7 (2003): <http://www.paclii.org/journals/fJSPL/vol07no2/3.shtml> and Farran, S., 'The Case of Pitcairn: A Small Island, Many Questions', *Journal of South Pacific Law* 11 (2007), 124–150.

[125] 999 UNTS 171.     [126] 993 UNTS 3.     [127] ETS No. 5.

[128] 1249 UNTS 13.

[129] General Assembly Resolution 48/104 (1993), in which the General Assembly recognized 'that effective implementation of the Convention on the Elimination of All Forms of Discrimination Against Women would contribute to the elimination of violence against women and that the Declaration on the Elimination of Violence Against Women, set forth in the present resolution, *will strengthen and complement that process*' (emphasis added). In a further preambular paragraph in this resolution, the General Assembly announced that it was 'convinced' that 'there is a need for a clear and comprehensive definition of violence against women, a clear statement of the rights to be applied to ensure the elimination of violence against women in all its forms, a commitment by States in respect of their responsibilities, and a commitment by the international community at large to the elimination of violence against women.' On the significance of the Declaration, see Charlesworth, H. and Chinkin, C., *The Boundaries of International Law: A Feminist Analysis* (Manchester: Manchester University Press, 2000), 75.

the implementation of this commitment; for example, Article 4(c) specifies that States should '[e]xercise due diligence to prevent, investigate and, in accordance with national legislation, punish acts of violence against women, whether those acts are perpetrated by the State or by private persons.'[130]

These provisions might be taken to suggest that the Government of the United Kingdom was, in law,[131] *obliged* to undertake the Pitcairn prosecutions; it would have certainly offended the letter as well as the spirit of the Convention if the Government had taken no action whatsoever. Yet, the practical matter was whether the Government *ought* to proceed in terms of criminal prosecutions—or whether it should act in some less dramatic way.[132] The Convention in question, necessarily drafted so as to express very general principles of action, with its requirement of taking 'all appropriate means',[133] provides no guidance. Much the same may be said of the 1989 United Nations Convention on the Rights of the Child,[134] Article 19(1) of which provides that: 'States parties shall take all appropriate legislative, administrative, social and education measures to protect the child from all forms of physical or mental violence, injury of abuse . . . including sexual abuse.' Article 19(2) envisages a wide range of possible protective measures, but, again, does not attempt to spell out in specific or concrete terms what is to be done in particular circumstances.

Perhaps these provisions ought to be connected to their overarching human rights context, in other words, and among other things, the 1966 United Nations Covenant on Civil and Political Rights.[135] When the United Kingdom ratified this Convention in May 1976, it appended to its ratification a list of named territories in respect of the geographical reach of its obligations. This list included one territory, that of

---

[130] See, further, Boyle and Chinkin, above note 15, at 299.

[131] Charlesworth and Chinkin suggest 'how evidence of *opinio juris* can be assembled in order to argue that the Declaration on the Elimination of Violence Against Women has contributed to customary international law'. Above note 129, at 76. Note, also, how the Declaration conceives of and portrays itself in respect of the Convention on the Elimination of All Forms of Discrimination Against Women: above note 129.

[132] Consider, for instance, the position of Herbert Ford, Director of the Seventh Day Adventist Pitcairn Islands Study Center at Pacific Union College in the United States, that 'a formal court trial that meets London standards will not recognize . . . the cultural differences of Pitcairn from much of the outside world.' See 'Academic Calls for "Restorative Justice" of Pitcairn Island' News Release, 7 July 2004 <http://library.puc.edu/pitcairn/>. A model of restorative, rather than adversarial, justice was therefore regarded as more appropriate: see Power, above note 1, at 616. [133] Art. 2.

[134] 1577 UNTS 3. [135] Above note 125.

the British Solomon Islands Protectorate, over which the United Kingdom did not exercise sovereignty, and it excluded a number of other territories—such as the British Indian Ocean Territory—over which it did. The Covenant did not include a Colonial Applications Clause, explicitly making extension to colonial territories optional, and in so far as the list excluded certain dependent territories, the United Kingdom was attempting to get around this fact and make its colonial application optional. Importantly, the list made explicit inclusion of Pitcairn Island, so that the Covenant would have had automatic application there upon ratification.[136] So we are in no doubt of the application of the Covenant to Pitcairn Island, and, to this end, it becomes important to quantify the scope of the right to a remedy for violations of the human rights itemized in the Covenant.

The Covenant is relevant to our assessments in one further respect, and that matter relates to the fact no copy of the Sexual Offences Act 1956—the legislation under which these prosecutions were brought—appears to have been placed on (or made present in) Pitcairn Island at the time when the offences were alleged to have been committed.[137] We are therefore concerned, here, with the rights of the accused,[138] who, it is plain, certainly had neither knowledge, nor means of knowledge, of the relevant statute or of the crimes contained therein. This has implications for the principle of *nulla poena sine lege*, spelt out in Article 11 of the 1948 Universal Declaration of Human Rights,[139] but which also finds expression in Article 15 of the 1966 United Nations Covenant on Civil and Political Rights: 'No one shall be held guilty of any

---

[136] See, further, Aust, A., *Modern Treaty Law and Practice* (Cambridge: Cambridge University Press, 2nd edn, 2007), 203.

[137] See Lord Hope on this point, that: 'Apart from one small book of Pitcairn laws, no legal texts, statutes or law reports were available on the island until about 1997.' Above note 14, at para. 59 (per Lord Hope). Apparently, the earliest provision of a copy of *Halsbury's Statutes* to Pitcairn Island occurred in 1997: Power, above note 1, at 622.

[138] Since there was no '*formal* use of a cultural defence': Power, above note 1, at 619 (emphasis in original); the main line of defence related to legality and promulgation matters, as well as abuse of process. See, further, Power, above note 1, at 610.

[139] UN General Assembly Resolution 217A (III), which provides that: 'No one shall be held guilty of any penal offence on account of any act or omission which did not constitute a penal offence under national or international law at the time when it was committed.' The Declaration, which is not of course a treaty, is understood to rank either as a statement of customary international law, or, alternatively, as an authoritative exposition of the references in the text of the United Nations Charter to human rights (on which, see above note 121). See, further, Meron, T., *Human Rights and Humanitarian Law as Customary International Law* (Oxford: Clarendon Press, 1989), 82–84.

criminal offence on account of any act or omission which did not constitute a criminal offence, under national or international law, at the time when it was committed,' and which goes on to provide that '[n]othing in this article shall prejudice the trial and punishment of any person for any act and omission which, at the time when it was committed, was criminal according to the general principles of law recognized by the community of nations.'[140]

One can appreciate the potential contributions that these provisions could have made in the jurisprudence that resulted from the prosecutions, but neither the Universal Declaration of Human Rights nor the Covenant were so much as mentioned in the Privy Council opinions. In fact, no reference at all is made in terms to public international law in the opinions of Lord Hoffmann,[141] Lord Woolf, or Lord Hope. To be sure, Lord Woolf and Lord Hope, who both penned their own concurring opinions, conceptualized their considerable anxieties over the legitimacy of the proceedings around the notion of abuse of process, and the principle of legality—or, as they put it, the rule of law: for Lord Woolf, '[t]he absence of the required knowledge as to the criminality of their actions and inaccessibility of information could be an appropriate basis for an allegation of abuse of process.'[142] However, he maintained that abuse of process had limitations as to the scope of its application:

Abuse of process should ... be reserved for cases where it would be an affront to justice for the person concerned to be prosecuted. To prosecute an individual for an offence of which he has no means of knowing the details is capable of being such a departure from the requirements of due process as to justify the prosecution being stayed. However, it is of the essence of an argument based on the lack of due process that the individual concerned would if the prosecution proceeded be treated unjustly and in this sense prejudiced. As in this case the appellants suffered no prejudice in view of their state of knowledge an argument based on abuse of process would not be established. It may be the case that the argument under this head could be freestanding and not based on abuse of process. However if this be so the need for prejudice would still be a requirement.[143]

Lord Hope, on the other hand, believed that '[t]he requirement of ascertainability is an essential component of the rule of law,' and that, this being so, 'in the case of statutes of general application in force in England, as the Governor should have known, it was incapable of being

[140] Above note 125.   [141] With whom Lords Steyn and Carswell concurred.
[142] Above note 14, at para. 44 (per Lord Woolf).   [143] Ibid.

met on Pitcairn'.[144] Taken together, the method of legislating for Pitcairn Island was regarded as 'unsatisfactory', and as the basis of considerable 'unease'.[145] Ordinarily, they would have led Lord Hope to
conclude that an abuse of process had indeed happened but, in view of
sections 48 and 52 of the Offences Against the Persons Act 1861,[146]
earlier emendations of the criminal law, Lord Hope went on to question
whether an abuse of process had happened as *a matter of fact*:

> It can be seen from the way these provisions are worded that they were not creating
> new crimes. They assume that the crimes of rape and indecent assault already exist,
> as indeed they did as they were already known to the common law. They were
> building on the common law to this extent only, that they were prescribing the
> penalties that were to attach to these offences . . . . The [relevant] offences men-
> tioned in [the Sexual Offences Act 1956] can therefore be traced back directly to
> the common law. There is an air of unreality about the objection that the appel-
> lants were disadvantaged by the fact that the provisions of . . . the 1956 Act are not
> ascertainable on Pitcairn . . . Here were are dealing with conduct which the com-
> mon law has regarded as criminal for centuries, and the appellants cannot have
> been in any doubt that what they were doing amounted to criminal conduct.[147]

---

[144] Above note 14, at para. 81 (per Lord Hope).

[145] Above note 14, at para. 82 (per Lord Hope).

[146] According to the Act, 'whosoever shall be convicted of the crime of rape shall be
guilty of a felony, and being convicted thereof shall be liable, at the discretion of the court,
to be kept in penal servitude for life or for any term less than three years, or to be
imprisoned for any term not exceeding two years, with or without hard labour' (s. 48);
'[w]hosoever shall be convicted of any indecent assault upon any female, or of any attempt
to have carnal knowledge of any girl under twelve years of age, shall be liable, at the
discretion of the court, to be imprisoned for any term not exceeding two years' (s. 52).

[147] Above note 14, at para. 84 (per Lord Hope). Note, also, the observations of Lord
Hoffmann:

> Their Lordships would accept that the fact that a law had not been published and
> could not reasonably have been known to exist may be a ground for staying a
> prosecution for contravention of that law as an abuse of process. It is however
> unnecessary to discuss the philosophical basis or legal limits of such a principle
> because, in the light of the concurrent findings of fact and the agreement of both the
> lower courts as to the exercise of what on any view is a discretion, their Lordships
> think that it is an impossible task to persuade the Board to interfere. They can find
> no error of principle in the way in which the discretion was exercised and on the
> facts as found would have exercised it in the same way. These were serious offences
> and the balance to which Lord Steyn referred in [*Regina v Latif* [1966] 1 WLR 104,
> 112–113] comes down firmly in favour of bringing them before a court of justice.

Ibid, at para. 24 (per Lord Hoffmann). The Privy Council did not advert to the fact
that the concept of incest, conceived as a crime, differs from culture to culture, and only
became a criminal offence in the United Kingdom in 1908.

We are left with the 1950 European Convention on Human Rights which, again, was nowhere mentioned in the jurisprudence of the Privy Council. This Convention is fundamentally different from such code as the 1948 Universal Declaration of Human Rights and the 1966 United Nations Covenants because of its institutional infrastructure which has made it possible to build up an elaborate jurisprudence concerning human rights, developing the generally stated provisions of the text of the Convention itself.[148] The Convention, as developed in this jurisprudence, is therefore capable of providing much more specific guidance as to the *obligations* of State Parties and, it is in this context, that we refer to Article 7(1) of the Convention ('No punishment without law'), which is identical to Article 15(1) of the United Nations Covenant on Civil and Political Rights. It provides that '[n]o one shall be held guilty of any criminal offence on account of any act or omission which did not constitute a criminal offence under national or international law at the time when it was committed'.[149] Article 7(2) is almost identical to Article 15(2) of the Covenant on Civil and Political Rights, for it provides that '[t]his article shall not prejudice the trial and punishment of any person for any act or commission which, at the time when it is committed, was criminal according to the principles of law recognized by civilized nations'.[150]

To be sure, the Privy Council did recall *dicta* from Lord Bingham in the House of Lords in *R v Rimmington* (2005),[151] but it did not cultivate that part of his ruling where close attention was paid to the function of Article 7 of the European Convention on Human Rights; there he said that Article 7:

[S]ustains [the] contention that a criminal offence must be clearly defined in law, and represents the operation of 'the principle of legal certainty' [which] enables each community to regulate itself 'with reference to the norms prevailing in the society in which they live. That generally entails that the law must be adequately accessible—an individual must have an indication of the legal rules applicable in a given case—and he must be able to foresee the consequences of his actions, in particular to be able to avoid incurring the sanction of the criminal law'.[152]

---

[148] See Steiner, H. J., Alston, P., and Goodman, R., *International Human Rights in Context: Law, Politics, Morals* (Oxford: Oxford University Press, 3rd edn, 2008), 933.
[149] Above note 127.        [150] Ibid.
[151] [2006] 1 AC 459. In the opinion of Lord Hope, that is: above note 14, Lord Hope at para. 81.        [152] [2006] 1 AC 459, at [30].

This might strike the reader as somewhat surprising, especially given the fact that, in the lower courts, it was conceded that the European Convention on Human Rights applied to Pitcairn Island.[153] Yet, as the case was presented and determined in the Privy Council, the Convention was treated as irrelevant on the grounds that this was a mistake; that it had never been extended to Pitcairn Island under Article 56(1) of the Convention, now called the Territorial Application provision, but originally and more realistically called the Colonial Applications Article.[154]

It is certainly the case that there has never been a notice of extension, and we have no concrete information as to why this never happened. One of us is on record as arguing that in the case of British overseas territories which are directly run from London, and which possess no democratic institutions or local autonomy arrangements, an extension is not required—but, in making the argument, Pitcairn Island was not singled out as one of the examples termed British non-autonomous overseas territories (or BNOTs).[155] This was because it does enjoy some limited measure of local autonomy. The function of the Colonial Applications Article in the Convention, the United Kingdom consistently argued in negotiations, was to enable the metropolitan government to consult with the colonial government, and only extend the Convention with local consent. So far as we are aware, no such consultation has taken place in the case of Pitcairn Island and it is a little short of bizarre that the United Kingdom Government should take the position that the residents there should be deprived of the protection of the Convention. It might be thought even more curious, in view of the fact that virtually identical provisions of the United Nations Covenant on Civil and Political Rights *do* apply there,[156] that there was no detailed appreciation of the human rights dimension to the prosecutions. But that, in the end, was the way in which the matter was handled.

To all of this we must add the accompanying silence in the jurisprudence of the Human Rights Act 1998—which, we can assume, did

---

[153] Case for the Appellants Stevens Christian and Len Brown, at p. 6.

[154] Originally numbered Art. 63. See, in particular, Simpson, A. W. B., *Human Rights and the End of Empire: Britain and the Genesis of the European Convention* (Oxford: Oxford University Press, 2001). See, also, Aust, above note 136, at 203.

[155] See Moor, L. and Simpson, A. W. B., 'Ghosts of Colonialism in the European Convention on Human Rights', *British Yearbook of International Law* 75 (2005), 121–193.          [156] Above note 136.

not apply. The Sexual Offences Act 1956 applied because it was regarded as a statute of general application, and, therefore, applied under the terms of section 14(1) of the Judicature Order 1970 ('[s]ubject to the provisions of the next succeeding subsection the common law, the rules of equity and the statutes of general application as in force in and for England *at the commencement of this Ordinance* shall be in force for the Islands').[157] The Sexual Offences Act was at that time in force, and we see a similar theme to the later legislation of the Judicature (Courts) Ordinance 1999. Section 16(1) of this Ordinance announced that '[s]ubject to the provisions of subsection (2) the common law, the rules of equity and the statutes of general application as in force in and for England for the time being shall be in force in the Islands'; according to section 16(2), these laws would be in force 'so far only as the local circumstances and the limits of local jurisdiction permit'. If the Human Rights Act is to be ranked as a 'statute of general application', then, it is clear, the Act would form part of the law that governs Pitcairn Island. However, if the Convention was not regarded as applicable—a point that might be inferred from the jurisprudence in the Privy Council—it would seem somewhat peculiar that the Human Rights Act, whose purpose in part is to incorporate the Convention into the law of the United Kingdom,[158] would nevertheless apply. For better or for worse, the point was not raised before the Privy Council, and so we are left in further doubt as to whether this is indeed the legal position, whether it should be so and, if so, the grounds on which the case is made that the Human Rights Act, and the European Convention on Human Rights for that matter, are not applicable to Pitcairn Island.

## Concluding Reflections

We conclude our contribution to this volume by emphasizing the anomalous and even unique nature of Pitcairn Island—and of the prosecutions for sexual offences relating thereto. However, historical

---

[157] Emphasis added.
[158] Consider Bamforth, N. C., 'Understanding the Impact and Status of the Human Rights Act 1998 within English Law', *NYU School of Law Global Law Working Paper* (2005), Series 60.

investigations of the territory, its population, and the changing config-
urations of its relationship with the United Kingdom, have helped
deepen our understanding of the full *extent* of this anomaly, of why it
has been what it has been—and of what it has in the end become. We
have attempted to chronicle the path of this relationship against the
backdrop of the provisions of public international law, but also *via* the
instructions and lessons of comparative example, and this has allowed us
an appropriate context, indeed an important platform, to develop our
critical appraisals of the situation. It ought to be evident from what we
have written that, as one comes into closer contact with the realities of
these prosecutions, this really was no straightforward assertion of jurisdiction by the United Kingdom—at the very least, it is one that res-
urrected and brought to the fore a labyrinthine past of actions and
interactions concerning the United Kingdom with both the place and
the people of Pitcairn Island.

   We have not just had reference to the provisions of public international law. We have had to enter—and to understand and
engage—the central elements and the dynamic of the legislative
relationship that the United Kingdom developed with the island and
its islanders. This has meant that the invocation of the Sexual
Offences Act 1956 could not be read in splendid (and convenient)
isolation; it has taken its place as the next chronological step in an
ongoing performance (or series of performances) of sovereignty. That
has been the occasion for some to tease out and to dwell upon the
colonial dimensions of this narrative—a sort of colonialism practiced
before, during, and after decolonization, as it were[159]—but, in this
situation, we have encountered the additional spark of the *origins* of
the settlement on Pitcairn Island of *British* nationals, and of the
*consequences* of it as a landing post for the mutineers on the
*Bounty*.[160] Through the telling idiom of jurisdiction, we have
explored the unfolding relationship between the United Kingdom
and Pitcairn Island and its islanders, leading us, in the penultimate
section of the chapter, to ask after the obligations that stem from any
attainment of sovereign title in public international law. With
reference to the specifications of human rights, we hope to have

---

[159] See Farran, above note 13, and, further, Angelo, T. and Wright, F., 'Pitcairn:
Sunset on Empire?', *New Zealand Law Journal* (2004), 431–432, and Winchester, S.,
*Outposts: Journeys to the Surviving Relics of the British Empire* (2004), 13.
   [160] Cf. Mason, above note 25.

demonstrated in some measure the *problematique* which the Pitcairn prosecutions have entailed for the very concept of law itself,[161] and of the demands of justice in what Lord Hope has called 'one of the most remote communities in the world'.[162]

[161] See the discussion at above notes 142–147 (and accompanying text). A theme superbly investigated and developed by Taggart, M., 'Ruled By Law?', *Modern Law Review* 69 (2006), 1006–1025.

[162] Above note 14, at para. 58 (per Lord Hope). See, also, above notes 12 and 20.

# 6

# 'A Million Mutinies Now': Why Claims of Cultural Uniqueness Cannot be Used to Justify Violations of Basic Human Rights

*Colm O'Cinneide*

The trial and successful prosecution of six male members of the Pitcairn Island community on charges of rape, indecent assault, and other sexual offences generated considerable media and academic interest. While the protracted and controversial case was ongoing, some commentators argued that the prosecution represented the imposition of a set of external and alien legal norms by a dominant and overbearing metropolitan authority upon a small and vulnerable community.[1] In the eyes

---

[1] See eg A. Trenwith, 'The Empire Strikes Back: Human Rights and the Pitcairn Proceedings' (2003) 7(2) *Journal of South Pacific Law*, Part V, available at <http://www.paclii.org/journals/fJSPL/vol07no2/3.shtml> (last accessed 12 February 2009) (hereafter 'The Empire Strikes Back'): '[T]he law that the United Kingdom seeks to impose is a foreign one; those subject to it have had little or no say in its creation, and will have almost no say in its implementation. Yet they are the ones who stand to lose the most—able-bodied men, such as those charged, are needed to man the longboats which form an integral part of Pitcairn's lifeline for re-supply. Without them, the island cannot survive . . . ' See also S. Farran, 'The Case of Pitcairn: A Small Island, Many Questions' (2007) 11(2) *Journal of South Pacific Law* 124–150, 143 (hereafter 'The Case of Pitcairn'): ' . . . consideration of the unique circumstances of Pitcairn and the damaging impact of the trial procedures have been ignored . . . '; and the comments of Herbert Ford reported in a press release, 'Academic Calls for "Restorative Justice" for Pitcairn Island', News Release, 7 July 2004, Pitcairn Islands Study Center, available at <http:library.puc.edu/pitcairn/> (last accessed 12 February 2009): 'The downtown London trial process as planned may well rip Pitcairn apart'. For media commentary in a similar vein, see Gordon McLaughlan, *New Zealand Herald*, 2 October 2004: 'Didn't someone in [the New Zealand] cabinet say, . . . "Why destroy one of the most remote communities in the world when we could perhaps do some healing here, support any people who feel they've been misused, and take steps to make sure women are not being preyed on, even if it is part of the longstanding mores of this society?".'

of these critics, the indicted islanders were effectively being penalized for sharing certain cultural and ethical assumptions which were very different from those prevailing within the metropolitan mainstream.[2] The argument was also made that the prosecutions endangered the continued survival of the unique community on Pitcairn: the laying of criminal charges against a substantial proportion of the adult male population could readily be seen as creating a serious risk that this small and unique island community would be endangered.[3]

These criticisms gave rise to a media and academic narrative about the case, which placed great emphasis on the isolation and uniqueness of Pitcairn. It depicted the trial process as a seemingly ludicrous spectacle, whereby the UK, remembering that it owned a remote Pacific outcrop, descended upon the islanders with the full controlling might of a modern prosecutorial system, and demanded conformity to metropolitan norms established many thousands of miles away.[4]

So is this narrative broadly true? Did the Pitcairn case involve the crushing application of metropolitan cultural norms by external legal *fiat* to a vulnerable and unique community? Were the critics of the prosecution correct in arguing that it constituted an overbearing and unjustified assault on the cultural specificity of the Pitcairn Island community?

This chapter concludes not. Instead, it argues unapologetically that the prosecution represented a legitimate intervention in the life of the Pitcairn community, on the basis that it served to protect and vindicate the basic human rights of the women on the island, whose rights to bodily integrity had been violated by the sexual abuse to which they had been subjected. The protection of such basic rights must take priority over the desire to insulate unique cultures such as that existing on Pitcairn against the shock of change.

---

[2] See eg Trenwith, 'The Empire Strikes Back', Part IV: 'The conflict that arises is with British culture, and although it is foreign to them, it is an inherent part of the law under which the defendants are to be tried.' See also Farran, 'The Case of Pitcairn', 142–144.

[3] See eg Trenwith, 'The Empire Strikes Back'; Farran, 'The Case of Pitcairn', 149–150.

[4] See eg Trenwith, 'The Empire Strikes Back', who refers in Part V to the legal basis for the Pitcairn proceedings as a 'hastily constructed edifice'; and A. H. Angelo and A. Townend, 'Pitcairn: A Contemporary Comment' (2003) 1 *New Zealand Journal of Public International Law* 229, 242. Farran goes so far as to suggest that 'The Pitcairn case however, appears to have provided the motive and opportunity for strengthening British jurisdiction over Pitcairn so that would appear to make any possibility of self-determination and perhaps even its survival unlikely in the foreseeable future': see Farran, 'The Case of Pitcairn', 150.

This argument is developed here through analysis of the 'cultural' dimension to the Pitcairn case. It is easy to portray the prosecutions brought against the Pitcairn Islanders as an exercise in cultural imperialism, but that is fundamentally misleading. To start with, as set out below, if one probes claims that the Pitcairn prosecution infringed important communal cultural rights, it rapidly becomes apparent that these claims are simply factually unsustainable. So too is the argument that the cultural specificity of Pitcairn Island should have been respected in an alternative approach to that adopted by the prosecution authorities, the trial judges, and ultimately, the Privy Council. These 'cultural' claims are rooted in a lazy and excessive reverence for cultural difference, linked perhaps to a stereotyped and simplistic view of Pitcairn culture. The Pitcairn prosecutions were not directed against victimless and harmless sexual practices peculiar to Pitcairn, but instead were targeted at abusive and exploitative behaviour by aggressive males that was little different from similar behaviour in any culture where the abuse of women is relatively unchecked. Sexual violence directed against woman lay at the heart of this case: four out of the six convicted males were found guilty of rape.

Therefore, if one peels away the outer wrapping of tropical cultural exoticism, the Pitcairn case begins to look much less like an alien attack upon a vulnerable culture and more like a necessary intervention to assist an exploited sub-group—the women—to vindicate their basic human rights. Even within the particular culture of Pitcairn, it appears as if the actions of the convicted males were regarded as 'wrong'. Therefore, the use of 'cultural' arguments to attack the prosecutions or the ultimate outcome of the Pitcairn case is ultimately incoherent.[5]

However, even if it could be argued that the prosecutions endangered the unique Pitcairn culture, the particular vulnerability of that culture cannot justify a refusal to vindicate basic rights. To borrow and apply out of its originating context a resonant phrase used as a book title by V. S. Naipaul, there are 'millions of mutinies now', in the form of a multiplicity of different claims of cultural distinctiveness.[6] Every culture

---

[5] See in general the nuanced analysis of the cultural issues at stake in H. Power, 'Pitcairn Island: Sexual Offending, Cultural Difference and Ignorance of the Law' (2007) *Criminal Law Review* 609–629 (hereafter 'Pitcairn Island').

[6] V. S. Naipaul, *India: A Million Mutinies Now* (London: Penguin, 2002), where Naipaul uses the phrase to refer to the dynamism of modern India and the assertiveness of its population.

can claim to be special: every culture can demand some form of special treatment. However, respect for basic human rights norms requires that they must 'trump' these multiple claims of cultural exceptionalism.

As a result, simplistic concepts of 'native' culture or the need to maintain cultural difference cannot be invoked to justify, excuse, or exculpate those who deny basic rights of bodily autonomy and human dignity. Pitcairn may be a unique place with a unique culture, but it can be argued that every culture is unique and different. Therefore, there is no reason why cultural exceptionalism can justify in itself a suspension of basic rights norms, for to accept such a suspension for one culture would invariably open the door for similar claims to be made in respect of every other cultural tradition that could claim to be vulnerable, endangered, or simply different.

## Narrating Pitcairn

Two different narrative strands ran through much of the media commentary on the Pitcairn case.[7] On the one hand, reporting of the case sometimes carried echoes of William Golding's *Lord of the Flies*: the prosecution was presented as peeling back the façade of an apparently idyllic island community and uncovering dark secrets.[8] This first strand portrayed the Pitcairn community as dominated by rapacious males and marooned in a pre-modern past, where sexual abuse and the exploitation of young girls were commonplace.[9] Within this narrative, the prosecution was justified as a necessary intervention by the sovereign authority to protect the victims of this abuse: the metropolitan centre was depicted as intervening to redress barbaric behaviour in the name of human rights, the protection of children, and gender equality.

---

[7] It is not suggested here that commentary on the Pitcairn case can be classified as adhering exclusively to one or the other of these two narrative strands. Instead, the two strands are presented as dominant themes in much of the reporting and analysis of the Pitcairn prosecutions, each made up a series of interwoven and interconnected tropes.

[8] See Power, 'Pitcairn Island', 614–618 for examples of reporting that emphasized the 'pathological' nature of elements of island life.

[9] See eg K. Marks, 'Pitcairn Trial Hears a Litany of Child Sex Abuse', *The Independent*, 3 October 2004.

However, an alternative counter-narrative also emerged, which in contrast painted a picture of tropical innocence (often drawing on narrative tropes associated with Ballantyne's *Coral Island*[10] or Melville's *Typee*[11]). Media reports presented the islanders as living in a self-sustaining community that was cut off from the modern world. Great emphasis was placed on the isolation, simplicity, and rootedness of life on Pitcairn, as well as on the uniqueness of the culture that had emerged on the island.[12] Comparisons were drawn with other Polynesian island cultures, regularly portrayed as prelapsarian oases insulated against the instrumental rationality and normative values of modernity.

This second narrative strand was not alone generated by external media reporting: it also emerged in the attacks on the prosecution mounted by anthropologists familiar with the Pitcairn culture, defence lawyers representing the accused, and islanders who were strongly opposed to the prosecution.[13] All emphasized the isolation and uniqueness of island culture. All also emphasized the gulf that was alleged to exist between the norms and values of the island community and those of the outside world. Specifically, the argument was repeatedly made that the sexual practices which triggered the prosecution should not be understood through a conventional lens: what might qualify as the abuse of underage children in European societies was in the context of Pitcairn an innocent result of customary Polynesian cultural practice and the tendency of young adults in such isolated island societies to reach precocious sexual maturity. In this way, the second narrative strand, with its emphasis on tropical innocence and the specificity of Pitcairn culture, tended to depict the prosecution as a brutal imposition of external cultural norms upon an insulated, isolated, and innocent cultural grouping.[14]

---

[10] R. M. Ballantyne, *Coral Island* (Edinburgh: W & R Chambers, 1857), text available at Project Gutenberg, <http://www.gutenberg.org/etext/646> (last accessed 12 February 2009).

[11] H. Melville, *Typee*, (1846) text available at Project Gutenberg, <http://www.gutenberg.org/etext/9269> (last accessed 12 February 2009).

[12] See again Power, 'Pitcairn Island', 614–18 for examples of reporting that emphasized the isolation and distinctiveness of the island community.

[13] See eg 'US Academic Says Holding Pitcairn Trial Without First Reviewing Documents Would Be Miscarriage Of Justice', News Release, September 2004, Pitcairn Islands Study Center, available at <http:library.puc.edu/pitcairn/> (last accessed 12 February 2009): 'Pitcairn Women Back Sex Trial Accused', *The Guardian*, 29 September 2004; 'Pitcairn Trial a Miscarriage of Justice, Says Former Islander', *New Zealand Herald*, 26 October 2004.

[14] See eg the material cited at note 1 above, which in general primarily adheres to the tropes of this second narrative.

The second narrative strand also surfaced in external media reporting, which contrasted the simplicity and rootedness of the culture of the Pitcairn islanders with the alleged heavy-handedness of the UK government's intervention, the artificiality of the trial process, and the surreal side-products of the prosecution (which included the construction at great cost of a special jail on the island and the eventual incarceration of one-quarter of its adult male population). As the legal process unfolded, the 'authentic' values of the islanders were even contrasted with the personal conduct of the chief prosecutor.[15]

Finally, the tropes of the second narrative strand loomed large in how commentators expressed concern that the unique cultural particularity of Pitcairn seemed to be seriously imperilled by the prosecution.[16] There was clearly some threat to the ongoing survival of the island community, as the imprisonment of so many of the island's adult male population could have rendered the largely subsistence-based economy of the island unsustainable. Media reports and some islanders themselves also expressed concern that the intrusive impact of the trial proceedings ran the risk of irrevocably changing the way of life of the islanders. The prospect of cultural annihilation was therefore raised: tropical innocence is often portrayed as fragile and precarious, and the second narrative strand tapped into this trope in depicting the unique and irreplaceable island culture as endangered by the clumsy prosecution.

### The alleged failure to respect the uniqueness of Pitcairn

The perspective of the Pitcairn case offered by the first narrative strand appeared to be vindicated by the outcome of the prosecution and the judgments of the various courts that adjudicated the matter. It is certainly reflected in Lord Hoffmann's conclusion that '[t]hese were serious offences and the balance ... comes down firmly in favour of bringing them before a court of justice'.[17]

However, the themes of the second narrative strand have been echoed in some (but certainly not all) of the academic commentary that has followed

---

[15] See eg the comments of an islander on the conduct of the Pitcairn Public Prosecutor quoted in K. Marks, 'Pitcairn Sex Trial Lawyers Caught In Fancy Dress', *The Independent*, 2 July 2003.
[16] See note 1 above; see also N. Squires, 'Sex Abuse Trial Threatens Pitcairn's Future', *The Telegraph*, 12 October 2002.     [17] *Christian v R* [2006] UKPC 47, para. 24.

the eventual determination of the case. Much of this commentary has taken the form of a groundswell of discontent about how the prosecution was handled. Different criticisms have been made about different aspects of the process. A recurring theme throughout much of this work is that to many commentators, the cultural specificity of Pitcairn appeared to have been wholly disregarded throughout the trial process.[18]

This apparent neglect of Pitcairn's uniqueness is alleged to have taken several forms. Some commentators (including several in this book) have claimed that the prosecution authorities and the courts failed to give serious consideration to the island's special history. Particular attention has been drawn to the question marks that surround the exact status of the UK's claim to exercise sovereignty over the island. Questions have also been asked as to whether there was a sufficient relationship of dependency and active support between the metropolitan centre and the island to justify the exercise of coercive power by the UK prosecution authorities, and whether there was a sufficient promulgation of the laws alleged to have been violated on the island, given the uniquely isolated nature of the Pitcairn community.

Many of these issues were ventilated during the course of the litigation, and are discussed elsewhere in this volume. However, most of these specific areas of concern, and in particular, the questions of the historical status of Pitcairn, the extent and sufficiency of the pre-existing relationship between UK public authorities and the islanders, and whether the laws in question were sufficiently promulgated could be seen as 'proxy' issues: these questions stand in for the deeper underlying question as to whether Pitcairn's cultural particularity and unique isolation were sufficiently recognized and appreciated in the course of the trial process.[19]

Legal argumentation 'translates' disputes about facts and the application of normative values into its own particular linguistic and

---

[18] See eg the materials cited in note 1 above.

[19] This is not to dismiss the separateness and importance of each of these distinct issues. However, Pitcairn's cultural uniqueness constitutes the unifying theme that links most of these specific arguments. For example, central to the question of promulgation is whether Pitcairn's isolation was adequately taken into account in the finding of the Judicial Committee of the Privy Council that no substantial issue arose as to whether the islanders could be deemed to have sufficient notice of the existence and implications of the relevant criminal legislation. The same point can be made about most of the other legal issues that arose during the litigation and which have been subsequently discussed in this book and elsewhere: they turn in one way or another on whether Pitcairn's uniqueness should have been accorded more weight in the deliberations of the prosecution authorities, the first instance tribunal, and the appellate courts.

seriously contrary to the criminal law it does not follow that there should be a prosecution, let alone a conviction and then punishment. If the investigators or prosecutors do not comply with the correct procedures—as in the most dramatic instance when they obtain cogent and reliable evidence by oppressive means such as torture—the defendant should not be convicted. And it denigrates the importance of the requirement of legality to say, as people do, that such acquittals are 'technical only', because although the defendant committed the offence, it is irrational for the prosecutors to treat the defendant in violation of the values *in the name of which* they pursue prosecution and conviction.[2] If you accept this argument, then I suggest you should accept the possibility that although the defendants on Pitcairn may have done wrong, there still could have been grounds for acquitting them.

With this in mind, I direct my argument to the question whether there was an 'abuse of legality' in applying 'British standards' in imputing knowledge of the law to the defendants in spite of strong evidence that they lived within a distinctly non-British culture of sexual conduct, encouraged in the absence of law enforcement mechanisms. There were two 'abuses' in my view. First, there was a plausible argument that the British Crown lacked jurisdiction over Pitcairn, even though the strong, and prevailing, view in all Pitcairn courts was that the British Crown did have jurisdiction. It was not disputed that Britain had barely contributed materially or spiritually towards its claimed possession in spite of Pitcairn's economic and social isolation, and special needs. In fact, it begs the question to assume that there was any relationship between the communities at all in calling the British failure to install the trappings of a British legal culture on the island a matter of 'neglect', since that word implies that there existed a relationship between Britain and Pitcairn giving rise to specific obligations. It is more realistic to suppose that, if there was neglect, it was that of the New Zealand government, whose officials actually did something from time to time in connection with the island. The nagging doubt that some semblance of a connection—something that would 'colour the right'—should have existed is something that we cannot merely wish away. I suggest that for Crown

---

[2] If, for example, the police assault a suspect and extract a confession, and then use that confession to secure the suspect's conviction for assault, this makes a mockery of the consistency and moral integrity of the legal system. If the defendant may not assault, neither may the police.

conceptual terms. At times, this can result in a strange distortion of the 'true' issues and the establishment of a reified conceptual framework that is divorced from the lived experience of those most directly affected by the trial. The Pitcairn Islanders who opposed the prosecution on the basis that British justice was suddenly sprung upon their island community must have been a little surprised to see this resentment transformed into the technical language of promulgation and assertions of continuing jurisdiction. Similarly, the argument that the sexual practices at issue were accepted and 'normal' within Pitcairn culture was never directly addressed by the courts: the 'proxy' arguments were deployed in its place.

Nevertheless, the proxy arguments became a way of articulating the concerns of islanders and external commentators about the prosecution. The Privy Council ultimately rejected these arguments, with only Lord Hope appearing to consider that they were worthy of close and sustained analysis.[20] However, the proxy arguments have resurfaced in academic commentary, much of which has been very concerned to find ways of giving shape to the troubling sense that Pitcairn's uniqueness had been given insufficient attention. In this way, the tropes of the second narrative, and in particular its concern that the unique island culture and island values had been trampled upon and disregarded by the prosecution, continue to resonate.

## The incoherence of the cultural narrative and the reality of the sexual abuse that occurred on Pitcairn

Both the first and second narratives present excessively one-sided accounts of the Pitcairn case. The simple 'bad men' analysis underlying Lord Hoffmann's brusque dismissal of the case may be a little reductionist: there are troubling aspects about the Pitcairn case.[21] However, the second narrative, with its concentration upon the island's isolation, its vulnerable culture, and the apparent arrogance of the metropolitan centre imposing external values upon largely innocent islanders, is riddled with problems and ultimately incoherent.

This incoherence manifests itself in a variety of ways, all linked to the uncomfortable lack of fit of the second narrative's tropes with the actual

---

[20] See the analysis in Power, 'Pitcairn Island', 620–629.
[21] Ibid., especially the excellent analysis at 626–629.

facts on the ground found to exist by the trial court, confirmed by the appellate courts, and subsequently unchallenged by the lawyers for the accused or academic commentators. The picture of the relationship between Pitcairn and the UK that emerges from the court findings is much more complex and well-developed than that depicted by the second narrative. UK criminal law had been recognized as applicable on Pitcairn at regular intervals over time.[22] UK public authorities have committed more resources to the Pitcairn community than is sometimes depicted as being the case.[23] In other words, there has been a consistent, accepted, and well-established link between the island community and the UK, which included the acceptance that UK criminal law was applicable on the island. Suggestions that the islanders lived in glorious isolation, wholly separate and detached from the UK and its criminal justice system, appear to be exaggerated.

In addition, it is apparent from reading the findings of fact made by the judges of the newly-appointed Supreme Court of Pitcairn Island sitting alone at first instance (reiterated in the subsequent appellate court decisions) that the island community itself certainly did not collectively subscribe to the tropes of the second narrative. The opponents of the prosecution dominated media headlines and reporting of the case. However, it is notable that in a closed and insular community, the prosecution were able to find victims of the crimes in question who were willing to testify. Without this willingness, the case would simply have collapsed. It is possible to infer from this that at least some islanders, and in particular the victims of the abuse in question, did not see the prosecution as an external imposition of alien values upon their vulnerable and unique culture, but rather accepted its legitimacy and necessity. The picture that occasionally surfaced in the second narrative of a unified island community resisting external pressure appears to be at best a considerable simplification: at worst, it may be a total distortion.[24]

---

[22] See *Christian v R (No.2)* [2005] PNSC 1, paras 96–110.

[23] Ibid, paras 111–47.

[24] Farran expresses concern that 'the private lives of Pitcairn islanders have been subject to the scrutiny of outsiders; they have been required to testify against relatives and neighbours; to give evidence in front of strangers; to be represented and judged by foreigners; and now must deal with a community torn by accusation and conviction': 'The Case of Pitcairn', 147. This may indeed be a perception shared by many islanders, but absent from this analysis of the impact of the prosecutions is any analysis of the perspectives and views of the victims who gave evidence against the accused, and who presumably would have a different view of the trial process.

Some of those who gave evidence appear to be islanders who had chosen to leave the island and reside elsewhere.[25] However, it should not be inferred from this that the prosecution was based upon the absorption of external values by individuals who had cut their ties with the island. Victims who left Pitcairn may have had good cause to do so. The findings of fact made at first instance make it very clear that serious sexual violence appears to have periodically taken place on Pitcairn.

As summarized in the judgment of the Supreme Court of the Pitcairn Island in *R v Christian (No. 2)*,[26] the trial judges concluded that non-consensual sexual assault and/or rape had occurred in five out of seven cases, of a type that no contemporary culture would readily claim to be 'acceptable' within its own set of ethical and moral self-understandings. Several of these assaults involved gang rape, violence, and forcible penetration. Of the six men convicted, one, Dennis Christian, was convicted only of the lesser charge of sexual offending as a result of having sex as a 15 to 17 year old with a girl who was between 12 and 14. He received a non-custodial sentence. The other five were convicted of rape and/or indecent assault.

This is an important point to emphasize: at times the second narrative presented the Pitcairn case as being all about consensual underage sex, but rape and indecent assault lay at the heart of the prosecution. The 'tropical innocence' trope of the second narrative, with its insistence that the prosecution was an attempt to criminalize innocent, accepted, and harmless Polynesian sexual practices between young girls and slightly older men, completely disregards the much darker reality.[27]

In addition, it is worth noting that not only were rape and serious assault the key elements of the prosecution 'package' of charges, but this behaviour had gone unchecked and unpunished for years prior to the prosecution. This casts a whole new light upon the apparently less troubling occurrences of some of the older men having consensual sex with very young girls.[28] However, the instances of underage sex that

---

[25] See K. Marks, *Trouble in Paradise* (London: Harper, 2008), chapter 8.

[26] [2005] PNSC 1, paras 20–41, available at <http://www3.paclii.org/pn/cases/PNSC/2005/1.html> (last accessed 23 January 2009).

[27] For example, Trenwith (admittedly writing before the first instance findings) states that the Pitcairn prosecutions 'predominantly involve complaints of sexual intercourse with underage girls': see Trenwith, 'The Empire Strikes Back', Part IV. This description leaves out any reference to the allegations of non-consensual sexual intercourse that formed the core of the prosecution case.

[28] Eg Dennis Christian, alone of the six convicted in *R v Christian (No. 2)* not to face charges of rape.

formed the basis of some of the prosecutions must have played out against the background of apparently unconstrained male sexual violence.

In general, therefore, the second narrative is radically misleading in the way in which it substitutes a picture of tropical innocence, self-contained cultural isolation, and arrogant metropolitan intervention for the much more complex and contested reality that existed on Pitcairn. In particular, it reveals itself to be pre-feminist in its failure to acknowledge that the unique sexual practices prevalent in Pitcairn culture may have been the product of embedded forms of sexual exploitation.

## The distorting influence of the emphasis on Pitcairn's isolation

If one accepts the existence of at least some consciousness of 'wrongness' of sexual assaults on the part of those responsible, and then takes into consideration the links that existed between the island and the wider world, the clear statements of the applicability of English law that had been made over time, and the ongoing if periodic interaction between the island and UK public authorities, then it makes sense to presume that the attackers knew that they were doing something that had the quality of a punishable 'wrong' if they were ever called to account for their acts. The myth of tropical innocence should not be allowed to cloud this logic. Some very compelling evidence should be available before one can assume that the isolation and remoteness of Pitcairn meant that the perpetrators of these violent acts had no real consciousness that they were committing punishable wrongs.

In his chapter in this book, Stephen Guest develops a rigorous analysis of the concept of promulgation of laws and raises interesting issues about what will qualify as adequate promulgation in isolated communities such as Pitcairn. However, when it comes to applying this analysis to the facts of the Pitcairn cases, much ultimately turns on the question whether it should be assumed that sufficient knowledge of the general contours of English law existed amongst the island community so as to make it unnecessary actually to publish the Sexual Offences Act or legal textbooks about it on the island. In general, legal systems operate on the basis that laws have been adequately promulgated, even in geographically remote communities. For example, recently arrived visitors or members of immigrant communities who may speak little or no English and live lives closed off from the mainstream community are deemed to have sufficient notice of the laws of England. Pitcairn is perhaps uniquely isolated. However, it makes sense to require pressing evidence before finding in such a case as this that the standard assumption of promulgation should not apply. It is difficult to see what evidence to that effect exists in the Pitcairn scenario, especially if one factors in the serious abuse suffered by some members of the island community and the inherently and obviously 'wrong' nature of some of the violent sexual assaults to which they were subject.

Similar issues may arise in respect of the argument made by George Letsas in his chapter that the UK authorities had failed to discharge their side of the 'social contract' bargain by not providing a sufficient level of state support to the islanders, and therefore were not entitled to prosecute the islanders for non-compliance with the laws of a state that had done little or nothing for them. Pitcairn is very remote and it received relatively little state support from the UK authorities, at least when compared with the support regularly now made available to inhabitants of the core territorial parts of the UK. However, one again has to be wary before inferring from this that the islanders lived in the state of tropical isolation and disconnect from the UK that is depicted by the second narrative. State support was provided at intervals to the islanders, when requested: the presence of the Kent Police officer which triggered the entire case was an example of that. The islanders were entitled to seek and expect help from the UK authorities, as they had done in the past when confronted with problems of crime.[29] Presumably, the expectation also existed that in case of a disaster they could rely on emergency assistance. The prosecutions themselves were an example of state intervention to fulfil its side of the bargain towards the islanders, in this case the islanders who had faced sexual abuse.

In other words, it is not at all clear that the Pitcairn community was as isolated and abandoned as the second narrative tends to suggest. It is necessary to avoid being sucked into assumptions that may be founded on myths of tropical isolation, remoteness, and innocence. The siren song of the second narrative must be resisted through a careful focus on the exact factual relationship between the islanders and the metropolitan centre. The reader can judge for herself whether the arguments made elsewhere in the book which question the legitimacy of the prosecutions succeed in doing this. It suffices to say that if one puts the

---

[29] See the findings in *Christian v R (No. 2)* [2005] PNSC 1, paras 111–147.

violent abuse suffered by some women on Pitcairn at the centre of the analysis, and casts a cold eye over the assumptions underlying much of the second narrative, then the case in favour of the prosecutions grows in strength.

## 'Cultural' Arguments in Relation to Pitcairn

The distorting effect of the second narrative can be detected when one turns to claims that the prosecution process was illegitimate because it did not sufficiently acknowledge (and perhaps even actively menaced) the unique and vulnerable culture of the Pitcairn community. As discussed above, these claims were made by some islanders opposed to the prosecutions before and during the trial process, and in some academic commentary. The idea that unique cultures, such as that of Pitcairn, deserve protection against intrusions from the outside world is attractive given the *ex post facto* realization of the devastation wrought on a multiplicity of cultures by colonial expansion over the last few centuries. These arguments lent considerable emotive power to the second narrative. However, once again, when one peels away the simplistic picture of the Pitcairn prosecutions that the second narrative initially presents, these culture-based arguments prove very deceptive.

At first glance, the Pitcairn prosecutions involve the imposition of dominant culture values on a vulnerable minority culture, whose specificity seemed to go largely unacknowledged in both the decision to bring the prosecutions and the subsequent judicial process. Given that the prosecution would result in the imprisonment of a substantial proportion of the island's male population, it is also easy to portray the intervention by the UK authorities as endangering the existence of the island's ongoing cultural separateness. While the trial process was ongoing, some commentators depicted the prosecution as threatening to end human habitation on Pitcairn.[30]

Taken together, these arguments can be classed as a 'cultural critique' of the prosecutions. On closer analysis, they are based on a combination of three distinct if interlinked sets of normative claim. *Firstly*, the cultural critique makes use of an element of 'minority group rights' analysis, which sees distinct cultural communities as possessed of some

---

[30] See eg the publications cited at note 1.

form of group right to protection against external interference which attacks or erodes their shared cultural practices. *Secondly*, this critique also draws upon the argument that the relevant cultural background must be taken into account and given due weight when the criminal justice system assesses the acts and motivations of accused persons, via the application of some form of 'cultural defence'. *Thirdly*, in suggesting that it is not appropriate to apply the values of the metropolitan centre in passing judgment on the acts of the islanders, the cultural critique also draws upon 'relativist' or 'particularist' approaches to the question of how and when to apply general norms within a legal system.[31]

Each of these three distinct types of normative claim is controversial, attracting both passionate support and intense opposition. However, all three have a well-established intellectual pedigree. The 'cultural critique' of the Pitcairn prosecutions relies upon a combination of arguments linked to all three types of claim. It therefore attempts to borrow some of their intellectual credibility. However, once again, the factual circumstances underlying the prosecution process wholly undermine the 'cultural critique'. Arguments rooted in 'cultural rights' claims or cultural relativism/particularism cannot meaningfully be used to attack the Pitcairn prosecutions. Even if such arguments are accepted as essentially valid in the abstract, they cannot be coherently applied to the Pitcairn case. They found no purchase in legal argumentation before the courts that heard the prosecutions and the subsequent appeals: furthermore, they have no purchase at the normative level either. The 'cultural critique' is essentially hollow: even on its own terms, it fails to provide a meaningful platform for challenging the convictions.

Even if the lawyers for the accused had wished to use elements of the 'cultural critique' in their legal arguments, they would have found little or no toehold in the applicable set of legal norms. Little basis exists for a claim in UK human rights law that a particular form of state action will deny minority groups the right to maintain their cultural identity. The provisions of Article 27 of the UN International Covenant on Civil and Political Rights (ICCPR),[32] which protect certain minority rights, are not incorporated into domestic UK law. The same is true for the UN

---

[31] See M.-B. Dembour, *Who Believes in Human Rights?* (Cambridge: Cambridge University Press, 2006), chapter 6 for an analysis of why the term 'particularist' is suitable.      [32] See chapter 5 for discussion of international law in relation to Pitcairn.

Declaration on the Rights of Persons Belonging to National or Ethnic, Religious and Linguistic Minorities, the Council of Europe Framework Convention for the Protection of National Minorities, or the OSCE Copenhagen Declaration of 1990. The European Convention on Human Rights (ECHR), as incorporated by the Human Rights Act 1998, guarantees individuals freedom of religion, freedom of association, and freedom from discrimination in the enjoyment of other Convention rights. However, the ECHR contains no guarantee of minority rights upon which individuals or groups can establish a case that their unique culture is endangered. Therefore, the minority rights avenue presented no possibility of a defence for the accused and the issue was not raised directly before the courts that dealt with the case.

The same goes for the 'cultural defence' line of argument. There is considerable debate in the United States, South Africa, the Netherlands, France, and elsewhere as to if and when an accused person can cite their particular cultural background as a defence by excuse or exculpation to a criminal charge.[33] There have been instances in these legal systems where such a defence has been recognized, and other instances where its existence has been decisively rejected. In contrast, debate on this issue has been more muted in the UK legal literature.[34] As Helen Power notes, 'the British legal system (in common with others in Europe) has barely acknowledged culture in its substantive criminal law'.[35] The availability of such a defence could create serious problems, even if in individual cases it might produce a justified and proportionate amelioration of the rigour of the criminal law: given these complexities, it is no surprise that, as Power again notes, citing Bovenkerk and Yesilgöz's analysis of the Dutch criminal justice system, '[j]udges tend to cling to the rules and generally hold their tongue.'[36]

A similar position exists with respect to the argument that there should be greater recognition of cultural particularism within the fabric of national legal systems. This issue is controversial and has generated

---

[33] For an overview, see W. I. Torry, 'Multicultural Jurisprudence and the Cultural Defense' (1999) *Journal of Legal Pluralism* 127–161; A. Dundes Renteln, *The Cultural Defense* (New York: OUP, 2004); Note, 'The Cultural Defense in the Criminal Law' (1986) 99 *Harvard Law Review* 1293–1311.

[34] See however A. Phillips, 'When Culture Meets Gender: Issues of Cultural Defence in the English Courts' (2003) 66 *Modern Law Review* 510; H. Power, 'Provocation and Culture' (2000) *Criminal Law Review* 871, 876–884.

[35] Power, 'Pitcairn Island', 619.          [36] Ibid.

highly charged discussions in both political debate and academic literature.[37] However, the day-to-day workings of a national criminal justice system are generally regarded as an inappropriate place to resolve these disputes. As with the issue of a 'cultural defence', judges and legislators are usually content to apply general norms to all caught up in the criminal justice system, save where the very odd exception which reflects the existence of cultural variation has entered the law via case law or legislation. No such exception was relevant in the Pitcairn cases.

As a consequence, again as noted by Power, it is not surprising that no attempt was made by lawyers for the accused to make any direct use of a cultural defence, notwithstanding the 'cultural critique' offered up by some media and academic commentators, and the insistence of the second narrative on the uniqueness of Pitcairn culture. Instead, as discussed above, other legal arguments stood in as proxies or substitutes for the cultural critique, to ultimately unsuccessful effect.

## Minority group rights claims

Any attempt to invoke a 'minority rights claim', whether via a hypothetical legal route or through normative argumentation, would also run into similar insurmountable obstacles. Such a claim would differ from a 'cultural defence' in that the accused would not be attempting to justify their own conduct, but would rather be challenging the prosecutions on the basis that they threatened the cultural identity of the distinctive Pitcairn community, who could be viewed as constituting a vulnerable minority within the UK. Article 27 of the ICCPR states that 'persons belonging to such minorities shall not be denied the right, in community with the other members of their group, to enjoy their own culture . . . ' In other words, a minority rights claim could only be sustained if the prosecutions could be presented as a threat to the right of the island community to enjoy their own unique and distinct culture.

---

[37] See Dembour, *Who Believes in Human Rights?*, at note 31 above: for some of the major contributions to this extensive literature, see B. Barry, *Culture and Equality: An Egalitarian Critique of Multiculturalism* (Oxford: Polity, 2000); S. Benhabib, *The Claims of Culture: Equality and Diversity in the Global Era* (Princeton, NJ: Princeton University Press, 2002); W. Kymlicka, *Multicultural Citizenship: A Liberal Theory of Minority Rights* (Oxford: Clarendon Press, 1995); J. Habermas, 'Multiculturalism and the Liberal State' (1995) 47(5) *Stanford Law Review* 849–853.

The existence of such a threat featured prominently in the excited rhetoric of the second narrative. As discussed above, particular emphasis was placed on the risk that the jailing of a substantial proportion of the adult male population of the island could make it effectively impossible for the unique Pitcairn community to remain on the island. In other words, the prosecutions were depicted as constituting a threat to the continued survival of the island community, and therefore to Pitcairn's cultural uniqueness and the rights of Pitcairners to 'enjoy' this culture. Academic commentators were particularly excited by this prospect, at times depicting the prosecutions as a crass imperialist intervention that ran the real risk of eradicating the vulnerable and precious culture of the island community.[38]

However, if one once again peels away the distortions and exaggeration endemic in the second narrative, the possibility of establishing a coherent minority rights claim disappears. The UK government adopted measures during and after the trial process to minimize the impact of the convictions. A special quasi-open prison regime was put into place to enable convicted individuals to continue to live and work on the island. New electronic communication and transport links were established, and the islanders were provided with additional and unprecedented levels of state support. This burst of state benevolence was doubtless motivated by guilt at previous neglect of Pitcairn. However, these measures appear likely to reduce the threat to the continued existence of the island community.

It should also be remembered that, as noted previously, the prosecutions were only possible because individual members of Pitcairn's community, or former members of that community who had moved abroad, were willing to give evidence against their abusers. As with the issue of cultural defence, this shows that there were islanders who were not convinced that the cultural survival of Pitcairn depended on avoiding any externally imposed prosecution process. The victims of abuse who gave evidence were in many ways reclaiming their rights to participate in the unfolding story of Pitcairn: they were asserting their entitlement to 'enjoy' their cultural context free of the shadow of sexual violence. Power in her cogent analysis once again hits the nail on the

---

[38] See in particular Trenwith, 'The Empire Strikes Back', at note 1 above; see also Farran, 'The Case of Pitcairn', also above at note 1.

head: '[d]espite the best efforts in some quarters to depict these proceedings as the last gasp of an Empire bullying its colonial dependents,
the uncomfortable fact remained that [the victims who gave testimony]
were one-time "insiders", asserting their rights to autonomy and
dignity.'[39]

The argument that the prosecutions are open to challenge because
they endangered the cultural rights of the Pitcairn community is
therefore highly problematic. There is also an inherent contradiction in
using claims rooted in human rights frameworks to argue for an end to
prosecutions brought to uphold the rights of women to live free from
violence and abuse. Minority rights claims are just one piece of the
human rights jigsaw: it makes little sense to permit tenuous and
unsubstantiated claims about threats to the cultural integrity of the
Pitcairn community to override the immediate and tangible need for
individual islanders to be protected against rape, sexual assault, and
exploitation.

Theorists such as Taylor and Kymlicka who have argued that dominant majority cultures should 'recognize' and respect the rights of
minority cultural groups to autonomy have by and large justified such
recognition of minority cultures on the basis that they provide an
essential locus for individual human flourishing.[40] As a consequence,
supporters of minority group rights tend on the whole to accept that
where the flourishing of individuals is impeded in a substantial manner
by oppressive manifestations of the minority culture in question, the
claims of groups to cultural autonomy can be overridden by the entitlement of individuals to assert more fundamental rights that protect
their basic human dignity.

Other theorists, including Waldron and Spinner-Halav, have been
more sceptical about the coherence and justification of 'group rights'
claims founded upon the special status of minority cultures, and tend to
argue that while the survival of distinct cultural identities might be

---

[39] Power, 'Pitcairn Island', 619.

[40] For example, Kymlicka argues that '"societal culture" ... provides its members
with meaningful ways of life across the full range of human activities, including social,
educational, religious, recreational and economic life, encompassing both public and
private spheres': see W. Kymlicka, *Multicultural Citizenship*, note 37 above, 76. Kymlicka
cites Avishai Margalit and Joseph Raz in support of this proposition: see A. Margalit and
J. Raz, 'National Self-determination' (1990) 8 *Journal of Philosophy* 439–461. See also
C. Taylor, 'The Politics of Recognition', in A. Gutmann (ed.), *Multiculturalism and
The Politics of Recognition* (Princeton, NJ: Princeton University Press, 1992), 25–73.

desirable, this interest lacks sufficient substance to overcome the more tangible claims of individuals asserting fundamental rights.[41]

As a result, very few theorists would consider minority group rights as sufficiently tangible to overcome or outweigh individual rights claims. Moshe Halbertal and Avishai Margalit have suggested that the right of a minority group to enjoy their own culture may justify 'an obligation to support cultures that flout the rights of [their individual members] in a liberal society'.[42] Kutkathas, while not a believer in minority group rights per se, nevertheless takes the view that the sum of the individual rights of the members of a group to enjoy their common culture may confer upon such a group of individuals the right to be 'left alone'.[43] However, even Kutkathas accepts that this is subject to 'individual acquiescence' in the cultural norms in question, and accepts that it 'is not always the case that the entire cultural community is eager, or even willing, to preserve cultural integrity at any price'.[44]

As a consequence, there is widespread agreement that minority group rights cannot trump fundamental individual rights to core entitlements such as bodily integrity and autonomy. Even most 'strong' advocates of minority group rights recognize the need for 'individual acquiescence' in cultural norms and the existence of limits on what is and can be justified in the name of preserving cultural integrity. So, for example, Gerald Doppelt advocates a 'culture/identity sensitive liberalism', but proceeds to argue that group rights are only justifiable when the legal and cultural requirements of a robust liberalism are already embedded in the relations and identities of individuals and groups. In the absence of this condition, group rights can impede justice.[45]

Rape, sexual assault, and underage exploitation constitute basic denials of fundamental individual rights. Therefore, it makes no sense to argue that the rights of the Pitcairn community at large 'to be left alone' can prevail over the rights of individuals to be free from the abuses sought to

---

[41] See J. Waldron, 'Minority Cultures and the Cosmopolitan Alternative', in W. Kymlicka (ed.) *The Rights of Minority Cultures* (Oxford: Oxford University Press, 1995), 93–119: J. Spinner-Halev, *Surviving Diversity: Religion and Democratic Citizenship* (Baltimore: Johns Hopkins Press, 2000), especially chapter 3.

[42] M. Halbertal and A. Margalit, 'Liberalism and the Right to Culture' (1994) 61 *Social Research* 491–510.

[43] C. Kutkathas, 'Are There Any Cultural Rights?' (1992) 20 *Political Theory* 105–139.        [44] Ibid., p. 114.

[45] G. Doppelt, 'Illiberal Conditions and Group Rights' (2002) 12 *Journal of Contemporary Issues* 661–692.

be rectified and prevented by the prosecution process. This is all the more true given that the cultural norms prevailing in Pitcairn are obviously the subject of contention, with the victims of the abuse at issue not wishing to accept the self-serving account of Pitcairn's cultural norms given by the dominant males responsible for that same abuse.[46]

## 'Cultural defence' claims

Even if the lawyers for the accused had found some way of putting legal flesh on the cultural critique, it may have been of little use to their clients. To start with, if any form of cultural defence is to be accepted within a national criminal justice system, the accused must be able to demonstrate that what would ordinarily constitute a criminal offence is in some way regarded as 'acceptable', 'normal', or even 'mandated' by the self-understanding of the particular culture to which the accused belongs. (If the accused was only able to show that the act in question was regarded as normatively justified within their own individual normative order, or that of a small group that did not form a distinct cultural entity, then this defence would be an unworkable *carte blanche* for any form of criminal activity.)

Therefore, if a cultural defence did exist in law, the accused in the Pitcairn prosecutions would have had to establish that the sexual practices at issue—rape and sexual assault—were in some way 'accepted' as normal by the Pitcairn community at large. This would have been frankly implausible, given the position of the women complainants in the case. The accused might have had a better chance of establishing that consensual underage sex with very young girls was tolerated on the island. However, as discussed above, given that the underage sexual activity in question took place against the background of unpunished and repeated sexual assaults by dominant males within the community, it would be very difficult to disentangle allegedly consensual sexual acts with girls aged 12 from the non-consensual abuse to which they were also vulnerable. Any attempt by the accused to claim island culture tolerated their activities would also be suspect on the basis of their status within Pitcairn society: as Power suggests, '[O]n Pitcairn, the "elders"

---

[46] Okin has argued that there is a need to be aware of the existence of power imbalances within cultural communities in responding to demands apparently emanating from such communities to be 'left alone': see S. M. Okin, 'Feminism and Multiculturalism: Some Tensions' (1998) 108(4) *Ethics* 661–684, 675–676.

themselves were on trial, and any attempt by them to give an account of the "Great Pitcairn Tradition", exonerating themselves, would hardly have appeared plausible, let alone authentic.[47]

Power also notes that attempts to make use of cultural defences in other criminal justice systems, such as that of the Netherlands, have usually involved defendants painting an essentialized and often wholly outdated picture of their 'home' culture, relying on outmoded stereotypes and the lack of readily available alternative accounts of their cultural background in a strategic attempt to excuse their actions.[48] However, as she highlights, on Pitcairn 'there were witnesses readily available who could testify to the contestability of the culture being asserted'.[49] It is clear from the first instance findings that the victims of the abuses in question did not perceive their treatment as 'normal' or 'acceptable'. On the contrary, their testimony clearly established their understanding of the 'wrongness' of what was done to them and their unwillingness to consent. Therefore, any attempt to invoke a cultural defence would run straight into contradictory accounts of what was acceptable behaviour within the Pitcairn community.

## 'Cultural relativism' claims

A similar logic applies to claims that the specific cultural context of Pitcairn should have been taken into account during the trial process, and that the accused should have been treated differently from individuals accused of similar crimes from a more 'mainstream' metropolitan cultural background.

Such 'cultural relativist' or 'cultural particularist' arguments often featured in the tropes of the second narrative. Cultural relativism/particularism is essentially based upon the idea that each culture has its own values, only understandable within their own terms, which are difficult to assess morally within the conceptual framework of another culture. Opponents of the Pitcairn prosecution used arguments rooted in this conceptual approach to claim that the behaviour of the islands could not be adequately judged and weighed by outsiders, which linked to the themes of innocence, isolation, and cultural uniqueness that ran throughout the second narrative. In other words, critics of the decision to initiate the prosecution suggested repeatedly that it was inappropriate

---

[47] Power, 'Pitcairn Island', 619.        [48] Ibid.        [49] Ibid.

to apply the norms of a society such as the UK to a society like that of Pitcairn.[50]

However, once again, the use of such arguments has been characterized by a troubling gap between rhetoric and reality, and they have also often been casually deployed without close analysis of their underlying premises.

Dembour suggests that the problem of cultural particularism can never be wholly discounted: 'minimal common standards are never entirely common: they always stand in the way of more peculiar, or particular norms', while legal systems must struggle to make a 'difficult and always controversial accommodation between unity and diversity in mankind'.[51] In contrast, in his chapter in this book, George Letsas has strongly criticized the theoretical foundations of 'cultural relativism'. Both Letsas and Dembour are correct. Letsas' criticisms of the underpinning normative foundations of 'cultural relativism' is accurate, while Dembour nevertheless reminds us that the problem of ensuring justice while also responding to human diversity is a constant challenge even in systems clearly committed to giving effect to a common or 'universal' framework of established norms.

The reader is referred to the Letsas chapter for an analysis of why the use of culturally relativist/particularist arguments to argue that the behaviour of the accused was in some way justified or incapable of condemnation as 'wrong' is wholly problematic. In what follows, the additional argument will be made that the Pitcairn trial process struck the right balance in reconciling the demands of universal justice with the need to reflect the particular circumstances of the unique factual and cultural scenario at issue. A successful resolution of the tension identified by Dembour was achieved and the criticism launched at the process on the grounds of cultural particularity was misguided.

If the Pitcairn trials had paid no attention to the particular circumstances of the island, then the concerns of the second narrative and the picture it painted of a blundering and interfering imperial power intervening in a context which it did not understand might have had some validity. However, in both the handling of the trial process itself and the subsequent sentencing decisions, the background context

---

[50] See in particular the arguments made by Trenwith, note 1 above.
[51] Dembour, *Who Believes in Human Rights?*, note 31 above, p. 155.

of the case received due weight. In particular, the establishment of the special prison arrangements on Pitcairn reflected a concern that the cultural specificity of the island (and its vulnerability) be taken into account.

In addition, the first instance findings of fact as recorded in the judgment by the Supreme Court of the Pitcairn Islands in *R v Christian (No. 2)* established clearly that non-consensual acts of sexual assault at least were perceived by the victims as violent, aggressive, and 'wrong'. In other words, as discussed above in the context of the cultural defence arguments, the women who suffered the abuse in question were clear that many of the acts at issue did not constitute culturally acceptable behaviour. Thus, Pitcairn cultural self-understanding was factored into the adjudication process, and the accused can have no complaints that they were simply subject to a wholly external and alien set of norms. In addition, as already discussed extensively above, the lack of a cultural defence poses no particular normative problems.

In sum, the second narrative's concern with the prospect of the imposition of 'external' norms upon the Pitcairn islanders rings hollow. There is little or no substantive evidence that the values of the Pitcairn culture were fundamentally different from that of other cultures. There is also no real indication that the UK criminal justice system was incapable of understanding the particular Pitcairn context, or that the actions and behaviour of the accused could not be judged within the established framework of the commonly applied norms of the UK criminal justice system.

The concerns about cultural particularism expressed via the tropes of the second narrative have served essentially as a smokescreen, obscuring the nasty reality of the abusive sexual practices at issue in this case. The exoticism of Pitcairn, its geographical isolation, and unique history have to some extent been smeared across much of the media and academic commentary. This has produced some troubling results. Many commentators have downplayed the extent of the sexual violence at issue. The prosecutions have been depicted as a threat to the cultural integrity of the island, when the reality is much more complex. The entire trial process has been characterized as an act of arrogant imperial folly, whereas the willingness of the victims of the sexual offences in question to give evidence paints a wholly different picture of how the prosecution might look to their eyes. The balance of human rights concerns in no way necessarily lies in favour of the accused.

## The Dangers of Exaggerated Respect for 'Culture'

In fact, the Pitcairn case can be seen as illustrating the validity of certain forms of 'universal' human rights-based approaches, even in circumstances of apparently strong cultural variation. In particular, it can be seen as an example of how external intervention via a legally structured trial process in the interest of protecting the human rights of abused and assaulted women can serve to expose oppressive and abusive power relationships which have otherwise sheltered under the cloak of cultural difference.

Communities cannot assert a right to insulate their particular cultures from externally-driven transformation, where to do so would involve a nullification of the reasons for recognizing cultural diversity in the first place. The concern to respect minority rights, and to take cultural particularism and cultural difference into account within criminal justice systems, is driven by a concern to recognize and give due weight to the role culture plays in shaping people's lives. However, concerns about external interference must not be allowed to prevent lawful, structured, and proportionate intervention directed towards upholding the most fundamental individual entitlements to dignity, respect, and freedom from abuse. This is all the more obvious when the community in question is divided, as was the case with Pitcairn, and those resisting external interference are precisely those who dominate, shape, and control existing cultural practices.

There is also a danger in giving cultural difference exaggerated respect. The Pitcairn case illustrates this perfectly. Well-established cultural practices can be riddled with exploitation. In fact, claims for special cultural exemptions, such as those that gave rhetorical force to much of the second narrative, invariably disclose a hidden set of assumptions that reflect conceptions of Western superiority that those concerned with imperial intervention, minority rights, and cultural relativism often tend to decry. Lurking at the heart of many such exemption claims is the assumption that Western cultures are eminently suitable for demands to comply with human rights standards: in contrast, other cultures are often treated as less mature, or uniquely exotic, or as existing in an unreal space of innocence and isolation, far removed from their complex reality.

Much of the rhetoric surrounding the Pitcairn case exemplifies this mindset. The Pitcairn islanders have often been deemed to be too isolated, innocent, and enmeshed in a unique cultural mindset to appreciate the inherent wrongness of non-consensual sexual assault and the possible exploitation of vulnerable underage girls. No one would make such arguments about Catholic priests abusing children in the UK, or permit a newly-arrived immigrant in England to justify rape on the basis of a cultural misunderstanding. Yet Pitcairn is deemed to be a special case, often because the nature of the sexual offences involved appear to have been downgraded in media and academic commentary from non-consensual assault to consensual sex between underage youngsters.

## Conclusion

There is no doubt that the language of human rights can be used to justify illegitimate intervention. There is also no doubt that metropolitan intrusions into isolated societies via the blunt instrument of the criminal law may produce unjustified results. Delineating how human rights standards should be applied in different cultural contexts is also difficult, especially when the criminal law is invoked by external interveners in the name of protecting basic rights, as was the case on Pitcairn. The challenge is to attempt to identify what constitutes a violation of universal fundamental rights norms in particular cultural contexts, and how the criminal justice system should respond in each particular context. In doing this, the accumulated perspectives built up by protracted debates on feminism, multiculturalism, imperialism, cultural difference, and minority rights are invaluable. The Pitcairn case illustrates this perfectly: the application of feminist analysis shows up the denial of equality and bodily autonomy inherent in the 'hidden' cultural specificity of Pitcairn Island.[52]

However, at the core of all human rights claims lies a presumption that a degree of near-universal applicability exists, at least where the essence of rights is concerned. Over-emphasizing cultural difference at the expense of basic rights to bodily autonomy, dignity, and respect leads towards incoherence. All individuals can claim to be embedded in a set of specific cultural practices: to return to Naipaul's phrase, there are 'a million mutinies now', in the form of multiple cultural claims to

---

[52] Okin has argued that many cultures have an interest in the domination and control of women: see S. M. Okin, 'Feminism and Multiculturalism: Some Tensions' (1998) 108(4) *Ethics* 661–684, 667–669.

difference and special treatment, as well as multiple different voices within cultures and communities giving different accounts of the internal values of their particular culture or community. Human rights norms cannot be applied to those cultures that we choose to regard as sufficiently similar to be claimed as recognizably 'ours', while suspended from being applied to other forms of cultural practice that we choose to define as 'different' or 'exotic'. Making allowances for different cultural backgrounds is one thing: permitting lazy rhetoric about cultural vulnerability and difference to block the application of the criminal law when its use is necessary to vindicate basic rights is another. Perhaps fortunately, the prosecution, trial judges, and the appellate courts who handled the Pitcairn case did not fall into this trap.

# 7

# Rights and Duties on Pitcairn Island

*George Letsas*

Desert island scenarios are the political philosopher's test tube. They are commonly used by philosophers in order to test theories about the proper way governments should treat their people and what people owe to each other, as well as theories of truth and knowledge.[1] Philosophers often use them as hypotheses or thought experiments in the hope that they will be able to isolate which facts count in favour of a particular principle, which facts count against it, and which are completely irrelevant. It is often difficult to determine what the morally right course of action is by looking at long-standing political communities that have a rich and complex history of social interaction. Political contingencies, acts of violence, and accidents of history may and often do create a multitude of reasons pulling in opposite directions, making it difficult for us to identify how abstract values of critical morality,[2]

---

[1] For instance, desert island scenarios have been used widely to test utilitarianism's account of the morality of promissory obligation. See eg Jan Narveson 'The Desert Island Problem', 23(3) *Analysis* (1963), pp. 63–67; James Cargile, 'Utilitarianism and the Desert Island Problem', 25 *Analysis* (1964), pp. 23–24. Other philosophers who have used desert island examples to illustrate a philosophical claim include David Hume, *An Enquiry Concerning the Principles of Morals: A Critical Edition* (Oxford: Oxford University Press, 2000), p. 25; Joseph Raz in *Morality of Freedom* (Oxford: Clarendon Press, 1986), p. 374; Ronald Dworkin in *Sovereign Virtue: The Theory and Practice of Equality* (Cambridge: Cambridge University Press, 2000), p. 66 and many others.

[2] Throughout this paper I shall be using the word 'morality' to refer to critical, rather than conventional morality. Roughly, conventional morality refers to a set of norms regulating activity that are endorsed and practised by people within a particular community. Critical morality refers to ideal norms which *ought* to regulate conduct, regardless of what conventional norms say, and which are justified by true and objective moral values whose validity does not depend on communal acceptance and practice. For example, conventional morality in Ancient Sparta required that all newly born babies that would not make good warriors be murdered by being thrown into a chasm. Needless to say, whatever Spartans thought (and anyone else for that matter), critical morality condemns such abhorrent practices.

like fairness and justice, impact on what is morally right here and now.

Desert island thought experiments offer a promising solution to this methodological problem: we are asked to imagine the human condition in its most elementary form, before any social interaction between people has taken place, and then test our intuitions about the moral difference the addition of this or that social fact would make. We can ask ourselves, for instance, whether there would be something morally wrong with an individual on a desert island not sharing the island's resources with other islanders. Or we can ask what benefits there would be if these individuals were to cooperate, to set up institutions, to obey the law and the like. The idea is that if we settle on our intuitions about what moral principles should govern the interpersonal relationships of individuals in the simple context of an imaginary desert island, we can then, by analogy, apply those principles to the more complex social settings in which we now live and discover what our own rights and duties are. This method of inquiry, elements of which can be seen in the social contract tradition of Thomas Hobbes, John Locke, and John Rawls, is characteristic of much of liberal political philosophy.

The story of Pitcairn Island may seem like a desert island thought experiment come true. In 1790, a small group of people consisting of nine British mutineers from the famous *Bounty* and 19 Tahitian men and women, settled on the small and uninhabited Pitcairn Island. In the more than two centuries since, the descendants of the original settlers have lived on the island continuously and with little interaction with the rest of the world. One would be inclined to think that the Pitcairn case would pose little difficulty from the point of view of legal and political philosophy. Yet Pitcairn Island is nothing like the clean slate of a philosopher's desert island: its history began with a mutiny against the British Crown and in conditions of injustice (many of the original Tahitian settlers had been kidnapped) and continued with incidents of violence, religious tensions, and a troubled relationship with the metropolitan state, resulting in the 2004 prosecutions on which much of the discussion in this book focuses. Pitcairn's social and political history has been anything but a simple, straightforward desert island scenario.

This chapter will attempt to identify and discuss some of the jurisprudential issues that the fascinating Pitcairn case raises. Like Professor Stephen Guest in chapter 8, I have much sympathy for the defendants in the case of *Christian and Others*. Like him, I believe that the moral wrongness of an act, including a particularly abhorrent one like rape, is a necessary but not a sufficient condition for legal punishment. But unlike Professor Guest, I wish to locate the unmet conditions of the justifiability of interference by the United Kingdom more in the issue of jurisdiction and the exercise of legal authority over Pitcairn rather than the issue of adequate promulgation of English criminal law on Pitcairn. I will also examine the issue of cultural relativism and how it bears on the Pitcairn case.[3] Two major philosophical debates will be used throughout this chapter as the basis of my analysis. The first is the debate between cultural relativism and moral universalism; the second is the debate between positivist and non-positivist accounts of law. Which school of thought one sides with in these debates has important consequences for one's view of the legitimacy of the Pitcairn prosecutions. This paper will side with moral universalism and against positivism.

In the next section, I begin with a discussion of the ideas of cultural relativism and moral universality and how they bear on the Pitcairn case. Section three looks at the debate between legal positivism and natural law and explains its relevance to the issue of the legality of the Pitcairn prosecutions. Section four develops a non-positivist argument in support of the view that the Crown lacked jurisdiction over Pitcairn Island.

## Cultural Relativism, Universality, and Blameworthiness

To people born and living in the west, like the author of this paper, it is no surprise that the culture of Pitcairn Island appears remote and strange. The mere fact that the island is geographically isolated means that there is very little cultural, economic, and socio-political interaction with the rest of the world, which in turn suggests the existence of a rather static culture. Societies that are open to outside influences often exhibit a faster pace of cultural and social change and more cross-cultural similarities than isolated ones. Size may also be crucial. Large political communities, no matter how isolated they are, are more likely to have a rich and dynamic culture, in the sense that they allow for a larger degree of cultural diversity and pluralism. In small communities by contrast, like that of Pitcairn (some 47 in total), cultural evolution and political innovation are harder to come by and there may well be

---

[3] See also chapter 6 by Colm O'Cinneide.

some biological basis behind this. To outsiders, it feels as if cultural and social time in small and isolated societies runs slowly compared to open and large ones, often triggering the rather imperialist comment that the latter are 'hundreds of years behind'.

But on top of these objective parameters of geographical isolation and the small size of its population comes another fact that has influenced, perhaps to a greater extent, the development of Pitcairn's culture in a way that perhaps makes it difficult for us to understand it. When the ancestors of the islanders settled on Pitcairn in 1790, the island was uninhabited. The settlers were culturally and ethnically mixed, comprised of nine British and 19 Tahitians. But they were not part of any official colonizing mission, and they were far from acting in the name of a standing political community with an established order of moral values—quite the opposite. The English settlers were mutineers of the *Bounty*, a ship of the Royal Navy, who were hoping to evade arrest and punishment by the British authorities, whereas the Tahitians were most likely kidnapped by the mutineers. Two crimes, kidnapping and mutiny, lie at the heart of the historical chain of events that led to the birth of the Pitcairn community, and there is no doubt that they have had a lasting influence on its culture. An attitude of insubordination and lawlessness, naturally inspired by the act of mutiny, was certainly strong in the first decades after the settlement and it survives symbolically in the annual burning of an effigy of the *Bounty*. This attitude was combined with the very 'liberal', by European Christian standards, sexual mores of the Tahitian culture which so much intrigued westerners since Gauguin's visit to Tahiti.[4]

It seems to me natural that the ethical ideas created by this cultural *mélange* of British insubordination and Tahitian sexual mores in circumstances of isolation, although initially short of constituting a full moral code, gradually took a life of their own, as all communal morals do. There is, I think, little sense in trying to disentangle the different cultural elements that have influenced the island's current practices; it is not purely colonial, nor post-colonial, nor indigenous, nor rebellious. It makes more sense to treat it as a unique culture that, after 219 years, has become much more than the sum of its original parts.

If this is true, and if we also take into account the size and geographical isolation of the island, we should not expect to be able to

---

[4] See Nancy Mowll Mathews, *Paul Gauguin: An Erotic Life* (Newhaven: Yale University Press, 2001).

understand, let alone endorse, the cultural practices of Pitcairn, including, most importantly, its sexual practices. This should make us extremely cautious in our moral assessment. In our culture with its very different history, we take underage and non-consensual sex to be serious moral wrongs that the law should prohibit and punish; but on Pitcairn Island it may well be the case that there was a time when such acts were considered, by both men and women, either minor moral harms which the law should punish lightly (eg as the crimes of sodomy and homo-sexuality were considered until recently in the UK) or minor moral wrongs that the law should not punish at all (eg like adultery). For obvious reasons this is not an assumption we should make lightly and it is one that should be subjected to empirical verification other than the defendants' say-so. For it is often the case that those who allege a widely held cultural or societal belief about the moral permissibility of a wrongful act are the very same people who commit it and that those who are harmed by it have a very different story to tell.[5]

Still, let us assume, for the sake of the argument, that at least as far as underage sex and indecent assault are concerned, Pitcairn Island has different conventional moral values from the ones currently shared by British people. Would it follow that it was wrong to intervene in the affairs of Pitcairn because it was a case of imposing 'our' values upon 'theirs'? Is cultural relativism an available argument against the moral justifiability of the Pitcairn prosecutions, even if we assume that the prosecutions were, technically speaking, lawful? In this section I would like to assess the argument from cultural relativism that, I will argue, ultimately fails to lend support to the view that moral wrongness is relative to each culture. My discussion will move on at the level of moral philosophy, leaving questions of legality and the moral justifiability of criminal punishment for the next section.

The doctrine of cultural relativism remains as popular as it is inconsistent. Bernard Williams once called it 'possibly the most absurd view to have been advanced ever in moral philosophy'.[6] The doctrine draws two inferences, both of which are philosophically unwarranted.

---

[5] Recall the old common law doctrine that a wife could not in law be raped by her husband which was fully abolished by the House of Lords in 1991 in *R v R* [1992] 1 AC 599, recognizing marital rape as a criminal offence. It was certainly not the case that the victims of marital rape thought that there was nothing wrong with it.

[6] Bernard Williams, *Morality: An Introduction to Ethics* (Cambridge: Cambridge University Press, 1972), p. 34. The next three paragraphs draw on Williams's insightful remarks in that book.

First, it seeks to infer moral relativism from the mere fact of moral diversity; it argues that since different societies have different views about what is right and what is wrong, it follows that rightness and wrongness are relative to each culture. It concludes that there need be no universal rights and wrongs and that what is wrong 'for us' (say rape) may not be wrong 'for them'. The second inference is that moral relativism entails a duty of toleration and non-interference. This is the idea that since what is right is relative to each culture we ought never to interfere with the affairs of other societies.

The doctrine is inconsistent because the second claim, that it is wrong to interfere with the practices of other societies, contradicts the first claim that rightness and wrongness are relative to each society. Clearly, the doctrine seeks to establish that it is objectively wrong *for anyone* to interfere with the practices of other societies, not just that it might be wrong *for us*. Think about it: if you genuinely believe that we ought not to interfere with the practices of other cultures then you must also think that they ought not to interfere with our practices, no matter what *they* think. For you are unlikely to change your mind and welcome outside interference with our practices (say by military invasion) if told that *for them*, it is morally right to attack us. You are likely to hold on to your belief that interference is still wrong even if other cultures think it is right. But if you believe *that* then you must also believe that interference in another culture is wrong no matter what *any* culture thinks, including yours. You believe, in other words, in an objective, non-relativized, notion of right and wrong and you have just abandoned the view that 'right' is relative to each society and that there are no universal rights and wrongs. On pain of inconsistency you cannot both morally oppose interference and believe that the whole of morality is relative to each culture.

Inconsistencies are of course things that perhaps only philosophers care about avoiding, and we must move on to examine the merits of the suggestion that we ought never to interfere with the practices of other societies. Williams called the attempt to ground an absolute duty of non-interference on the mere fact of moral diversity 'vulgar relativism' because it advocates a very controversial position without any moral argumentation.[7] Indeed, it would be strikingly presumptuous, not just

---

[7] Ibid, p. 39.

inconsistent, to condemn the Pitcairn prosecutions by offering as a justification the short statement that morality is not universal.

Can a more sophisticated relativism, one that does not deny the existence of *some* universal rights and wrongs, fare any better in advocating non-interference? An improvement on vulgar relativism is one that tries to maintain a degree of cultural relativism, albeit against the background of some universal moral truths. It argues that there are some things that are universally wrong across cultures (for instance, genocide) but that within a wide range of societal practices, from sexual morality to food and clothes, there is no right answer as to how each society should conduct its affairs. H. L. A. Hart once argued that given various facts about human nature, there are some things that positive law must, to some extent, protect if we are to live together at all, like personal safety and property, which he called the 'the minimum content of natural law'. He wrote:

Reflections on some very obvious generalizations—indeed truisms—concerning human nature and the world in which men live, show that as long as these hold good, there are certain rules of conduct which any social organization must contain if it is to be viable. Such rules do in fact constitute a common element in the law and conventional morality of all societies which have progressed to the point where these are distinguished as different forms of social control. With them are found, both in law and morals, much that is peculiar to a particular society and much that may seem arbitrary or a mere matter of choice. Such universally recognized principles of conduct which have a basis in elementary truths concerning human beings, their natural environment, and aims, may be considered the *minimum content* of Natural Law.[8]

Hart was quite generous about what things are, as he put it, 'peculiar to a particular society', 'arbitrary', or 'a mere matter of choice'. The suggestion is that beyond those minimum essentials for human cooperation and survival, it makes little sense to speak of universal rights and wrongs: polygamy, underage sex, genital mutilation, sodomy, pornography are just different, equally acceptable, practices that societies may endorse as 'their' sexual morality or non-moral practices; our more sophisticated relativist would argue that we should not take for granted that our way of doing things is the only acceptable way.

This more sophisticated relativism is on the right track because it captures an important distinction between practices that are wrong no

---

[8] H. L. A. Hart, *The Concept of Law* (2nd edn, Oxford: Clarendon Press, 1994), p. 193.

matter how much societies value them and practices whose value (or disvalue) depends—either partly or entirely—on societal approval. Most of us would be abhorred if we were to find out that there is a society in the Amazon that practices human sacrifice. We would not think that the practice of human sacrifice has any value, value *for them*, because they approve it, while it has none for us because we condemn it; rather, we would think it has no value whatsoever and that those who practice it have badly misunderstood what can be of value to humans. By contrast, we take an attitude of respect towards things like rules of etiquette, food, and music preferences, or clothing fashions that differ so much around the world. As the HSBC commercial reminds us in one of its many examples of funny cross-cultural differences, showing the soles of one's feet causes offence in some parts of the world but is interpreted positively as a sign of relaxation in others. We realize that, as much as we may dislike and oppose what other cultures eat, listen to, or treat as offensive, these are practices that—unlike murder and human sacrifice—may acquire moral value *because* a society approves and practices them.

This sensible point immediately calls for some respect and refraining from interfering, without having to assume, as the relativist might, that we cannot take cultural practices out of context and compare their moral merits. For we clearly can. We can say, for example, that hereditary privileges and titles are in tension with the value of equality of persons and that states which have abolished them are closer to the full realization of that value. We take the exact same critical attitude about our own culture and politics whenever we reform a long-standing practice of ours that we have found to be morally deficient.[9]

The distinction between the things that are wrong, no matter how much societies value them, and things on which societal approval can confer value, is as important as it is difficult to draw with precision. The development of international human rights law is an ongoing attempt to specify the list of things that clearly fall under the first category. Yet we must be careful not to make one serious mistake when we go about drawing this distinction, one often encouraged by naïve arguments from cultural relativism. This is the mistake of categorizing practices that have value because societies accept them by using as a criterion what

---

[9] The recent reform of the House of Lords and the strengthening of the idea of the separation of powers in the UK is a good example of a people's critical attitude towards one's own political culture.

societies *themselves* think; that if, for example, a society takes female genital mutilation to have value for them because they approve it, then it follows that we must not treat genital mutilation as a human rights violation and that we should respect it. The mistake is one that philosophers call *circularity*: we are asking what the relevance of societal approval is regarding the moral value of various practices and we answer that question by saying that the relevance is determined by what societies themselves approve of. To avoid the charge of circularity, we need some objective criterion, one that makes no reference to societal approval at all. Without such an objective criterion we are unable to know which practices call for respect and non-interference and which ones may prima facie justify interference. Just like the critical attitude towards our own culture, a critical attitude towards other cultures must move beyond what people think or have thought and offer reasons *for* believing or doing something (justifying reasons) rather than descriptive facts about people's beliefs and actions (explanatory reasons).

Now, do the crimes that the defendants in *Christian and Others* were convicted of constitute objective moral wrongs that no amount of societal approval can cure? There is no doubt that the moral equality of persons and the objective value of each human life ground universal moral reasons against murder, assault, and rape. There is also little doubt that humans around the world and throughout history have the capacity to appreciate that such reasons exist, even when bias, self-interest, and instinct lead them to restrict the application of these reasons to their own family, social class, ethnic group, or gender. There is no serious debate to be had as to whether murder, rape, and assault are objective moral wrongs—of course they are. People have a moral duty not to rape and assault others and a corresponding moral right not to be raped and assaulted.

Nor is there any reason to think that rape and torture are not objective moral wrongs if the perpetrators honestly hold the—irrational—belief that such things are only wrong when done to people of their own gender, race, or class. Whether or not the perpetrators of such wrongs held an honest belief that they were not acting wrongly has relevance for issues of moral *blameworthiness* rather than wrongfulness. The distinction between blameworthiness and wrongness is an important moral distinction which positive criminal law in most countries tracks: the concept of wrongness applies to those *actions* that harm fundamental interests of individuals or violate their rights; the concept of blameworthiness, on the other hand, refers to a judgement about someone's moral *character* and to whether she can be held responsible for an act which, we have already established, constitutes wrongdoing.

It seems to me that cultural relativism gets its traction more by our uneasiness about blaming people in other cultures than our doubts about the existence of universal rights and wrongs. Blaming and holding others accountable involves a *personal* attitude of resentment or indignation towards someone's character that few of us feel confident in expressing towards strangers, whose particular circumstances we may well ignore or fail to understand. The cultural relativist wishes to draw our attention to the difficulties surrounding cross-cultural judgements of blame and call for caution in moving too quickly from findings of wrongdoing to judgements of blame. And she is, in that respect, right. For we do display a similar restraint towards, and we feel sympathy for, people who lived at a time and place where nobody thought there was anything wrong with what we now think are moral atrocities, like slavery. Aristotle, one of the greatest minds ever, was unable to think beyond the social and political ideas that served the interests of male Athenians and their empire, and sought to provide a moral defence of slavery; seeing the problems in trying to justify the morality of slavery on the conventional ground that it was at the time legal, he turned to nature and argued that some people are simply born without the ability to think properly and need a master to tell them what to do.[10] We feel, very plausibly, that it is wrong to blame Aristotle for owning slaves and for not realizing that slavery is morally atrocious; that we are unjustified in holding reactive attitudes, like resentment and indignation towards him.[11] But doubts about attributing moral blame (or full moral blame) to people because of what it is reasonable to expect of them to do and think, do not cast any doubt on what counts as *wrongdoing*: the moral fact is that slavery was, is and will always be wrong regardless of what people think. It was wrong in Aristotle's time as much as it is now, even

---

[10] Aristotle, *Politics*, eds R. F. Staley and E. Barker (Oxford: Oxford University Press, 1998) I.5 1254b20–1254b23.

[11] Although some commentators do pass negative judgement on Aristotle for defending slavery, though perhaps short of attributing moral blame. John McDowell finds Aristotle's defence of slavery 'an embarrassing feature of Aristotle's thinking', in J. McDowell, 'Eudaimonism and Realism in Aristotle's *Ethics*', in R. Heinaman (ed.), *Aristotle and Moral Realism* (London: University College London Press, 1995), pp. 201–218. Richard Kraut calls it 'a deeply disturbing feature of his political thought', in R. Kraut, *Aristotle: Political Philosophy* (Oxford: Oxford University Press, 2002), p. 277.

if no moral blame should be attributed to him. The idea of blameless wrongdoing is not an oxymoron.

Of course some conditions for *applying* correctly the universally valid concepts of wrongfulness and blameworthiness are culture-specific. For example, what exactly is the age below which it is wrong to take one's consent to sexual intercourse as autonomous and freely given varies and should vary from one place to another. For consent to be genuine and autonomous, one must have the intellectual maturity and the ethical sensibility that are necessary in order to understand that sexual intercourse is a significantly intimate way of disposing one's body with serious consequences for one's self-respect and one's relationships with others as well as with material consequences that may affect one's future well-being, such as pregnancy and parenthood. At what age one attains an adequate level of intellectual maturity and ethical sensibility is a matter of degree and it depends not only on biological factors but also on many cultural ones such as the general availability of education and information. But other things too, like average life expectancy and shared expectations about marriageable age and reproductive ethics, are morally relevant in setting the age of consent as a matter of law, quite apart from actual levels of intellectual maturity. What is important to stress though is that the fact that the appropriate age of consent is culture-specific does not mean that cultures cannot go wrong in setting it. We may still pass judgement on other cultures and claim, after taking into account all the relevant circumstances, that they have set the age of consent so low that they are wronging their younger members. The appropriate age of consent may be relative to each culture but the judgement as to what counts as genuine consent in each culture (the absence of which creates a moral wrong) is no less objective.

Looking at the actions for which the defendants were prosecuted in *Christian and Others* and setting aside the question of *legal* punishment and responsibility, it is rather difficult to deny that they constituted *moral* wrongdoing. Four of the defendants in *Christian and Others* were convicted of raping girls as young as 10 years old, on counts brought against them under section 1 of the Sexual Offences Act 1956. Three of them were convicted of indecent assault against girls as young as five years old. Setting aside for a moment the question of moral blame or excuse, there is no doubt that rape and indecent assault are violations of fundamental rights and that the wrongdoing character of them does not depend on cultural acceptance or knowledge. A societal practice, in which 10-year-old girls are forced to have sex or to be subjected to other forms of sexual abuse, is not simply morally imperfect or deficient; it is a practice that is morally unacceptable, a case of gross injustice towards the victims that we hope will stop at once. I can think of no argument that the cultural relativist can offer in support of the view that rape and indecent assault are not, in themselves, universal moral wrongs and we should be firm in our moral condemnation of them wherever they occur.

But we may take a less critical attitude towards the defendants, as far as moral blame is concerned. Clearly, the degree of knowledge and awareness of the moral wrongness of the crimes they committed was far lower on Pitcairn than it is in any western state; other objective factors that influence sexual practices are also relevant, such as the small size of the population and the ratio between men and women.[12] The lack of education and of a public culture that would mould the appropriate sexual morality, as well as the existence of biological factors that make some moral wrongs (like underage sex) more likely to occur, suggest that less than full moral blame is warranted. In my view, this is one of the intuitions that drives the attempts to criticize the Pitcairn prosecutions either on the grounds of cultural relativism or on the grounds of lack of promulgation.[13] To be sure, the lack of proper promulgation of the Sexual Offences Act is not only relevant for the *legality* of punishment but also for our assessment of the degree of the defendants' moral blameworthiness. But it is only one factor amongst many others and it is plausible that promulgation would not have removed all the normative constraints to attributing full moral blame to the defendants. Cultural and political isolation and the United Kingdom's failure to establish an institutional presence on the island that would create essential public goods (of the kind people enjoy in the metropolitan state), are relevant in assessing how far we may hold the islanders accountable for acts of wrongdoing. And in my view, we cannot go very far given the institutional neglect that the United Kingdom has shown towards Pitcairn until the rape prosecutions of 2004.

It is also important to stress that the United Kingdom could have condemned the wrongs it discovered on Pitcairn in 2004 and

---

[12] In 1989 there were twice as many women on Pitcairn as men. The population of Pitcairn was 55, 18 of whom were men and 37 were women. Out of 37 women, nine were girls under 16.

[13] See Professor Guest's illuminating discussion of *mala in se* and *ignorantia* in chapter 8 below.

attributed—publicly—moral blame to the perpetrators, without prosecuting them. Given the discretionary character of prosecutorial powers in the UK legal system, such an option would have been both possible and sensible. The attribution of criminal responsibility, though dependent on notions of moral responsibility, involves an additional element of moral disapprobation as well as criminal sanctions that were disproportionate to the degree of the defendants' moral blameworthiness.

In this section I have tried to show that cultural relativism lends no support to the view that rightness and wrongness are relative to each culture and no support to the view that we ought never to interfere in the affairs of other cultures. I distinguished between wrongness and blameworthiness and argued that, though the Pitcairn offences were universal moral wrongs, less than full moral blame was warranted. The option the United Kingdom government took, to prosecute the offenders under the Sexual Offences Act, was disproportionate to the degree of blameworthiness involved. In the remainder of this paper, I will shift focus to examine whether the Pitcairn prosecutions were inappropriate quite apart from whether the defendants were morally blameworthy or not.

## Legal Positivism and Natural Law

Historically, legal positivism and natural law have been seen as conflicting, mutually exclusive, positions about the nature of law. Yet the divide between positivism and natural law is not easy to draw, at least not in a way that will meet every legal theorist's agreement. But some general remarks are in order, in order to understand how the debate bears on the Pitcairn case.

First, it is no longer the case, if it ever was, that what separates the two schools of thought is the belief in moral objectivity. Some moral sceptics have in the past been drawn to legal positivism thinking that statements about what the law is and what functions law performs are factual and value-free. They were motivated by the belief that the study of law can be objective in a scientific sense, insulated from the threatening scepticism and the pervasive disagreement that plugs moral argumentation.[14]

---

[14] Hans Kelsen is an example of a legal theorist whose theory of law was driven by the rejection of the idea of moral objectivity. Karl Marx's account of law, as causally determined by whatever economic relations are in force, is also often seen as driven by a value-free sociological positivism that rejects the possibility of evaluative objectivity.

But of course some of the most well-known analytic legal positivists are not moral sceptics. Jeremy Bentham, the founder of utilitarianism, which is one of the most comprehensive moral and political theories, certainly was not. He took the principle of maximizing happiness for the greatest number to be an objective moral principle, one whose validity does not depend on what people say or think. Nor is Joseph Raz a moral sceptic: his work in moral and political philosophy (perfectionism) has had a huge impact in the field and is perhaps better known than his theory of law. Utilitarians and perfectionists are moral cognitivists who believe that there are objective moral values (eg utility or well-being), which determine the truth (or falsity) of moral propositions. There might be a link between legal positivism and utilitarianism (or perfectionism) but that link is not to be found in the rejection of moral objectivity.

Likewise, it is no longer the case that what is distinctive of natural law theories is the belief that there are objective moral norms and values which are independent of and superior to those recognized by man-made law. Though some natural lawyers, like Michael Moore,[15] emphasize their commitment to moral realism as a distinctive position of natural law, contemporary natural lawyers, like John Finnis, are more interested in how positive law can promote objective moral goods rather than whether there are any in the first place.[16] On John Finnis' view it is constitutive of law that it be put in the service of the common good but he accepts that very often actual legal systems fail badly in their constitutive aim.

Most legal theorists moreover, and indeed most people, think that man-made law can range from being perfectly just and fair at one end of the moral spectrum, to being average and morally imperfect albeit tolerable in the middle, to being morally evil and wicked at the other end. Most of us do not assume that the legality of a norm is the only standard of its legitimacy, that the law has the final word on what is right and

---

[15] See Michael Moore, 'Law as a Functional Kind' in Robert P. George (ed.), *Natural Law Theories: Contemporary Essays* (Oxford: Clarendon Press, 1992), pp. 188–242; Michael Moore, 'Moral Reality', *Wisconsin Law Review* (1982), p. 1061; Michael Moore, 'Moral Reality Revisited' 90 *Michigan Law Review* (1992), p. 2424.

[16] See John Finnis, *Natural Law and Natural Rights* (Oxford: Clarendon Press, 1980). Finnis takes these goods to be 'self-evident'.

what is wrong. The phrase 'morally unjustified law', as John Gardner puts it, is not an oxymoron.[17]

Nor do we assume that the standards by which we judge the legitimacy of a legal system are necessarily internal to the society in which that system is in force; that the only way, for instance, in which Iranian law can be illegitimate is by falling short of cultural and religious ideas prevalent in Iranian society. We believe that it is both intelligible and meaningful to make cross-cultural judgements about whether governments treat their people justly and we believe that it is possible for the majority of a society to hold beliefs that are morally abhorrent and that inflict great moral harm to minorities or outsiders. A state may be unjust and inflict great moral harm by violating principles that are not shared by the people who live in it.

What are we then to make of the old debate between legal positivism and its rivals and how does that impact on the Pitcairn case?

Recall Austin's motto that 'the existence of law is one thing, its merits or demerits another'.[18] Contemporary legal positivists believe that the Austinian position has become something of a trivial thesis about law that no one seriously denies, not even contemporary natural lawyers.[19] They take for granted that the validity of legal norms is a matter of social facts, which does not depend on moral evaluation. And they illustrate this point by a set of propositions that aim to show how there is only a *contingent* link between legality and morality. First, the mere fact that a putative norm is a morally good norm does not suffice to turn it into a legally valid one. For example, the fact that freedom of speech is a morally good norm does not make freedom of speech a legally binding norm in China. A norm is a legally valid one if, and only if, it comes from a source that norm-applying institutions of a country recognize and use in their adjudicative practices (rules of recognition). Second, the mere fact that a norm is legally valid does not suffice to turn that norm into a morally good one. The validity of the race discrimination laws in Apartheid South Africa for example did not, in the slightest bit, change

---

[17] See John Gardner, 'Law's Aim in Law's Empire' in Scott Hershovitz (ed.), *Exploring Law's Empire* (Oxford: Oxford University Press, 2006), p. 207, at 217.

[18] John Austin, *The Province of Jurisprudence Determined* (Cambridge: Cambridge University Press, 1955), p. 184.

[19] See John Finnis, 'The Truth in Legal Positivism' in Robert P. George (ed.), *The Autonomy of Law* (Oxford: Oxford University Press, 1996), pp. 195–214.

the fact that these laws were morally abhorrent. Law *promises* justice,[20] but we know that some of the greatest injustices in human history were inflicted by law. To sum up, positivists believe in the truth of the following two propositions: the morality of a norm is neither a necessary nor a sufficient condition for the validity of a norm; and the legal validity of a norm is neither a necessary nor a sufficient condition for the morality of a norm.

That is not to say of course that legal positivists do not have a story to tell about when it is justified to follow the law. The most well-known story is Joseph Raz's normal justification thesis, according to which it is a necessary condition for the legitimacy of an authority that:

> [ ... ] the subject would better conform to reasons that apply to him anyway (that is, to reasons other than the directives of the authority) if he intends to be guided by the authority's directives than if he does not.[21]

But legal positivists insist that the legitimacy of enforcing legal norms depends on reasons other than the fact that they are legal. By contrast, the validity of law is considered to be a matter of empirical fact and does not depend on the truth of moral propositions. Legal *validity* of a norm is independent of its content and it is derived from factual criteria used in practice by norm-applying and norm-enforcing institutions in a given territory. On the positivist view, what makes some normative system the legal system of the UK is the fact that it is practised by officials and that people living in the UK by and large obey the norms. Hart writes:

> There are therefore two minimum conditions necessary and sufficient for the existence of a legal system. On the one hand, those rules of behavior which are valid according to the system's ultimate criteria of validity must be generally obeyed, and, on the other hand, its rules of recognition specifying the criteria of legal validity and its rules of change and adjudication must be effectively accepted as common public standards of official behavior by its officials.[22]

What would the legal positivist position be with respect to whether English law was valid on Pitcairn? One question is what the relevant position is from the point of view of English law. There are two

---

[20] Cf. Jeremy Waldron, 'Does Law Promise Justice?', 17 *Georgia State University Law Review* (2001), p. 759.

[21] Joseph Raz, 'The Problem of Authority: Revisiting the Service Conception', 90 *Minnesota Law Review* (2006), p. 1003, at 1014.

[22] H. L. A. Hart, *The Concept of Law* (2nd edition, Oxford: Clarendon Press, 1994), p. 116.

possibilities here. First, if UK officials (most importantly, courts) had in the past explicitly treated Pitcairn Island as falling within the jurisdiction of the UK, then legal positivists would assert that, from the point of view of English law, the Sexual Offences Act was legally valid on Pitcairn and that the prosecutions were lawful. Having said that, however, they may well agree with the conclusion reached in the previous section, namely that, *morally* speaking, legal punishment of the islanders was disproportionate and hence morally objectionable; legal positivists are not moral sceptics. They can, in the same breath and without any inconsistency, assert the lawfulness as well as the inappropriateness of the Pitcairn prosecutions and convictions.

If, on the other hand, there was no clear precedent or statute to the effect that Pitcairn was within the jurisdiction of the UK for the purposes of applying criminal law, then the legal positivist would assert the existence of a 'gap' in the law of the United Kingdom which courts in *Christian and Others* filled retrospectively by creating new law. If that is the case, then—before *Christian* was decided—it was neither true nor false that the British Crown had jurisdiction over Pitcairn. But after the Privy Council's judgment in *Christian*, English law does provide for the British Crown's jurisdiction over Pitcairn. Under this second possibility, legal positivists would probably be even more critical in their moral assessment of what courts decided, given that the judges' task would not be one of applying pre-existing law but one of acting as a lawmaker who has to take into account all the relevant circumstances without being bound by any text or precedent. And given the severe criminal sanctions that would (and did) follow upon the retrospective, 'gap-filling' judgment that Pitcairn is within the criminal jurisdiction of the UK, legal positivists may well condemn the judicial outcome on the ground that courts exercised their judicial discretion in a morally deficient way.

There is a further complication however. Whether, from the point of view of English law, the British Crown has jurisdiction over Pitcairn is one thing. But whether the English legal system is *in fact* the legal system of Pitcairn Island is another. It is wrong to infer the latter from the former. As Professor Guest puts it, reminding us of Hart's related critique of Kelsenian positivism, 'saying so does not make it so'.[23] It is clearly not the case that if the Westminster Parliament passes an Act tomorrow extending its jurisdiction over the territory of Zimbabwe, the

---

[23] See Guest, chapter 8 below.

English legal system will *ipso facto* become the legal system in force in Zimbabwe (however desirable such a thing would be). This is because the scope of jurisdiction that a legal system claims for itself need not be coextensive with the jurisdiction that a legal system in fact has. This is an important intuition that most legal theorists share (Kelsen aside), positivists and not positivists alike.

The way legal positivists try to accommodate this intuition is by introducing two further criteria that a legal system must meet in order to be the system *in force* in a particular territory and to constitute the legal system of a particular class of persons. First, the norm-applying institutions must practice the system's criteria of validity when settling disputes between the people living in that territory;[24] second, the latter must by and large obey the laws made by those who are authorized to enact valid law under the legal system's criteria of validity. To use the same example, if courts in Zimbabwe were to practise the criteria of validity of the English legal system, applying Westminster statutes *and* people in Zimbabwe were to obey whatever the Queen in Parliament enacts, then the English legal system would become the legal system in force in Zimbabwe. Likewise, if Pitcairn courts practice the criteria of validity of the English legal system and Pitcairn islanders by and large obey English law, then—according to the legal positivist—the English legal system is the legal system in force on Pitcairn. On the positivist view, both these conditions are matters of *empirical* fact, a matter of what the 'facts on the ground' of Pitcairn are, rather than a matter of what English law says or what the Crown officials believed.

Interestingly, the Privy Council did not seem to acknowledge the possibility that, despite all the Orders in Council made under the British Settlements Act 1887 and relevant statements made by the executive, the English legal system was not *in force* on Pitcairn. The Privy Council only looked at matters 'from the point of view of English law'. Delivering the judgment of the Privy Council, Lord Hoffmann opined:

Mr Cook QC proposed to take their Lordships to the history of the island to demonstrate that the islanders never acknowledged allegiance to the Crown. Their Lordships declined to investigate this question because it appears to them that the legal status of the island as a British possession is concluded by

---

[24] See Joseph Raz, *Practical Reasons and Norms* (Oxford: Oxford University Press, 1999), pp. 123–177.

successive statements of the executive, starting with the direction of the Secretary of State in 1898 and ending with the making of the 1970 Order in Council [ . . . ] For over a hundred years Pitcairn has been administered by the Crown as a British possession and whatever its history or the inclinations of its people may have been, it is unthinkable that the Judicial Committee of Her Majesty's Privy Council would not accept an executive statement affirming it to be part of the territory of the Crown.[25]

This position may be understandable given that the Privy Council is primarily a court within the UK legal system and its institutional structure. It contradicts however the positivist distinction between the scope of jurisdiction of a legal system as proposed by norms within that system, and the actual jurisdiction over a territory or group of people as a matter of *empirical* fact. And it is possible for a legal positivist to argue that the English legal system was not in force on Pitcairn before *Christian* was decided and that a separate 'Pitcairn legal system' existed. Would she be right? Regarding whether the two conditions above were met, the answer is definitely not obvious but a negative one seems more likely. First, the islanders never explicitly acknowledged allegiance to the Crown; and clearly most of them did not take for granted that the Crown had jurisdiction over the island when criminal charges were brought against the defendants under English law. Second, there is little evidence of a systematic judicial practice, say by the Island Magistrate, of settling disputes between the islanders using English law. There was moreover evidence of applying what was known on Pitcairn as 'island laws'.

Such empirical facts, however, may be hard to establish and I do not mean to take a definitive stance on whether the positivist's conditions for the existence of a legal system were met in the case of Pitcairn. This is mainly because, as far as the *legitimacy* of the prosecutions and convictions is concerned (which is what interests me in this chapter), it matters little to a legal positivist whether the English legal system was in force on Pitcairn. Recall that the legal positivist takes the existence of law (or lack thereof) to be a matter of fact, which does not, by itself, provide any moral reasons regarding whether a particular law should be followed and applied. Legal positivists do not aim at providing an answer to the question of legitimacy and they do not think that lack of a de facto Crown jurisdiction over Pitcairn would immediately taint the legitimacy of the prosecutions. And the other way around: they do not think that a clear existence of Crown jurisdiction over the islanders

---

[25] *Christian and Others*, para. 10.

would immediately confer moral legitimacy on the prosecutions. The positivist dissociation of the issue of legal jurisdiction from the legitimacy of the prosecutions seems to me to be a mistake. It would be surprising if the finding that the English legal system was not the actual legal system of the islanders, had no impact on whether the Crown prosecutions in *Christian* were legitimate. In the next and final section I shall explore a non-positivist argument against the legitimacy of applying English law in the Pitcairn case.

## Legality and Community

In the previous section I identified an important intuition that legal theorists try to capture: acts enacted by legislatures within a particular legal system setting out its jurisdictional scope, and relevant statements made by officials on behalf of the legal system, are not determinative of whether that legal system applies in a given territory or class of persons; whether, that is, it is the legal system *of* those persons. This intuition can be fleshed out as follows: there is a sense in which there must be a *special* relation between rulers and ruled, between coercers and coercees, in order for the latter to be under the legal authority of the former. No such special relation is created between individuals and a government by the mere fact that the latter intends to enact norms that bind the former. For example, no special relation would be created between British people and the Chinese government if the latter passed a law making Chinese law applicable in Britain. Such law would not suffice to bring British people under the legal authority of the Chinese government.

Now, legal positivists try to account for this special relationship through the idea of de facto authority: a body has de facto authority over a class of persons when first, it *claims* legitimate (*de jure*) authority and it is 'in fact followed or at least conformed with by considerable segments of the population'.[26] A special relation is created when the population conforms with the laws made by a body that claims legitimate authority over that population. And we saw in the last section that, for positivists, the existence of such relation is a matter of empirical fact. But can it be something more than that? Are the mere facts of individuals in a given territory complying with the laws of a legislature

[26] Joseph Raz, 'The Problem of Authority: Revisiting the Service Conception', 90 *Minnesota Law Review* (2006), p. 1036.

and of courts applying its laws, enough to establish a relationship of legal authority between them?

The alternative, non-positivist, account of the special relation that must exist between the rulers and the ruled treats that relation not as a matter of empirical fact, but rather as an *evaluative* question. To provide an analogy: it is not a matter of empirical fact whether two persons who spend time together are really friends; whether this is the case depends on whether their behaviour and attitudes instantiate the ethical value of friendship, whether, that is, their relationship meets a *moral* test furnished by our best understanding of the value of friendship. This is the line of argument I wish to explore in relation to the Pitcairn case, because I believe that it does a better job than legal positivism in explaining why law does not exist unless there is some kind of special relation between the rulers and the ruled.[27] If there is a *moral* test governing whether individuals are under the legal authority of a government, and that test was not met in the case of Pitcairn, then the prosecutions lacked the moral legitimacy that would have existed had this moral test been meet.

My starting point is the idea that both the notion of legality and that of criminal punishment presuppose the existence of a distinct political community with its own collective practices and historical ties. Legal punishment, particularly when it involves imprisonment or other forms of deprivation of liberty, is a case of collective use of coercive force exercised *in the name* of a political community. Contrast legal punishment to the following cases: victims of injustice who seek self-redress; private avengers hired to inflict harm on wrongdoers; religious fundamentalists who take themselves to have the power to punish sinners in the name of God; individuals to whom others have voluntarily granted permission to inflict physical harm. We would not characterize any of these acts as cases of criminal punishment because they are not done in the name of a political community nor are they authorized by it to do so. It is essential to legal punishment that it be administered by representatives of the people as a whole, in the name of the people as a whole.

The power to punish and coercively to enforce laws is therefore a *normative* power that depends on there being a *political* community between the rulers and the ruled. Whether or not such political community exists, moreover, is not a descriptive matter. A group of people

---

[27] My interest here is mainly to contrast the positivist and the non-positivist position on this rather than provide a defence of the latter.

interacting with each other does not necessarily amount to a political community. There is no political community between slave owners and slaves or between mafia extortionists and their victims. Some *moral* conditions must be met for any form of social organization to count as a political community in the right sense, ie in the sense that it is necessary for legal authority to exist and for law to create obligations on individuals.

Ronald Dworkin sets out two conditions that a community must meet if its decisions are to be legitimately enforced upon individuals *qua* law. The first one is empirical: the community in question must have a historical and geographical continuity over time. It must first be, as Dworkin calls it, a *bare* community.[28] Second, the community must also meet the moral requirements of a *true* community, one in which genuine political obligations and rights exist between its members and can be legitimately enforced through collective force. Dworkin claims that there are four requirements for the existence of a true community. First, the relationship within the community is *special* and does not hold towards individuals outside it. Second, the relationship is *personal*, 'established directly from each member to each other'. Third, there is *reciprocal* concern for the well-being of other members of the community. And fourth, the community displays an attitude of *equal concern* towards all its members.[29] On Dworkin's view, only true communities can create obligations on its members to respect the legal rights and duties that flow from its past political decisions and only true communities have legitimacy to coerce their members in the name of law. Dworkin calls the value that governs how true communities may coercively enforce their decisions using collective force *legality*.[30] Since for him law, properly understood, only exists when there is a true community, legal obligation is also a *moral* obligation and state enforcement of the law is prima facie morally *legitimate*. But when the community is not a true one, lacking one or more of the above requirements, then its laws create no moral obligation and legal coercion carries no title of moral legitimacy. Unlike legal positivism, this view does not separate

---

[28] Ronald Dworkin, *Law's Empire*, (Oxford: Hart Publishing, 1986), p. 199ff.

[29] The requirement of equal concern is that of a genuine and honest egalitarian attitude towards people rather a requirement of *actual* equal distribution of burdens and benefits and just treatment. It is therefore compatible with some injustice in those political communities.

[30] See Ronald Dworkin, *Justice in Robes* (Cambridge, Mass: Harvard University Press, 2006).

the existence of law and legal authority on one hand from the legitimacy of state coercion and legal enforcement on the other.

Applying the above non-positivist remarks to the Pitcairn case, it seems to me plausible that no 'true' community existed, at the time of the prosecutions, between the United Kingdom and the islanders, even if we do accept that a 'bare' relationship had been established over time through the British Settlements Act 1887 and the various Orders in Council made under it. There was little sense in which the islanders and the British people shared a personal and special concern for each other's well-being.[31] First, the islanders felt little allegiance towards the Crown and counted their internal relationships as more special and important than their relation to the British people. John Stuart Mill's account of a people's culture, which he calls 'nationality' is here illuminating:

A portion of mankind may be said to constitute a Nationality, if they are united among themselves by common sympathies, which do not exist between them and any others—which make them cooperate with each other more willingly than with other people, desire to be under the same government, and desire that it should be government by themselves, or a portion of themselves, exclusively. This feeling of nationality may have been generated by various causes. Sometimes it is the effect of identity or race and descent. Community of language, community of religion, greatly contribute to it. Geographical limits are one of its causes. But the strongest of all is identity of political antecedents; the possession of national history, and consequent community of recollections; collective pride and humiliation, pleasure and regret, connected with the same incidents in the past. None of these circumstances, however, are necessarily sufficient by themselves.[32]

Clearly, taking Mill's criteria into account would weigh heavily in favour of there being a Pitcairn 'people' and a Pitcairn community with its own

---

[31] That is not to say of course that a *true* community necessarily existed between the Pitcairn Islanders. To the extent that immoral practices, such as sexual abuse and rape, were widely and systematically practised on the island as conventional 'legal' norms, then 'Pitcairn law' generated no moral rights and obligations, even if it was accepted by the majority of the islanders. But in my view, even if the value of legality did not apply to the community of Pitcairn, for lack of reciprocal egalitarian concern between its members, this does not automatically licence the coercive intervention of another legal system. The upshot of this account is that there may be a sense in which Pitcairn was lawless, ie that neither English law nor Pitcairn law created any moral obligations (and rights) for the islanders.

[32] J. S. Mill, 'Considerations on Representative Government', in J. M. Robson (ed.), *John Stuart Mill: Collected Works* (Toronto: University of Toronto Press, 1977), vol. XIX, p. 546 as quoted by John Rawls, *The Law of Peoples* (Cambridge, Mass: Harvard University Press, 1999), p. 23.

special collective memory and sense of identity and pride that are separate from, and are not shared with, the United Kingdom. There was moreover no relationship of *reciprocity* between the islanders and the British people, no sense in which UK policies that promote the well-being of British people must show due regard to the interest of the islanders and vice versa.

But more important than these more or less psychological elements is the fact that the British government had done very little by way of providing *institutional support, welfare protection*, and *political representation* to the islanders. What the British government has shown towards Pitcairn is at best institutional neglect and at worst total absence of political engagement and institutional presence. There was no sign of a commitment on the part of the British government to showing *equal* concern to the islanders, of a commitment that their well-being and voice matters in principle as much as those of any other British subject. And in practice, very few of the rights and benefits that people in the United Kingdom enjoy in virtue of being British citizens were ever extended to the islanders. Pitcairn islanders did not stand to gain or lose anything by how resources and other benefits were allocated in the United Kingdom nor were they ever asked to have a say as to how some of these resources may be spent to improve the quality of life on the island. Nor did they have access to the full institutional machinery that supports the exercise of rights of private law in the United Kingdom, such as a land registry, a wills registry, police protection, bailiffs, judicial remedies, and so on and so forth.

In my view, the case is strong that no true community, as defined above, ever existed between the United Kingdom and Pitcairn. On a non-positivist account of legality, this entails that English law created no duties for Pitcairn islanders and that coercive enforcement of English law against them lacked the moral legitimacy that legal enforcement always carries.[33] It entails, in other words, that the Crown had no legal authority over Pitcairn, and hence no legitimacy to prosecute, despite the existence of some statutory texts and executive statements to the

---

[33] I will not discuss in this paper what permissible grounds exist for coercive interference and punishment of moral wrongs other than the existence of legal obligations within a true political community. Clearly, violations of international law (such as genocide and other crimes against humanity) may justify coercive interference and punishment by external agents despite the absence of a special relation between the intervening agent and the coercees. It suffices to say that the character and scale of the Pitcairn offences do not fall within the category of wrongs for which that kind of intervention is warranted.

contrary. On the non-positivist view I have sketched, the impact of these statutes and statements must be seen in the light of the value of *legality*, which imposes a *moral* test on coercive enforcement of past political decisions: it is a necessary (though not sufficient) condition that the coercee is an equal member of a true political community. I have argued that this condition was not met in the Pitcairn case and that therefore the relevant English statutes and statements conferred no legitimacy on the Pitcairn prosecutions *qua* legal actions. This argument supports the defendants' case and it is quite independent of the argument from promulgation: even if the United Kingdom had clearly promulgated the Sexual Offences Act on Pitcairn this would not have been enough to meet the conditions for the existence of a true community within which legal coercion can be justified.

Sadly, the argument from lack of jurisdiction received the least attention in the Privy Council's judgment, and was dismissed quickly on the grounds that judicial notice had been taken of all the relevant constitutional documents and executive statements.[34] A more detailed examination of the issue would perhaps have revealed the difficulty (and the paradox) in taking those documents and instruments as determinative of the existence of jurisdiction. It would have been neither inconsistent nor absurd for English courts to have found the prosecutions unlawful for lack of jurisdiction by elaborating on the idea that the mere existence of a legal norm in the UK extending jurisdiction to a particular territory or class of persons is not enough to establish the actual existence of jurisdiction. Though both positivists and non-positivists would have been happy with such a finding, only an *evaluative*— rather than *factual*—conception of jurisdiction, one that draws on the value of legality and what counts as a true political community, would truly justify it. Had the Privy Council followed such an evaluative conception of jurisdiction, the outcome of the case could have been different. In the absence of a special political relation between the islanders and those on behalf of whom the criminal charges were brought and the penalties were imposed, we may question not only the legitimacy of the Crown's intervention but also its *legality*.

---

[34] See Lord Hoffmann's remarks in *Christian*, para. 9.

## Conclusion

I have argued in this chapter that there are universal moral wrongs, of the kind committed by the defendants on Pitcairn, whose existence does not depend on cultural practices and societal approval. The cultural relativist has no hope of opposing external interference with cultural practices on the ground that morality is not universal. By contrast, judgements of moral blameworthiness can be culture-specific, requiring a detailed and careful examination of local circumstances. In my view the circumstances on Pitcairn Island were such that less than full moral blame was warranted. The British government's decision to prosecute the offenders for the moral wrongs they had committed and to impose legal punishment involved a distinctive element of moral disapprobation that was disproportionate to their degree of blameworthiness. In addition, I argued that prosecuting and convicting the defendants under English law was illegitimate *qua* an exercise of legal authority, on the ground that no relationship of political community existed between the islanders and the British government of the kind that can justify coercive enforcement of law. The existence of legal authority over a territory or class of person is not an empirical matter, as legal positivism assumes, but an evaluative one which imposes normative conditions for the enforcement of valid legal norms.

Some may argue that even if we concede the lack of legal authority, the Crown was morally justified in intervening in order to prevent further abuse and protect the victims. Legality, they may argue, is not the only acceptable moral ground for punishment. This may well be the case and in fact it may also be the case that the Pitcairn case will mark the beginning of a new political relationship between the United Kingdom and Pitcairn, one closer to the ideal of equal respect and concern. Indeed let us hope that this will happen sooner rather than later. Nevertheless, it is important, I think, to note that a kind of injustice towards the defendants was committed in *Christian and Others*, an injustice which may be outweighed, but will not be extinguished, by future beneficial consequences for the island. We must emphasize this claim of injustice if we care about legality and if we care about justifying the exercise of state coercion to those who are subject to it, no matter how terrible the moral wrongs that they have committed are.

# 8

# Legality, Reciprocity, and the Criminal Law on Pitcairn

*Stephen Guest*

In this paper I suggest some arguments in favour of the defendants in the case of *Steven Raymond Christian & Others v The Queen.*[1] My account is of a broad 'natural law' sort although I mean by that no more than 'non-positivist'. (Not that the term 'non-positivist' is entirely clear but it is clearer than the term 'natural law'.) I would add that I do not condone rape or the various sexual assaults as defined by the Sexual Offences Act 1956 which were the basis for the convictions. Nor should I be understood to be in any sense 'anti-feminist' when expressing disapproval of the use of the criminal law in dealing with the widespread sexual abuse that occurred on the island for many years. (And so I am neither a cultural nor moral 'relativist'.) My objections to the prosecutions are primarily on the two non-chauvinist grounds that due consideration should have been given to the crucial requirements of legality before bringing the prosecutions, and that the criminal law was, in the peculiar circumstances of Pitcairn, an inappropriate tool for bringing about the necessary change of sexual culture. On the point of legality, it is important to remember that, outside of very special circumstances such as war, or genocide, we don't generally think that because someone has acted in an undesirable way (by 'undesirable' we could add any number of definitions which might include 'anti-social', 'generally accepted as wrong', or even just 'wrong') that fact is in itself sufficient for us to say it was *illegal*. We may actually go further than this. If someone does something even

[1] [2006] UKPC 47.

jurisdiction over Pitcairn there should have been argumentative attention paid towards evidence of a more fairly integrated relationship between Britain and Pitcairn than was apparent from the 'paper trail' of constitutional enactment and appointment. The argument concerns the nature of legality and, in particular, why punishing people in the name of law demands something over and above the existence of isolated, unjust acts, albeit that they represented serious breaches of morality.

Second, even if we assume British jurisdiction, it was not clear that the English criminal law was sufficiently brought to the attention of the defendants, this being the issue advanced in *Christian*—at all hearings—that there was insufficient promulgation of the law applying on the island. Relevant content, including penalties, of the Sexual Offences Act 1956 may not have been sufficiently clear to the defendants in a sizeable number of instances given, first, an 'enculturation' in the defendants of 'Tahitian' sexual custom, including a confused belief that even non-consensual sex with girls over the age of puberty was not particularly serious,[3] and, second, the absence of police and a court structure, the existence of an unused jail, and almost no sign of willingness on the part of the Pitcairn community or authorities anywhere, either in New Zealand, or Britain, to bring an end to this culture.

Three further points concern the nature of the criminal law. The first is to remind us that the criminal law is a blunt instrument whose purpose is primarily the enforcement of external compliance with a desired social norm. Its job is to announce that certain acts 'not be done' and to furnish a motive for compliance in the form of social stigma or punishment.[4] Where means less intrusive of personal freedom may be used, it follows that this will be preferable, particularly where a change in *internal* attitude is crucial. The second is an argument against the increasingly popular view that the criminal law should in large part be concerned with justice to the victims of crime. According to this view, victims 'secure justice' only when the perpetrator of the crime against them is pursued and punished. A more emphatic version of that view claims that victims have 'rights' both to the fact of punishment, as well as to its degree. Questions of jurisdiction aside, if the victims had such

---

[3] The only relevant Pitcairn criminal offence was that of 'unlawful carnal knowledge' of girls over 12.

[4] See, generally, Hart, H. L. A. *Punishment and Responsibility*, revised edn (2008) Oxford: OUP.

rights, that would support the criminal prosecutions. On the other hand, if, as I maintain, victims have no such rights to prosecution or to the punishment of their tormentors but only rights to fair treatment, it is not necessary to suppose that the only way of improving the situation was through the criminal law. Other solutions were an amnesty, followed by counselling and compensation to victims, or even perhaps a South African style 'truth and reconciliation' procedure. The third is an argument that, given the draconian nature of the criminal law, a principle of *certainty* should be observed as much in the criminal law as it is admired in property law. If a person cannot reasonably know what it is they must do—that is, how they should modify their behaviour to avoid conviction—it cannot be fair to convict.[5]

## Crown Jurisdiction in Pitcairn: Community and Legal Theory

The jurisdiction of the British Crown over Pitcairn has never been clear because of the ambiguity inherent in the long historical connection between Britain and Pitcairn. The Pitcairn community was tainted with rebellion from the community's formation following the *Bounty* mutiny. That ambiguity remains, the taste of rebellion renewed each year in the ceremonial burning of an effigy of the *Bounty* on the island bay. Yet the islanders refer to themselves as British—as one imagines the original mutineers did—and they display a British-derived flag.[6] The almost total lack of contact between the island and Britain has been striking. Precisely what one would expect that contact to be is a difficult question, given the isolation, but the reality was, and to a large extent still is, only via some electronic connection (Internet and shortwave radio) and passing cruise ships. The occasional administrative direction comes from New Zealand and not Britain. Any input to law creation through the Island Council was to the laws drawn up by the Island Governor who does so in the British High Commission in Wellington, 2,200 miles to the southwest. The island community is conspicuously small in territory (two square miles) and population (47 people) and there are only four families, with strong evidence of inbreeding.

---

[5] This formulation covers strict liability offences; these, in my view, are compatible with responsibility where they reasonably impose duties 'to find out'.

[6] The flag is a British ensign with a burning *Bounty* imposed on top.

Although it is as small as the tiniest of English villages, that comparison omits its dramatic isolation, for Pitcairn's nearest neighbour is the relatively empty and barely populated Easter Island, over 1,000 miles to the east. Pitcairn Island is generally thought to be the most isolated community in the world.

Imagine a ship that leaves Britain under a naval captain who represents the sovereign at high seas. The ship becomes stalled, radio contact is lost, and the ship roams free like *The Flying Dutchman*. After a long time, when the ship is becalmed, it becomes stuck on a rock, and coral gradually anchors it to the seabed and it becomes a tiny island supporting a tiny population of the descendants of the ship's sailors.[7] There will come a point in the interpretation of this chain of events that the past becomes only of detached historical interest. Similarly, think of George Washington's axe, the head and handle of which were replaced several times since he chopped down the cherry tree. What principle of historical interpretation should—if it should—link this present axe with the one that Washington once held in his hands? Both analogies suggest that the mere recital of a chain of events is insufficient; that something extra is needed to say why this or that chronology is significant in showing why the island is still ruled by the ship owners, or why this axe is the same as Washington's, or even that certain events constitute a 'chain' or a 'chronology'. As the colour of historical connection fades, the question of the criteria of significance looms. Given that the Pitcairn defendants were charged with criminal offences, and so were potentially liable to punishment, what role do past events play? The answer must lie in an account of the most basic conditions for making a justifiable claim of law; in other words, the answer must lie in a convincing account of the meaning of *legality*. The Pitcairn prosecutions raised this, and related issues, very acutely.

To say that 'the law says', or that 'the defendant has contravened a legal provision, or committed a legal offence' must, I suggest, be to claim wrongful non-compliance on the part of some person with a requirement that is in some sense issued on behalf of—or in the name of—a community. It would follow that to make a *legal* claim in Pitcairn's case would be to announce that the community represented by

---

[7] The analogy is apt given the British propensity for having treated remote islands as ships; examples are: HMS Diamond Rock, a lump of granite in the Grenadines; the HMS Atlantic Isle, which was, both before and after the Second World War, Tristan da Cunha. Most well known is Ascension Island, originally known as HMS Ascension.

the British Crown was justified in applying coercive power against the defendants (we may leave open, for now, what that community was). We should note, of course, that the legal claim is different from the announcement that the defendants had acted wrongly. The 'legal' claim requires something more than that, the focus being not on the wrongness of the act itself—for acts can be wrong but not illegal—but on a community's collective right to use its coercive powers. Further, in any legal system, the claim of legality will imply some minimal relationship between the body making the claim and the people to whom that claim is directed. Even in uncivilized legal systems in which there are absolute monarchies and dictatorships, the fact that the monarch or the dictator 'has spoken' means they 'speak for' the state. Again, that claim is different from the bare claim that the subject did something wrong. In civilized legal systems, I believe it is reasonable to conclude that a claim of law has the colour of a *moral* claim, for instance, that the ruler acts with moral legitimacy, say, in accordance with principles of decency, or in recognition of fundamental rights, or principles of democracy. If so, we may learn from those legal theorists who emphasize links between governments and the communities they purport to govern. One such theorist was Lon Fuller who consistently maintained that we cannot make any sense of legal systems unless we understand them to aspire to certain ideals of morality.[8] (And, in the example of uncivilized legal systems above, what sense can we truly give to the idea that community-wide obligations are imposed by mere claims?) The most abstract formulation of Fuller's ideal was what he referred to as the necessity of 'reciprocity of expectation' between law-makers and those subject to laws, disparagingly terming the idea of law as a one-way set of orders as 'law as managerial direction' only. The clearest statement of his view is in his *The Morality of Law*,[9] where he argued that the more a community loses 'interactivity' or 'reciprocity of expectation' between ruler and ruled, the more a legal system's moral power to impose obligations and confer powers declines: '. . . the existence of a relatively stable reciprocity of expectations between lawgiver and subject is part of the very idea of a functioning legal order'.[10]

---

[8] Fuller founds his theory on a distinction between the 'moralities' of 'aspiration' and of 'duty'. See Fuller, L. L. *The Morality of Law*, revised edn (1969) New Haven and London: Yale University Press, chapter 1.

[9] 'Reply to his Critics', in Fuller, L. *The Morality of Law*, note 8.          [10] Ibid.

Fuller leaves the territorial and communal reach of this view unspecified. But the thrust is clear, and the contrast between the 'relatively stable reciprocity of expectations' between the British Government and people in Britain and the conspicuous absence of such expectations on Pitcairn must cause us to pause on the question of British jurisdiction. In considering this, we should realize that Fuller thought that such expectations, based on fairness between rulers and ruled, went directly to the question whether there was law or not. For his theory is one of what legality, properly understood, means.[11]

A not dissimilar view concerning the moral background to legality is advanced by Ronald Dworkin and in some variants by others, including this author.[12] While also viewing law as an 'aspirational' concept, Dworkin is more direct than Fuller, proposing that the importance of legality lies in the relatively conservative idea of uniting of a community's past with its present. It follows, he says, that the best view of law is through the means by which that ideal would be best achieved. We should do this by interpreting the legal practices of the community as morally coherently as we can. For him, this means reading those practices on the assumption that they treat all members of the community as

---

[11] Ibid. Other similar quotations are: '...the basic difference between law and managerial direction [is that] law is not, like management, a matter of directing other persons how to accomplish tasks set by a superior, but is basically a matter of providing the citizenry with a sound and stable framework for their interactions with one another.' (210). '[T]he Rule of Law demands of a government that it...legitimate its actions towards citizens.' (211). 'The publication of rules plainly carries with it the "social meaning" that the rule maker will himself abide by his own rules.' (217). '[W]e must not ignore the reality of the commitment implied in lawmaking, nor forget that it finds expression in empirically observable social processes.' (218). '[T]he functioning of a legal system depends upon a cooperative effort—an effective and responsible interaction—between the law-giver and subject.' (219). 'If we could come to accept what may be called broadly an interactional view of law, many things would become clear that are now obscured by the prevailing conception of law as a one-way projection of authority.' (221). Compare this with the German jurist Jürgens Habermas who goes a little further in claiming that: 'The modern legal order can draw its legitimacy only from the idea of self-determination: citizens should always be able to understand themselves also as authors of the laws to which they are subject as addressees.' *Beyond Facts and Norms* trans. Rehg, (1996) Cambridge, Mass: MIT, 449.

[12] Allan, T. *Law, Liberty and Justice: the Legal Foundations of British Constitutionalism*, (1993) Oxford: OUP; Ashworth, A. *Principles of Criminal Law* (2003) Oxford: OUP; Dworkin, R. 'Political Judges and the Rule of Law' in Dworkin, R. *A Matter of Principle* (1985) Cambridge, Mass: Harvard University Press, 9–32; Dworkin, R. *Justice in Robes* (2006) Cambridge, Mass: Harvard University Press; Guest, S. 'Why the Law is Just' [2000] 31 *Current Legal Problems*; Tamanaha, B. *The Rule of Law* (2004), Cambridge: CUP; Tribe, L. 'Revisiting the Rule of Law' (1989) 64 *New York University Law Review* 726.

having moral rights to be treated as equals, and that they 'speak' to all members of the community 'with one voice', that assumption providing us with the critical tool to ensure whether the community acts 'on principle'. There is clearly a relationship between treating all members of the community as equals, and Fuller's idea of a reciprocity, since the moral entreaty to treat the ruled as equals would require a two-way response between rulers and ruled (in Dworkin's account, it requires the reciprocal relationship of a democracy). If there is insufficient reciprocity, or insufficient 'treatment as equals', then the conditions of legality are insufficiently met for both distinguished jurists. In an early account of legality, found in his Maccabaean lecture to the British Academy in 1977, Dworkin contrasted two versions of legality, one a 'formal' or 'rule-book' version that depended on the law being identified without moral judgement, and the other that depended on identifying law only through the moral rights it enforces. The moral conception is the more 'ambitious', he says, because:

It assumes that citizens have moral rights and duties with respect to one another, and political rights against the state as a whole. It insists that these moral and political rights be recognized in positive law... The rule of law on this conception is the ideal of rule by an accurate public conception of individual rights. It does not distinguish, as the rule book conception does, between the rule of law and substantive justice; on the contrary, it requires, as part of the ideal of law, that the rules in the rule-book capture and enforce moral rights.'[13]

Claims of law must conform to a set of moral principles which together constitute what we mean by the 'rule of law', he says. These principles are the abstract and familiar personal rights to dignity, equality, and freedom, and support the democratic legitimacy of the community. Although this account relegates non-democratic legal systems to a lesser status of legality or even to a failure of legality, we can still trace a connection to the uncivilized rule of absolute monarchs and dictators. As I have pointed out, in common with democratic laws and dictatorial decrees there is reference, albeit often cynical, to the points of view of those subject to it (Hitler: 'I speak on behalf of the German people'). This argument is not a sleight of hand, for our language is sufficiently flexible and rich to enable us to understand a dictator's commands as law in some sociological sense, that is, without our having morally to justify

---

[13] Dworkin, R. 'Political Judges and the Rule of Law', note 12, 12; Habermas, J., note 11.

it. If we accept the collection of moral principles behind the rule of law, then these principles will colour the significance with which we both regard and interpret law. It must follow that we reject *as law* the idea of those 'laws' that do not embody such principles. Where this leaves Pitcairn is to some extent problematic; both jurists propose theories that place the Pitcairn prosecutions only at the margin of legitimate legality.

There is little in the cases or the Pitcairn recent history to indicate that relevant officials in Britain, New Zealand, and Pitcairn discerned a connection between British neglect and British jurisdiction. But there was a prevalent view that British neglect was one of the causes of continuance of the sexual culture. Lord Hope in the Privy Council said: '[T]he fact that this scale of offending... was tolerated for so long in such a small, isolated and closely knit community is an indication of the poor state of supervision exercised over its affairs by the colonial authorities.'[14] Similarly, the Legal Adviser to Pitcairn in a letter written in 2000 to the Acting Governor of Pitcairn said: '[I]t is possible, although perhaps unpalatable, to attribute a degree of responsibility for the unbridled sexual licence of Pitcairn men over past generations to the absence of any meaningful civil authority and actual system of justice representing the guidance and supervision of the colonial power.'[15] But British neglect did not affect the question of British jurisdiction. Lord Hope thought British law applied, in spite of neglect, asserting that 'long standing practice has established Pitcairn's status as a settled colony', and so he was not willing to question the Governor's 'legislative authority' to incorporate such law onto the island.

It is a shame that there was no discussion of the relevance of colonial neglect to the question of jurisdiction. To take the extreme case, let us imagine that Britain had no legitimate claim over Pitcairn, and Pitcairn is a foreign state, as foreign as France, or the United States. What, then, would Britain be doing there? It would have as much right to prosecute as would a French prosecuting authority, or the Santa Barbara District Attorney's office. The British Crown needed to argue the case other than through historical chronology, as the examples of the marooned *Flying Dutchman* and George Washington's axe show, and both Fuller's and Dworkin's suggested connection between legality (establishing

---

[14] *Christian*, 2006, para. 56.
[15] A letter from the legal adviser Paul Treadwell to Karen Wolstenholme, the Acting Governor of Pitcairn, whose office was in Wellington, dated 29 April 2000. See Appendix II, Document (b).

jurisdiction) and moral legitimacy seems to me to be a very plausible way of doing that.

There is a contrasting theoretical account of law, particularly useful because it explains a mode of reasoning permeating decisions at all levels in the Pitcairn courts. It is a very English account, traceable to the legal positivist school deriving from Bentham's teachings and, in the twentieth century, from its foremost scholar, H. L. A. Hart. While appreciating the importance of moral reflection upon the law, this school's main thesis was, to quote Hart, 'that it is by no means a necessary truth that laws reproduce the claims of morality although they have often done so'.[16] The coherent message of this school, and the one popularly understood, is that to identify laws we need to determine whether they meet the criteria of valid law identifiable from an empirically described official practice of identifying law, a process sometimes referred to as identifying the law's 'pedigree'.[17] Bentham, as well as his protégé John Austin, claimed that this pedigree was located in the 'command of the sovereign'—a description suiting the rule of monarchs and dictators. Hart thought that the pedigree of law lay in his 'rule of recognition'—a rule formulated from an 'empirical' and 'factual' description of what judges accepted as constituting the criteria of legal validity. And agreeing with Hart, Raz described the facts that gave rise to the rule of recognition as the 'social sources' of law, those practices of legal officials in identifying and applying law.[18] According to these philosophers, to claim that some requirement had 'legal validity' meant no more than it met the criteria actually in use by legal officials. Accordingly, because the British legal officials as a matter of practice recognize statutes and other constitutional instruments, the British Crown clearly had the *legal* authority, in their eyes, to impose its laws by virtue of its incorporation by the Pitcairn Governor. In practical 'real' terms, the theory says that working out what British rules applied on Pitcairn was a matter of finding a 'paper trail'.

Consider the nature of historical analysis implied by this theory, which focuses on the tests for law in an empirically described official practice. This mode of argument is apparent in all the judgments, including the Pitcairn Court of Appeal, its Supreme Court, and in the Privy Council. The judgments trace the historical derivation of British

---

[16] Hart, H. L. A. *The Concept of Law*, 2nd edn (1994) Oxford: OUP.

[17] See Dworkin, R. *Taking Rights Seriously* (1977) London: Duckworth, chapter 2.

[18] Raz, J. 'The Rule of Law and its Virtue' in *The Authority of Law* (1979) Oxford: OUP.

jurisdiction through application of the British Settlements Act 1887 as purely an algorithmic exercise. Notable is Lord Hoffmann's remark that the Pitcairn situation fell squarely within the 'doctrine' that what is a territory of the Crown is a matter of which the Court 'takes judicial notice'. He thought that constitutional instruments such as directions made in 1898 by the Secretary of State as well as various Orders in Council would be the subject of such judicial notice.[19] He assumed, in other words, that a 'paper trail' of historical documents was conclusive evidence of the legal position. This approach makes quite irrelevant any discussion of neglect of the island by the British Crown. It also appears to deny the possibility of *interpretation* of these constitutional instruments.

It is important to consider, first, whether it is fair to legal positivism to charge it with supporting 'paper-trail' type judgements about law. But Hart is clear, time and again, that the determination of the criteria of legal validity in any legal system amounts to no more than a report (which may be complex, of course) of the observable practice of 'officials', 'officials' referring in large part to judges.[20] One might wonder in relation to Pitcairn what those facts of official practice would be. Was the question whether British laws applied to Pitcairn merely a matter of reporting—a 'reading off'—what British legislation *said*, since that legislation appears to meet the positivist criteria? Pitcairn makes us question this seeming orthodoxy, for the circumstances there make it easier for us to sense that something is going on that transcends the mere recording of 'what official British practice was' and 'what the British laws say'. Any judge, any official, would reasonably be expected to go beyond that suspiciously clear-seeming enterprise and, rather, try to make some sense of that practice (for example, ask whether it makes sense for it to extend to Pitcairn, given the circumstances there).[21] At

---

[19] A judge must of course take 'judicial notice' of all laws (Ordinances, Orders in Council, and the Sexual Offences Act 1956, for example) and consider himself bound by them; but he must interpret them first before he can say what they are conclusive *of.*

[20] See *The Concept of Law*, 2nd edn (1994), note 16, 12, footnotes to chapter V.

[21] A useful case—one which demonstrates the damage that can be caused by supposing that law may just be 'read off' the paper—is *Al-Kateb v Godwin* 208 (2004) ALR 124. Justice Kirby's dissenting judgment has great power (see 156). He condemns the expressed view of the majority that because the statute was 'clear' any attempt at interpretation by judges as to its meaning would undermine the legislature. Justice Kirby must be right in thinking that to declare a statute as having any meaning, clear or unclear, is still to engage in an act of interpretation. That an interpretation is 'clear' could mean a number of things but not that interpretation was unnecessary. Justice Kirby thought that judges should interpret statutes in the light of prevailing principles (in his case, drawn from international law).

any rate, an appreciation of the difficulties in this point should draw us to non-question-begging questions about the lack of significant connection between officials in charge of the day-to-day administering of Pitcairn and those 'officials' who regularly apply tests of legal validity.

The positivist must maintain that certain mechanisms of law are in place, namely, that there are appropriate 'officials' actually operating something that can be interpreted as a 'system' in which there is both the creation and application of rules over a relatively well-defined 'territory', and over which the rules are relatively 'effective'.[22] Using the *Flying Dutchman* example once more, legal positivism, viewed as a descriptive account of law, appears less compelling the more the ship's crew and passengers regard the historical origin of the regulations governing them as insignificant, and the more they are ready to discard the authority of the captain to be that of the British Crown. Taken to the extreme, is it unquestionable that we must characterize anyone as a legal official under British law if no one at all on the island regarded such a person as an official? Maybe the naked claim of the British Crown to be the official legal authority is sufficient, but one feels the need for more.[23] While the making of the claim might be a necessary condition for the Crown's legal authority, it is difficult to see how it could be any more than that, and it is certainly not sufficient. In any case, what 'claiming authority' means is a highly moot point. It seems possible for someone to be an official (such as a much-loved charismatic ruler, for example) without anyone having to contend that such an official has 'claimed' authority. In sum, in the story outlined so far, the question of legal authority over Pitcairn is not clearly settled. That is a matter of interpretation of the facts of settlement, and there is no obvious reason why Crown jurisdiction obtains by a default 'because the paper trail says so'.

---

[22] These are common (and sensible) requirements of, anyway, Austin, Kelsen, Hart, and Raz.

[23] See Raz's various comments concerning the relationship between 'claiming' authority and 'having' authority in 'Authority, Law and Morality' in his *Ethics in the Public Domain* (1994) Oxford: OUP. He says, for example, that 'the law must be, or at least be presented as being, an expression of some people or of some institutions on the merits of the actions it requires'. He goes on to say: 'Such attributions can only be based on factual consideration. Moral argument can establish what legal institutions should have said or should have held but not what they did say or hold.' (215). Note that his clearly positivist account still requires a separate 'factual consideration' as to whether the 'expression' of an institution applies appropriately to a remote territory. Raz must have in mind the usual sort of legal system in which the connection between 'officials' and subjects is relatively uncontroversial.

One way to probe jurisdiction is to distinguish the criteria of legal validity from the conditions under which we would identify legal systems. First, 'saying so does not make it so'.[24] Hart took this line in criticizing Hans Kelsen's doctrine that municipal legal systems are a subset of an international legal system.[25] To use Hart's now-dated example, if the UK legislature passed a 'Soviet Laws Validity Act' which purported to validate the law of the Soviet Union by providing that laws currently effective in the Soviet territory are valid, that would not mean that Soviet law 'derived its validity' from the UK, or that UK law was 'the reason for the validity' of Soviet law. Hart thought this argument was 'clear and compelling': the courts and law-enforcing agencies of the Soviet Union would not recognize the force of that UK law. He concluded that the criteria for the identity of a legal system are different from those identifying the 'relationship of validating purport':

No doubt we could collect all laws between which the relationship of validating purport holds, irrespective of the legal system from which they come, and call the group of laws so collected 'a single legal system'. This would be to introduce a new meaning for the expression 'legal system'; for a group of laws lined together solely by the relationship of validating purport would not correspond to the concept of a legal system that lawyers and political theorists or any serious thinkers about law and politics actually use ... *recognition by the law-identifying and law-enforcing agencies effective in a given territory is of crucial importance in determining the system to which the laws belong.*[26]

It is important to disentangle threads here by emphasizing that the point of my introducing this particular argument is to draw attention to the possibility of Pitcairn's having a distinct legal system. For, under Hart's account, British law could still extend to Pitcairn. He thought the question of legal validity was a matter of conformity to the criteria of legal validity evidenced in the 'facts' of what 'officials' of the British legal system declared it to be, and so British laws *could* apply to Soviet territory (and, as they do for murder, apply all over the world). On the other hand, legal systems, he thought, were defined in a different kind

[24] Britain's attempt to deny that there were any laws made in Southern Rhodesia is a good example. See the Southern Rhodesia (Constitution) Order 1965.

[25] Kelsen, H. *Introduction to the Problems of Legal Theory*, ed. & trans. Paulson (2002) Oxford: OUP.

[26] Hart, H. L. A. 'Kelsen's Doctrine of the Unity of Law' from *Essays in Jurisprudence and Philosophy* (1983) Oxford: OUP, 335–336. My emphasis, to bring out what is relevant to Pitcairn.

of way, not by 'chains of validity' but by a 'descriptive sociology' of officialdom and effectiveness.[27] So we should not take more from Hart than he suggests. On the other hand, if there was a separate operating legal system on Pitcairn—and that idea, as I have suggested, appears to have initial plausibility—the view of what was legally valid from the point of view of Pitcairn could have been at odds with the British law, and the official British view of things. Of course, how a genuinely separate and distinct Pitcairn legal system would view things is a problematic—and probably unanswerable—question given that the judges, and Office of Public Defender, created to represent the defendants if they so wished, were appointed by the British Crown, to enforce 'the law applying to Pitcairn'. The ambiguity in that idea is very difficult to disentangle if, indeed, it can be disentangled. And we should not assume that legal positivism is right in its insistence on drawing a distinction between the criteria of legal validity and the conditions at the root of defining a legal system.

How, without begging questions as to their status, did those officials administering Pitcairn law—those 'on the ground'—view the English criminal law? The islanders themselves, and so presumably the Island Magistrate, always spoke in terms of 'Island law'; so there was at least no clear evidence that the island administrators believed themselves to be acting purely within the scope of jurisdiction granted to them by the British Crown. Pitcairn was (and is) not that sort of place. 'Island law' was understood to be that which was written out in a special book of summary offences, available on the island and created by the island Governor, and it included various laws written by ship captains, notably the captain of the HMS *Fly* in the early nineteenth century. In this context, the English common law was clearly not understood to be part of 'Island law'. I cannot further see how simply renaming certain courts in New Zealand as being 'Pitcairn Courts' (and 'giving' them retrospective jurisdiction)[28] could answer that fundamental problem unless judges were prepared to go beyond the paper trail. To repeat: mere historical chronology does not seem sufficient to the task. In clear cases, I believe, the moral judgements are buried, although present, but in a

---

[27] For the same thesis, see Raz, J, *The Concept of a Legal System* (1970) Oxford: OUP.

[28] For Pitcairn, a community of only 47, to have its own separately identifiable three-tier system of judicial appeal—a Court of Appeal, a Supreme Court, and then recourse to the Privy Council—seems ludicrous.

case of Pitcairn's complexity, some willingness to be explicit on the moral position would have helped immensely in sorting out the question of legitimacy, including the Crown's right to govern, its right to institute courts, and ultimately, its right to punish.[29]

## Mala in se

Let us assume that these suggestions have merit and that the British Crown had no jurisdiction over Pitcairn, or that there was insufficient promulgation of the Sexual Offences Act 1956 to make it a valid law or to make the prosecutions fair, or that the English common law of rape had not been exported to Pitcairn. Even then, it remains an important question whether criminal liability could be imposed on the defendants by *anyone*. That any legal system would have no criminal provision for serious sexual offences is an odd idea, and one that throws light on the startling omission in the island law for sexual offences against children under 12 (there were sexual offences against children over that age). Can we say that some acts are either so morally pernicious that their legal status is assured independently of having been adopted or claimed as offences by any particular community? Or, perhaps, that their very perniciousness alone outweighs the requirement of legality? Perhaps we can learn a lesson from Fuller, who thought that the more wicked the act, the less need there would be for publication. There are difficulties in the approach. One is over what counts as a 'wicked act'—an act that is 'wrong in itself' or *mala in se*—because of the variation of that idea from culture to culture (in the Muslim world, the depicting of Muhammad is regarded as a wicked act) and so the idea that there is 'world interest' in imposing criminal liability on Pitcairn for the doing of 'wicked' acts requires something more. In practical terms, adding a requirement of being common to all legal systems would perhaps suffice. More important, however, is the general undesirability of the idea, already discussed, that because an act is wicked, or immoral, it *therefore*

---

[29] Note Dworkin, R. *Justice in Robes* (2006) Cambridge, Mass: Harvard University Press, at 170:

'We understand legal practice better, and make more intelligible sense of propositions of law, by pursuing an explicitly normative and political enterprise: refining and defending conceptions of legality and drawing tests for concrete claims of law from favored conceptions. There is no question of taking theories of law constructed in this way to be merely "descriptive".'

should be regarded as illegal and criminal. (It is through this thought, as I have discussed, that we arrive at the importance of legality).

In some cases—extreme ones—it is reasonable to suppose that right-minded people think that certain acts such as genocide, the waging of aggressive war, and torture are so very bad that it is difficult to imagine a legal system in which such offences could never be prosecuted as a *matter of law*. The idea of crimes 'against humanity' makes good sense in this context. It is not just that the acts are *mala in se* but that they are of such a nature that the world community can condemn them *in its name*; this is what gives it the quality of legality, and it explains why we are minded to say such crimes are 'against humanity' and constitute a breach of 'universal laws'. We may answer the objection that Nuremberg-type defendants are then prosecuted retrospectively either by arguing that these universal laws existed before concretization for specific purposes or, more simply, by the argument that these crimes were so terrible that the moral importance of prosecution outweighed the moral principle of *nulla poena*.[30]

Did the sexual abuse on Pitcairn fall into the same category as crimes against humanity? The question might reasonably be disputed. Of special significance would be the *weight* attached to the particular circumstances, for there is a difference in seriousness between rapes as there is in murder; a statutory rape (as in some jurisdictions) between two consenting fifteen-year-olds is clearly different in kind from a non-consensual and violent rape between strangers, or a young girl or woman and a much older man. Murder clearly comes in different degrees (once described that way), and it is not too difficult to draw a line between the sorts of violent and sadistic murders committed in Nazi concentration camps and some forms of kindly intentioned euthanasia.

The situation in Pitcairn should make us confront the genuine question whether there was a different set of sexual norms that prevailed in the 'pre-political correctness' period of the 1960s, 70s, and early 80s, and whether 'Pitcairn sexual norms' were different from those existing in Britain. It seems to me that it could be unfair to make a retrospective judgement about the extent of how bad or reprehensible the defendants' conduct was in 1963 (when the first alleged offence occurred) by the later norms of 1999 and after, particularly on the basis of the significantly developed mainstream views on sexual abuse that had

---

[30] See Hart, *The Concept of Law*, note 16, chapter 9, particularly the last sentence.

developed in the interim in Britain. It is not necessary for this argument to absolve the defendants of *all* moral blame, for there is evidence of admissions amongst them that they believed that what they were doing was wrong at the time.

To explore how we might view our treatment of moral wrongness in another culture, imagine that in a remote British settlement, officials discover a tribe whose predominantly male culture endorses female circumcision, and decide to prosecute the tribal elder who performs ritual circumcisions. We think of him as unfeeling, and ignorant of the damage he does; but we can also see that he is not motivated by malice, and only performs the procedures because it is so much part of his culture; he has done it many times, over many years. I suggest it is not a simple matter of showing that he has met the conditions required by section 18 of the Offences Against the Person Act 1861; that it would not be fair to charge him with the standard offence of maliciously[31] causing grievous bodily harm, with intent to do such harm, although clearly, had he performed ritual circumcision in Surrey, he would have committed the offence. There would be an air of inappropriateness about such a prosecution in spite of his having the *mens rea* and, it is suggested, the criminal law would be inappropriate for dealing with the situation. Because the culture so permeates the tribal elder's actions, it does not seem fair to prosecute him. It would not occur to him that what he did matched, say, the violence the young men of his tribe inflict on one another. He is wrong to think this, but our realization does not remove our feeling that there exists a degree of ignorance in his actions that deserves something less than the full operation of section 18. I would emphasize, though, that these remarks do not endorse cultural and (therefore, some might think) moral relativism. Rather, my view is that a sensitive and sympathetic appreciation of personal responsibility in morally bad cultures should encourage the shifting of the burden of correction away from the processes of the criminal law.

### The importance of promulgation

The answer may lie in the attention we should pay to promulgation. The case of the 'different culture' indicates that, where someone is

---

[31] 'Malicious', of course, has a standard meaning for s. 18 of having an intention or being reckless. That the tribal elder is not malicious in the popular sense would not save him from criminal liability.

enculturated to a lesser degree of understanding of wrongness, a greater degree of promulgation is required; in order for the criminal law to announce that certain acts 'not be done'—to use Hart's term—extra effort needs to be put into carrying that message more clearly to the enculturated intended addressees.

And so, in Pitcairn, the suggestion that there was a different prevailing sexual culture may determine the degree and kind of promulgation required. There was some attempt at engaging with the problem in 1970 during discussion at an Island Council where the Deputy Governor and others raised the matter of sexual conduct towards the island children. But it was a feeble attempt at altering behaviour; in any case, no one pursued the matter. That little was done for the following 29 years speaks volumes about the existing culture.[32] The view that there were different sexual mores in Pitcairn from those in England is supported by the report of a study carried out by Neville Tosen, the island's pastor, in 2000. He confirmed anecdotal evidence that most women had their first child between the ages of 12 and 15. Clearly Tahitian influence from the genesis of human habitation on Pitcairn permeated island culture, and it is a fairly persuasive argument that the historical background to the sexual practices of the island was Tahitian—where it is widely known (Gauguin is a good reference) that sex was 'freer'.[33]

Aside from questions of a theoretical nature, concerning both positivist and non-positivist accounts of jurisdiction, there was the particular legal question raised and discussed in all the Pitcairn courts: whether there was sufficient 'promulgation' of the English Sexual Offences Act, 1956. In some sense, of course, the defendants 'could' have found out what this statute said. They were not incompetent, and it was physically possible to obtain the knowledge by shortwave radio, or by letter. And it is true that there was a public notice displayed on Pitcairn for some time (although faded by weather) stating, in as many

---

[32] Acknowledged, too, in official correspondence, eg, that between the Island Governor (Williams) and the Foreign and Commonwealth Office in 2000, speaking of two cases of sexual misconduct on the island: 'I have no doubt that these are not unique cases. It is far more likely that they are a continuation of a pattern that has been going on for 200 years.' Vol. 8b of the Pitcairn Privy Council Record, 3668 (PC disk).

[33] Marks, K. 'The Paradise That's Under a Cloud' *The Independent*, January 23, 2002. A significant proportion—perhaps as much as half—of the original eighteenth century inhabitants were from Tahiti, as either wives of the *Bounty* mutineers, or brought for work.

words, that British law, both statutes and the common law, applied on Pitcairn. What was the reality, however? Pitcairn was even more isolated 20 years ago than it is now, with only recent Internet connection, and available well after any of the alleged offences occurred. It was then an extraordinarily isolated community only remotely in touch with the 'host' kingdom through shortwave radio and contact with the occasional cruise ship. The islanders were, significantly, not conversant with law other than 'Island law', and they had little knowledge of how law was generally viewed, administered, policed, enforced, and discussed in Britain.

Nevertheless, the Pitcairn courts made findings of fact that there was sufficient promulgation, and so it was relatively easy for Lord Hoffmann to conclude that it was unnecessary to discuss 'the philosophical basis of legal limits' of the principle.[34] Can one truly set 'philosophical' questions aside like this? Possibly Lord Hoffmann meant to imply, as Fuller was explicit, that the more serious the offence the less there was a need for detailed promulgation, because he went on to say that these were 'serious offences', and so the balance came down 'firmly in favour of bringing them before a court of justice'. But he certainly took no account of anything like 'enculturation', from which a plausible Pitcairn perspective existed that these were less serious offences.

## Promulgation and *ignorantia*

It is common for legal systems to enshrine a principle that defendants may not offer as a defence that they were ignorant of the law that purportedly governed their conduct (*ignorantia juris non excusat*). It is a well-established principle of the English criminal law. We might be seduced into thinking this principle covers the situation of inadequate promulgation simply because, as a result of poor or non-existent promulgation, the defendants are ignorant of the law. But if the promulgation could not have been reasonably known, the principle of *ignorantia* may not be so straightforwardly applied, because we could then say that the defendant's ignorance of the law is reasonable where the law is inadequately promulgated. The ignorance of the law principle is still one of personal responsibility. It creates a duty in the defendants

---

[34] *Christian*, 2006, para. 24. His position reflected his argument concerning judicial notice of the 'fact' of British jurisdiction.

to have reasonably considered the lawfulness of their actions. Where that duty is discharged, any remaining ignorance should in fairness excuse. It is instructive to see the intimacy of the link between fairness and promulgation here. Because (as it were) unreasonable promulgation makes ignorance of the law reasonable, whether someone is criminally liable in such cases is a direct question about what is fair in the circumstances, and whether it is fair to prosecute. We can enhance the intimacy by imagining what sort of community it would be where little or no regard is paid to promulgation. Try to imagine, as Fuller did, a legal system in which there were no publicly expressed laws at all, one in which all laws are secret and unpublished; even if one could construct such a system on paper, it makes absolutely no sense in the real world. And so it must be a virtue of the 'natural law' approach that this seemingly intimate connection between law and morality is more easily explained.[35]

What about the 'positivist' approach, given its connection with the 'paper trail' method of establishing jurisdiction on Pitcairn? Some theorists professing a 'positivist' position and often called 'soft' positivists (or 'inclusive' positivists, or 'incorporationists')[36] *do* acknowledge the intimacy of law and morality in difficult cases. But it is precisely because they do, that their theory becomes destructive of their goal of maintaining a separation between morality and law. For they claim that moral argument only becomes part of the law when particular moral rules and principles are identifiable by reference to a non-morally defined and descriptively identified 'social source' of law such as a judicial decision, a statute, or general recognition by judges. In such cases, these 'soft' positivists argue, the law 'includes' or 'incorporates' morality but not in other cases; so since morality is only there, as it were, at the 'invitation' of law, the distinction between law and morality can be maintained, even though the

---

[35] See Aquinas, T. *Summa Theologica* (c. 1266–1273), Vol. 28, Question 90, Art. 4. Also see Fuller, L. *The Morality of Law*, note 8, 49, and Hobbes, T. *Leviathan* (1651) ch. 31 para. 20 (quoted by Lord Hope in *Christian & Others v R* Judgment of the Privy Council, 30 October, 2006 [2006] UKPC 47, para. 48).

[36] 'Soft' positivism is first referred to by Dworkin in *Law's Empire* as 'soft conventionalism'. Hart in his *Postscript* to *The Concept of Law*, note 16, uses 'soft positivism' in his defence of his theory against Dworkin. The same idea has variously been adopted as 'incorporationism' by, for example, Coleman, J. *Practice of Principle: In Defence of a Pragmatist Approach to Legal Theory* (2001) Oxford: OUP, and as 'inclusive positivism' by, for example, Waluchow, W. *Inclusive Legal Positivism* (1994) Oxford: OUP.

identification of law, because a controversial question in the difficult cases, remains 'soft'.

This argument cannot work. First, we are struck by a virtue of clarity in positivism's apparently bright line between the law's requirements and morality's requirements. Clarity in that distinction would assist the criticism of law, and it would also encourage the understanding of law in those to whom it is addressed.[37] But soft positivists do not appear to think that their theory has practical virtue. Rather, they view the theory as only 'descriptive' of law (as Hart in his *Postscript* claimed) and so, for them, the 'descriptive fact of the matter' is just that there are no 'bright lines'. A second point is fatal, however. Soft positivism has a Trojan virus. Once morality is incorporated into law, its power becomes unstoppable. No 'social source' fact can restrain it from undermining the authority of the social source itself. Take the favourite of all positivist accounts, the morally evil system. Imagine that the judge is required to give effect to a barbaric statutory provision—one, say, like that of the 1935 Nuremberg decree that prohibited marriage between Jews and German citizens—and to do so, as we can easily hypothesize, 'with due attention to equity and justice'.[38] Soft positivism provides no reason why that requirement, of making moral judgements relevant in determining the question of *law*, would prevent the judge from concluding that the law of barbaric content was itself contrary to 'equity and justice'; indeed, soft positivism can offer no reason that would prevent the judge from concluding that the institution issuing the law—that body identified by the relevant social source—lacked all the legal authority to make any such law. The point fatal to all versions of soft positivism is that morality is not a kind of 'add-on' to other systems but is a freestanding generator of first-order universal judgements which are morally sovereign. Coming to this argument from the other end, since there seems no reason why the legal incorporation of moral standards should not be *implicit*, as something to be 'read into' the 'social sources' of law, soft positivism cannot tell us why moral standards are not fundamental to identifying law in all cases.

---

[37] Two arguments used by Bentham in favour of a positivistic account (see later).

[38] Even the supposed Law for the Protection of German Blood and German Honour of 1935 appeared to allow that innocent marriages between Jews and German citizens (ie, ones that were not intended to evade the prohibition) would be recognized if they were celebrated outside Germany; that spark of recognition of personal responsibility—of morality—could be kindled to good use.

## Two values of promulgation and legal positivism

We should therefore look for better versions of positivism to understand the significance of promulgation. 'Harder' versions claim as a virtue the clarity—the 'non-softness'—of the distinction between law and morality; the metaphor urges the idea that law is a 'hard' object, ultimately identifiable by reference to an empirically describable social source such as a practice amongst judges.[39] The value of the clarity in distinction is, I suggest, two-fold: it aids the *efficiency* in carrying out the law's purposes, and it establishes the *moral independence* of the addressee of law.

Efficiency requires promulgation because the addressees of law have to be aware of what it requires or empowers them to do. According to this interpretation of positivism, the argument is not to say that laws are 'invalid' because they are not promulgated. Rather, it is that a failure of efficiency represents a failure of law in a respect that legal positivism, under this interpretation, makes significant; it is a defect that goes to the heart of what this form of positivism says is law's inherent aim. Bentham stressed that framing laws was not enough, and that the legislator also had to attend to making those laws clear to those affected.[40] He also thought that the law should pursue utilitarian ends: if most of us accepted that law could be identified and dealt with independently of morality, the clarity of mind and subsequent critical awareness we would gain would contribute to the greater happiness of the greatest number.[41]

A second practical virtue of legal positivism, also present in Bentham's work, is that through the clarity of hard positivism's distinction, the moral independence of individuals is preserved in the intellectual

---

[39] The most well-known 'hard' positivist is Raz, J. 'Authority, Law and Morality' in his *Ethics in the Public Domain* (1994) Oxford: OUP, and Raz, *The Authority of Law* (1979) Oxford: OUP, chapter 3, especially at 50–52. The only sensible interpretation of Hart's theory, I believe, is that it is one of 'hard' positivism. Waluchow, note 36, uses the term 'exclusive' for 'hard' positivism, to distinguish it more sharply from 'inclusive' positivism.

[40] He did this by likening the unmindful legislator to the ostrich which '. . . leaves its eggs in the sand, unmindful that the passing foot may crush them . . . the legislator who, after having framed his laws, abandons their promulgation to chance, and thinks that his task is finished when the most important of his duties has only begun, would have been represented by the ostrich'. 'Of promulgation of the law and promulgation of the reasons thereof.' Vol. I Bowring *Edition of Bentham's Works* (1843) Part I. Texas CUWS website.

[41] See Postema, G. *Bentham and the Common Law Tradition* (1986) Oxford: OUP. Note Postema's reference in chapter 9 to Bentham's remark in a letter to Voltaire of 1776: 'I have built solely on the foundation of utility.'

separation of the state's legal demands from those of individual conscience. This value supports promulgation because it requires that people know the law in order to be able, morally, to detach themselves from it. Once more, this is not to say that an unpromulgated law is not a valid law, but to emphasize that the lack of promulgation expresses a failure in a fundamental defining aim of this version of positivism. In the event of failure, of course, a question concerning the fairness of prosecution under such a law needs resolving. Hart was particularly clear about how he perceived this particular moral value of his theory in *The Concept of Law.*[42] In chapter IX, he explicitly chooses between two conceptions of law: one which combines law with moral judgement (a 'narrow' conception), and a 'wider' one which distinguishes sharply between the two. He chooses the latter way to characterize law on the explicit ground that there are 'practical merits' in thinking that law could be wicked. His summing up is in a passage stating most forcefully what is, in my view, the central thesis of *The Concept of Law*:

> What surely is most needed in order *to make men clear-sighted in confronting the official abuse of power*, is that they should preserve the sense that the certification of something as legally valid is not conclusive of the question of obedience, and that, however great the aura of majesty or authority which the official system may have, its demands must in the end be submitted to moral scrutiny.[43]

Hart's insight is that if we can clear-sightedly identify law we can more easily distinguish its specific demands from those of our personal moral conscience. In civilized communities, these two requirements are, for the vast majority, merged within one rough set of convictions; most people accept in these cases that the community is entitled to make reasonable, and sometimes disagreeable, demands. But the theory requires the distinction, and this leaves space between saying what the community has demanded, and what the individual's own moral convictions demand. Where people are not given that chance of 'clear-sighted' identification of the law's demands, their inability to scrutinize what the community demands again raises the issue whether it was fair to prosecute.

This argument is morally significant when compared with efficiency. Efficiency seems compatible with morally unjustifiable ends whereas the

---

[42] *The Concept of Law*, note 16.    [43] Ibid. Emphasis added.

enhancement of moral independence is not. It is one matter for a legal system to be inefficient but another that a legal system fail to place the issue of legality before an individual recognized as personally responsible to their own conscience, and capable of confronting 'the official abuse of authority'. If we constantly defer to the law for what we must morally do, then we will begin to assume that we should just accept what is 'handed down from on high'. This is what tends to occur in totalitarian systems, or in religious oligarchies, under which the individual has continually to guess what the state wants. It was against this sort of reductive and illiberal thinking that Hart, I believe, evolved his analysis and endorsement of legal positivism. For him, the virtue of requiring law to be clear and certain was paramount, and so, too, a recognition that this virtue would come at a 'cost', that of allowing people to be free unless there were clarity and certainty about what the state required of them.

A brief excursus would be helpful. It is widely believed that Hart's theory of law is a purely descriptive one, not intended to impute to law any particular value. The argument is sometimes confused between the question whether this was what Hart intended or whether his theory makes best sense as a descriptive theory, although it is mostly concentrated on the former question, and supported by well-known remarks by Hart both in the early stages of *The Concept of Law* and his posthumously published *Postscript*. If it is true that it is merely a matter of 'descriptive fact' that law is efficient, and that it enhances moral independence, then where the law is unclear there is nothing to say about it, except that 'the law is like that' as 'a matter of fact', or that this is 'just how law is' at its descriptive 'fringes' or 'penumbra' (Hart's words). I don't believe this argument is sustainable.[44] Imagine a society where people believe and live according to a conception of law that God is the source of all of our obligations, including our legal obligations. We may also imagine that priestly 'interpreters' of God's law inconclusively identify these obligations, and there is perhaps evidence for them in a Holy book. It is, in fact, a sketch of the ideal Islamic system of law. Hart's account of law fails to describe this system centrally as law

---

[44] Nor does Finnis, in *Natural Law and Natural Rights* (1980) Oxford: OUP, chapter 1, nor Dworkin, in *Law's Empire* (1986), Cambridge: Harvard University Press, chapter 1.

because one of the significant features of his central case will be missing; now, the ultimate source of our legal obligations is God's commands, and not a factually identifiable human 'rule of recognition'. I should add that it would be facile to say, in defence of Hart, that the rule of recognition is the concordant and factually identifiable practice amongst human officials in identifying God as the source of law. If we identify God's commands with the requirements of morality then we would not be able to distinguish them from law, which distinction is the mark of legal positivism. (It would also, very probably, be highly blasphemous to declare that God's authority to make law derived solely from human will).

If we take the practical—non-descriptive—interpretation of Hart to be the better one, legal positivism sits very well with the liberalism rightly associated with the rest of Hart's work, on criminal responsibility, on punishment, on the enforcement of morality, and other matters. This liberalism relies on the view that our moral obligations are a function of our independently conceived personal consciences, a characteristic thought of the Enlightenment, and the basis of our conception of personal responsibility. Understood in this straightforward way, Hart's *The Concept of Law*, far from being a 'morally neutral and descriptive theory', *joins sides*. It says that on occasions it will be morally good to *break* the law, an idea that is surely inconceivable in the purely Islamic legal system, because it would praise disobedience to God. In essence, Hart's book enjoins you, the emancipated individual, to ignore the law where your personal convictions demand it. In fact, my personal impression of Hart was that this was his moral take on law. I personally believe the *Postscript* to be an unfortunate aberration that was wrongheadedly aimed at winging Dworkin. It is better, in my view, that Hart be remembered as presenting the best interpretation of Bentham's positivist doctrine, one that has a clear moral point.

## Return to Pitcairn

If these arguments are correct, and positivism's only coherent justification lies in its promoting efficiency and moral independence through the clarity of its famous distinction, those twin values needed more recognition in the particular circumstances of Pitcairn. For the evidence of promulgation was some distance from achieving efficiency in effecting change or ensuring the moral independence of the defendants.

One of the more interesting items in this hugely documented case[45] is the extensive cross-examination by the Pitcairn Public Defender of the Pitcairn Island legal adviser, Paul Treadwell, who was a solicitor practising in a small town about 150 miles north of Auckland in New Zealand, and some 1,800 miles from Pitcairn.[46] (I mention distances and geographical locations to emphasize the element of surreality in this case.) The line of questioning was designed to show that since the official Pitcairn legal adviser was not himself aware of what law applied on the island—for example, he admitted he was unaware of the English Sexual Offences Act 2003—in order to show that it could hardly then be said that the defendants were or could be assumed to be aware of the relevant law. It was only after Mr Treadwell had consented to being legal adviser that he discovered that he had the powers, in relation to Pitcairn, of the Attorney-General of England and Wales. It was revealed that he had not given any legal advice to the Island Magistrate, although he knew at the time that the Island Magistrate was only a layperson, the island's teacher. And although Mr Treadwell had asked whether he might visit Pitcairn, this request was apparently refused. In 1997, his expressed view to the Governor of Pitcairn in Wellington was that the only law the islanders were aware of in relation to sexual assault was section 88 of the Justice Ordinance, passed by the Pitcairn Governor, which made it an offence to have intercourse with a female of or over the age of 12.[47] He thought it 'a very unsatisfactory situation' that offences against girls under 12 were covered by an English act, and that offences against those of 12 or over was the subject of a local statute. More to the point, he thought that even stocking a public library on Pitcairn with the written laws—kept up to date—would not go far enough to inculcate appreciation of what was required in the islanders. He recommended that the Governor should 'provide codes of criminal law, criminal procedure, evidence in criminal cases and a workable system of judicial organisation'. Indeed, he went on to say: 'This may seem like a hefty exercise for such a tiny jurisdiction but

---

[45] The Pitcairn case at the Privy Council was the first case in which the full public record of its proceeding was put on disc. It contains an enormous amount of information, much of it providing a detailed documentary history of Pitcairn. The disc contains 1.4 gigabytes of information, translating into many thousands of pages. It is a fascinating read.

[46] The evidence of this cross-examination was not discussed in the Privy Council because the Privy Council took the Pitcairn Court of Appeal findings as settled.

[47] An offence apparently referred to on the island colloquially as 'cardinal' knowledge. The Ordinance laws comprised what was known locally as the 'Island laws'. See Appendix II, Document (a) below.

of course it will take only another single incident of serious crime on Pitcairn from which there may well be no simple means of disposal . . . in order to create a situation of great difficulty, expense and perhaps international embarrassment.'[48]

Of course, if we reject the idea that positivism must have some practical value, and maintain, as many do, that the theory is intended only to offer a general 'descriptive' account, we may show its support of the 'paper trail' method of establishing Crown jurisdiction (where 'saying so' appears to 'make it so'). Nevertheless, to raise the familiar objection from natural law, it remains for it to be made obvious why a mere description of 'the way things are' gives rise to obligations and powers that are not 'paper only', including, of course, the right to prosecute and punish. The point is that, contrary to what people often think about legal positivism, its account of law—that is to say the conception of law it chooses and invites us to accept—rests firmly on moral beliefs about the right relationship between the citizen and the law-creating state.

We might, therefore, try to put the legal positivist position in two ways, each relevant to Pitcairn. I realize that many positivists will find the argument outrageous here because it will seem like turning positivism into natural law; but this is what I am trying to do. Positivism is a theory of law. If the conditions for law according to this theory are to serve a practical point, the less that point is served, the more positivism must deny its status centrally as law. Positivists can only retreat from this position by claiming the theory to be 'descriptive only'; this position, of course, has its own special difficulties in failing to characterize adequately some aspects of law, particularly the evaluative nature of legal argument (which, as I argued, soft positivism cannot cope with) and the status of purely theistic Islamic-type systems. First, efficiency is

---

[48] Letter to the First Secretary of the British High Commission in Wellington dated 5 January 1997. See Appendix II, Document (a). (Recall that the first investigations against the Pitcairn defendants began two years later in 1999 when a member of the Kent constabulary visited the island.) Also note that Karen Wolstenholme who was Deputy Governor until 2002 wrote to the Foreign Office in May 2000 outlining serious deficiencies in the way Pitcairn was governed. She noted that the Governor and other senior officials lived 2,200 miles away, in New Zealand, visiting only 'irregularly' and for short periods. The resident Government adviser, who doubled as the teacher, was not regarded as a figure of real authority. She said that the island lacked 'civil authority' and that it perhaps was 'not altogether surprising if the community does not see the laws as applicable to them'. See the *Auckland Herald* April 22, 2005.

a major aim of law, and so, less efficient law is to that extent *less law*, and completely inefficient law is not law at all. (And so we can say *something* like there is 'less of an obligation' *or* 'the question of obligation requires something more than an unqualified statement of what has been declared as law'.) If efficiency is necessary to law, or is 'part of the "concept" of law', then where efficiency is lacking, so, to that extent, is it 'less law' or closer to, in Hart's terms, the '*pre*-legal'.[49] Second, clarity about what the law requires represents a moral value of 'knowing where you stand' so that law that is not particularly clear (eg the common law according to Bentham) is also lesser law, and completely unclear law is not law at all. One way of putting it is to say that the first reason for requiring promulgation—efficiency—looks at the law primarily from the point of view of the legislator, and the second reason looks at the law from the point of view of the legal individual. If Hartian legal positivism includes the proposition that individuals have rights to individual conscience, and that the 'abuse' of the state against conscience is wrong, it is not a big step to say that positivism demands *in some way* that law be fair. Applying this line of reasoning to criminal prosecution, if it is not possible for a person to escape criminal conviction even though he could not reasonably have expected criminal consequences for his conduct, the law fails to meet its own standard of legality. The Rule of Law, according to legal positivism, then, not only requires promulgation but on one strong interpretation does so by making fairness to the Pitcairn defendants relevant.

## Fairness

This brings us to the question: what was 'fair' on Pitcairn? Herewith are relevant subsections of section 14 of the Sexual Offences Act 1956:

(1) It is an offence, subject to the exception mentioned in subsection (3) of this section, for a person to make an indecent assault on a woman.

(2) A girl under the age of sixteen cannot in law give any consent which would prevent an act being an assault for the purposes of this section.

---

[49] *The Concept of Law*, note 16, 94, emphasis added.

for at least the first 40 years,[6] guns and practices of domination by force, a kind of solidarity (among some of the women, at least, if their rebellions are any evidence[7]), and some dogmas about 'family'. Above all, despite 'insubordination',[8] they had what must have given them a certain purchase on the passing ships and the Royal Navy that brought them into British view:[9] they had law. I do not mean in the sense of the 'personal law'[10] that was the view from the Crown; nor do I simply mean that for the English speakers it was a term in their vocabulary.

Rather, one could speculate as to whether or not it would even cross the minds of the mutineers and their descendants that they did not recognize rules and conventions in general. If knowingly or not the British had common law, as Lord Hope observes, the Tahitians came from a chiefly polity with its own protocols of sanctity and concerns about breaking taboos. I would render much more strongly what is found tentatively in some of these chapters, the observation that the islanders must have built up a normative order.[11] Let me enlarge on this in relation to sexual mores.

We know that for a spell there was a Court of Elders,[12] for another a parliament.[13] More germane, from the outset they specifically had the *Bounty* Bible, parts of the Anglican *Book of Common Prayer*[14] with its table of kindred and affinity, and then subsequently the precepts of the Seventh Day Adventist Church.[15] At the period, for example, when government was theocratic and patriarchal,[16] it cannot have failed to address notions of legitimacy and degrees of consanguinity in the handling of sexual unions, whether within marriage or outside it. Indeed, following other imaginings about different norms between men and women,[17] one could imagine arrangements building on a kind of legal pluralism[18]—marriage according to British conventions and premarital liaisons according to Polynesian conventions (where binding to secrecy can be part of the encounter). I say marriage as a gloss on whatever regular conjugal relations were considered to be, and acknowledge that we are dealing with a changing society and that what may have once prevailed in Tahiti can only give clues to Pitcairn's

---

[6] Chapter 4: 69–70.   [7] Chapter 3: 46.   [8] Chapter 7: 160.
[9] Chapter 3: 53.   [10] Chapter 4: 67, 68.   [11] Chapter 4: 85; chapter 7: 161.
[12] Chapter 5: 112.   [13] Chapter 3: 56.   [14] Chapter 3: 48; chapter 5: 112.
[15] Chapter 3: 56.   [16] Chapter 5: 112.   [17] Chapter 4: 73.
[18] Chapter 4: 89–90; compare chapter 8: 2, 11.

We might begin by asking what, according to the English law, was an indecent assault on Pitcairn? Lord Ackner approved a test in 1989 for indecent assault as something that 'taking into account the surrounding circumstances' would be 'regarded by ordinary right-thinking people as an indecent assault'.[50] Applying this test retrospectively to Pitcairn in 1963, when the earliest of the offences occurred, it is extremely difficult to imagine either the thoughts, or composition, of a contemporary Pitcairn jury (all of whom would be Seventh Day Adventists, of course). It must then be reasonable to ask, in determining the question of sufficiency of promulgation, how precise knowledge of section 14 had to be. We cannot assimilate simple belief that a certain act was 'wrong', to a reasonable understanding of the precise nature of the offence. Take the set of facts giving rise to Dave Brown's 10 counts of sexual assault. These were allegedly committed over the period 1972–1974 when he was aged 15–17 and the victim was aged 12–14, at a time when in other countries, notably Spain, the age of consent was 12. Is it fair to have imputed to him the knowledge that what he was doing was contrary to the particular prohibitions spelled out in section 14 and that whether his victim consented or not was irrelevant? In Lord Hope's terms: 'There is no evidence that anyone on Pitcairn was aware of the provisions of sections 1 and 14 of the Sexual Offences Act 1956 prior to the commencement of the police investigation in 1996.'[51]

When coupled with the penalties, there is a degree of specificity to these offences that the defendants could not have known. Were they 'fairly labelled' in the 'reasonable scenario' of the defendants' imputed knowledge? What if someone thought—because of hypothetical lack of cultural awareness—that 'having carnal knowledge' with a girl over 12 was something wrong, but nothing like 'indecent assault' since the idea of indecency never enters their head, nor the idea that there could possibly be an assault simply because the victim apparently consented?

In support of this line of argument, I would note Ashworth's belief that the mere 'announcement in advance' of a set of stable rules would be insufficient for establishing legal liability; he argues for 'greater judicial activism' in developing a richer account of the idea of legislative supremacy and what counts as a fair warning to the addressees of the criminal law. He thinks that attention to the cultural and social values

---

[50] *R v Court* [1989] AC 28, 48. He also thought that the question was solely one for a jury.    [51] *Christian*, para. 68.

held within the jurisdiction are relevant to determine liability. Such
values are, he says:

> [S]ometimes described by the phrase 'the rule of law', but that phrase is unsa-
> tisfactory because of its varying uses. In its narrowest, neutral sense it connotes a
> fairly stable set of clear and general laws announced in advance. More appro-
> priate here is a wider concept which encompasses such values as formal justice
> (treating like cases alike), respecting vested rights, non-retroactivity, maximum
> certainty, fair labelling, and the presumption of innocence . . . The values are not
> absolute *but should be linked to the social and legal culture of the jurisdiction.*[52]

Of relevance to Pitcairn on this latter point is the question whether
sections 1 and 14 of the Sexual Offences Act 1956 constitute 'fair
labelling', that is to say, give a fair and accurate description of what, on
Pitcairn, constituted an indecent assault, a statutory rape, and a lack of
consent.[53]

Lord Hope came nearest to seeing the difficulty. He was impressed by
the idea that there may be some sleight of hand in supposing that the
Sexual Offences Act 1956 applied on Pitcairn, providing a strong lead to a
major argument of this chapter ('The requirement of the ascertainability is
an essential component of the rule of law. But in the case of statutes of
general application in force in England, as the Governor should have
known, it was incapable of being met on Pitcairn'). He managed to evade
the difficulty, however, by arguing that because the 1956 statute was in
effect no different from the common law ('they were not creating new
crimes') other than prescribing penalties, and, since the common law was
known to have been part of the island's law, it did not particularly matter if
the defendants were reasonably unaware of the existence or terms of that
statute. But with some respect, to substitute the supposedly already existing common law of rape does not circumvent the point. For the conces-
sion that the Sexual Offences Act 1956 might not have been sufficiently
promulgated because of its over-specificity, does not lead to the conclusion
that the common law was sufficiently promulgated, for that, too, is at least
equally unascertainable, but through *under-specificity* rather than over-
specificity. As a general principle, we can't suppose the common law to be
as specific as, or more so than, statute. That is not in its nature (and some
would say is its virtue). Lord Hope's instincts seemed right and so it is a
pity he failed to take the argument to its predictable conclusion. Rather, he

---

[52] Ashworth, A. 'Interpreting Criminal Statutes: a Crisis of Legality' [1991] *Law
Quarterly Review*, 419, at 440. Emphasis added. Also see Tamanaha, B. *The Rule of Law*
(2004) Cambridge: CUP.          [53] See further, Ashworth, note 52, 442.

left that argument when, in discussing Blackstone's argument that uninhabited countries 'discovered and planted' by English subjects were controlled by the common law, he reminded us that, however, in Pitcairn 'the decision was taken to prosecute the appellants under the English statute, not the common law'.[54]

We may wonder also whether we should ignore the general question whether penalties are part of the meaning of an offence for the purposes of promulgation; penalties have the important function of indicating the seriousness of the offence. And there is, of course, the problem with what the common law precisely requires. The power of Lord Hope's argument derives from the fact that rape is a generally recognized moral wrong and so its function in the argument is that rape is a crime of 'natural notoriety'.[55] Lord Hope's instincts that his argument is not quite satisfactory is revealed in his speech:

> As a general rule the prosecutor is tied to the ground that he chooses to fight on. If he decides to prosecute under a statute, it is not open to him to ask for a conviction under the common law unless the statute in question provides for this as an alternative. But I do not need to resolve this issue as I have concluded, although not without difficulty, that as sections 1 and 14 of the 1956 Act were not creating new crimes it was open to the prosecutor to bring the prosecutions under the statue notwithstanding its lack of promulgation.[56]

Imputing knowledge of the common law to the defendants is easier than imputing knowledge to them of the penalty. While the defendants knew that rape was wrong in someone's law (although I'm sure none of them knew what 'common law' meant), it is very doubtful any of them knew, or had reason to know, that the offence was liable to life imprisonment. For all they had experience of, over many years, was the offence of carnal

---

[54] *Christian*, para. 71.

[55] Note Bentham:

> There are some laws which seem to have a natural notoriety: such as those which concern crimes against individuals; as theft, personal injuries, fraud, murder, etc. But this notoriety does not extend to the punishment, which, however, is the motive upon which the legislature relies for procuring obedience to the law. It does not extend even to those circumstances, often so delicate, which must be noticed before the line of demarcation can be traced among so many crimes differently punished, nor even to those actions which are either innocent or meritorious.'

Also see Glanville Williams' 'Convictions and Fair Labelling' [1993] *Cambridge Law Journal*, 85, and see Ashworth's reference to the principle of 'fair labelling': Ashworth, A. 'Interpreting Criminal Statutes: a Crisis of Legality', above n 52.

[56] Para. 86.

knowledge, the penalty for which was—clearly set out in the book of 'Island law'—only three months' imprisonment.[57]

It is instructive for my argument how Douglas Husack in his discussion of *ignorantia* echoes Fuller's sentiments on reciprocity; in fact, he sums up the general position very well:

> Deciding how much blame persons deserve for being ignorant of the law without evaluating the quality of the state's effort to inform persons of their obligations is like deciding how much blame persons deserve for being illiterate without evaluating the quality of the state's schools. Good citizens make an effort to learn the law of the state. But duties inhere in both directions. Good states make an effort to teach citizens the law.[58]

## The Limits of Criminal Law

What is criminal law for? Characteristically, as I said earlier, it announces that various acts should not be done, and supplies reasons for not doing those acts in the form of the imposition of penalties in the case of irresponsible non-observance of its rules. Proceeding by way of penalty, including the stigma of conviction, it is a relatively draconian instrument of social change. Given its connection with punishment, I suggest the criminal law is not suited merely to making announcements 'for symbolic effect'.[59] A blanket view of legislation that its point is to 'send out a message' is undesirable, because it makes certainty and particularity about the conduct it criminalizes slide to an inferior position to the message, and therefore subverts principled decision-making. Legislation as 'symbolic of change' crudely and efficiently—by the writing of some words alone— addresses the often short-term political problem of placating a vociferous section of the public. That can be achieved by the mere publication of the intention to produce legislation, maybe of a non-criminal sort and, unfortunately, an effective means of doing so will be underscoring the announcement with the promise of punishment. But of course there is a sharp distinction between 'making an example' of someone in order to 'make an announcement' to the community at large that certain conduct will not be tolerated within the community, and the justice of any

---

[57] The transcripts of the police interrogations reveal that the defendants were stunned by how seriously their conduct was regarded. There was some feeling of injustice amongst Pitcairn women about the way the defendants were treated: see Marks, K. *Pitcairn: Paradise Lost* (2008) Australia: Harper Collins, especially chapter 16 entitled 'Interdependence + Silence = Collusion'.

[58] Husack, D. 'Ignorance of Law and Duties of Citizenship' (1994) 14 *Legal Studies*, 105.          [59] See Fieschi, C. 'Symbolic Laws' (2006) 119 *Prospect*.

particular prosecution and conviction. If it were otherwise, prosecution decisions, and convictions, would be justified in proportion to how well the 'message got across'. (And to take this point to its logical conclusion, the conviction and punishment of innocent people could, if concealed, 'send out' the desired 'message'.)

It would be misleading, however, to think that 'getting the message across' by means of punishment was impermissible on all occasions. There are occasions when it must be made clear that prosecutions will be pursued. And in determining criminal sentences, after conviction, sending an 'exemplary' message out may, on some occasions, be justified. Unusually high sentences were handed down to offenders in the Notting Hill race riots in 1958, sentences which were at odds with the sentencing norms of the time; the justification was that a clear signal had to be given that repeat of this conduct was a risky enterprise. But the Notting Hill riots were a different sort of case altogether; racial tension was at a peak and there was a very high risk of escalation. There was nothing of that sort of situation on Pitcairn. Given the smallness of the community, the extensive publicity and investigation, and clear institution of prospective criminal laws were alone likely to have changed the community's future pattern of conduct dramatically (if not, as some prominent officials contemplated, destroy the community altogether). It must be true to say there was a nil risk of reoffending.[60] The Notting Hill race riots case

---

[60] Note Claire Short's letter to Jack Straw (Privy Council disc 8-38832) of 5 August 2001, where she voiced concern that prosecutions might not take place: 'Failure to act means that abuse may well continue and those who have made allegations might be subjected to pressure to withdraw.' See Appendix II, Document (d) below. She was Secretary of State for International Development and the Foreign Secretary at the time. In an earlier letter to Jack Straw (PC disc 8-3860) dated 25 June 2001, she said:

> I suggest we need to face up to the reality that the Pitcairn community is probably so socially dysfunctional that we should cease to plan to support and sustain it, and should instead consider supporting resettlement alongside psychological help and counselling for those who need it. I would not favour providing budgetary support.

Her rather drastic view of the island came in for some criticism from Governor Williams in a letter written in response two days later (PC disc 8-3863):

> Ms Short seems to have decided already that the islanders are incapable of mending their ways. Is this fair? The visits so far by the social workers seem already to have had an impact. We need to keep up the educational process. But the community should be given the chance to show it can reform with more help from HMG (Her Majesty's Government) than in the past.

Clare Short had earlier, without consultation (according to a letter written to her by Robin Cook, then Foreign Secretary), suspended the £800,000 work on the road (the Hill of Difficulty which traversed the area where the longboats came in to the centre of Adamstown), on the grounds that the community might be disbanded as a result of the impending prosecutions, and that the money might need to be used for various social works. Robin Cook protested in a letter of 23 February 2001 (see PC disc 8-3845).

concerned quantum of punishment rather than the desirability of prosecution, and concerned a situation where there was no doubt that
prosecutions were justified. It was also a difficult matter to see what other
quick means for preventing violent race riots there were. In the case of
Pitcairn, an entirely different situation, it should not be automatically
thought that the only way to deal with matters was by criminal
prosecution.

If these arguments against 'symbolic' law are valid, then 'making an
example' of the Pitcairn defendants 'to send a message' out would not
have been justified. It is necessary to labour this essentially simple point
for two reasons. First, there is an element of 'political correctness' that
inevitably adheres to contemporary understanding of what sexual
offences mean in England that was clearly not present in Pitcairn at the
relevant times. Second, this motive for understanding legislation as a
way of 'getting a message across' is in danger of victimization—treating
some people as means and not ends—and so contravenes a basic
requirement of fairness.

## Rights of victims

It is a popular idea that victims now have rights, not just to prosecution
but even to the type and degree of punishment meted out to a defendant. It is a retrograde idea, in my view, an idea that was pleasingly
subdued in the history of English criminal law by the emergence of the
concept of the 'King's Peace'. Crimes were no longer offences against
subjects, but offences against the community at large. But that is not to
say that victims have no rights at all in the criminal justice system, just
that their rights must be qualified by the rights of decency and equality
of respect that all people have, including criminal suspects and offenders. A victim's right to respect cannot include a right to the operation
of the criminal law and a particular exercise of the functions of criminal
justice. That is not an argument against the bringing of private prosecutions, because the most sensible rationale for this relatively rare procedure is not that it vindicates a victim's right to punishment but that it
prevents the arbitrary exercise of a discretion to prosecute; it is thus a
right that all citizens have, whether or not victims. A stronger idea is that
all citizens—not just victims—have a right that their community not be
'dislocated'. A letter from the British Foreign and Commonwealth
Office to the Acting Governor in 2000, reported: 'Ministers want justice to be done fully, freely and without constraint, even if this leads to

the dislocation of the community.'[61] That pursuit of criminal prosecution seems overly single-minded. It is a drastic vision of justice, indeed, that it be pursued at the expense of the stability of the community.

What else could have been done? Some practical solutions were proposed by the Pitcairn legal adviser to the then-Acting Governor of Pitcairn in 2000. In a reflective and perceptive letter,[62] Treadwell expressed his belief that it was perhaps 'unpalatable to impose criminal responsibility' for the sexual behaviour of Pitcairn men 'in the absence of any meaningful civil authority and actual system of justice representing the guidance and supervision of the colonial power'. He therefore suggested a 'general amnesty', or something along the lines of a 'truth and reconciliation' procedure as in South Africa,[63] a suggestion that the Acting Governor, Karen Wolstenholme, endorsed and communicated to the Foreign Office. The Island Commissioner, Leon Salt, took the same line in a letter to the Governor, Mr M. J. Williams, in 2000.[64] There was a suggested cut-off date (1 January 2000) and it was suggested that such a procedure could be accompanied by conditions, the first being that it would cease to apply to any recidivist, the second being that the British Government should provide an ongoing professional police presence for the 'viable future'. The Commissioner also thought that the 'needs and rights of the victims' might be addressed by establishing a special commissioner of inquiry 'to ascertain privately the merits of allegations of sexual offences made', such a person being a judicial officer who could determine individual claims giving rise to compensation. He thought the inquiries could be private and protected from publication.[65] It is difficult to see why this sensible and

---

[61] See the reference to the letter from Stephen Evans of the UK Overseas Territory Department to the Acting Governor of Pitcairn, Karen Wolstenholme (Privy Council disc at 8-3833).

[62] This is in my view one of the most remarkable documents in the case, worth reading in full. See the Appendix.     [63] See Appendix II, Document (b) below.

[64] See Privy Council disc at 8-3779. Appendix II, Document (b) below.

[65] Also see the NZ *Listener* 26 July–1 August 2003 Vol.189, No.3298 <http://www.nzlistener.com/issue/3298/features/384/the_pitcairn_problem,2.html> in which it is reported that the education officer and government adviser on the island, Pippa Foley, wrote to the British Government advising that there should be a 'truth and reconciliation' commission to which she received only a 'polite reply'. Also see the account published in *Vanity Fair* of the Pitcairn trials <http://www.vanityfair.com/culture/features/2008/01/pitcairn200801>. There it is reported that, in 2000, the British Ambassador to New Zealand, Martin Williams, urged London to devise a Nelson Mandela-type amnesty, and that Baroness Scotland QC, the Minister for Overseas Territories at the time, and an expert on child law, 'bluntly' refused the suggestion in a meeting with Williams. (See Appendix II, Documents (a), (b), and (c).) This thoughtful and well-researched article is one of the very few which tries to understand Pitcairn from the point of view of the defendants.

humane proposal, supported by significant officials, close to ground, as it were, was not pursued.

## The value of certainty in the criminal law[66]

As a general rule, hard cases would not make bad law if judges fully appreciated that hard cases are hard precisely because they involve issues of principle. The temptation in the very hardest of cases—which Pitcairn exemplifies—is to value decisiveness over a careful examination of the issues. Of course, that is not to say that decisiveness is not a value in itself. An obvious example is the procedural principle of majority rulings; whether or not the reasons that the majority advances (or could have advanced) are the right ones, it is the fact that the predominance of judgment goes in that direction that is decisive. Decisiveness is also a mark of the legal cast of mind. It is not enough to say—as a philosopher, or an historian might—'well, it could be this, because . . . ' or 'it could be that, perhaps, since . . . ', because a decision precipitating immediate consequences not wanted by at least one of the parties to the dispute is required by fairness. And why fairness? First, it is because decisiveness alone cannot be a value, for it is consistent with arbitrary and evil rule. Many a dictator's political life was marked by decisiveness, but evil is frequently a characteristic of such rule. Second, it is natural to think that the governing principle of judicial decision-making is to be fair to the parties before the court, both in the interpretation and application of the law, and the exercise of judicial discretion when the law permits. Decisiveness will therefore only be a value when there are no reasons available as to why one party rather than the other should win; in rare cases, if they exist, fairness may consist in simply leaving the matter to equal chance, such as by deciding on the toss of a coin. Criminal cases are quite different, however, for fairness would not be served where the reasons were equally balanced and a coin was tossed. The social stigma attached to conviction requires the prosecutor's case to be free of 'reasonable doubt'; so in spite of there being good reasons in favour of the conviction of the defendant, the matter should be resolved in such cases in favour of the defendant. That principle states that a defendant should not be liable for conviction on the basis of a law

---

[66] We should remind ourselves of the 1966 Practice Statement of the House of Lords in which 'the especial need for certainty as to the criminal law' is enshrined: [1966] 3 All ER 77.

the interpretation of which fails to pass a threshold of ambiguity or obscurity to a layperson (since the criminal law is directed to all). It matches the requirement that a defendant should not be convicted on the basis of a reasonable doubt as to the facts that allegedly support conviction, but as I describe it, it applies to questions of law. There seems every reason why that level of reasonableness should match the test for reasonableness in cases of fact.

## Summary and Conclusion

Using the popular expression, I have favoured a 'natural law' approach because it makes more sense of what legality meant on Pitcairn and, particularly, directly offers fair treatment to the defendants. The opposite approach, legal positivism, would, according to a mainstream understanding of what positivism means, allow the conviction and subsequent punishment of the defendants, through a 'paper trail' line of reasoning. But, as I have argued, deeper examination shows that the only credible version of positivism is a non-descriptive, and *practical*, one that favours (that is, this theory makes a significant feature of law in general) both efficiency and fairness, from the same root of clarity that supports paper trail-type law. Because of inefficient promulgation, partly brought about through lack of fair notice to the defendants, constituted by both the absence of precision in the specification of the offences, the likely penalty, and the significant absence of any enforce-ment mechanism, 'practical' legal positivism does not well typify what law was on Pitcairn. Hence my view gains some support—admittedly weaker—from the better interpretation of positivism; there is still valid law, but the theory fails to characterize it as good law. It was a question of abuse of legality and not a question of invalidity, and that was, of course, the Public Defender's main contention. In sum, although all the arguments are *in* 'natural' law, here is an additional argument from the opposite camp providing some support for the same conclusion.

What even very good jurists don't understand is that legal positi-vism—the theory of law that says that law and morality are distinct—may be a morally good and practical way of viewing law; that is, a proposal for, and not a description of, how we should view law. The difficulty arises because it is thought 'how can a theory that separates law from morality be a moral theory?' But the aroma of contradiction is not the same as contradiction. Bentham clearly thought belief in legal positivism would further moral aims (he thought that the clear-mindedness that acceptance of positivism would achieve would promote the 'greatest happiness of the greatest number') and that is surely an accessible and highly practical idea, well outside the category of the merely esoteric. All the Pitcairn judges, excepting Lord Hope and Lord Woolf, gave positivist-inspired judgments that had serious effects on the future of the defendants. So legal theory—getting it right about justifying the coercive power of the state—certainly is of great practical importance to this case. One of the perceived attractions of positivism is that judges feel that to 'let in' arguments of 'fairness and justice and morality' would be to make legal argument a dangerous free-for-all. But this is an exaggerated worry, and something less than a free-for-all but much more than the application of a 'paper trail' would have had better effect on the sorry situation on Pitcairn, a situation that, I believe, deserved more sensitive treatment.[67]

[67] I was British Academy/Leverhulme Trust Senior Fellow while I wrote this paper. I am grateful for their financial assistance.

# *Afterword*

MARILYN STRATHERN

## How are Islands Made?

Given the invitation to comment, it might be thought a social anthropologist would broaden the picture by putting the Pitcairn incident into some kind of 'wider' context, to muse, say, on the propensities of human nature or to draw the reader's eye to practices in Polynesia. However, I also seize an opportunity. I take the phenomenon presented in these pages—arguments surrounding the rejection of an appeal questioning the validity of the way the law had been applied—as itself forming a kind of offshore island. Offshore, because of the significant intellectual dividends to be gained by retrospectively contemplating the whole sorry state of affairs while being removed from any input into the case, it being the removal of course that enables the arguments to be rehearsed in an open away. Island, because of the self-referential nature of the judgments and the attempts in these chapters to subject them to broader scrutiny within the specific compass of legal debate. For there is something here to be learned about isolation.

Suppose, as in a court hearing, all we know is what is presented in these pages. What would a social scientist/anthropologist make of it? Obviously the book cannot be isolated from its readers and their expectations, which, in a nutshell, is essentially its own argument about legal process and those affected by it. But for my part I am reluctant to swamp the narrative, even if I could, with learning from elsewhere. I responded to this generous invitation not quite sure knowing what landfall I would find and, being much enchanted by my sojourn on this island, instead work largely—but not uncritically—within its confines. The invitation is in any case big enough: what more is there to say about the way the law was applied, and about how it has been debated?

The comments divide into two parts, the first the lengthier, but alas not long enough to dispatch avoidable solecisms in chronology and historical epoch I know are there. For the unavoidable ones of ignorance I beg allowance.

## Speculations

The principal comment to make about human nature is in relation to the size of the population. While the numbers on Pitcairn might correspond to the kind reconstructed for certain societies, the chances are that bands of its size would be roaming over large territories. Reports of tiny groups of forest-dwellers surface from time to time, but these are often in contact with other peoples as well; and, while Polynesia is populated with minute islands and atolls, trade with neighbours everywhere echoes the inter-island voyaging that accompanied the original settling of the Pacific. The situation on Pitcairn is truly remarkable: a radical isolation indeed,[1] with a tiny population confined to a tiny island. No neighbours. A space station might be the nearest analogue, though people there would be organized by task and project. On Pitcairn Island, I surmise that the human capacity for social organization itself would be challenged—not because the islanders were in any kind of state of nature (as some of the accounts hint), idyllic or savage,[2] but because of the limitations of their resources. We know some were concerned about its reproduction as their 'community'.[3]

I speculate that what would be most challenging would be the cultural legacy[4] of those inhabitants imagining themselves either tied in some way to being British or thinking back to Tahiti. For neither arena would provide the kind of solution to which very small populations have sometimes resorted: developing the capacity to internally differentiate in order to create the possibility of future relationships between 'different' persons. They could have invented a kinship system, for example, that 'cut off' blood ties at certain points in order for those now created 'non-blood' kin to marry, but it is doubtful whether these people had the conceptual resources. Neither on populous Tahiti nor in Britain had anyone needed to conceptualize their relations with one another in such terms. In any event, how they handled procreative unions is (on the island that this book creates) largely unknown. One hint from the book is that although among the long-term residents everyone is related, there are today seven apparently distinguishable families.[5]

The islanders came with (and built up over time) other capacities, and with other resources for survival, including literacy, two languages

[1] Chapter 5: 97, 128; chapter 8: 186.    [2] Chapter 7.    [3] Chapter 1: 14.
[4] See chapter 7: 60.    [5] Chapter 1: 3.

subsequent evolution.[19] However, while this is not really the business of this book,[20] perhaps it should have been the business of the law. For what is not considered are the claims men had on women, that is, the relationship of men to one another with respect to women, in the light of which the local law about unlawful intercourse with a girl over 12[21] might make some sense[22]—and opens up an unsuspected set of issues to feminist criticism. The local law hints at a division between very young girls and older ones over whom men began to assert claims. That is, this particular rule may have been addressing relations between men, as much as relations between men and women. There is, however, some information on the concept of sexual age,[23] on the age of first child-bearing,[24] on the ratio between the sexes,[25] on early cohabitation,[26] and on the much later Judicature Ordinance, supposedly reflecting local mores in its penalties for cohabitation and adultery.[27]

Running through all the chapters is the question of the constitutional (and international)[28] basis on which the Sexual Offences Act 1956 was applied to Pitcairn. The above leads me to a footnote on this. I wish to make a specific point out of the general observation that the courts showed little interest in investigating what practices prevailed in the community,[29] and properly so according to chapter 6. It is noted that acknowledging the criminality[30] or illegality[31] of an act is a separate matter from conceiving it as a wrong, as is the separation of blame from wrong-doing.[32] Questions about applying different values,[33] or whether in practice Pitcairn had an English legal system,[34] or what might be legally valid on the Island,[35] are raised. But in the case of sexual mores, one thing that the court did not investigate can also barely make it to our island. The contributors to the book are not in a position to dwell on the relationship between the alleged abuse, indecent assault, rape, and incest, of which almost all of the Island's men were suspected, and Island rules about conjugal and other kinds of liaisons.

If on Pitcairn the acts of the accused were breaches, what rules were being observed in the breach? If they were not, then what kind of rule did they encode? One can enquire without presupposing moral

[19] Chapter 7: 3.   [20] Though see chapter 8, and for a contrary view chapter 6.
[21] Chapter 8: 208.   [22] Chapter 8: 197, 200, 208   [23] Chapter 4: 85.
[24] Chapter 8: 200.   [25] Chapter 7: 168.   [26] Chapter 3: 46, 47.
[27] Chapter 3: 58; also see chapter 3:12.   [28] Chapter 5.
[29] Chapter 4: 70; chapter 8: 211.   [30] Chapter 4: 84–85; chapter 8: 183.
[31] Chapter 7: 170–171; chapter 8: 183–184.   [32] Chapter 7: 169.
[33] Chapter 7: 161; chapter 6: 151.   [34] Chapter 7: 172–173.   [35] Chapter 8: 192.

judgement.[36] However, I introduce the term 'rule' provocatively. The truth is there is no conclusive evidence either way as to whether, in this matter, the Pitcairn Islanders were ever lawless. I use the term in the ordinary sense of the word and not with Lord Hoffman's meaning.

Perhaps, to speculate to the contrary, it actually contributed to the islanders' isolation to understand themselves as already having law.[37] This is, of course, a separate question from how exploitative[38] or morally abhorrent,[39] or indeed otherwise, their law might be. We are dealing with an evolving and changing situation over time[40] and different epochs in the Island's history,[41] but, putting aside caveats about anachronism, there are comparisons with colonial situations elsewhere. For example, in being only too ready to castigate themselves for *not* previously 'having law', subject peoples have been known to embrace, to the point of imitation, forms of introduced or colonial law; the shadow or obverse of this is the colonial idea that of course these people always had law of sorts, an idea that they may equally embrace themselves. Out of such interactions comes the state's creation of the notion of customary law ('customary law'[42] being an artefact of state law). Is it out of this too that comes a phenomenon reported for Pitcairn, echoed elsewhere? Once the need to avoid detection subsided, people sought to attach themselves to an outside authority or power. Yet was it to authority or to power? Was the motivation to validate what they already knew about themselves as rule-bound? Or was it a question of the power that those who could tap into it thereby acquired (another point of potential feminist interest)?

Not just law is at issue but laws. In the early years, islanders made use of naval captains to ratify 'local lawmaking'.[43] Now the use of these outsiders (in almost classical Polynesian manner, as Captain Cook knew) does not necessarily imply that it was English law that prevailed,[44] nor that there was the kind of relationship between Britain and Pitcairn that could create a legal community.[45] The requests for recognition, and an apparent desire to make regulation explicit, may have reflected as much on those elements on Pitcairn who tried to impose their vision on fellow islanders.[46] Indeed there seems, as far as one can tell from these accounts, no great break at the juncture when 'Island Law' was

---

[36] Chapter 7: 163–165.    [37] Chapter 3: 53.    [38] Chapter 6: 154.
[39] Chapter 7: 171.    [40] Chapter 1: 7.    [41] Chapter 3.
[42] Chapter 4.    [43] Chapter 3: 53; chapter 4: 72–73; chapter 5: 113.
[44] Chapter 7: 172–173.    [45] Chapters 7–8, esp. chapter 7: 176–180.
[46] Chapter 4: 80–81, chapter 5: 113.

introduced, that is, the special regulations or 'local laws' first established
in the period of settled government and subsequently by, and they were
always outsiders, Island Governors.[47] Whatever the view from Britain or
passing ships' crews, from the islanders' point of view one would want to
know if they entertained any sense of the exotic, of anomaly, or indeed
of remoteness in these arrangements. Had they in effect also helped
create *themselves* as a legal island? Here it is worth noting that at times
size can be irrelevant: a singular (ie. unique)[48] community is capable of
thinking of itself as a whole world. (Although many left Pitcairn, a
population was twice taken off the island only to return.[49]) In other
words, did they once exist—survive, flourish—in a thoroughly self-
referential way, where laws beyond the Island would have been
superfluous?

Possibly something along these lines really did contribute to what was
also a self-grown or self-nurtured isolation, to what made this island an
island. If so, the dismal tale of years of British administrative neglect[50] is
to be seen partly in this light (though not today's failure of the judicial
system to act as a conduit in considering public international law and
human rights protocols, especially with regard to women[51]). The term
neglect of course begs the question of a community of interests.[52] The
point to bring to conclusion builds on the question of the distinctiveness (distinct from English) of a Pitcairn legal system.[53] 'Local law'
seems to have meant different things at different times, from informal
conventions and customary law[54] to the promulgated Island Law,[55] a
boundary object recognized from several sides and over several epochs
though never for quite the same qualities. At any rate, perhaps it was the
ready—or too ready—construction of 'local law' that helped contribute—both positively and negatively—to some of the islanders' sense
of legal self-sufficiency.

## Comparisons

The island that the book creates has its own organizational complexity.
Its scope is divided, between the Privy Council judgment (itself not a

---

[47] Chapter 3: 57–58; chapter 8: 187, 196, 208.      [48] Unique, chapter 7: 160.
[49] Chapter 3: 52, 54.
[50] Chapters 2–3; chapter 4: 88; chapter 5; chapter 7: 180; but see chapter 6: 137.
[51] Chapter 5: 120–121.      [52] Chapter 7:177–180; chapter 8: 183, 184.
[53] Chapter 8: 196.      [54] Chapter 4.      [55] Chapter 5; chapter 8.
[56] Chapter 2:23.

unitary artefact)[56] and the commentaries on it, between the differing views of diverse authors,[57] and between opposed views of what constitutes fairness in legal hearings. Indeed, on this last point, the editor suggests there is a divide, in terms that could be put in what was once jargon from economic anthropology, between formalist and substantivist approaches to the law.[58] So I think I might want to add that on the evidence here, given all the questions that are being asked, it is unfair[59] to brand as 'legalistic' the formalist viewpoint.[60] This formalist viewpoint may have an isolating effect, but obviously it is not isolated from other approaches—or the book would not exist. It is clear that debates can be wide-ranging, raising profound or radical points, be multi-faceted, equivocal, critical, and still be legal debates! Indeed one of the guiding precepts of the lawyer-contributors (the islanders on this book) is to air some of the discussion that seems to have been so peremptorily closed down by the Privy Council's Judicial Committee.[61] They raise diverse legal questions, such as the choice of normative order and the flat preference for English state law,[62] what exactly was the lineage of title to the Island,[63] in what possible sense did the Crown have jurisdiction in the first place,[64] and whether a regime of distinct infrastructures of governance did not count as an instance of intra-territoriality.[65] Yet, however theoretically or philosophically formulated,[66] the burden of the book is that these queries have at least as much bearing on (assessing) the outcome of the adjudication as the paper trails so assiduously laid out.

Now an interesting issue is raised by those paper trails, to pick the term up from chapter 8. It is what is rather scathingly referred to as the court keeping its colonial or legal paperwork in order[67] or as the judgment relying on paperwork and executive statements.[68] While I cannot possibly make any comment on the disciplinary arguments about legal positivism and its rivals,[69] I can mention current anthropological interest in the role documents play in the formation of states and their governments, and draw attention to one of the present government's offspring, audit trails.

The law and order concerns articulated here obviously long pre-date

---

[57] Chapter 6.    [58] Chapter 2: 28.    [59] After chapter 8: 198.
[60] Chapter 1: 10; see also 'formal legal doctrine', chapter 4: 87, 91.
[61] eg chapter 4: 85; chapter 8: 192–193.    [62] Chapter 4: 89.    [63] Chapter 5: 108–109.
[64] Chapter 7: 180–181; chapter 8: 184–187.    [65] Chapter 5: 117.    [66] Chapter 8: 192.
[67] Chapter 1: 3, 9–10.    [68] Chapter 2: 25, 26–27.
[69] Chapters 7–8.

the contemporary predilection for regulating by systems of account-ability: perhaps, rather, the impetus to measure practices by their demonstrable outcomes, where targets substitute for principles, is encouraged by the possibilities of formalism inherent in legal process. In fact, one could think of the court's decision as a kind of reverse audit or possibly an end-point of audit: rather than having to produce the paper trail in order to back up claims about meeting targets, satisfying per-formance indicators and the like, the paperwork is already in place. It then has to be matched retrospectively to the events on the ground. But fancy aside, perhaps contemporary practices allow one to reflect back on the relationship between law, government, administration, and accountability.

In any event, given its focus on whether the colonial paperwork as such had complied with the requirements of the law (the paperwork being subjected, as it were, to performance scrutiny), the kind of loop created by the judgment[70] has to outsiders a self-sufficient quality. It creates an island. At least it does so in so far as the court gives effect to legal paperwork that has been produced by its own government, with no recourse to independent principles.[71] Could we even say that this was done in a thoroughly self-referential way, where sources of law beyond the island created by the judgment would have been super-fluous? In declaring to the contrary that there are questions to be debated,[72] this collection makes it clear that it is important to be aware of the sea out of which an island is formed and to appreciate that, unless you are actually living on Pitcairn, everyone has neighbours. And that this goes too for the conceptual resources that are brought to the consideration of cases in court.

## End

If I may finally bring the volume back to the Foreword, Lord Hope makes it clear that the interest of this case (beyond the lives of the convicted) was never in the verdict: it was in the routes that the judges took and could have taken, and for what one might learn about the application of law and its applicability. There may indeed be a lesson about isolation here. How and where do we create islands, and to what good or ill effect?

[70] And compare the comment in chapter 5: 101.     [71] Chapter 1: 7.
[72] eg chapter 1: 6–7, 16.

No doubt the concept of an island has been worked too hard. It will be appreciated that I refer not to the pristine thought experiment mentioned by one of the contributors but to the self-referential nature of debate. Yet putting the Pitcairn islanders in this regard side by side with the judiciary, and indeed the legal debating within this book, brings me to a final point. For all the negative connotation of isolation, and the way people can cut themselves off thereby, we should not overlook the cultivation of inner resources either. People thrown back on their own resources often (by no means always, as we also know) can come up with interesting solutions. So although there are several interpretations I might want to make that imply some criticism of the lawyers' (diverse) positions, equally I have found within these legal considerations many resources for creating a community of concerns that go beyond the law.

It was never the book's intention to describe Pitcairn in terms of people's obligations to one another, the licences and freedoms they allowed, religious observance, the internal organization of its population, or the kinds of relationships they created. Nor indeed was it concerned to ask about the numbers of unmarried men, how sexual affairs were arranged in general, and what might or might not be regarded as incest. This is partly because of its focus on the judgment reproduced here and not on those of the lower courts (Pitcairn Supreme Court and Court of Appeal) at which a vast amount of information denied on this occasion had been aired then. However it does something else.

It might be thought that pursuing issues for their interest or curiosity, especially when they involve the fortunes of others, is of only academic, that is, remote, concern. But it is precisely that view that cuts off interest and curiosity, and *makes* other people seem remote. It is in the spirit of Lord Hope's remarks to observe that interest and curiosity and to exercise the imagination. And imagination is the first resource any of us have for including others, any others, within our purview. This book has been just such an imaginative exercise.

Marilyn Strathern
Cambridge University[73]

[73] Acknowledgement: I am grateful to the editor for this invitation and opportunity. It will be appreciated that this is indeed written as though I were an island, and the inspiration of numerous colleagues in social anthropology are not mentioned.

# Steven Raymond Christian and Others v The Queen (The Pitcairn Islands) [2006] UKPC 47 (30 October 2006)

JUDGMENT OF THE LORDS OF THE JUDICIAL COMMITTEE
OF THE PRIVY COUNCIL

Delivered the 30th October 2006
- - - - - - - - - - - - - - - - -
Present at the hearing:-
Lord Hoffmann
Lord Woolf
Lord Steyn
Lord Hope of Craighead
Lord Carswell
- - - - - - - - - - - - - - - -
**[Delivered by Lord Hoffmann]**

1. This is an appeal by special leave from the Pitcairn Court of Appeal (Henry P, Barker and Salmon JJA) affirming the convictions of the six appellants by the Pitcairn Supreme Court on charges of rape, indecent assault and incest. The issues upon which leave was given do not concern the merits of the convictions but relate to the validity of the laws creating the offences and the question of whether the bringing of the prosecutions was an abuse of process. ....

2. Pitcairn is a small and remote island in the South Pacific between New Zealand and Chile. It was occupied in 1790 by a group of mutineers from HMAV *Bounty* and some Polynesian men and women. In 1856 the small population removed itself to Norfolk Island but a few families returned two or three years later and re-established themselves. In the nineteenth century the forms of government were rudimentary, consisting of rules drawn up locally or with the assistance of the commanding officers of ships of the Royal Navy which made infrequent visits.

3. In 1893 Her Majesty in Council made the Pacific Order in Council to provide a system of government for British settlements in the Pacific. The Order was made under the British Settlements Act 1887, which gave power to establish 'all such laws and institutions' as might appear to Her Majesty

in Council to be 'necessary for the peace, order and good government of Her Majesty's subjects and others within any British settlement.' A 'British settlement' was defined as any British possession 'which has not been acquired by cession or conquest' and which did not have its own legislature.

4. Article 6(1) of the Order provided that, until otherwise directed by the Secretary of State, jurisdiction should be exercised only over certain islands which did not include Pitcairn, but article 6(2) gave the Secretary of State power to direct that other British settlements in the Pacific should be added. In 1898 the Secretary of State directed that the Order should apply to Pitcairn. The direction was therefore a statement by the Crown that Pitcairn was a British settlement.

5. The Order set up a High Commissioner's Court for the Western Pacific with criminal and civil jurisdiction. Article 20 provided that such jurisdiction should be exercised 'so far as circumstances admit ... upon the principles of and in conformity with the substance of the law for the time being in force in and for England.'

6. The application of the Pacific Order in Council to Pitcairn was revoked by the Pitcairn Order in Council 1952, which provided that the Governor of Fiji should also be Governor of Pitcairn and some neighbouring uninhabited islands ('the Islands') and have power to make laws for the 'peace order and good government' of the Islands. A savings clause provided that until the Governor made other provision, the jurisdiction of the High Commissioner's Court and the law which it applied should continue in force. Other provision was made by Judicature Ordinance 1961, which replaced the jurisdiction of the High Commissioner with that of the Supreme Court of Fiji. The Ordinance also dealt with the law to be applied in Pitcairn:

7. Subject to the provisions of section 8 of this Ordinance the substance of the law for the time being in force in and for England shall be in force in the Islands.

8. All the laws of England extended to the Islands by this Ordinance shall be in force therein so far only as the local circumstances and the limits of local jurisdiction permit and subject to any existing or future Ordinance and for the purpose of facilitating the application of the said laws it shall be lawful to construe the same with such formal alterations not affecting the substance as to names, localities, courts, offices, persons, moneys, penalties and otherwise as may be necessary to render the same applicable to the circumstances.

7. The independence of Fiji in 1970 meant that new provision had to be made for the governorship of Pitcairn. The Pitcairn Order 1970, made in exercise of the powers vested in Her Majesty by the 1887 Act 'or otherwise' replaced the 1952 Order and provided for a Governor appointed by Her Majesty with the same power, in section 5(1), to make laws for 'the peace, order and good government of the Islands'. By section 5(3), all such laws made by the Governor were to be 'published in such manner and at such place or places

in the Islands as the Governor may from time to time direct.' The Governor made the Judicature Ordinance 1970, which repealed the 1961 Ordinance and created a Supreme Court having the same jurisdiction in Pitcairn as the High Court of Justice in England. Section 14 dealt with the law which the Supreme Court was to apply:

(1) Subject to the provisions of the next succeeding subsection the common law, the rules of equity and the statutes of general application as in force in and for England at the commencement of this Ordinance shall be in force in the Islands.

(2) All the laws of England extended to the Islands by the last preceding subsection shall be in force therein so far only as the local circumstances and the limits of local jurisdiction permit and subject to any existing or future Ordinance and for the purpose of facilitating the application of the said laws it shall be lawful to construe the same with such formal alterations not affecting the substance as to names, localities, courts, offices, persons, moneys, penalties and otherwise as may be necessary to render the same applicable to the circumstances.

8. This Ordinance was duly published in accordance with section 5(3) and was in force at the time when the offences were committed. The appellants were charged under provisions of the Sexual Offences Act 1956, which was a law of general application in force in England at the time of the commencement of the Ordinance.

9. The first point taken by the appellants is that the 1970 Ordinance was *ultra vires* the 1887 Act, either because Pitcairn was never a British possession at all or, alternatively, because it had been acquired by cession and was therefore outside the definition of a 'British settlement'. In support of the first argument, Mr Cook QC proposed to take their Lordships to the history of the island to demonstrate that the islanders never acknowledged allegiance to the Crown. Their Lordships declined to investigate this question because it appears to them that the legal status of the island as a British possession is concluded by successive statements of the executive, starting with the direction of the Secretary of State in 1898 and ending with the making of the 1970 Order in Council. In *The Fagernes* [1927] P 311, 324, Atkin LJ said:

'What is the territory of the Crown is a matter of which the Court takes judicial notice. The Court has, therefore, to inform itself from the best material available; and on such a matter it may be its duty to obtain its information from the appropriate department of Government. Any definite statement from the proper representative of the Crown as to the territory of the Crown must be treated as conclusive.'

10. This is not the occasion on which to explore the limits of this doctrine, but their Lordships consider that the present case falls squarely within it. For over a hundred years Pitcairn has been administered by the Crown as a British possession and whatever its history or the inclinations of its people may have been, it is unthinkable that the Judicial Committee of Her

Majesty's Privy Council would not accept an executive statement affirming it to be part of the territory of the Crown. The directions of 1898 and the Orders in Council of 1952 and 1970 are statements of this kind.

11. The argument that the Crown acquired Pitcairn by cession is a novel one. Cession by whom? The notion of cession contemplates a transfer of sovereignty by one sovereign power to another. . . . the question appears to their Lordships to be quite academic, since there is no doubt that the power of the Crown to legislate for a conquered or ceded possession is more extensive than its power to legislate for a settled colony: see Blackstone's *Commentaries* (4th ed 1770) at p. 107. As the 1970 Ordinance was made under the powers vested in Her Majesty by the 1887 Act 'or otherwise', it is valid whether Pitcairn was settled or ceded.

12. Mr Cato submitted next for the appellants that the language of section 14 of the 1970 Ordinance was too imprecise to incorporate the 1956 Act as part of the law of Pitcairn. What was a statute 'of general application'? And there could be much dispute over whether 'local circumstances' made it appropriate for the law to apply. But this language has been used in legislation for British overseas possessions for many years without causing any difficulty. As Sir Kenneth Roberts-Wray said in his book on *Commonwealth and Colonial Law* (1966), at p. 545:

> 'It has been in use for many decades, it has been the subject of judicial interpretation, it does not appear to have given the courts serious trouble, and it has much the same effect as the common law rule. So a change of formula may do more harm than good.'

13. Similar language was considered by the Court of Appeal in *Nyali Ltd v Attorney-General* [1956] 1 QB 1, where Denning LJ said (at p. 17) that the task of making qualifications to English law to suit the circumstances of overseas territories called for wisdom on the part of their judges. But he described it (at p. 16) as a 'wise provision' and did not suggest that it was incapable of application. Their Lordships think that there can be no doubt that the 1956 Act is an act of general application and that there are no local circumstances which make it inappropriate to apply the provisions about rape, indecent assault and incest.

14. Mr Cato also submitted that the phrase 'the substance of the law for the time being in force in and for England' in section 7 of the 1961 Ordinance and the 'statutes of general application' in section 14(1) of the 1970 Ordinance did not incorporate the criminal law. He contrasted this language with section 20 of the 1893 Order in Council, which referred expressly to civil and criminal jurisdiction. Their Lordships think that there is nothing in this point. 'The law' obviously means the whole of the law and 'statutes' means all statutes. Indeed, if it did not incorporate the criminal law, it is hard to see how, by the same process of reasoning, it could have incorporated the civil law.

15. Mr Cato also submitted that, at the time when the offences were committed, the 1956 Act and all other English statutes creating indictable offences failed the test of suitability to local circumstances because until the creation of the Pitcairn Court of Appeals by the Pitcairn Court of Appeal Order 2000, there was no right of appeal against a conviction by the Supreme Court. In their Lordships' opinion, the right of appeal is a question of procedure which has no connection with the applicability of the substantive law. If there is a need for a right of appeal (as to which their Lordships express no opinion) that requirement arises at the time of conviction. . . .

16. Mr Perry, for the appellant Carlisle (Terry) Young, submitted that the 1956 Act could not apply because it had not been published in accordance with section 5(3) of the 1970 Order in Council. But that subsection applies to laws made by the Governor in the exercise of his powers under section 5(1). Under that section the Governor made the 1970 Ordinance, which was duly published, but obviously not the 1956 Act. Mr Perry submitted that in the peculiar circumstances as they existed on Pitcairn, section 5(3) should be read as applying not only to laws made by the Governor but also to any laws incorporated by an Ordinance as part of the law of Pitcairn. Quite apart from the fact that this is not what section 5(3) says, their Lordships think that such a construction would be quite unrealistic. Section 14(1) incorporates not only statutes but also the common law and the rules of equity, which hardly admit of 'publication'. It is true that if, contrary to Mr Cato's argument, Pitcairn was a British settlement, the settlers would have taken the rules of common law and equity to the island without the need for express legislation. Nevertheless, the Ordinance purports to incorporate them.

17. Furthermore, if section 5(3) is to be read as requiring publication of incorporated statutes, the same construction must have applied to section 5(3) of the 1952 Ordinance. At that time, English statutes applied to Pitcairn by virtue of the 1893 Pacific Order in Council. Assuming that Order to have been validly made and applied to Pitcairn, as their Lordships think it was, there is no dispute about the validity of its incorporation of English law. At the time of the Judicature Ordinance 1961, therefore, the substance of English statute law applied to the island. But Mr Perry's submission is that once the Governor, by that Ordinance, exercised his power to bring the application of the 1893 Order in Council to an end, English statute law ceased to apply except in so far as each statute was subsequently published on the island. Their Lordships think it unlikely, in the absence of express language, that such a result was intended. And so far from there being express language, the result can be achieved only by a bold process of implication into the language of the 1952 and 1970 Orders. For these reasons, which are the same as those of

the Court of Appeal (see paragraphs 34 to 37) their Lordships reject the submission.

18. Their Lordships pass to the alternative ground of appeal, that the prosecution was in all the circumstances an abuse of the process of the court. The chief reasons put forward are that the Sexual Offences Act 1956 had not been published in the island and that the rudimentary policing of the inhabitants gave the impression that English law would not be enforced, but there were other grounds such as delay and inequality of arms.

19. In *Regina v Latif* [1996] 1 WLR 104, 112–113 Lord Steyn said that a judge had power to stay a criminal prosecution on broad considerations of 'the integrity of the criminal justice system' when there has been an abuse of process which 'amounts to an affront to the public conscience'. In exercising this discretion, it was necessary for the judge to weigh in the balance 'the public interest in ensuring that those who are charged with grave crimes should be tried' and the competing public interest in not conveying an impression that 'the end justifies the means'.

20. The Supreme Court was referred to the principle stated in *Latif* and invited to exercise its discretion to stay the proceedings. It examined all the grounds with great care and declined to do so. The Court of Appeal re-examined those grounds and concluded (at paragraph 150):

> 'Even viewed cumulatively, the alleged grounds for abuse of process do not militate against a fair hearing. The proceedings were instituted and prosecuted in accordance with the true purpose of criminal proceedings, that is, to hear and determine the charges against the accused and to assess punishment of those found guilty. The appellants did not show that they will suffer serious prejudice if the proceedings were allowed to proceed.'

21. In support of the exercise of its discretion, the Supreme Court made certain findings of fact. Their Lordships set out those which they consider to be the most important:

> [108] When considering the material placed before us as a whole, we are satisfied that the evidence establishes that at all relevant times Pitcairn was a developed society in which rape and various sexual offending were known to be criminal. There is no reason to doubt that this knowledge of rape extended to sexual offending generally, including indecent assault and incest.
>
> [110] We find that English administration of justice over Pitcairn Island was not a paper administration operating in an occasional and ad hoc way, but a reality when considering how civil and criminal disputes were dealt with throughout the 20th century.
>
> [118] We do not accept the suggestion that Pitcairn may in some way be an anarchic or lawless society. Over the years the roles of the Island Police officer and the Island Magistrate have frequently been of high profile and the law, and enforcement of the law, has loomed large in Pitcairn affairs.

22. The findings on knowledge of the criminality of rape, indecent assault and incest were upheld by the Court of Appeal (see paragraphs 114 and 115) which went on to say:

> [116] Faced with this factual situation it becomes unreal to contend that it was unfair or unjust to commence these prosecutions because the 1956 Act or a summary of its provisions had not been separately published locally. There was never any contention that the appellants, or any of them, did not or could not reasonably have known that the allegations against them constituted serious criminal offending ...
>
> [117] Counsel for the appellants also relied on an absence of knowledge of the penalties provided by the 1956 Act. While we agree that the penalty factor is something to be taken into account in the overall assessment, we do not see it as having any significant effect on the present argument. It was self-evident that for rape a substantial term of imprisonment would be available to the sentencer ... The other maximum penalties of two years' imprisonment could not be regarded as unforeseeable.

23. The findings on policing were similarly upheld. The Crown conceded that the standard of policing had been 'variable, to say the least' but the Court of Appeal said:

> [134] ... we see at best no prejudice to the accused of a sufficient weight as to stay the prosecution on abuse of process on this ground. The lack of an English police presence did not mean that the appellants could not and did not receive fair trials. Lack of policing could not possibly immunise serious offenders from prosecution.

24. Their Lordships would accept that the fact that a law had not been published and could not reasonably have been known to exist may be a ground for staying a prosecution for contravention of that law as an abuse of process. It is however unnecessary to discuss the philosophical basis or legal limits of such a principle because, in the light of the concurrent findings of fact and the agreement of both the lower courts as to the exercise of what on any view is a discretion, their Lordships think that it is an impossible task to persuade the Board to interfere. They can find no error of principle in the way in which the discretion was exercised and on the facts as found would have exercised it in the same way. These were serious offences and the balance to which Lord Steyn referred in *Latif* comes down firmly in favour of bringing them before a court of justice.

25. That leaves the subsidiary grounds upon which it was submitted that the prosecutions should have been stayed. One was the delay which occurred between the time when the accused were first notified that they might be charged and the time when they were indicted. The main period of delay (between a year and two years) was caused by the need to determine a venue for the trials and appoint Supreme Court judges to conduct them. This required a diplomatic agreement between the United Kingdom and

New Zealand, followed by primary legislation by the New Zealand Parliament. These arrangements were, all things considered, carried through with remarkable speed but the appellants say that it all took a good deal longer than it would have done if the necessary institutions had already been up and running when the charges were first investigated. That is no doubt true, but the Supreme Court found that the delay had not caused prejudice to the fairness of the trials and although there was for a year or so uncertainty about when and where the appellants would be tried, their Lordships agree with both of the lower courts that the period was nowhere near long enough to make the prosecutions an abuse of process.

26. Finally, the appellants argued that (1) the legislation passed after the appellants had been charged to establish a suitably fair trial procedure and a right of appeal 'compromised the appearance of even-handed justice' and suggested inequality of arms (2) the Supreme Court judges should have come from the United Kingdom rather than New Zealand and the new laws should have been based on United Kingdom rather than, as they were, on New Zealand models (3) the appellants were prejudiced by the appointment of a Public Defender some time after the appointment of a public prosecutor, resulting in a period before the trial when there was inequality of arms. It is hard to take any of these points seriously. There is no dispute that the new legislation made the trial and appeal process fair. There is no suggestion of any lack of competence on the part of the judges or a restriction on the Governor's power of appointment on grounds of nationality. And there is no dispute that the Public Defender had all the time he required to prepare the defences.

...

29. Their Lordships will humbly advise Her Majesty that the appeals should be dismissed.

## Judgment by Lord Woolf

30. I have had the advantage of reading in draft the opinion of the Board prepared by my noble and learned friend Lord Hoffmann and I am in agreement that the appeals should be dismissed for the reasons he gives. I have also had advantage of reading the judgment of my noble and learned friend Lord Hope of Craighead. I shared Lord Hope's concerns about the issue involving the appellants' lack of knowledge of the provisions of sections 1 and 14 of the Sexual Offences Act 1956. However with the assistance of the additional facts that Lord Hope has set out so clearly in his judgment I am able to briefly set out my views on this issue.

...

33. ... In my view the evidence that Pitcairn is and was at all relevant times a British possession was overwhelming and so I agree with Lord Hoffmann, that for the purposes of determining these appeals, it is not necessary to

explore the limits of the act of state doctrine. Where this is not the position, in my view it would be necessary to carefully re-examine the authorities including those cited by Lord Hoffmann which support the contention that an act of state is to be regarded as conclusive on issues as to the status of alleged British possessions overseas. Recent developments, mainly in relation to judicial review have demonstrated a greater willingness on the part of the courts to scrutinise the use by the Crown of prerogative powers and so far the limits, if any, of the courts' power of review has not been clearly determined. So today it can no longer be taken for granted that the courts will accept that there is any action on the part of the Crown that is not open to any form of review by the courts if a proper foundation for the review is established.

34. Having made those preliminary remarks I turn to the issue about which I was primarily concerned, namely the fact that the Sexual Offences Act 1956 was never promulgated on Pitcairn. I start with the fact that the offences in respect of which the appellants were charged, indicted and convicted were offences under sections 1 or 14 of that Act. This being the position it was essential for the Crown to establish that the Act was in force on Pitcairn at the time of the alleged offences. If the Act was not then in force this is fatal to these convictions. In my view having been indicted or tried on the statutory offences of rape and indecent assault the appellants could not be convicted of common law or other offences of a similar nature.

35. In view of this, there are two questions that have to be answered positively if the convictions are to stand. They are:

   a) Was the Sexual Offences Act 1956 part of the law of Pitcairn at the time of the offences?

   b) Were the appellants sufficiently aware of nature of the offence of rape and indecent assault charged respectively under sections 1 and 14 of the Sexual Offences Act 1956 to justify prosecuting them on the charges on which they were convicted?

36. Mr David Perry, who represented Carlyle Terry Young, advanced an argument that the Sexual Offences Act never became part of the law of Pitcairn. This was based on article 5 (3) of the Pitcairn Order in Council 1970 that was made under the British Settlements Acts of 1887 and 1952. His argument was adopted by the other appellants.

37. Lord Hope sets out the legislative history fully in his judgment. Briefly, article 5 (1) of the Pitcairn Order 1970 (the same is true of the earlier Order of 1952) gave the Governor power to make laws for the peace, order and good government of the Island. Article 5 (3) requires laws made by the Governor to be published in such manner and in such place or places in the Island as the Governor may from time to time direct. As a result of

article 5 (4) a law comes into operation on the date on which it is published.

38. In the case of the Judicature Ordinance 1970, section 14 provided that 'the common law, the rules of equity and the statutes of general application as in force in and for England at the commencement of this ordinance' were to be in force in the Island so far only as local circumstances permit. The earlier legislation made similar provision for the incorporation of the laws of England. Mr Perry, correctly in my view, does not dispute that an incorporation by a general reference of this nature is permissible. There was a specific offence under section 88 of the Pitcairn Ordinance of 1966 of having unlawful sexual intercourse but no legislation dealing with offences as serious as rape or indecent assault. And so, as there is nothing that would make offences set out in sections 1 and 14 of the Sexual Offences Act inappropriate to the circumstances in Pitcairn, sections 1 and 14 of the Sexual Offences Act 1956 were as a result of the general words capable of being made part of the law in force in Pitcairn at the relevant times.

39. However, Mr Perry relies on the fact that that the Act of 1956 was never published·on Pitcairn so he submits sections 1 and 14 never came into force on Pitcairn. I have no hesitation in agreeing with Lord Hoffmann and Lord Hope, that Mr Perry's submission that article 5 of the Pitcairn Order 1970 (and the 1952 Order) required all the laws of England or at least the Sexual Offences 1956 to be published on the Island before they came into force on the Island is incorrect. The proper interpretation of article 5 is that what are required to be published are the Judicature Ordinance and not all the laws of England incorporated by reference. This answer accords with the language of the Orders. In addition it is the only practical answer, if the Orders were to operate in a practical manner. The corpus of English law could not realistically be published on Pitcairn and even if it was attempted to achieve this by having, for example, all the volumes of Halsbury's Laws and Statutes gathering dust on the island, this would not be more than a meaningless gesture and not what the Orders intended. The first of the two questions I identified above is, accordingly, answered positively.

40. The issues raised by the second question are not so straight forward. The more general argument advanced in the courts below and relied upon by Mr Perry is not a matter of interpretation. It is based on the principle that it is a requirement of almost every modern system of criminal law, that persons who are intended to be bound by a criminal statute must first be given either actual or at least constructive notice of what the law requires. This is a requirement of the rule of law, which in relation to the criminal law reflects the need for legal certainty. As the Supreme Court in its judgment of 24th May 2005 recognised (para.155) governments must

ensure adequate publication or at least reasonable access to the criminal laws which they wish to enforce.

41. I have no difficulty with the generality of this freestanding argument, but in my view it has no application on the facts to the present appeals. I say this despite the fact that on the findings of the Supreme Court it is clear that the appellants were probably unaware of the terms of the Sexual Offences Act or even that there was legislation of that name or the sentences that could be imposed for those offences. They were aware, however, that their conduct was contrary to the criminal law. The community of Pitcairn may be small in numbers and isolated but it is not the appellants' contention that rape and indecent assault was conduct which was regarded as being other than criminal on Pitcairn. Furthermore, while the precise terms of the 1956 Act had not been published on the island, the fact that there were offences such as rape and possibly indecent assault which had to be dealt with by the Supreme Court because they required greater punishment than was possible otherwise was generally known. In addition, the Supreme Court came to the conclusion (paragraph 145) that 'Pitcairn Islanders have had free access to information about their laws through the Government Advisor, the Commissioner and Legal Advisor'. This was because the Supreme Court was left in no doubt that 'the British Administrators recognised and appreciated that because of Pitcairn's physical isolation and small population, the law significantly affected each individual's life and therefore dealt with even minor matters . . . if asked to assist. All Pitcairn Islanders had access to the law' (paragraph 147). The Court of Appeal was unimpressed by this finding (paragraph 108), but it appears to be justified by the evidence and of the greatest significance. As Lord Bridge of Harwich pointed out in this context in *Grant v Borg* [1982] 1 WLR 638, 646, if information is accessible, a defendant is deemed to know of it. This must be the appropriate approach. The problems of obtaining knowledge of the contents of the law in Pitcairn are not the same as those, for example, in a very different society such as England but in both there are problems. The sheer volume of the law in England, much of which would be inapplicable and have no application to Pitcairn, creates real problems of access even to lawyers unless they are experts in the particular field of law in question. The criminal law can only operate on Pitcairn, as elsewhere, if the onus is firmly placed on a person, who is or ought to be on notice that conduct he is intending to embark on may contravene the criminal law, to take the action that is open to him to find out what are the provisions of that law.

42. The Supreme Court (at paragraph 96 of the judgment of 24th May 2005) correctly raised the question whether the 'degree of publication' together with the other factors to which the Court referred in their judgment

accords knowledge that is sufficient to alert the appellants to the fact that rape, indecent assault and incest are crimes punishable, if committed on the island, under English law. While the appellants needed to know that rape and indecent assault were contrary to the criminal law, they did not need to know of the precise provisions of sections 1 and 14 of the Sexual Offences Act 1956 which produced this result. It was sufficient that they could have obtained detailed information relating to the Act if they had wanted to do so. Obtaining that information could be a more protracted exercise on Pitcairn because of its inaccessibility, but the fact that information could be obtained suffices to make the appellants responsible for their conduct.

43. The argument on lack of publication therefore is defeated by the findings of the Supreme Court as to the knowledge of the islanders and availability of information if it was wanted. Lord Hope also regards as being critical the fact that the 1956 Act was not creating in sections 1 and 14 new offences. He is right, that rape and indecent assault were not new offences so far as English law is concerned but I am not sure why this assists. Even though the antecedents of those sections included like offences this does not alter the fact that the prosecution was based on the 1956 Act and the appellants would not be any more aware of the position under the earlier Act or at common law.

44. The absence of the required knowledge as to the criminality of their actions and inaccessibility of information could be an appropriate basis for an allegation of abuse of process. Abuse of process should however be reserved for cases where it would be an affront to justice for the person concerned to be prosecuted. To prosecute an individual for an offence of which he has no means of knowing the details is capable of being such a departure from the requirements of due process as to justify the prosecution being stayed. However, it is of the essence of an argument based on the lack of due process that the individual concerned would if the prosecution proceeded be treated unjustly and in this sense prejudiced. As in this case the appellants suffered no prejudice in view of their state of knowledge an argument based on abuse of process would not be established. It may be the case that the argument under this head could be freestanding and not based on abuse of process. However if this be so the need for prejudice would still be a requirement. The great majority of criminal offences require *mens rea*. If you do not know and are not put on notice that the conduct with which you are charged was criminal at the time you are alleged to have committed the offence, it can be the case that you do not have the necessary criminal intent. Whether or not this is the situation will very much depend on the facts and in this developing area of criminal law it is undesirable to generalise.

45. I would dismiss these appeals.

**Judgment by Lord Hope of Craighead**

46. The judgment of the Board has been given by Lord Hoffmann. But I have been much more troubled by some of the questions raised by these appeals than the way he has dealt with them in his judgment might be thought to indicate. So I should like to explain in my own words why, in the end, I have come to be of the opinion that the appeals should be dismissed.

47. In order to set the scene for what I wish to say I must first deal more fully with the facts. The circumstances which gave rise to these prosecutions are highly unusual—almost certainly unique in the Board's experience. They raise some fundamental issues about the rule of law in remote communities and about the responsibilities of the colonial power which seeks to exert its authority over them. I agree with all that Lord Hoffmann has said in his judgment on the question whether the Judicature Ordinance 1970 was ultra vires the British Settlements Act 1887. In my opinion the evidence shows that Pitcairn was established by settlement. As para 800 of 6 Halsbury's Laws of England (4th ed, 2003 Reissue) puts it, every colony must be assigned to one or other of two classes, either (1) settled or (2) conquered or ceded. This is a classification of law, and once made by practice or judicial decision it will not be disturbed. Much interesting historical research has been laid before us. But, as long standing practice has established Pitcairn's status as a settled colony, it must be held to be irrelevant to the issue of classification raised in these appeals. I agree that the Governor had legislative authority to enact laws for the peace, order and good government of Pitcairn.

48. But the vesting of legislative authority in the Governor is one thing. The manner of its exercise is quite another. It is this aspect of the case that I have found much more difficult. As I shall show in my account of the facts, the central question is whether sections 1 and 14 of the Sexual Offences Act 1956, a United Kingdom statute, were in force on Pitcairn at the time when the offences were committed. Let me not mince words. This case is about child sexual abuse on a grand scale. The extent to which it was practised on Pitcairn is deeply disturbing. Conduct of that kind cannot be regarded as other than criminal and deserving of punishment. But abhorrence at the nature of these crimes must not blind us to the rule of law. Thomas Hobbes, Leviathan (1651), Ch 31, para 3, made this point as clearly as anyone when, having declared in Ch 30, para 20 that a good law is 'withal perspicuous', he wrote: 'To rule by words, requires that such words be manifestly made known; for else they are no laws: for to the nature of laws belongeth a sufficient, and clear promulgation, such as may take away the excuse of ignorance; which in the laws of man is but of one only kind, and that is, proclamation, or promulgation by the voice of man.'

49. The issue on which I wish to concentrate, then, is whether the legislative technique that was adopted by the Governor was sufficiently well adapted

to conditions on Pitcairn for it to be possible for us to say that the 1956 Act was in force there at the relevant time, with the result that the Supreme Court had jurisdiction to entertain the charges that were laid against the appellants under the statute. I agree with the way Lord Hoffmann has disposed of the other issues in these appeals.

The offences

50. I must now set out the offences of which the six appellants were convicted in greater detail. This needs to be done to reveal the extent of the problem which lay beneath the surface when an allegation of rape was brought to the attention of the Foreign and Commonwealth Office in 1996 and Kent Police were asked to provide personnel to investigate the allegation. Following an investigation which was conducted on Pitcairn by two officers of Kent Police in September 1996 it was decided that there was insufficient evidence to prosecute the suspect for the offence of rape. But he had admitted consensual intercourse with the complainant on six occasions before and after her 12th birthday. This was contrary to section 88 of the Justice Ordinance 1966, which makes it an offence on Pitcairn for any male person to have carnal knowledge with a female child of or over the age of 12 years. It was also contrary to section 5 of the Sexual Offences Act 1956, assuming it to be part of the laws of Pitcairn, under which it is an offence for a man to have sexual intercourse with a girl under the age of thirteen.

51. For the reasons explained by Paul Treadwell, the legal adviser to the Governor of Pitcairn, in his letter to the first secretary in the British High Commission in Wellington dated 5 January 1997, it was decided that the suspect should be formally cautioned but not prosecuted for these offences. Section 88 of the Justice Ordinance 1966 does not prohibit intercourse with a girl below the age of 12 years. So it was decided to draft an indictment under sections 5 and 6 of the Sexual Offences Act 1956. But Mr Treadwell thought it fair to assume that the offender was unaware of the terms of these provisions of the 1956 Act and of the very substantial penalties attaching to them. Furthermore no United Kingdom statutes were available to the public on Pitcairn. It was a moot point whether they would be understandable by members of the public, even if they were. As he put it, the decision not to prosecute was taken out of concern for the current state of the criminal law on Pitcairn, and for its implications for the liberty of Her Majesty's subjects on the island.

52. There had never been any British police presence on Pitcairn until the arrival of the Kent Police in 1996. So, following this investigation, it was decided that a police officer should be sent to Pitcairn for a three month tour of duty to train and support the existing Island officer who up until then had the sole responsibility of policing the island. WPC Gail Cox was selected for this duty and she made her first visit to Pitcairn in October

1997. It was as a result of her painstaking investigation under very difficult circumstances that the extent of the child sexual abuse being practised on the island was revealed and the prosecutions brought that have led to these appeals.

53. Four of the appellants were convicted of rape on counts brought against them under section 1 of the Sexual Offences Act 1956.

(a) Len Carlyle Brown ('Len Brown'), who was born in March 1926, was convicted of two offences of rape committed between January 1969 and June 1972 when he was aged between 42 and 46, on each of which he was sentenced to 2 years' imprisonment. The complainant, who was the same individual in both cases, was aged between 15 and 18 years when the offences were committed against her.

(b) Stevens Raymond Christian, who was born in January 1951, was convicted of four offences of rape committed against one complainant between September 1964 and October 1968 when he was aged between 13 and 17 and she was aged between 11 and 15 years, on each of which he was sentenced to 2 years' imprisonment. He was also convicted of one offence of rape committed between February 1972 and February 1973 when he was 21 or 22 against a different complainant who was 12 or 13 years old, for which he was sentenced to 3 years' imprisonment.

(c) Carlisle Terry Young ('Terry Young'), who was born in October 1958, was convicted of repeatedly raping the complainant between December 1977 and December 1981 when he was 19 to 23 and she was aged between 12 to 15 years, for which he was sentenced to 5 years' imprisonment.

(d) Randall Kay Christian, who was born in March 1974, was convicted of four offences of rape committed between September 1994 and October 1996 when he was 20 to 22 and the complainant, who was the same individual in all four cases, was aged between 10 and 12 years, on each of which he was sentenced to 6 years' imprisonment.

54. Three of the appellants were convicted of indecent assault on counts brought against them under section 14 of the 1956 Act.

(a) Dennis Ray Christian pleaded guilty to one count of indecent assault under section 14 of the Sexual Offences Act 1956 and two counts of incest between February 1972 and March 1974 when he was aged 15 to 17 and the complainant was 12 to 14 years old, for which he was sentenced to 300 hours of community work and placed under supervision for two years.

(b) Len Calvin Davis Brown ('Dave Brown'), who was born in October 1954, pleaded guilty to two offences of indecent assault under section

14 of the 1956 Act against one complainant and one against another which were committed between January 1986 and January 1987 when he was aged 31 to 32 and the complainants were aged 14 and 15 at the time of the offences. He was found guilty on a further six counts of indecent assault between December 1989 and December 1991 when he was aged 35 to 37 and the complainant was aged between 13 and 15 years. The Public Prosecutor conceded that the conduct in relation to four other counts of indecent assault which were proved against him came within section 88 of the Justice Ordinance 1971, with the result that those counts were dismissed as they were out of time. For the offences of which he was convicted he was sentenced to 400 hours of community work and placed under supervision for two years.

(c) Carlisle Terry Young was convicted of six counts of indecent assault under section 14 of the 1956 Act in addition to that of rape. The indecent assaults were committed against three different complainants between December 1972 and December 1991 when he was aged 14 to 33. In one case the complainant was only 5 years old when he began to touch her. In all the other cases the complainants were under 15 years old. He was sentenced to six months imprisonment on the indecent assault charges, to be served concurrently with the sentence of 5 years on the charge of rape.

(d) Randall Kay Christian was convicted of four counts of indecent assault under section 14 of the 1956 Act committed between October 1998 and February 1999 when he was 24 and the complainers were aged 14, for which he was sentenced to 12 months' imprisonment to be served concurrently with his sentence of six years for rape.

55. Some indication of the scale of the sexual abuse that was found to have been perpetrated on Pitcairn can be gathered from the ages of the men who were engaging in this practice and the dates between which the offences were committed that were found to have been proved. The ages of the perpetrators range from 13 in the case of Stevens Christian to 46 in the case of Len Brown. The offences were committed between September 1964, more than 38 years before the charges in these proceedings were laid in Pitcairn Magistrate's Court in April 2003, and February 1999. Between them the appellants were convicted on thirty counts, several of which involved a course of conduct that was repeated many times over against the same complainant. It is impossible to believe that the appellants were not aware that what they were doing was wrong. The Supreme Court was satisfied, after considering the material placed before it, that at all relevant times Pitcairn was a developed society in which rape and sexual offending generally was known to be criminal: para 108 of its judgment of 24 May 2005 as to promulgation of laws and related issues.

56. But the fact that this scale of offending, of which the offences that have been proved in this case was almost certainly the tip of the iceberg, was tolerated for so long in such a small, isolated and closely knit community is an indication of the poor state of supervision exercised over its affairs by the colonial authorities. To put the scale of offending into context it should be noted that the population of Pitcairn in 1964 was 90, of whom 34 were men and 13 were girls under 16: A Guide to Pitcairn, Revised edition, 1970, Appendix 1. By 1989 it had fallen to 55, of whom 18 were men and 9 girls under 16: A Guide to Pitcairn, 5th edition, 1990, Appendix 1. On the figures that the Board has been given it appears that the appellants comprise about a third of the adult male population of Pitcairn. Further proceedings are currently in progress against three men in New Zealand. It is scarcely credible that the population of the island as a whole was unaware of what was going on. The Supreme Court, after studying the evidence in great detail in its judgment on the promulgation of laws and related issues, concluded that in a community the size of Pitcairn issues of law and order and of punishment could not have escaped the notice of the community at large, including youths as they grew up: para 129. Nevertheless no steps were taken to deal with these offences until Kent Police began their investigation. The development of the Island's legal system

57. The Board was provided with a wealth of material about the history and social conditions on Pitcairn from the date when it was first settled to the present day, all of which was considered by the judges in the Supreme Court and in the Court of Appeal with great care and attention to detail. It is impossible to summarise this material in a few paragraphs, and I shall not attempt to do so. But a few points which stand out from the rest must be mentioned to provide the necessary background.

58. Pitcairn, which is one of four widely scattered islands comprising the Islands of Pitcairn, is one of the most remote communities in the world. It lies approximately midway between New Zealand, some 3,000 miles to the west, and Chile, some 4,000 miles to the east. Pitcairn is the only one of the islands in the group that is inhabited. The nearest inhabited island lies in the Gambia Archipelago, some 300 miles to the north-west. It is also very small, but quite high and rugged. It is about two and a half miles long and one mile wide, extending to about 1,100 acres. Much of the land slopes steeply to a peak of 1,140 feet, and only about 39 per cent of the island is comparatively flat and arable. Consequently, although the soil is fertile and it has a favourable climate, the island has never been able to sustain a population of more than about 200 people. In recent years the population has declined sharply as islanders seek their fortunes elsewhere, particularly in New Zealand

59. When Pitcairn was settled in about 1790 by 9 male Bounty mutineers, who were well aware that the Admiralty would seek to bring them to

justice, and the 19 Polynesians (13 women and 6 men) they brought with them it was deliberately chosen as a place where they could avoid detection. It remained isolated from the rest of civilisation for nearly two centuries. The shoreline is steep and rocky and there are no harbour or port facilities. Nor are there facilities for any type of aircraft. Until about 1985 the islanders had no means of communicating with the outside world, other than by transacting with visiting ships, except by radio using the Morse code. They had no operative internal legal system for almost all the period of the island's habitation other than a local island magistrate assisted by two assessors, none of whom had any legal training. Apart from one small book of Pitcairn laws, no legal texts, statutes or law reports were available on the island until about 1997.

60. From time to time however various measures affecting Pitcairn have been passed in the exercise of the authority conferred on Her Majesty in Council by section 2 of the British Settlements Act 1887 and the authority given to it to delegate the power of making laws under section 3. The history was reviewed in detail by the Supreme Court in its judgment on the promulgation of laws and related issues. It is unnecessary to repeat all but a few of these details. The Pacific Order in Council 1893 applied English law to a defined area in the Western Pacific which did not include Pitcairn. It conferred jurisdiction to deal with offences committed within that area on the Court of the High Commissioner for the Western Pacific in Fiji. In 1898, following the murder of Clara Warren and her one year old daughter on Pitcairn Island by Harry Christian, the 1893 Order was extended to include the area in which Pitcairn is located so that he could be put on trial for these crimes. A new legal code and rules of procedure for the High Commissioner's Court was introduced by the Pitcairn Island Government Regulations 1940. It provided, among other things, for the election, powers and procedures of a Council for the island and for the conduct of cases before the Island Court. All cases not within the jurisdiction of the Island Court were to be heard and determined by the High Commissioner's Court for the Western Pacific in Fiji.

61. The Pacific Order in Council 1893 was revoked by the Pitcairn Order in Council 1952 which provided that the Governor of Fiji was to be the Governor of Pitcairn. Section 5(1) of the 1952 Order provided that it was to be lawful for the Governor to make laws for the peace, order and good government of the Pitcairn Islands. Section 5(2) provided that, without prejudice to the generality of the power conferred by subsection (1), the Governor was to have power to constitute a court in and for the islands with such jurisdiction as he might think fit. Section 5(3) provided that all laws made in the exercise of that power conferred by the Order were to be published in such manner and at such place or places in the Islands as he

might from time to time  direct and section 5(4) provided that every law was to come into force on the date when it was published.

62. The Judicature Ordinance 1961 terminated the Pitcairn jurisdiction of the High Commissioner's Court for the Western Pacific, conferred jurisdiction over Pitcairn on the Supreme Court of Fiji and constituted a Subordinate Court for the Pitcairn Islands in addition to the Chief Magistrate's Court constituted by the Pitcairn Island Government Regulations 1940, which was to be presided over by a magistrate. By sections 7 and 8 of the 1961 Ordinance the substance of the law for the time being in force for the time being in and for England was declared to be in force in the Pitcairn Islands, but so far only as the local circumstances and the limits of the local jurisdiction permitted. At first sight this appears to be a general importation of the whole of English law into Pitcairn, subject to that proviso. But its primary purpose, as indicated by its title, was to confer jurisdiction on the Supreme Court, to constitute an intermediate court 'and for matters relating thereto'.

63. On 14 April 1966 the Justice Ordinance 1966 was enacted by the Governor of Pitcairn relating to the administration of justice and the preservation of order on the Islands. It provided for the constitution of an Island Court, which was to comprise an Island Magistrate to be assisted by two assessors. It was to have jurisdiction in both criminal and civil matters. But the maximum penalty that it could impose in the exercise of its criminal jurisdiction was a fine of £25 or 100 days' imprisonment, and it was not to hear or determine proceedings for any offence unless the complaint relating to it was brought within six months after the time when the matter of the complaint arose. Part X of the Ordinance contains a series of what may be described as local offences dealing with a variety of matters such as contempt of court, perjury, assault, disorderly conduct and stealing.

64. Among the offences in Part X of the 1966 Ordinance is section 88, which provides:

'Any male person who shall have carnal knowledge of any female child of or over the age of twelve years shall be guilty of an offence and liable to imprisonment for a hundred days.' Section 1 provides that the word 'child' means any person who is under the age of 15 years. Section 82, which provides that a person who without lawful excuse assaults another person shall be guilty of an offence and is liable to a fine not exceeding ten pounds, contains this proviso:

'Provided that if such assault is of such an aggravated nature, either by reason of the youth, condition or sex of the person assaulted or by reason of the nature of the weapon used or the violence with which the assault has been committed, that in the opinion of the Court such penalty is inadequate the court may substitute for such penalty a fine not exceeding twenty five pounds or imprisonment for any period not exceeding one hundred days.'

65. When Fiji became an independent state in 1970 the administration of the Pitcairn Islands was transferred to New Zealand. The Pitcairn Order 1970

was made by Her Majesty in Council in the exercise of the powers conferred by the British Settlements Act 1887 and 1952. It revoked the Pitcairn Order in Council 1952, but without prejudice to the continued operation of any laws made there under and having effect as part of the law of the Islands immediately before the appointed day: section 3(2). Section 4 of the Order provided that there was to be a Governor of the Pitcairn Islands appointed by Her Majesty. In practice the Governorship of Pitcairn has been conferred on the holder of the office of High Commissioner for the United Kingdom in Wellington. Section 5(1) provided that the Governor was to have power to make laws for the peace, order and good government of the Islands. Section 5(2) provided that, without prejudice to the generality of the power to make these laws, he was to have power, by any such law, to constitute courts for the Islands with such jurisdiction as he might think fit. Section 5(3), repeating the equivalent provision in the 1952 Order, provided:

'All laws made by the Governor in the exercise of the powers conferred by this Order shall be published in such manner and at such place or places in the Islands as the Governor may from time to time direct.'

66. In 1970, in the exercise of the powers conferred on him by the 1970 Order the Governor of Pitcairn made the Judicature Ordinance 1970. It repealed the Judicature Ordinance 1961 which conferred jurisdiction on the Supreme Court of Fiji, and created in its place a Supreme Court for the Pitcairn Islands with all the powers, jurisdiction and authorities of the High Court of Justice in England which was to be deemed duly constituted notwithstanding any vacancy in the office of any judge. It continued the jurisdiction of the Island Magistrate's Court. Sections 7 and 8 of the 1961 Ordinance to the effect that the law for the time being in force in England were to be in force in the Islands so far only as the local circumstances and the limits of local jurisdiction permit were re-enacted by section 14. But section 14(1) was more specific than the 1961 Ordinance had been as to what these laws were. It provided that the laws that were to be in force in the Islands were to comprise:

'the common law, the rules of equity and the statutes of general application as in force in and for England at the commencement of this Ordinance'.

67. The Supreme Court was provided with evidence showing the steps that were taken to publish, among other measures, the Judicature Ordinances 1961 and 1970. The Judicature Ordinance 1961 was forwarded to the Chief Magistrate on Pitcairn under cover of a letter written on the directions of the Governor which requested that one copy of it be published on the public notice board and that the date of publication be notified by radio. By telegram dated 9 October 1961 the Chief Magistrate confirmed that it had been published on the notice board on 8 October 1961. The

Magistrate confirmed by telex that the enactment of the Judicature Ordinance 1970 on 27 October 1970 was followed by its publication on the notice board on 4 March 1971.

68. There had therefore been proper publication of the making of these Ordinances, as required by the Pitcairn Order in Council 1952 and the Pitcairn Order 1970. But the Supreme Court accepted in para 95 of its judgment as to promulgation of laws and related issues that at no time during the currency of the accused's offending was English law itself published on the Islands. None of the relevant statutes or legal texts were sent to the island. Nor had any publications such as Halsbury's Laws of England been provided. There is no evidence that anyone on Pitcairn was aware of the provisions of sections 1 and 14 of the Sexual Offences Act 1956 prior to the commencement of the police investigation in 1996.

69. The position as to the promulgation of the Justice Ordinance 1966, which contained the series of local laws already referred to, was markedly different. In March 1965 a draft of the Ordinance was discussed on Pitcairn with the Island Council. Among other matters the law as to sexual offending was discussed. In a letter dated 22 November 1965 the Council were advised in general terms that if there was any matter not covered by the law of Pitcairn the law of England could be invoked. They were also advised that the wording of section 88 had been left as the Council in March had wanted it but that they should remember that, as English law also applied, a male who had carnal knowledge of a female child under the age of 12 would be liable to be prosecuted under the English law of rape. At a meeting of the Island Council on 8 December 1965 the Government Adviser, who chaired the meeting, read through the draft ordinance. A motion that it be approved was accepted. On 10 December 1965 a telegram was sent from the Magistrate to the Commissioner reporting to him that it had been approved in full by the Council.

70. The situation throughout the period of offending can therefore be summarised in this way. All the formal steps that were needed to provide a workable legal system in the exceptional circumstances of Pitcairn had been taken before September 1964 when the first of the series of offences was committed. The orders that provided for the setting up of that system had been duly promulgated. The wording of the Justice Ordinance 1966, which set out the local offences that were thought at the time to be appropriate for Pitcairn, was discussed in detail with the Island Council before the Ordinance was enacted by the Governor. But no steps were taken to bring to the notice of the Island's Council or its inhabitants, other than in the most general way, any of the laws of England that might be invoked on Pitcairn to deal with any serious criminal matter not covered by the Ordinance.

The prosecution

71. The offence of rape was known to the common law of England long before it was provided for by statute. So too was the offence of assault with all its aggravations, including that of indecency. It was not until they were made statutory offences by sections 48 and 52 of the Offences Against the Person Act 1861, which sections 1 and 14 of the 1956 Act replaced, that the common law offences fell out of use in England. The settlers of Pitcairn took the common law with them when they decided to settle there. As Blackstone, Commentaries on the Laws of England, 4th ed 1770, Vol 1, p 107, puts it:

' . . . it hath been held that if an uninhabited country be discovered and planted by English subjects, all the English laws then in being, which are the birthright of every subject, are immediately there in force.'

So these offences, like murder, were already common law crimes on Pitcairn long before they were made statutory offences in England. But the decision was taken to prosecute the appellants under the English statute, not under the common law.

72. It appears too that many of the offences of which the appellants were convicted under the 1956 Act could have been charged against them under the Justice Ordinance 1966, although the sentences that could have been imposed would of course have been much more lenient and questions would have arisen as to whether the prosecutions were out of time. The offences of which they were convicted under section 14 of the 1956 Act could have been charged against them as aggravated assaults contrary to section 82 of the Ordinance. Seven of the twelve offences of rape of which they were convicted could have been brought against them under section 88 of the Ordinance, as in those cases the complainers were all of or over the age of twelve years. No complaint on the grounds of non-promulgation or abuse of process could have been made if these offences had been prosecuted in the Islands Court under the 1966 Ordinance. But the decision was taken to prosecute all but a handful of these offences under the 1956 Act. How did this come about?

73. Reference is made in the written case for Stevens Christian and Len Brown to the documentary evidence that was before the Supreme Court as to discussions that took place in correspondence between the Governor of Pitcairn and the Foreign and Commonwealth Office ('the FCO') in London about the action that ought to be taken when the first of these offences came to light. In a letter to the FCO dated 16 December 1999 the Governor noted that the sentences that were available under the existing laws in Pitcairn (under the Justice Ordinance 1966) were quite inadequate to the seriousness of the offences. In a letter to the Deputy Governor dated 29 April 2000 Paul Treadwell, the legal adviser, said that the public

interest required that such serious offences against the person should be detected and punished, even though the destruction that might result within the tiny island community seemed incalculable. He also mentioned that there were obvious reasons for searching for a path of compromise, among which was the fact that it was possible to attribute a degree of responsibility for the unbridled sexual licence of Pitcairn men over past generations to the absence of any meaningful civil authority and actual system of justice representing the guidance and supervision of the colonial power.

74. In a further letter to the FCO dated 1 May 2000 the Acting Governor expressed concern as to whether it would be practicable or desirable to investigate a whole raft of offences going back many years when, given the timescale, it would be difficult to treat everyone even-handedly. She also acknowledged the validity of Paul Treadwell's suggestion that the situation was partly of the colonial power's own making:

'There is no civil authority on the island. Governors, Deputy-Governors and Commissioners reside 3,000 miles away in New Zealand, visit irregularly and for short periods of a few days only. The schoolteacher (from New Zealand) doubles as the Government Adviser. But is not viewed by the islanders as being in a position of real authority. We rely on a local Police Officer—who is related to every member of the community they serve—to uphold the law which, until we began a comprehensive review with the assistance of the Good Government Fund (in 1998), was in any case unworkable. Recent media reports have underlined the islanders' views on their remoteness from the UK. Perhaps, therefore, it is not altogether surprising that if the community does not see the laws as applicable to them.'

She concluded however that all the allegations had to be investigated thoroughly, and that if, as had been suggested, the line of offending that had been revealed was a cultural trait, an end had to be put to it once and for all.

75. Suggestions that the offenders should be offered an amnesty were rejected and the matter was put into the hands of the public prosecutor. One can infer that the decision to bring these prosecutions under the 1956 Act was reached out of a desire to deal even-handedly with all the offenders, and to root out the cultural trait once and for all by seeking convictions under legislation that would enable sentences to be imposed that gave full weight to the gravity of the crimes that had been committed. These were laudable aims. But they give rise to an important and difficult issue as to whether the law under which the offenders were to be prosecuted had been sufficiently promulgated in Pitcairn for it to be permissible for them to be dealt with in this way.

Incorporation by reference

76. The method that was chosen to make laws for Pitcairn by means of the Judicature Ordinance 1970 was incorporation by reference, in the most

general terms, of all the statutes of general application in force in England at the commencement of the Ordinance but only so far as local circumstances permit. The problem does not lie in the meaning of the words that were used in section 14 to bring this about. Sir Kenneth Roberts-Wray, Commonwealth and Colonial Law, 1966, p 545 said that if the phrase 'statutes of general application' were to be offered as a novelty to a legislative draftsman today he would disclaim responsibility for its consequences unless it were defined. But he acknowledged that it had been in use for many decades, that it does not appear to have given the courts serious trouble and that it has much the same effect as the common law rule by which the English law taken by the settlers is both the unwritten law (common law and equity) and the statute law in force at the time of settlement: see p 540.

77. A survey of cases in New Zealand and Pacific countries of decisions where this criterion for a source of law has been considered has revealed that, without exception, all the statutes in question applied to matters other than the criminal law: Tony Angelo and Fran Wright, Pitcairn: sunset on Empire? (2004) NZLJ 404, 405. The writers of this note suggest that one reason for this is perhaps to be found in the principles of legality, due process and the protection of human rights. I agree that these principles must not be overlooked, but I do not think that they justify excluding the whole of the criminal law from the generality of the phrase. A more likely reason is the other one that they give, which is that the usual practice was for a colony to have its own criminal law so resort to the criminal law of England was unnecessary. The Sexual Offences Act 1956 is a public general Act which extends to the whole of England and Wales without qualification. In my opinion it is a statute of general application within the meaning of section 14 of the 1970 Order.

78. As for the qualification in section 14(2) that the law thus imported was to be in force only so far as 'local circumstances' permit, Sir Kenneth Roberts-Wray said at pp 544–545 that this amounted to no more than the rounding off of a common law rule and that all the circumstances are to be taken into account including the local relevance or otherwise of circumstances in England which explain a particular law. In *Nyali Ltd v Attorney-General* [1957] 1 QB 1, 16 Lord Denning, speaking about the common law, said that this qualification was a wise provision, and that it should be liberally construed as a recognition that the common law cannot be applied in a foreign land without considerable qualification:

'Just as with an English oak, so with the English common law. You cannot transplant it to the African continent and expect it to retain the tough character which it has in England.'

How statutes of general application in force in England are to be qualified in the light of local circumstances is less clear. Sir Kenneth notes at p 548 that in a few cases the uncertainty has been reduced by legislative intervention locally. But none of these problems affect the provisions of the Sexual Offences Act 1956 which were invoked in this case. As I have said, it is a statute of general application. While some of the sections that it contains such as those about abduction and the keeping of brothels might have no relevance on Pitcairn, that is not so in the case of the sections under which these prosecutions were brought. There are no circumstances either locally on Pitcairn or in England which require the provisions of either section 1 or section 14 to be qualified in any way.

The promulgation issue

79. Mr Perry, who appeared for Carlisle Terry Young only but whose argument on this issue was adopted by counsel for the other appellants, said that he was not attacking the principle of incorporation by reference. This was, he said, a legitimate device, subject always to the requirement of legal certainty. His point was that Pitcairn was a wholly exceptional case, and that it was unreasonable to expect an island community of about 50 people to absorb the entirety of a legal system designed to meet the needs of more than 50 million people in England and Wales. He also submitted that, as the Governor was required by article 5(3) of the Pitcairn Order 1970 to publish all laws made by him in the exercise of the powers conferred on him by the order and the date when every such law is to come into operation was to be the date when it was published, publication was an essential requirement of each and every law that he chose to enact for Pitcairn. So the fact that the 1956 Act had never been published even in summary form on Pitcairn meant that sections 1 and 14 of the Act were not in force in the islands when these offences were committed.

80. The question whether, as a matter of form, the requirements of article 5(3) of the 1970 Order were satisfied is relatively easy to answer. As the Court of Appeal pointed out in paras 37 and 38 of its judgment of 2 March 2006 on abuse of process and the conviction appeals, these requirements extend not just to statutes of general application but also to the common law and to the rules of equity which are not susceptible to publication in the way that this argument contemplates. Furthermore the laws that are to be published are those made by the Governor. The law which he was seeking to make by means of the Judicature Ordinance 1970 was really no more than declaratory of the existing situation at the commencement of the Order. He was not making new laws but was providing for the continuation of existing laws, many of which had been part of the law of Pitcairn since the earliest days of the settlement. It was his own law that he was required to publish, not all the law that he was incorporating by reference.

81. But meeting the formalities that the 1970 Order lays down is one thing. Satisfying the principles on which the rule of law is founded is another. It is here that this method of legislating in the exceptional circumstances of

Pitcairn seem to me to be highly questionable. There is no evidence that the Governor ever applied his mind to the question whether it was appropriate to apply the Sexual Offences Act 1956 to Pitcairn, and if so which parts of it were appropriate for application there and which were not. Of course it can be said that the method of legislating that he chose to adopt made it unnecessary for him to do this. But it is one thing for this well-established method of legislating to be used in circumstances, such as in New South Wales or New Zealand, where ample resources existed for finding out what the law was and for obtaining advice about it in case of doubt. It is quite another to use it in the circumstances of a tiny, remote and isolated community like Pitcairn, where at the relevant time these resources were entirely absent. As Lord Diplock observed in *Fothergill v Monarch Airlines Ltd* [1981] AC 251, 279, elementary justice requires that the rules by which the citizen is bound should be ascertainable by reference to sources that are accessible. In *R v Rimmington* [2005] UKHL 63; [2006] 1 AC 459, 482, para 33 Lord Bingham of Cornhill said:

> 'There are two guiding principles: no one should be punished under a law unless it is sufficiently clear and certain to enable him to know what conduct is forbidden before he does it; and no one should be punished for any act which was not clearly and ascertainably punishable when the act was done.'

The requirement of ascertainability is an essential component of the rule of law. But in the case of statutes of general application in force in England, as the Governor should have known, it was incapable of being met on Pitcairn.

82. The use of this method for legislating about the criminal law in the circumstances of Pitcairn is made all the more unsatisfactory in the light of the steps that were taken when the Judicature Ordinance 1966 was under preparation to ensure that all its provisions were understood and were acceptable to the Island Council as representing the whole community on the island. The differences between penalties for committing the offences described in sections 82 and 88 of the 1966 Ordinance and those which apply to the overlapping offences described in sections 1 and 14 of the 1956 Act are substantial. The fact that no attempt was made to reconcile the terminology of the 1966 Ordinance with that of the 1956 Act, or to explain the circumstances in which the more severe penalties laid down in the Second Schedule to the 1956 Act would be invoked in place of those provided for by the Ordinance is a further ground for unease.

The turning point

83. These considerations would have led me to conclude that it was an abuse of process for these prosecutions to be brought under sections 1 and 14 of the 1956 Act, but for one fact which in the end has persuaded me that the

use of these provisions can be reconciled with the principles of legality. It is to be found in the language of sections 48 and 52 of the 1861 Act, from which these sections were derived. Section 48 of the 1861 Act provides:

'Whosoever shall be convicted of the crime of rape shall be guilty of a felony, and being convicted thereof shall be liable, at the discretion of the court, to be kept in penal servitude for life or for any term less than three years, or to be imprisoned for any term not exceeding two years, with or without hard labour.'

Section 52 of the 1861 Act provides:

'Whosoever shall be convicted of any indecent assault upon any female, or of any attempt to have carnal knowledge of any girl under twelve years of age, shall be liable, at the discretion of the court, to be imprisoned for any term not exceeding two years.'

84. It can be seen from the way these provisions are worded that they were not creating new crimes. They assume that the crimes of rape and of indecent assault already exist, as indeed they did as they were already known to the common law. They were building on the common law to this extent only, that they were prescribing the penalties that were to attach to these offences. Sections 1 and 14 are differently worded, but their function was to identify—as was necessary in the days when the 1956 Act was passed—which of the offences it contained was or was not a felony and to provide, when read together with section 37 and the Second Schedule, for the prosecution and punishment of these offences. They did not create new crimes, any more than the 1861 Act had done. The offences mentioned in sections 1 and 14 can therefore be traced back directly to the common law. There is an air of unreality about the objection that the appellants were disadvantaged by the fact that the provisions of sections 1 and 14 of the 1956 Act were not ascertainable on Pitcairn. This case is quite unlike *R v Rimmington* [2006] 1 AC 459, where the objection was to the enlargement of the common law crime of causing a public nuisance. Here we are dealing with conduct which the common law has regarded as criminal for centuries, and the appellants cannot have been in any doubt that what they were doing amounted to criminal conduct.

85. This feature of the legislation makes it possible to reconcile the failure to promulgate the fact that the 1956 Act was to be part of the laws of Pitcairn with the principle of legality. The islanders brought the common law of England with them when they settled there. Rape and indecent assault were part of the criminal law of the island long before the Justice Ordinance 1966 and the Judicature Ordinances 1961 and 1970 were enacted. No objection could have been taken on the ground of lack of promulgation if the prosecution of the appellants had been brought under the common law. The only practical difference that resulted from bringing the prosecutions under the statute was as to the sentences that

were available. But the effect of the statute was simply to replace the common law, under which there was no limit to the length of any sentence that could be imposed, by the statutory maxima. Substitution of the statutory system for the common law which leaves everything to the judge's discretion works in favour of the accused, not against him. This reduces the risk of any unfairness. It is not possible to detect any unfairness in the sentences imposed on any of the appellants, which were not challenged in the Court of Appeal. My noble and learned friend Lord Woolf is not sure why this assists: see para 14. The answer, I suggest, is to be found in the point which he makes in the next paragraph. We are dealing here with acts which were wrong in themselves. So I do not think that it was an affront to justice for them to be prosecuted for such acts under the statute.

86. It would have been open to question whether these convictions could have been sustained on the ground that the offences were contrary to the common law and that it was unnecessary to proceed under the statute. As a general rule the prosecutor is tied to the ground that he chooses to fight on. If he decides to prosecute under a statute, it is not open to him to ask for a conviction under the common law unless the statute in question provides for this as an alternative. But I do not need to resolve this issue as I have concluded, although not without difficulty, that as sections 1 and 14 of the 1956 Act were not creating new crimes it was open to the prosecutor to bring the prosecutions under the statute notwithstanding its lack of promulgation.

87. I wish finally to associate myself with all that Lord Woolf has said about the way in which these proceedings were conducted by both sides and by the courts below. I also pay tribute to the careful way in which the papers were prepared both in hard copy and electronically for our use by both sides in these appeals, and to the conspicuous fairness and sensitivity with which these proceedings have been conducted throughout by the Public Prosecutor.

# APPENDIX II

# Official Correspondence

## Contents

(a) Paul Treadwell to C.D. Shute, 5 January 1997
(b) Paul Treadwell to Karen Wolstenholme, 29 April 2000
(c) Martin Williams to Karen Wolstenholme, 2 May 2000
(d) Clare Short to Robin Cook, 8 February 2001

Robin **Cook**: Secretary of State for Foreign and Commonwealth Affairs

Simon Eisdell **Moore**: Pitcairn Public Prosecutor, member of the Auckland law firm Meredith Connell mainly doing Crown Solicitor's work

Leon **Salt**: Commissioner for Pitcairn Island, Office of the Governor of Pitcairn, Henderson, Ducie, and Oeno Islands

Clare **Short**: Secretary of State for International Development

C.D. **Shute**: First Secretary, British High Commission, New Zealand

Paul **Treadwell**: Honorary Legal Adviser to the Governor, Acting Governor of Pitcairn Island

Martin **Williams**: Governor of Pitcairn Island

| | |
|---|---|
| BHC | British High Commission |
| EU | European Union |
| FCO | Foreign and Commonwealth Office |
| HMG | Her Majesty's Government |
| KCC | Knowledge and Communications Department (a department within Department for International Development) |
| OTD | Overseas Territory Department |
| PQ | Parliamentary Question |
| S of S | Secretary of State |

# Document (a)

Paul Julian Treadwell O.B.E. LL.B.
Barrister

P.O. Box 572
Kerikeri
Tel: 09 407 9818
Fax: 09 407 9498

380/001/97

PO1/P/370/2

5 January 1997

C.D. Shute Esq.
First Secretary
British High Commission
P.O. Box 1812
Wellington

Dear Chris

Pitcairn: Alleged Serious Crime

I am afraid that I have taken more than a little time to reply to the second paragraph of your letter of 21 November about my report on the disposal of the police enquiry.

The reason for my comments of 29 October was that it became necessary to draft an indictment of the offender under sections 5 and 6 of the Sexual Offences Act 1956 of Great Britain. It is safe to assume that the offender was unaware of the terms of these provisions or the very substantial penalties attaching to them. There are no British statutes available to the public on Pitcairn. Even if there were, it is a moot point that they would be understandable by members of the public.

The only provision of law known to the islanders is section 88 of the Justice Ordinance, which they refer to as 'cardinal knowledge'. On the face of the Justice Ordinance, it is something of a mystery that it is unlawful by section 88 to have intercourse with a female of or over the age of 12 years but not with a female below that age. I myself raised this apparent anomaly some years ago, when it was pointed out to me, correctly, that although there is no local provision prohibiting intercourse with a female under 12 the provisions of section 14(1) of the Judicature Ordinance have the effect of applying section 5 of the Sexual Offences Act 1956.

I suppose that the ideal answer to your question is that both Halisbury's Statutes and Halisbury's Law of England, which run to many score of volumes, should be available to the public of Pitcairn because of the terms of section 14(1) of the Judicature Ordinance. It is to be noted, however, that the rules of equity and the statutes of general application which are applied by this subsection are those in force in England on the 1st of January 1983. It would therefore be necessary to install a legal library showing the laws in force in England at that time.

In the present context we are, however, concerned with the criminal law and its implications for the liberty of Her Majesty's subjects on Pitcairn. The dating of any relevant publication is crucial for the reason mentioned above. I was able to lend an appropriate textbook to Detective-Superintendent McGookin, namely *An Introduction to Criminal Law* by Cross and Jones being an edition fairly close before the cut-off date and therefore setting out with accuracy the rules of procedure, principles and substance of the criminal law of England which would be in force on Pitcairn.

However, even if such a textbook were available to and understandable by the inhabitants of Pitcairn, it is still a very unsatisfactory situation that intercourse with girls of 12 years and over is forbidden by a local statute and intercourse with girls under that age is prohibited by the Sexual Offences Act in England.

I warmly agree with your observation that at the very least the written laws of Pitcairn should be on the shelves of the public library and should be kept up to date meticulously as they are kept at the Commissioner's office in Auckland. However, in my view this does not go far enough. It is my opinion and recommendation that ordinances should be made by the Governor to provide codes of criminal law, criminal procedure, evidence in criminal cases and a workable system of judicial organisation. This may seem like a hefty exercise for such a tiny jurisdiction but of course it will take only another single incident of serious crime on Pitcairn from which there may well be no simple means of disposal as occurred last year, in order to create a situation of great difficulty, expense and perhaps international embarrassment. I would, with great respect, have thought that the experiences we shared last year should be regarded as some sort of warning which behoves HMG to put its legal and judicial house on Pitcairn in order now.

I should be glad to discuss these issues further if you desire. There must be an abundance of material available from other dependent territories which would serve as a model for Pitcairn.

Kind regards.

Sincerely,
Paul

## Document (b)

Paul Julian Treadwell O.B.E. LL.B.                    PO Box 572
Barrister                                             Kerikeri

                                                     Tel: 09 407 9818
                                                     Fax: 09 407 9498
                                                     Email: purini@xtra.co.nz

29 April 2000

Mrs K. Wolstenholme
Acting Governor of Pitcairn
British High Commission
P.O. Box 1812
WELLINGTON 1

By Fax: 495 0831

Dear Karen
                    Re: Pitcairn—Potential prosecutions

I am writing about your letter of 28 April to Simon Moore and his to Leon of the same date, both copied to me. We are all concerned at the grassfire of old sexual crimes revealed so far and the possibility of more to come. The public interest, which embodies the protection of the helpless, requires that such serious offences against the person be detected and punished. The destruction which may result within this tiny island community, offenders, victims and their families seems incalculable.

I am required to advise you, subject to the views of the Public Prosecutor, as to the public policy as well as the legal requirements of the criminal justice system in the same way that the Minister would be advised by the Attorney-General in England. I begin by saying that I would not be party to the concealment of the offences, nor would I expect to be asked to be. The plight of females, most of them children, in a British dependent territory, who have been sexually abused with impunity by adult males for some decades, makes this course unthinkable. I believe, with due diffidence, that it may however be possible to offer them a kind of recognition and solace, without prosecuting any of the offenders.

The reasons for searching out a path of compromise are obvious. The financial cost of mounting a raft of individual prosecutions in the Supreme Court of Pitcairn is the least of them. A reflection of considerably greater importance is that it is possible although perhaps unpalatable, to attribute a degree of responsibility for the unbridled sexual licence of Pitcairn men over past generations to the absence of any meaningful civil authority and actual system of justice representing the guidance and supervision of the colonial power. Hindsight, at the hands of international commentators, will ensure that this particular bolt is shot well and truly home.

I offer for consideration the device of a general amnesty. This would be declared by proclamation of the Governor, on the instructions of the Secretary of State, to render immune from prosecution all previous offences against the criminal law not at this time the subject of conviction and punishment prior to the date of the proclamation. The 'cut-off' date might well be, for presentational effect, 1 January 2000. Such an amnesty would need to be accompanied by conditions.

The first condition could be that the amnesty would cease to apply for the benefit of any recidivist. A second might be that HMG will provide an ongoing professional police presence (eg community constable) on a continuous basis for, say, two years, or whatever period is seen as the viable future of the island community.

It may be acceptable to address the needs and rights of the victims in a further condition of the proclamation establishing a special commissioner of inquiry to ascertain privately the merits of allegations of sexual offences made by or on behalf of the victims concerned. Such a commissioner would be a judicial officer reporting at intervals to the Minister or the Governor. He or she would determine individual claims on the balance of probabilities. In the case of accepted complaints, the commissioner would recommend the payment of compensatory damages, within a fixed limit, to the victim and HMG would agree to be bound by that finding. The content of the inquiry would of course be private and protected from publication.

No recourse to the courts would be available but perhaps the Governor or the Chief Justice might have the power to review the commissioner's decision in any case.

I have had little time to look at the details of this proposal. It is submitted in haste as a possible way through a distressing dilemma. The fact that an earlier complaint in this field in 1996 was in part compromised by the absence of a workable system of criminal, or any, justice lends no comfort now to our position (except that that particular complainant must be catered for). I take no credit for having drawn this situation to your attention as early as 1987, only for not having strenuously followed it up, except with the help of John Yapp, in the succeeding years. I am conscious that the proposal I now suggest is as far I am aware, without precedent, but so is the present situation of Pitcairn.

Sincerely,
Paul

cc: S. Eisdell Moore, Meredith Connell
Leon Salt, Pitcairn Administration

## Document (c)

2 May 2000

To:
Karen Wolstenholme
BHC, Wellington, NZ
Fax No: 00 64 4 495 0831

From:
Martin Williams
c/o HOMS, FCO, SW1
Fax: (020) 7270 3974

We had our meeting today with Baroness Scotland. The conclusion was we proceed with the court cases as seriously and urgently, but also as sensitively as possible, no matter the cost or the implications for Pitcairn's future. OTD will do a submission to S of S. No question of an amnesty.

OTD will aim to get investigators, suitably experienced (probably but not necessarily from KCC) to NZ in time for 22 May sailing. If there is a trial, or trials, we shall need to consider if our judge's experience is sufficient in relevant fields: if not, perhaps a suitable judge from England.

Lots of other issues; this is a quick initial read out.

Yours truly,

Martin Williams

# Document (d)

8 February 2001
Development (Short) to Foreign Secretary (Cook)

131184/01

From the Secretary of State

The Rt Hon Robin Cook MP
Secretary of State for Foreign & Commonwealth Affairs
King Charles Street
London
SW1A AA

Dear Robin

PITCAIRN ISLAND

Our respective officials are in touch about investigations currently being conducted by Kent Constabulary, into alleged child abuse on island. I understand the police team will be concluding their investigations and reporting their findings within the next few weeks.

I have suspended the Hill of Difficulty road and jetty project on island for two reasons. First, if the child abuse allegations prove to have foundation we shall want to understand the impact that prosecutions (and possible imprisonment) may have on so small a population. We and the EU will not want to build a £0.8 million road for a population which is seriously depleted and/or economically unsustainable and if the findings are very bad, maybe it would not be wise to help sustain such an unhealthy community. Secondly, depending on the seriousness of the situation, we may need to redirect available resources into social interventions, designed to put in place child protection measures.

The Pitcairn Council and Mayor have been advised by Martin Williams (Governor) of our decision to suspend the road project 'until decisions have been taken on the investigations currently in progress, and possible judicial proceedings'. My officials have also advised the project's engineering consultants, who in turn have told those companies based in New Zealand who were preparing tenders for the project.

There have already been some calls to our Enquiry Point, asking for information about our decision to halt the road project. *The Times* have also published an article written by their correspondent in Wellington about a rape case (which we believe to be connected to the child abuse concerns). I think it would be useful for you to inform the House of Commons by way of an arranged PQ that all this is going on. Taking no action risks embarrassing the Government if the story blows up and possible accusations of a Government cover up. In fact we have nothing to lose by being completely open about the child abuse investigations at this stage. FCO were expeditious in taking the necessary police action.

Yours,
Clare

Clare Short

# Outline: Pitcairn Island Chronology

| | |
|---|---|
| 1790 | Uninhabited Pitcairn Island settled by nine of the English *Bounty* mutineers, led by Fletcher Christian, with six Polynesian men and twelve Tahitian women, and a child. They burned the *Bounty*. (Their arrival was subsequently claimed by the UK to amount to the creation of a colony by settlement.) |
| 1808 | An American vessel 'discovered' Pitcairn to be inhabited. By then, John Adams was the only surviving mutineer. The other mutineers had been murdered, committed suicide, or died of disease. Adams had become the patriarch of the community. (He died in 1829.) |
| 1814 | Pitcairn 'discovered' by HMS *Briton*. Until then the UK did not know, officially at least, what had become of the mutineers. Its population was then 40. |
| 1831 | The community emigrated to Tahiti in March but returned to Pitcairn over the next few months. |
| 1838 | HMS *Fly*, under Captain Eliott, visited the island, gave them a Union Jack, wrote a constitution providing for universal adult suffrage, some laws including local laws, a requirement for schooling for all children, and provision for annual election of a Magistrate. (This may be interpreted as cession or an act of annexation of the island.) |
| 1852 | George Nobbs appointed Church of England Chaplain of Pitcairn. |
| 1856 | Population moved by the Crown to Norfolk Island, a former penal colony, as the island's resources were inadequate to sustain the size of population. |
| 1858–1864 | Some Pitcairners returned to Pitcairn from Norfolk Island |
| 1886–1890 | Pitcairners adopted Seventh Day Adventist practices, including Saturday worship, not eating pork, no smoking, and no alcohol. |
| 1887 | British Settlements Act gave power by s. 2 to Her Majesty in Council to establish 'all such laws and institutions necessary for the peace, order and good government of Her Majesty's subjects and others within British settlements', ie British possessions not acquired by cession or conquest. |

1893        The Pacific Order in Council was made under the 1887 Act. It did not initially apply to Pitcairn. It established a High Commissioner's Court for the Western Pacific with both civil and criminal jurisdiction which was empowered to apply the law for the time being in force in and for England so far as circumstances permitted.

1898        In reliance on a provision in the 1893 Order empowering him to extend the Order to other British Settlements in the region, the Secretary of State directed that the Order should apply to Pitcairn.

            Harry Christian was convicted by the High Commissioner's Court sitting on Pitcairn of the murders on Pitcairn of Clara Warren and her child Eleanor under the 1893 Order in Council.

1952        The Pitcairn Order in Council was enacted. The Governor of Fiji became the Governor of Pitcairn, with power to make laws 'for the peace, order and good government of [Pitcairn]'.

1956        English Sexual Offences Act passed. It provides by sections 1 and 14 for the prosecution and punishment of rape and indecent assault as criminal offences. (The defendants were convicted of offences under these sections.)

1958        The last visit to Pitcairn by a government legal adviser, Mr McLoughlin.

1961        Judicature Ordinance, made by the Governor, provided that 'the substance of the law for the time being in force in and for England shall be in force in [Pitcairn]'.

1965        Island Council met to consider a draft of what became the Justice Ordinance 1966. The meeting discussed, among other things: the law relating to sexual offences; the fact that English law applied; and that carnal knowledge of a female under twelve would be an offence of rape. A motion to approve the draft Ordinance was accepted and the Magistrate informed the Commissioner.

1966        Justice Ordinance made by the Governor. (The prosecutions were not brought under this Ordinance.)

1970        The Pitcairn Order in Council was enacted. No consultation took place, unlike the process in 1965, for the making of the Justice Ordinance 1966. Governorship of Pitcairn was conferred upon the UK High Commissioner based in Wellington, New Zealand. The same power to make laws was conferred on the Governor as that in the 1952 Order.

The Governor:

(i) enacted the Judicature Ordinance 1970 (which was still in force at the time of the offences). It provided in s. 14(1): '... the common law, the rules of equity and the statutes of general application as in force in and for England at the commencement of this Ordinance shall be in force in [Pitcairn]', this being amended in 1984 by the substitution of 1 January 1983 for the date of commencement of the 1970 Ordinance;

(ii) established a Supreme Court of Pitcairn with the jurisdiction of the High Court in England. (No judge was appointed to the court until 2000, for the trials of six men for offences against the English Sexual Offences Act.)

| | |
|---|---|
| 1973 | Only recorded visit of Governor of Pitcairn to the island, by Sir David Scott. |
| 1996 | Two Kent police officers sent to Pitcairn by the UK to investigate allegations that a young girl had been raped. The suspect was cautioned for underage sex. The police officers reported to the UK that police training was required. |
| 1997 | WPC Gail Cox spends time on Pitcairn training the island police officer. |
| 1999–2000 | WPC Gail Cox returns to Pitcairn to train the police officer, and receives complaints of sexual abuse of two girls on the island. She takes statements and reports back to the Foreign and Commonwealth Office (FCO). |
| 2000 | The start of 'Operation Unique'. The FCO sent two Kent police officers to investigate further. They interviewed complainants and men against whom complaints were made in Australia and in Norfolk Island. They interviewed all twenty women who had grown up on Pitcairn since 1980. All stated that they had been victims of various kinds of sexual abuse, including non-consensual rape and indecent assault, the abuse for some women having started when they were between three and five years old. The police officers decided to draw a line at 1960: they identified 31 victims, including two men, and some 30 named accused, of whom 27 were native Pitcairners— nearly every Pitcairn male. Some 12 women accused their brothers, uncles, or first cousins. |

Kent police reported on their findings to the FCO. Baroness Scotland, the minister in the UK Cabinet with responsibility for overseas territories, demanded prosecution. The British Cabinet decided that the legal machinery should be put in place to facilitate a prosecution. An agreement was reached with New Zealand that their judges would sit as the Pitcairn Supreme Court for the trials, and as the Pitcairn Court of Appeal to hear the expected appeals. A Pitcairn Public Prosecutor was appointed. A Pitcairn Bar was established and New Zealand lawyers were called to it.

2003    Trials were started by the laying of charges in the Pitcairn Magistrate's Court. Six men were convicted of offences including rape, indecent assault, and incest. Trials took place on Pitcairn Island, legal argument being reserved for hearing in New Zealand.

2005    Pitcairn Supreme Court sitting in New Zealand gives judgment on legal issues, finding for the prosecution.

2006    Appeals by the defendants were dismissed by the Pitcairn Court of Appeal.

The Judicial Committee of the Privy Council upheld the convictions. The men served their sentences of imprisonment (four defendants) and community service (two defendants) on Pitcairn.

2008    A Criminal Injuries Compensation Scheme was introduced for victims of sexual abuse on the island who had cooperated with the prosecution.

# *References*

## Chapter 1: Problems on Pitcairn

Birkett, D., *Serpent in Paradise* (New Zealand: Anchor Books, 1997).

Fullerton, W. Y., *The Romance of Pitcairn Island* (London: Carey Press, 1921).

Lummis, T., *Life and Death in Eden: Pitcairn Island and the Bounty Mutineers* (Aldershot: Ashgate, 1997).

Marks, K., *Trouble in Paradise: Uncovering Decades of Sexual Abuse on Britain's Most Remote Island* (London: Harper Perennial, 2008).

## Chapter 2: The Pitcairn Prosecutions, Paper Legal Systems, and the Rule of Law

Marks, K., *Trouble in Paradise: Uncovering Decades of Sexual Abuse on Britain's Most Remote Island* (London: Harper Perennial, 2008).

## Chapter 3: Pitcairn's Tortured Past: A Legal History

Alexander, C., *The Bounty* (New York: Viking Books, 2003).

Becke, G. L., and W. Jeffery, *The Mutineer: A Romance of Pitcairn Island* (London: Fisher Unwin, 1898).

Beechey, *Narrative of a Voyage to the Pacific . . . to Co-operate with the Polar Expeditions* (London: Colburn and Bentley, 1831).

Blackstone, W., *Commentaries on the Laws of England*, Vol. 1 (Oxford: Oxford University Press, 1st edition, 1765).

Blackstone, W., *Commentaries on the Laws of England, with notes and additions by Edward Christian* (London: Cadell, 12th edn, 1793–5).

Bligh, W., *A Voyage to the South Sea* (London: George Nicol, 1792).

Brodie, W., *Pitcairn's Island and the Islanders* (London: Whittaker, 1851).

Christian, E., *The Charge of the Chief Justice Edward Christian, Esq. to the Grand Jury at the Assizes held at Ely . . . on 9th of March 1804* (Cambridge: Hodson, 1804).

Christian, G., *Fragile Paradise* (London: Hamish Hamilton, 1st edn, 1982; Sydney and London: Doubleday, 2nd edn, 1999; The Long Riders Guild, 3rd edn, 2005).

Clay, J., *Maconochie's Experiment* (London: John Murray, 2001).

Curry, K., ed., *New Letters of Robert Southey*, vol I., 1792–1810 (New York: Columbia University Press, 1965).

Hawkesworth, J., *An Account of the Voyages Undertaken by the Order of His Present Majesty for making Discoveries in the Southern Hemisphere etc.*, 3 vols, (London: Strahan and Cadell, 1773), vol 1.

Hayes, W., *The Captain from Nantucket and the Mutiny on the Bounty* (Michigan: Ann Arbor, 1996).

Hughes, R., *The Fatal Shore* (London: Collins Harvill, 1986).

Lummis, T., *Life and Death in Eden: Pitcairn Island and the Bounty Mutineers* (Aldershot: Ashgate, 1997).

Maude, H. E., 'History of Pitcairn Island' in *Introduction to the Pitcairnese Language*, eds A. S. C. Ross and A. W. Moverley (London: André Deutsch, 1964), 45–101.

McLoughlin, D., 'The Development of the System of Government and Laws of Pitcairn Island From 1791 to 1971' in *Laws of Pitcairn, Henderson, Ducie and Oeno Islands*, ed. D. McLoughlin (Govt. of the Islands of Pitcairn, Henderson, Duecie & Oeno, rev. edn, 1971), online at <http://library.puc.edu/Pitcairn/pitcairn/govt-history01.shtml>.

Pocock, T., *A Thirst for Glory: The Life of Sir Sydney Smith* (London: Aurum Press, 1996).

Ross, A. S. C. and A. W. Moverley, eds, *Introduction to the Pitcairnese Language* (London: André Deutsch, 1964).

Scott, Sir David, *A Window into Downing Street* (London: The Memoir Club, 2003).

Sobel, D., *Longitude* (London: Fourth Estate, 1996).

Waldegrave, W., 'The Pitcairn Islanders', *Journal of the Royal Geographical Society of London* 3 (1833).

## Chapter 4: Pitcairn Island Law: A Peculiar Case of the Diffusion of the Common Law

Adams, J., 'Novanglus' in *The Works of John Adams*, ed. Charles Francis Adams (Boston: Little, Brown & Co. 1851), Vol IV, 3–177 (first published 1775).

Allott, A. N., *Essays in African Law* (London: Butterworths, 1960).

Allott, A. N., *New Essays in African Law* (London: Butterworths, 1970).

Amirthalingam, K., 'Culture, Crime, and Culpability: Perspectives on the Defence of Provocation' in *Multicultural Jurisprudence: Comparative Perspectives on the Cultural Defense*, eds A. Renteln and M.-C. Foblets (Oxford: Hart Publications, 2009).

Angelo, T. and F. Wright, 'Pitcairn: Sunset on Empire?', *New Zealand Law Journal* (2004), 431.

Baker, J. H., 'Custom and Usage' in *Halsbury's Laws of England*, 4th edn, 1998 re-issue, 12(1), 153–259.

Barrow, J., 'Recent Accounts of the Pitcairn Islanders', *Journal of the Royal Geographical Society of London* 3 (1833), 156–168.

Bartholomew, G. W., 'English Law in *Partibus Orientalium*' in *The Common Law in Singapore and Malaysia*, ed. A. J. Harding (Singapore: Butterworths, 1985), 1–30.

Bennion, F. A. R., *The Constitutional Law of Ghana* (London: Butterworths, 1962).

Blackstone, W., *Commentaries on the Laws of England*, Vol. 1, (Oxford: Clarendon Press, 1st edn, 1765).

Blackstone, W., *Commentaries on the Laws of England*, ed. E. Christian (London: T. Cadell, 12th edn, 1793).

Brown, K., *Reconciling Customary Law and Received Law in Melanesia: the Post-Independence Experience in Solomon Islands and Vanuatu* (Darwin: Charles Darwin University Press, 2005).

Castles, A., *An Introduction to Australian Legal History* (Australia: Law Book Co., 1971).

Corrin-Care, J., T. N. Cain, and D. Paterson, *Introduction to South Pacific Law* (London: Cavendish Publishing, 1999).

Corrin-Care, J. and J. G. Zorn, 'Legislating Pluralism: Statutory "Developments" in Melanesian Customary Law', *Journal of Legal Pluralism* 46 (2001), 49–101.

Coté, J. E., 'The Reception of English Law', *Alberta Law Review* 15 (1977), 29–92.

de Sousa Santos, B., *Toward a New Legal Common Sense: Law, Globalization and Emancipation* (London: Butterworths, 2nd edn, 2002).

Dinnen, S., 'Sentencing, Custom and the Rule of Law in Papua New Guinea', *Journal of Legal Pluralism* 27 (1988), 19–54.

Doucet, M. and J. Vanderlinden, eds, *La réception des systèmes juridiques: implantation et destin,* (Brussels: Bruylant, 1994).

Finnis, J. M., 'Commonwealth and Dependencies', in *Halsbury's Laws of England*, 4th edn, Vol. 6, 2003 Reissue, Part 5, 'The Extension of English Law', 515.

Fuller, L. L., *The Morality of Law* (New Haven and London: Yale University Press, rev. edn, 1969).

Janssen, H., *Die Übertragung von Rechtsvorstellungen auf fremde Kulturen am Beispiel des englischen Kolonialrechts: ein Beitrag zur Rechtsvergleichung* (Tubingen: Mohr Siebeck for Max-Planck-Institut fur auslandisches und internationalisches Privatrecht, 2000).

Joyce, R. B., 'British New Guinea: Government' in *Encyclopaedia of Papua and New Guinea*, Vol. 1, Gen. Ed. P. Ryan (Clayton, Victoria: Melbourne University Press in Association with the University of Papua and New Guinea, 1972).

Law Commission, New Zealand, *Converging Currents: Custom and Human Rights in the Pacific*, Study Paper 17. (Wellington, New Zealand: Law Commission, 2006).

Llewellyn, K., 'The Normative, the Legal, and the Law-Jobs: The Problem of Juristic Method', *Yale Law Journal* 49 (1940), 1355–1400.

Lummis, T., *Life and Death in Eden: Pitcairn Island and the Bounty Mutineers* (Aldershot: Ashgate, 1997).

McNeil, K., *Common Law Aboriginal Title* (Oxford: Clarendon Press, 1989).

Park, A. E. W., *The Sources of Nigerian Law* (London: Sweet & Maxwell and Lagos: African Universities Press, 1963).

Patchett, K., 'Reception of Law in the West Indies', *Jamaican Law Journal* (1973), 17–35, 55–67.

Prochnau, W. and L. Parker, 'Trouble in Paradise', *Vanity Fair* (January 2008), 95–103, 136–139.

Renteln, A. D., *The Cultural Defense* (New York: Oxford University Press, 2004).

Roberts-Wray, K., *Commonwealth and Colonial Law* (London: Steven and Sons, 1966).

Simpson, A. W. B., 'The Common Law and Legal Theory' in *Oxford Essays in Jurisprudence*, ed. A. W. B. Simpson (Oxford: Clarendon Press, 1970), 77–99.

Twining, W. L., 'Diffusion of Law: A Global Perspective', *Journal of Legal Pluralism* 49 (2004), 1–45.

Twining, W. L., 'Social Science and Diffusion of Law', *Journal of Law & Society* 32 (2005), 203.

Waldegrave, W., 'Extracts from a Private Journal Kept on Board H.M.S. *Seringapatam*, in the Pacific, 1830', *Journal of the Royal Geographical Society of London* 3 (1833).

Wanitzek, U. and G. R. Woodman, 'Relating Local Legal Activity to Global Influences: A Theoretical Survey' in *Local Land Law and Globalization: A comparative study of peri-urban areas in Benin, Ghana and Tanzania*, eds G. R. Woodman, U. Wanitzek, and H. Sippel (Münster: LIT Verlag, 2004), 1–79.

Watson, A., *Legal Transplants: An Approach to Comparative Law* (Edinburgh: Scottish Academic Press, rev. edn, 1993).

Wesley-Smith, P., 'The Reception of English Law in Hong Kong', *Hong Kong Law Journal* 18 (1988), 183–217, 207–210.

Woodman, G. R., 'Some Realism about Customary Law: The West African Experience', *Wisconsin Law Review* (1969), 128–152.

Woodman, G. R., 'Judicial Development of Customary Law: The Case of Marriage Law in Ghana and Nigeria', *University of Ghana Law Journal* 14 (1977), 115–136.

Woodman, G. R., 'Customary Law, State Courts, and the Notion of Institutionalization of Norms in Ghana and Nigeria' in *People's Law and*

*State Law: the Bellagio Papers*, eds A. Allott and G. R. Woodman (Dordrecht: Foris, 1985), 143–163.

Woodman, G. R., 'How State Courts Create Customary Law in Ghana and Nigeria' in *Indigenous Law and the State*, eds B. W. Morse and G. R. Woodman (Dordrecht: Foris, 1988), 181–220.

Woodman, G. R., 'The Peculiar Policy of Recognition of Indigenous Laws in British Colonial Africa. A preliminary discussion', *Verfassung und Recht in Übersee* 22 (1989), 273–284.

Woodman, G. R., 'Folk Law' in *Dictionnaire encyclopédique de théorie et de sociologie du droit*, dir. A.-J. Arnaud (Paris: Librairie Générale de Droit et de Jurisprudence, 2nd edn, 1993), 262–265.

Woodman, G. R. 'The Involvement of English Common Law with Other Laws' in *La quête anthropologique du droit: Autour de la démarche d'Étienne Le Roy*, eds C. Eberhard and G. Vernicos (Paris: Éditions Karthala, 2006), 477–500.

Woodman, G. R., 'The Culture Defence in English Common Law: The Potential for Development' in *Multicultural Jurisprudence: Comparative Perspectives on the Cultural Defense*, eds A. D. Renteln and M.-C. Foblets (Oxford: Hart Publications, 2008), 7–34.

Zorn, J. G. and J. Corrin-Care, *Proving Customary Law in the Common Law Courts of the South Pacific* (London: British Institute of International and Comparative Law, 2002).

## Chapter 5: The Pitcairn Prosecutions: An Assessment of Their Historical Context by Reference to the Provisions of Public International Law

Alexander, C., *The Bounty: The True Story of the Mutiny on the Bounty* (New York: Viking, 2003).

Angelo, A. H. and A. Townend, 'Pitcairn: A Contemporary Comment', *New Zealand Journal of Public International Law* 1 (2003), 229–243.

Angelo, T. and F. Wright, 'Pitcairn: Sunset on Empire?', *New Zealand Law Journal* (2004).

Anghie, A., *Imperialism, Sovereignty and the Making of International Law* (Cambridge: Cambridge University Press, 2005).

Aust, A., 'Lockerbie: The Other Case', *International & Comparative Law Quarterly* 49 (2000), 278–296.

Aust, A., *Modern Treaty Law and Practice* (Cambridge: Cambridge University Press, 2nd edn, 2007).

Bamforth, N. C., 'Understanding the Impact and Status of the Human Rights Act 1998 within English Law', *NYU School of Law Global Law Working Paper* (2005), Series 60.

Banner, S., *Possessing the Pacific: Land, Settlers, and Indigenous People from Australia to Alaska* (Cambridge, MA: Harvard University Press, 2007).

Beckett, W. E., 'The Exercise of Criminal Jurisdiction over Foreigners', *British Yearbook of International Law* 6 (1925), 44–60.

Birkett, D., *Serpent in Paradise* (London: Picador, 1997).

Bligh, W. and E. Christian, *The Bounty Mutiny* (New York: Penguin, 2001).

Bockarth, J., 'Law on Remote Islands: The Convergence of Fact and Fiction', *Legal Studies Forum* 27 (2003), 21–81.

Bowett, D. W., 'Jurisdiction: Changing Patterns of Authority over Activities and Resources', *British Yearbook of International Law* 53 (1982), 1–26.

Boyle, A. and C. Chinkin, *The Making of International Law* (Oxford: Oxford University Press, 2007).

Brownlie, I., *Principles of Public International Law* (Oxford: Oxford University Press, 7th edn, 2008).

Carteret, P., *An Account of the Voyages Undertaken by the Order of His Present Majesty for Making Discoveries in the Southern Hemisphere, and Successively Performed by Commodore Byron, Captain Carteret, and Captain Cook, in the Dolphin, the Swallow and the Endeavour: And Successively Performed . . .* (London: W. Strahan & T. Cadell, 1773).

Cassese, A., *International Law* (Oxford: Oxford University Press, 2nd edn, 2005).

Charlesworth, H. and C. Chinkin, *The Boundaries of International Law: A Feminist Analysis* (Manchester: Manchester University Press, 2000).

Clark, R. S., 'Steven Spielberg's *Amistad* and Other Things I Have Thought About in the Past Forty Years: International (Criminal) Law, Conflict of Laws, Insurance and Slavery', *Rutgers Law Journal* 30 (1999), 371–440.

Cormack, B., *A Power to Do Justice: Jurisdiction, English Literature, and the Rise of the Common Law, 1509–1625* (Chicago: University of Chicago Press, 2007).

Crawford, J., *The Creation of States in International Law* (Oxford: Clarendon Press, 2nd edn, 2006).

Curtis, G. T., *The Case of the Virginius, Considering with Reference to the Law of Self-Defence* (New York: Baker, Voorhis & Co., 1874).

de Deckker, P., 'Decolonisation Processes in the South Pacific Islands: A Comparative Analysis Between Metropolitan Powers', *Victoria University of Wellington Law Review* 26 (1996), 355–371.

Elias, T. O., 'The Doctrine of Intertemporal Law', *American Journal of International Law* 74 (1980), 285–307.

Farer, T. J. and F. Gaer, 'The UN and Human Rights: At the End of the Beginning' in *United Nations, Divided World: The UN's Roles in International Relations*, eds A. Roberts and B. Kingsbury (Oxford: Clarendon Press, 2nd edn, 1993).

Farran, S., 'The Case of Pitcairn: A Small Island, Many Questions', *Journal of South Pacific Law* 11 (2007), 124–150.

Farran, S., 'The "Re-Colonising" of Pitcairn', *Victoria University of Wellington Law Review* 38 (2007), 435–464.

Ford, R. T., 'Law's Territory (A History of Jurisdiction)', *Michigan Law Review* 97 (1999), 843–930.

Franck, T. M. and P. Hoffman, 'The Right of Self-Determination in Very Small Places', *New York University Journal of International Law & Politics* 8 (1976), 331–386.

Gaston, Jèze G., *Etude théorique et pratique sur l'occupation comme mode d'acquérir les territoires en droit international* (Paris: Giard & Brière, 1896).

Grey, F. T. and H. H. L. Bellot, 'The Relations of the Executive and the Judiciary', *Transactions of the Grotius Society* 15 (1929), 139–161.

Hall, W. E., *A Treatise on International Law*, ed. A. P. Higgins (Oxford: Clarendon Press, 8th edn, 1924).

Harris, D. J., *Cases and Materials on International Law* (London: Sweet & Maxwell, 6th edn, 2004).

Harvard Project on Jurisdiction with Respect to Crime, *American Journal of International Law* (Supplement) 29 (1935), 435–651.

Higgins, R., *Problems and Process: International Law and How We Use It* (Oxford: Clarendon Press, 1994).

Jennings, R. and A. Watts, eds, *Oppenheim's International Law* (Vol. I: Peace) (London & New York: Longman, 9th edn, 1992).

Jennings, R. Y., 'Extraterritorial Jurisdiction and the United States Anti-Trust Laws', *British Yearbook of International Law* 33 (1957), 146–175.

Jennings, R. Y., *The Acquisition of Territory in International Law* (Manchester: Manchester University Press, 1963).

Jessup, P. C., 'The Palmas Island Arbitration', *American Journal of International Law* 22 (1928), 735–752.

Johnson, K. and J. Dougherty, 'Sect's Children to Stay in State Custody for Now', *New York Times*, 19 April 2008, A11.

Knop, K., *Diversity and Self-Determination in International Law* (Cambridge: Cambridge University Press, 2002).

Kontorovich, E., 'The Piracy Analogy: Modern Universal Jurisdiction's Hollow Foundation', *Harvard International Law Journal* 45 (2004), 183–237.

Koskenniemi, M., *The Gentle Civilizer of Nations: The Rise and Fall of International Law 1870–1960* (Cambridge: Cambridge University Press, 2002).

Lauterpacht, H., *Oppenheim's International Law: A Treatise* (Vol. I: Peace) (London: Longmans Green & Co., 7th edn, 1948).

Lauterpacht, H., 'Revolutionary Activities by Private Persons Against Foreign States', *American Journal of International Law* 22 (1928), 105–130.

Lee, S., 'Continuing Relevance of Traditional Modes of Territorial Acquisition in International Law and A Modest Proposal', *Connecticut Journal of International Law* 16 (2000), 1–22.

Lewis, G. C., *On Foreign Jurisdiction and the Extradition of Criminals* (London: J.W. Parker & Son, 1859).

Lim, C. L., 'Neither Sheep Nor Peacocks: T. O. Elias and Post-colonial International Law', *Leiden Journal of International Law* 21 (2008), 295–315.

Mason, A., 'The Rights of Indigenous People in Lands Once Part of the Old Dominions of the Crown', *International & Comparative Law Quarterly* 46 (1997), 812–830.

McLoughlin, D., 'The Development of the System of Government and Laws of Pitcairn Island from 1791 to 1971' in *Laws of Pitcairn, Henderson, Ducie and Oeno Islands*, ed. D. McLoughlin (Govt. of the Islands of Pitcairn, Henderson, Duecie & Oeno, rev. edn, 1971), 34.

Meron, T., *Human Rights and Humanitarian Law as Customary International Law* (Oxford: Clarendon Press, 1989).

Moor, L. and A. W. B. Simpson, 'Ghosts of Colonialism in the European Convention on Human Rights', *British Yearbook of International Law* 75 (2005), 121–193.

Moore, J. B., *Report on Extraterritorial Crime and the Cutting Case* (Washington, DC: US Dept. of State, 1887).

Murray, T. B., *Pitcairn: The Island, the People, and the Pastor: To Which Is Added A Short Notice of the Original Settlement and Present Condition of Norfolk Island* (New York: E. S. Gorham, 1909).

Orent, B. and P. Reinsch, 'Sovereignty over Islands in the Pacific', *American Journal of International Law* 35 (1941), 443–461.

Perreau-Saussine, A., 'British Acts of State in English Courts', *British Yearbook of International Law* 78 (2007), 176–254.

Power, H., 'Pitcairn Island: Sexual Offending, Cultural Difference and Ignorance of the Law', *Criminal Law Review* (2007), 609–629.

Raustiala, K., *Does the Constitution Follow the Flag? Territoriality and Extraterritoriality in American Law* (New York: Oxford University Press, 2009).

Roberts, A. and B. Kingsbury, eds, *United Nations, Divided World: The UN's Roles in International Relations* (Oxford: Clarendon Press, 2nd edn, 1993).

Roberts-Wray, K., *Commonwealth and Colonial Law* (London: Stevens & Sons, 1966).

Salomon, C., *L'occupation des territoires sans maître. Etude de droit international* (Paris: Giard, 1889).

Schine, C., 'Adventures in the Opium Trade', *New York Review of Books*, Vol. LVI, No. 1, 15 January–11 February 2009, 39–41.

Shaw, M., 'Speaking Volumes: The Acquisition of Territory in International Law', *Times Higher Education Supplement*, 17 November 1995.

Shaw, M., *International Law* (Cambridge: Cambridge University Press, 6th edn, 2008).

Simpson, A. W. B., *Human Rights and the End of Empire: Britain and the Genesis of the European Convention* (Oxford: Oxford University Press, 2001).

Smith, II, G. P, 'From Cutlass to Cat-O'-Nine Tails: The Case for International Jurisdiction of Mutiny on the High Seas', *Michigan Journal of International Law* 10 (1989), 277–303.

Steiner, H. J., P. Alston, and R. Goodman, *International Human Rights in Context: Law, Politics, Morals* (Oxford: Oxford University Press, 3rd edn, 2008).

Sureda, A. R., *The Evolution of the Right of Self-Determination. A Study of United Nations Practice* (Leiden: Sijthoff, 1973).

Taggart, M., 'Ruled By Law?', *Modern Law Review* 69 (2006), 1006–1025.

Trenwith, A., 'The Empire Strikes Back: Human Rights and the Pitcairn Proceedings', *Journal of South Pacific Law* 7 (2003), online at <http://www.paclii.org/journals/fJSPL/vol07no2/3.shtml>.

Wahlroos, S., *Mutiny and the Romance in the South Seas: A Companion to the Bounty Adventure* (Topsfield, MA: Salem House Publishers, 1989).

## Chapter 6: 'A Million Mutinies Now': Why Claims of Cultural Uniqueness Cannot be Used to Justify Violations of Basic Human Rights

Angelo, A. H. and A. Townend, 'Pitcairn: A Contemporary Comment', *New Zealand Journal of Public International Law* 1 (2003), 229.

Ballantyne, R. M., *The Coral Island* (Edinburgh: W & R Chambers, 1857), text available at Project Gutenberg: <http://www.gutenberg.org/etext/646>.

Barry, B., *Culture and Equality: An Egalitarian Critique of Multiculturalism* (Oxford: Polity, 2000).

Benhabib, S., *The Claims of Culture: Equality and Diversity in the Global Era* (Princeton, NJ: Princeton University Press, 2002).

Dembour, M.-B., *Who Believes in Human Rights?* (Cambridge: Cambridge University Press, 2006).

Doppelt, G., 'Illiberal Conditions and Group Rights', *Journal of Contemporary Issues* 12 (2002), 661–692.

Dundes Renteln, A., *The Cultural Defense* (New York: OUP, 2004).

Editorial Note, 'The Cultural Defense in the Criminal Law', *Harvard Law Review* 99 (1986), 1293–1311.

Farran, S., 'The Case of Pitcairn: A Small Island, Many Questions', *Journal of South Pacific Law* 11(2) (2007), 124–150.

Gutmann, A., ed., *Multiculturalism and The Politics of Recognition* (Princeton, NJ: Princeton University Press, 1992), 25–73.

Habermas, J., 'Multiculturalism and the Liberal State', *Stanford Law Review* 47 (5) (1995), 849–853.

Halbertal, M. and A. Margalit, 'Liberalism and the Right to Culture', *Social Research* 61 (1994), 491–510.

Kutkathas, C., 'Are There Any Cultural Rights?', *Political Theory* 20 (1992), 105–139.

Kymlicka, W., *Multicultural Citizenship: A Liberal Theory of Minority Rights* (Oxford: Clarendon Press, 1995).

Kymlicka, W., ed., *The Rights of Minority Cultures* (Oxford: Oxford University Press, 1995).

Margalit, A. and J. Raz, 'National Self-determination', *Journal of Philosophy* 8 (1990), 439–461.

Marks, K., *Trouble in Paradise: Uncovering Decades of Sexual Abuse on Britain's Most Remote Island* (London: Harper, 2008).

Melville, H., *Typee*, (1846) text available at Project Gutenberg, <http://www.gutenberg.org/etext/9269>.

Naipaul, V. S., *India: A Million Mutinies Now* (London: Penguin, 2002).

Okin, S. M., 'Feminism and Multiculturalism: Some Tensions', *Ethics* 108(4) (1998), 661–684.

Phillips, A., 'When Culture Means Gender: Issues of Cultural Defence in the English Courts', *Modern Law Review* 66 (2003), 510.

Power, H., 'Provocation and Culture', *Criminal Law Review* (2000), 871.

Power, H., 'Pitcairn Island: Sexual Offending, Cultural Difference and Ignorance of the Law', *Criminal Law Review* (2007), 609–629.

Spinner-Halev, J., *Surviving Diversity: Religion and Democratic Citizenship* (Baltimore: Johns Hopkins Press, 2000).

Taylor, C., 'The Politics of Recognition' in *Multiculturalism and The Politics of Recognition*, ed. A. Gutmann (Princeton, NJ: Princeton University Press, 1992), 25–73.

Torry, W. I., 'Multicultural Jurisprudence and the Cultural Defense', *Journal of Legal Pluralism* (1999), 127–161.

Trenwith, A., 'The Empire Strikes Back: Human Rights and the Pitcairn Proceedings', *Journal of South Pacific Law* 7(2) (2003), Part V, available at <http://www.paclii.org/journals/fJSPL/vol07no2/3.shtml>.

Waldron, J., 'Minority Cultures and the Cosmopolitan Alternative' in *The Rights of Minority Cultures*, ed. W. Kymlicka (Oxford: Oxford University Press, 1995), 93–119.

## Chapter 7: Rights and Duties on Pitcairn Island

Aristotle, *Politics,* eds R. F. Stalley and E. Barker (Oxford: Oxford University Press, 1998).

Austin, J., *The Province of Jurisprudence Determined*, ed. W. Rumble (Cambridge: Cambridge University Press, 1955, first published 1832).

Cargile, J., 'Utilitarianism and the Desert Island Problem', *Analysis* 25 (1964), 23–24.

Dworkin, R., *Law's Empire* (Oxford: Hart Publishing, 1986).

Dworkin, R., *Sovereign Virtue: The Theory and Practice of Equality* (Cambridge: Cambridge University Press, 2000).

Dworkin, R., *Justice in Robes* (Cambridge, MA: Harvard University Press, 2006).

Finnis, J., *Natural Law and Natural Rights* (Oxford: Clarendon Press, 1980).

Finnis, J., 'The Truth in Legal Positivism' in *The Autonomy of Law*, ed. Robert P. George (Oxford: Oxford University Press, 1996), 195–214.

Gardner, J., 'Law's Aim in Law's Empire' in *Exploring Law's Empire*, ed. S. Hershovitz (Oxford: Oxford University Press, 2006).

George, R. P., ed., *The Autonomy of Law* (Oxford: Oxford University Press, 1996).

Hart, H. L. A., *The Concept of Law* (Oxford: Clarendon Press, 2nd edn, 1994).

Heinaman, R., ed., *Aristotle and Moral Realism* (London: University College London Press, 1995).

Hershovitz, S., ed., *Exploring Law's Empire* (Oxford: Oxford University Press, 2006).

Hume, D., *An Enquiry Concerning the Principles of Morals: A Critical Edition* (Oxford: Oxford University Press, 2000).

Kraut, R., *Aristotle: Political Philosophy* (Oxford: Oxford University Press, 2002).

McDowell, J., 'Eudaimonism and Realism in Aristotle's *Ethics*' in *Aristotle and Moral Realism*, ed. R. Heinaman (London: University College London Press, 1995), 201–218.

Mill, J. S., 'Considerations on Representative Government' in *John Stuart Mill: Collected Works*, ed. J. M. Robson (Toronto: University of Toronto Press, 1977), vol. XIX.

Moore, M., 'Moral Reality', *Wisconsin Law Review* (1982), 1061.

Moore, M., 'Law as a Functional Kind' in *Natural Law Theories: Contemporary Essays*, ed. R. P. George (Oxford: Oxford University Press, 1992), 188–242.

Moore, M., 'Moral Reality Revisited', *Michigan Law Review* 90 (1992), 2424.

Mowll Mathews, N., *Paul Gauguin: An Erotic Life* (Newhaven: Yale University Press, 2001).

Narveson, J., 'The Desert Island Problem', *Analysis* 23(3) (1963), 63–67.

Rawls, J., *The Law of Peoples* (Cambridge, MA: Harvard University Press, 1999).

Raz, J., *Morality of Freedom* (Oxford: Clarendon Press, 1986).

Raz, J., *Practical Reasons and Norms* (Oxford: Oxford University Press, 1999).

Raz, J., 'The Problem of Authority: Revisiting the Service Conception', *Minnesota Law Review* 90 (2006), 1003.

Robson, J. M., ed., *John Stuart Mill: Collected Works* (Toronto: University of Toronto Press, 1977).

Rumble, W., ed, *John Austin, The Province of Jurisprudence Determined, 1832* (Cambridge: Cambridge University Press, 1955).

Stalley, R. F. and E. Barker, eds, *Aristotle, Politics* (Oxford: Oxford University Press, 1998).

Waldron, J., 'Does Law Promise Justice?', *Georgia State University Law Review* 17 (2001), 759.

Williams, B., *Morality: An Introduction to Ethics* (Cambridge: Cambridge University Press, 1972).

## Chapter 8: Legality, Reciprocity, and the Criminal Law on Pitcairn

Allan, T., *Law, Liberty and Justice: the Legal Foundations of British Constitutionalism* (Oxford: Oxford University Press, 1993).

Aquinas, T., *Summa Theologica* (c. 1266–1273).

Ashworth, A., 'Interpreting Criminal Statutes: a Crisis of Legality', *Law Quarterly Review* (1991), 419–449.

Ashworth, A., *Principles of Criminal Law* (Oxford: Oxford University Press, 2003).

Coleman, J., *Practice of Principle: In Defence of a Pragmatist Approach to Legal Theory* (Oxford: Oxford University Press, 2001).

Dworkin, R., *Taking Rights Seriously* (London: Duckworth, 1977).

Dworkin, R., 'Political Judges and the Rule of Law' in *A Matter of Principle* (Cambridge, MA: Harvard University Press, 1985), 9–32.

Dworkin, R., *Law's Empire* (Cambridge, MA: Harvard University Press, 1986).

Dworkin, R., *Justice in Robes* (Cambridge, MA: Harvard University Press, 2006).

Fieschi, C., 'Symbolic Laws', *Prospect* 119 (2006).

Finnis, J., *Natural Law and Natural Rights* (Oxford: Oxford University Press, 1980).

Fuller, L. L., 'Reply to his Critics' in *The Morality of Law*, The Yale Storr Lectures (New Haven: Yale University Press, rev. edn, 1963).

Fuller, L. L., *The Morality of Law* (New Haven and London: Yale University Press, rev. edn, 1969).

Guest, S., 'Why the Law is Just', *Current Legal Problems* (2000), 31–52.

Habermas, J., *Beyond Facts and Norms*, trans. Rehg (Cambridge, MA: MIT, 1996).

Hart, H. L. A., 'Kelsen's Doctrine of the Unity of Law' in *Essays in Jurisprudence and Philosophy* (Oxford: Oxford University Press, 1983), 335–336.

*References* 283

Hart, H. L. A., *The Concept of Law* (Oxford: Oxford University Press, 2nd edn, 1994).

Hart, H. L. A., *Punishment and Responsibility* (Oxford: Oxford University Press, rev. edn, 2008).

Hobbes, T., *Leviathan* (1651).

Husack, D., 'Ignorance of Law and Duties of Citizenship', *Legal Studies* 14 (1994), 105–115.

Kelsen, H., *Introduction to the Problems of Legal Theory*, ed. and trans. Paulson (Oxford: Oxford University Press, 2002).

Postema, G., *Bentham and the Common Law Tradition* (Oxford: Oxford University Press, 1986).

Raz, J., *The Concept of a Legal System* (Oxford: Oxford University Press, 1970).

Raz, J., *The Authority of Law* (Oxford: Oxford University Press, 1979).

Raz, J., 'The Rule of Law and its Virtue' in *The Authority of Law* (Oxford: Oxford University Press, 1979).

Raz, J., *Ethics in the Public Domain* (Oxford: Oxford University Press, 1994).

Tamanaha, B., *The Rule of Law* (Cambridge: Cambridge University Press, 2004).

Tribe, L., 'Revisiting the Rule of Law', *New York University Law Review* 64 (1989), 726–751.

Waluchow, W., *Inclusive Legal Positivism* (Oxford: Oxford University Press, 1994).

Williams, G., 'Convictions and Fair Labelling', *Cambridge Law Journal* 42(1) (1983) 85–95.

# Index

**Abuse of process**
  basis of claim 82–89
  case raised in *Steven Raymond
    Christian and Others v The
    Queen* 28–35
  finding of Judicial Committee 29–30
  sovereign title and obligations 123
**Act of State doctrine**
  Lord Woolf's judgment in *Steven
    Raymond Christian and Others v
    The Queen* 27
  territorial acquisition 107
**Age of consent** 167, 211
**Amnesties**
  consideration by FCO 14
  rejection as alternative to
    prosecution 34
**Annexation** 75–76, 88
**Anthropology and sociology**
  absence of information about law 31
  central questions 5
  debate about absence of justice system 28
  formalist and substantivist approaches
    compared 226–228
  speculations on human nature 222–226
  unjustified claims of cultural
    uniqueness 135
**Appeals**
  establishment of Pitcairn Court of
    Appeal 16
  *Steven Raymond Christian and Others v
    The Queen*
    absence of criminal justice
      system 27–28
    colonial status of Pitcairn 24–27
    general procedure 23–24
    legality and rule of law 28–35
    Privy Council decision 231–258
    reflections on alternative judicial
      approaches 35–36
    subsequent measures by British
      Government 36–37
**Austin, J.** 171

**Barristers**
  absence on Islands 3

absence prior to 1996 59
appointment by Crown 196
cross-examination of Island legal
  adviser 208
**Bentham, J.** 170, 192
**Blackstone, Sir W.** 67, 71, 72
**Blameworthiness**
  effects of cultural relativism 159–169
  introduction 157–159
**Bligh, W.** 39–40
**Books** *see* **Law books**
  absence on Islands 3, 59
  promulgation of law 141
**British government** *see* **Crown; Great
  Britain**

**Carswell, Lord** 24
**Certainty** *see* **Legal certainty**
**Cession** 78–80, 109
**Choice of law**
  cultural differences 65–66
  general principles 63–64
  private international law 64–65
**Christianity**
  early teachings on Pitcairn 48
  Seventh Day Adventism
    arrival on Pitcairn 56
    fairness 211
    statement on British position 60
**Chronology** 267–270
**Civil and political rights**
  cultural arguments 144
  introduction 18
  sovereign title and obligations
    119–128
**Coercive powers** 188
**Colonial power**
  arguments against abuse of
    process 86–87
  central questions 4–5
  cession 78–80, 109
  choice of law 66
  coercive powers 188
  early British claims 3
  problem with state laws 83–84
  provision of institutions 74

**Colonial power** (*cont.*)
  requirement for community
    relationship 176–181
  settlement 24–27, 61, 67–71
  statutory authority of Great Britain
    over Pitcairn 56–60
  thought experiment for British
    Crown 5–10
  unjustified claims of cultural
    uniqueness 137
**Colonial status**
  case raised in *Steven Raymond Christian
    and Others v The Queen* 24–27
  Privy Council view 78–81
  sources of law 66
**Common law**
  adoption by settlors 2
  diffusion on Pitcairn Island
    abuse of process 82–89
    conclusions 89–91
    history and sources of law 66–66
    introduction 63–66
    law originally in force 67–71
    legal development after
      settlement 72–82
  imputations of fairness 213
  Lord Hope's view on prosecution 33
**Community**
  campaign against prosecutions 14–15
  measure put in place after
    convictions 36–37
  Pitcairn's tainted history 186
  special relationship between rulers and
    rules 176–181
  thought experiment for British
    Crown 7
  wrongs which override community
    culture 35
**Community Police Officer** 36–37
**Compensation**
  measure put in place after
    convictions 37
  thought experiment for British
    Crown 6
**Conquest** 109
**Consent**
  introduction 4
  jurisdiction 102, 126
  sexual behaviour
    blameworthiness 198
    'cultural defence' claims 151
    fairness 210–212
    freely given 167

  possible presumption 8
**Constitution**
  contribution from Captain Elliott 26
  early status of Pitcairn 50–51
  rules for Chief Magistrate 54
**Convictions**
  anticipation of 28
  arguments against 183–186
  lawfulness 35–36, 173, 175
  minimization of impact 147
  no lawyers resident 3
  overview 15–16
  political pressures 6
  stigma 214, 218–219
  subsequent measures by British
    government 36–37
  trial process 15–16
  unusualness 93
**Correspondence**
  acknowledgments of sexual
    misconduct 200
  conducted through visitors 44–45
  reasons for prosecution 33
**Criminal Injuries Compensation** 37
**Criminal justice system**
  absence on Islands 3
  case raised in *Steven Raymond Christian
    and Others v The Queen* 27–28
  legal positivist approach 173–175
**Criminal law**
  abuse of process 29, 82–87
  'cultural defence' claims 145
  jurisdiction 27
  knowledge of conduct 30
  legality and reciprocity
    conclusions 219–220
    Crown jurisdiction 186–197
    fairness 210–214
    introduction 183–186
    legal certainty 218–219
    limits of criminal law 214–216
    *mala in se* 197–199
    promulgation of law 199–207
    rejection of positivism 207–210
    rights of victims 216–218
  only prior prosecutions 57, 59
  precedent for jurisdiction 173
  recognition of UK law on Pitcairn 139
  weak state on Pitcairn 13, 37
**Crown**
  *see also* **Great Britain**
  absence on Islands 3
  appointment of judiciary 196

case raised in *Steven Raymond Christian and Others v The Queen* 24–27
failure to annex Pitcairn 75
legality, reciprocity and the criminal law 186–197
'Cultural defence' claims 145, 150–153
Cultural imperialism 133, 155
Cultural relativism 159–169
Culture
  abuse of women and children 32
  choice of law 65–66
  influences on police 12
  normative orders 63–64
  problem with state laws 83–84
  relativism 4
  thought experiment for British Crown 8–9
  unjustified claims
    alleged failure to acknowledge uniqueness 136–138
    alternative media narratives 134–136
    arguments particular to unique cultures 143–146
    conclusions 155–156
    'cultural defence' claims 150–153
    dangers of exaggerated respect 154–155
    distorting influence of isolation 141–144
    incoherent narrative ignoring sexual abuse 138–141
    introduction 131–134
    minority rights 146–150
  wrongs which override community culture 35
Customary law
  artefact of state law 225
  diffusion of common law on Pitcairn
    abuse of process 82–89
    conclusions 89–91
    history and sources of law 66–66
    introduction 63–66
    law originally in force 67–71
    legal development after settlement 72–82
  local law 226
  status of common law 17–18, 35

Deference
  opinions in *Steven Raymond Christian and Others v The Queen* 26

sources of law 69
territorial acquisition 108
Democracy
  moral claims 188, 190
  need to deal with deep issues 10
  thought experiment for British Crown 9
  withering in remote island 2
Discrimination 18
Dworkin, R. 178, 189–190

Evidence
  absorption of external values 140
  abuse of process 29
  Act of State doctrine 108
  application of personal law 70
  aspirations of independence 113
  awareness of Sexual Offences Act 1956 211
  constituents of sexual offences 85
  cultural values 153
  by defendants 4
  development of local customary law 18
  distorting influence of isolation 141
  effects of prosecution 38
  girl victims 12–15
  history of island 25–27
  impact on Lord Hope 32
  'Island law' 196
  knowledge of law 84
  lawlessness on Pitcairn 225
  legal validity 195
  obtained by oppressive means 184
  'paper trail' of documents 193
  persons who had moved abroad 147
  Pitcairn flag 73
  promulgation of law 8, 31, 142, 207
  settlement 78
  use of English law 175
  wrongdoing 199

Fairness 210–214
Family and Community Adviser 36
Feminist critique 120, 141, 150, 155, 183, 224–225
Finnis, J. 67, 170, 170–171, 206
Fletcher Christian
  death 42–43, 45
  mutiny on Bounty 39–41
  pretensions to gentility 41
  sons 49

Folk law 64
Foreign and Commonwealth Office
　correspondence in 2000 216, 262–265
　executive statements 26
　'Operation Unique' 13–15
Fuller, L. 21, 84, 188–191, 197,
　　201–202, 214

Girls *see* Women and girls
Governance
　formalist and substantivist approaches
　　compared 227
　history and development 10–13
Great Britain
　*see also* Crown
　absence of Crown presence 3
　claim to colonial power 3
　commitment of resources to
　　Pitcairn 139
　failure to discharge 'social
　　contract' 142
　intervention in Pitcairn: 1856–98 54
　lax approach to Pitcairn 61
　measures put in place after
　　convictions 36–37
　passing of decision to courts 36
　patriotism towards 3–4
　Pitcairn Island website 37
　recognition of Pitcairn:
　　1814–56 51–54
　significance of neglect 191
　statutory power over
　　settlements 56–60

Harry Christian 17, 48, 57, 111
Hart, H. 173, 192–193, 205–207
Hobbes, T. 10, 35, 72, 158, 202
Hoffmann, Lord
　brusque dismissal of case 138
　finding on abuse of process 29
　judgment 243–258
　legality of statute and
　　Ordinances 28–29
　*Steven Raymond Christian and Others
　　v The Queen*
　　main advice 24
　views on colonial status 80
Hope, Lord
　alleged failure to acknowledge
　　uniqueness 136
　arguments against abuse of
　　process 86–87

*Steven Raymond Christian and Others v
　The Queen*
　references to evidence 26
　separate opinions 24
　concern about rule of law 31
　concern about unjusticiability 35–36
　fairness 212–213
　fundamental issues about rule of
　　law 90
　interest of case 228–229
　judgment 243–258
　need to understand history of
　　Island 39
　positivist approach 35
　sovereign title and obligations 123
　territorial acquisition 107
　views on colonial status 78–79
　views on promulgation 34–35
　views on prosecution 32–33
Hosti humani generis 101
Human rights 119–120
　sovereign title and obligations 118–127
　unjustified claims of cultural
　　uniqueness
　　alleged failure to acknowledge
　　　uniqueness 136–138
　　alternative media narratives
　　　134–136
　　arguments particular to unique
　　　cultures 143–146
　　conclusions 155–156
　　'cultural defence' claims 150–153
　　distorting influence of isolation
　　　141–144
　　incoherent narrative ignoring
　　　sexual abuse 138–141
　　introduction 131–134
　　minority rights 146–150

Ignorance of the law 84, 201–203
　*see also* Promulgation of law
Indecent assault *see* Sexual offences
International law
　choice of law 64–65
　early status of Pitcairn 55
　jurisdiction under public
　　international law
　　conceptual analysis 96–106
　　conclusions 127–129
　　introduction 93–96
　　sovereign title and obligations
　　　119–127

territorial acquisition 106–119
**Intertemporal law doctrine** 109–110

**Judicial Committee of Privy Council**
  *Steven Raymond Christian and Others v
    The Queen*
    absence of criminal justice
      system 27–28
    colonial status of Pitcairn 24–27
    general procedure 23–24
    Law report 231–258
    legality and rule of law 28–35
    reflections on alternative judicial
      approaches 35–36
    subsequent measures by British
      Government 36–37
  culmination of drama 4
**Judiciary**
  absence on Islands 3
  appointment by Crown 196
  Carswell, Lord
    unanimous opinion 24
  deference
    opinions in *Steven Raymond
      Christian and Others v The
      Queen* 26
    sources of law 69
    territorial acquisition 108
  Hoffmann, Lord
    brusque dismissal of case 138
    finding on abuse of process 29
    judgment 231–238
    legality of statute and
      Ordinances 28–29
    main advice 24
    views on colonial status 80
  Hope, Lord
    alleged failure to acknowledge
      uniqueness 136
    arguments against abuse of
      process 86–87
    concern about rule of law 31
    concern about
      unjusticiability 35–36
    fairness 212–213
    fundamental issues about rule of
      law 90
    interest of case 228–229
    judgment 243–258
    need to understand history of
      Island 39
    positivist approach 35
    references to evidence 26

separate opinions 24
  sovereign title and obligations 123
  territorial acquisition 107
  views on colonial status 78–79
  views on promulgation 34–35
  views on prosecution 32–33
  positivist inspired judgments 220
  Steyn, Lord
    unanimous opinion 24
  Woolf, Lord
    concerns about
      unjusticiability 35–36
    finding on abuse of process 30
    judgment 238–242
    references to evidence 26–27
    sovereign title and obligations 123
    unanimous opinion 24
    views on abuse of process 84
    views on colonial status 78–79
**Jure gentium** 101
**Jurisdiction**
  case raised in *Steven Raymond Christian
    and Others v The Queen*
    absence of criminal justice
      system 27–28
    colonial status 24–27
  Judicature Ordinance 1961 76–77
  legal positivist approach 173
  legality, reciprocity and the
    criminal law
    conclusions 219–220
    Crown jurisdiction 186–197
    fairness 210–214
    introduction 183–186
    legal certainty 218–219
    limits of criminal law 214–216
    *mala in se* 197–199
    promulgation of law 199–207
    rejection of positivism
      207 210
    rights of victims 216–218
  moral wrongfulness and
    blameworthiness distinguished
    effects of cultural relativism
      159–169
    introduction 157–159
  public international law
    conceptual analysis 96–106
    conclusions 127–129
    introduction 93–96
    sovereign title and obligations
      119–127
    territorial acquisition 106–119

Jurisdiction (*cont.*)
    requirement for community
        relationship 181
    Supreme Court of Fiji 58
Justice *see* Criminal justice system

Kelsen, H. 169, 173–174, 194–195

Law
    central questions 4–5
    diffusion of common law on Pitcairn
        abuse of process 82–89
        conclusions 89–91
        history and sources of law 66–66
        introduction 63–66
        law originally in force 67–71
        legal development after
            settlement 72–82
    jurisdiction under public
        international law
        conceptual analysis 96–106
        conclusions 127–129
        introduction 93–96
        sovereign title and obligations
            119–127
        territorial acquisition 106–119
    lacking at early stage 2
    legal positivism and natural law
        compared 169–176
    legality, reciprocity and the
        criminal law
        conclusions 219–220
        Crown jurisdiction 186–197
        fairness 210–214
        introduction 183–186
        legal certainty 218–219
        limits of criminal law 214–216
        *mala in se* 197–199
        promulgation of law 199–207
        rejection of positivism 207–210
        rights of victims 216–218
    prohibition on more settlors 56
    thought experiment for British
        Crown 6
'Law and order'
    Lord Hope's view on prosecution 33
    meaning 31
Lawyers
    absence on Islands 3
    absence prior to 1996 59
    appointment by Crown 196

cross-examination of Island legal
    adviser 208
not resident at convictions 3
Legal certainty
    legality, reciprocity and the criminal
        law 218–219
    thought experiment for British
        Crown 7
Legality
    case raised in *Steven Raymond Christian
        and Others v The Queen* 28–35
    reciprocity and the criminal law
        conclusions 219–220
        Crown jurisdiction 186–197
        fairness 210–214
        introduction 183–186
        legal certainty 218–219
        limits of criminal law 214–216
        *mala in se* 197–199
        promulgation of law 199–207
        rejection of positivism 207–210
        rights of victims 216–218
        requirement for community
            relationship 176–181
        sovereign title and obligations 123
Living law 64
Locke, J. 73, 158

Magistrate
    constitutional requirements 54
    finding of Judicial Committee 29
    'Island law' 196
    role 12
Mala in se
    abuse of process claims 84–85
    arguments against abuse of
        process 85–86
    legality, reciprocity and the criminal
        law 197–199
    rejection of claims of cultural
        uniqueness 141
    thought experiment for British
        Crown 6
    wrongs which override community
        culture 35
Mayor 12
Media reporting 134–136
Mill, J.S. 179
Minority rights 146–150
Morality
    legal positivism and natural law
        compared 169–176

legality, reciprocity and the
criminal law
conclusions 219–220
Crown jurisdiction 186–197
fairness 210–214
introduction 183–186
legal certainty 218–219
limits of criminal law 214–216
*mala in se* 197–199
promulgation of law 199–207
rejection of positivism 207–210
rights of victims 216–218
thought experiment for British Crown
7, 9
wrongfulness and blameworthiness
distinguished
effects of cultural relativism
159–169
introduction 157–159
Mutiny
events on Bounty 39–41
jurisdiction under public international
law 101
origins of settlement 2

Nationality
acceptance of colonial status 81
jurisdiction under public international
law 99–103
requirement for community
relationship 179
Natural law
legal positivism compared 169–176
legality, reciprocity and the
criminal law
conclusions 219–220
Crown jurisdiction 186–197
fairness 210–214
introduction 183–186
legal certainty 218–219
limits of criminal law 214–216
*mala in se* 197–199
promulgation of law 199–207
rejection of positivism 207–210
rights of victims 216–218
New Zealand
handing over of administration 58–59
importation of justice system 27–28
occasional administrative
interventions 186
remoteness of Pitcairn 40
residence of Governor 11

Norfolk Island
interviews of complainants 14
move to 17, 54–56
Norms
arguments against abuse of
process 85–86
integral part of culture 63–64
legal positivism and natural law
compared 169–176
objectives of state law 91
requirement for community
relationship 177–178
sexual behaviour in Pitcairn
198–199
unjustified claims of cultural
uniqueness
alleged failure to acknowledge
uniqueness 136–138
alternative media narratives
134–136
arguments particular to unique
cultures 143–146
conclusions 155–156
'cultural defence' claims 150–153
dangers of exaggerated respect
154–155
distorting influence of isolation
141–144
incoherent narrative ignoring
sexual abuse 138–141
introduction 131–134
minority rights 146–150
wrongfulness and blameworthiness
distinguished
effects of cultural relativism
159–169
introduction 157–159

Occupation 109
Official correspondence 259–265
acknowledgments of sexual
misconduct 200
reasons for prosecution 33
Operation Unique 13–15

Pacific Islands
criminalization of kidnapping 102
depopulation 119
intervention on Pitcairn 54
Paper administrations
applicable law 9
finding of Lord Hoffmann 29

**Paper administrations** (*cont.*)
  formalist and substantivist approaches
    compared 227–228
  involvement in Pitcairn 11
  Operation Unique 13
  Pitcairn Supreme Court 12
  reliance on colonial paperwork 24–37
  sovereignty claims 7
  UK approach 3, 6
**Paper trails** 185, 192–196, 202, 209,
  219–220, 227–228
**Particularism** 144–145, 151–154
**Personal law** 67–70
**Pitcairn Island**
  diffusion of common law
    abuse of process 82–89
    conclusions 89–91
    history and sources of law 66–66
    introduction 63–66
    law originally in force 67–71
    legal development after
      settlement 72–82
  early history
    biblical monarchy 48–51
    conclusions 61
    importance 39
    intervention by British
      Government: 1856–98 54
    mutiny on Bounty 39–41
    recognition by Great Britain:
      1814–56 51–54
    settled government:1898-
      present 56–60
    settlement: 1790–1814 39–40
  Government website 37
  location 2
  problems on Pitcairn
    governance of Island 10–13
    introduction 1–5
    Operation Unique 13–15
    overview of book 16–21
    thought experiment for colonial
      power 5–10
    trials and convictions 15–16
  remoteness 40
  unjustified claims of cultural
    uniqueness
    alleged failure to acknowledge
      uniqueness 136–138
    alternative media narratives
      134–136
    arguments particular to unique
      cultures 143–146

  conclusions 155–156
  'cultural defence' claims
    150–153
  dangers of exaggerated respect
    154–155
  distorting influence of isolation
    141–144
  incoherent narrative ignoring
    sexual abuse 138–141
  introduction 131–134
  minority rights 146–150
**Police**
  case raised in *Steven Raymond Christian
    and Others v The Queen* 27
  finding of Judicial Committee 29
  no presence prior to 1996 12
  Operation Unique 13–15
**Political rights** *see* **Civil and political
  rights**
**Population**
  development 2–3
  effects of cultural relativism 160
  normative orders 63–64
  problem with state laws 83–84
**Positivism**
  approach of Lord Hope 35
  laws and morality 192–195
  legal positivism and natural law
    compared 169–176
  legality, reciprocity and the
    criminal law
    ignorance of the law 202–203
    support of 'paper trail'
      method 209
    two values of promulgation
      204–207
  legality and community relationship
    176–181
**Privy Council** *see* **Judicial Committee of
  Privy Council**
**Promulgation of law**
  adequacy in Pitcairn 141–142
  basis of abuse of process claim
    82–83
  case raised in *Steven Raymond Christian
    and Others v The Queen* 28
  contribution from Captain Elliott 26
  effect of customary law 85
  finding of Judicial Committee 30
  Judicature Ordinance 1970 34
  legality, reciprocity and the
    criminal law
    ignorance of the law 201–203

importance 199–201
introduction 185
two values and legal positivism
204–207
Lord Hope's view 34–35
need to understand history of
Island 39
thought experiment for British
Crown 8
views of Court of Appeal 84
**Prosecutions**
absence of local involvement 12
legality, reciprocity and the
criminal law
conclusions 219–220
Crown jurisdiction 186–197
fairness 210–214
introduction 183–186
legal certainty 218–219
limits of criminal law 214–216
*mala in se* 197–199
promulgation of law 199–207
rejection of positivism 207–210
rights of victims 216–218
opinion of Lord Hope 32–33
prior to 1996 59
thought experiment for British
Crown 5–10
**Public international law**
conceptual analysis 96–106
conclusions 127–129
introduction 93–96
sovereign title and obligations
119–127
territorial acquisition 106–119
**Punishment** *see* **Sentences**

**Rape**
arguments against abuse of process 87
finding of Judicial Committee 29–30
jurisdiction under public
international law
introduction 93–96
moral wrongfulness and
blameworthiness distinguished
effects of cultural relativism
159–169
introduction 157–159
sovereign title and obligations
118–127
unjustified claims of cultural
uniqueness

alleged failure to acknowledge
uniqueness 136–138
alternative media narratives
134–136
arguments particular to unique
cultures 143–146
conclusions 155–156
'cultural defence' claims 150–153
dangers of exaggerated respect
154–155
distorting influence of isolation
141–144
incoherent narrative ignoring
sexual abuse 138–141
introduction 131–134
minority rights 146–150
**Rawls, J.** 158, 179
**Raz, J.** 148, 157, 170, 172, 192, 194,
196, 204
**Relativism**
central questions 4
effects of cultural relativism 159–169
fundamental issues about rule of
law 90
**Religion**
*see also* **Seventh Day Adventism**
early Christian teachings on
Pitcairn 48
source of all obligations 206–207
sources of law 69
**Rule of law**
case raised in *Steven Raymond Christian
and Others v The Queen* 28–35
central questions 4–5
conformity with moral principles 190
fundamental issues 90
sovereign title and obligations 123

**Scotland, Baroness** 14, 217
**Sentences**
effect of common law 88–89
fairness 211–214
'getting the message across' 215
Lord Hope's view on prosecution 33
overview 15–16
requirement for community
relationship 177
**Settlement**
case raised in *Steven Raymond Christian
and Others v The Queen* 24–27
early history
conclusions 61

**Settlement** (*cont.*)
  early history of Pitcairn
    biblical monarchy 48–51
    intervention by British
      Government: 1856–98 54
    mutiny on Bounty 39–41
    recognition by Great Britain:
      1814–56 51–54
    settled government:1898–
      present 56–60
    ten years of savagery 41–48
  legal development after
    settlement 72–82
  origins 2
  sources of law 67–71
**Seventh Day Adventism**
  arrival on Pitcairn 56
  fairness 211
  statement on British position 60
**Sexual conduct**
  arguments against abuse of process 87
  case raised in *Steven Raymond Christian
    and Others v The Queen*
    legality 28–35
  choice of law 65–66
  concerns of Lord Hope 32
  fairness 210–214
  finding of Judicial Committee 30
  jurisdiction under public
    international law
    introduction 93–96
  *mala in se* 197–199
  moral wrongfulness and
    blameworthiness distinguished
    effects of cultural relativism
      159–169
    introduction 157–159
  role of governing Council 11
  sovereign title and obligations 118–127
  thought experiment for British
    Crown 5–10
  unjustified claims of cultural
    uniqueness
    alleged failure to acknowledge
      uniqueness 136–138
    alternative media narratives
      134–136
    arguments particular to unique
      cultures 143–146
    conclusions 155–156
    'cultural defence' claims 150–153
    dangers of exaggerated respect
      154–155

  distorting influence of isolation
    141–144
  incoherent narrative ignoring
    sexual abuse 138–141
  introduction 131–134
  minority rights 146–150
  whether Judicature Ordinances
    applied 77
**Short, C.** 215, 265
**Sociology** *see* **Anthropology and
  sociology**
**Sources of law**
  colonial status 66
  settlements 67–71
**Sovereignty**
  acceptance of colonial status 81
  annexation of Pitcairn 75–76
  early status of Pitcairn 50–51, 55
  jurisdiction under public
    international law
    conceptual analysis 96–106
    conclusions 127–129
    introduction 93–96
  sovereign title and obligations
    119–127
  territorial acquisition 106–119
  recognition of Pitcairn 51–54
  sources of law 68
  statement of Seventh Day
    Adventists 60
  statutory authority of United Kingdom
    Crown over Pitcairn 56–60
  unjustified claims of cultural
    uniqueness 137
***Steven Raymond Christian and Others v
  The Queen***
  absence of criminal justice
    system 27–28
  colonial status of Pitcairn 24–27
  general procedure 23–24
  legality and rule of law 28–35
  report of Privy Council decision
    231–258
  reflections on alternative judicial
    approaches 35–36
  subsequent measures by British
    Government 36–37
**Steyn, Lord** 24
**Symbolic law** 214, 216

**Tahiti**
  effects of cultural relativism 160

influences on Island culture 200
origins of mutiny 39–40
sexual customs 185
**Terra nullius** 55, 98
**Territorial acquisition**
assertions of jurisdiction 106–119
introduction 18
**Theocratic government** 112, 223
**Truth and reconciliation**
alternative approach 21, 186, 217
consideration by FCO 14

**United Kingdom** *see* **Crown; Great Britain**
**United Nations**
admission of independent Pitcairn 94
Convention on Rights of Child 1989 121
Covenant on Civil and Political Rights 1966 18, 121, 125–126
Covenant on Elimination of discrimination against Women 1979 18, 120
Declaration on Sovereignty 1945 119–120
Law of the Sea 99
**Universal rights**
moral wrongfulness and blameworthiness distinguished 159–169
problems of relativism 90
sovereign title and obligations 118–127
thought experiment for British Crown 8–9
**Utilitarianism** 170

**Victims**
arguments against abuse of process 86
influence on prosecutions 33
legality 216–218
legality, reciprocity and the criminal law
introduction 186
problems of relativism 90
rejection of claims of cultural uniqueness 139–140

**Visitors to Pitcairn**
first ten years 41–48
official visits 59–60

**Women and girls**
arguments against abuse of process 85
concerns of Lord Hope 32
conflicts with early settlors 46–47
early treatment by settlors 45
effects of cultural relativism 161
fairness 210–214
sovereign title and obligations 118–127
thought experiment for British Crown 6
unjustified claims of cultural uniqueness
alleged failure to acknowledge uniqueness 136–138
alternative media narratives 134–136
arguments particular to unique cultures 143–146
conclusions 155–156
'cultural defence' claims 150–153
dangers of exaggerated respect 154–155
distorting influence of isolation 141–144
incoherent narrative ignoring sexual abuse 138–141
introduction 131–134
minority rights 146–150
**Women's' rights** 18, 120
**Woolf, Lord**
*Steven Raymond Christian and Others v The Queen*
references to evidence 26–27
unanimous opinion 24
concerns about unjusticiability 35–36
finding on abuse of process 30
judgment 238–242
sovereign title and obligations 123
views on abuse of process 84
views on colonial status 78–79